THE IMAGE OF ARISTOCRACY
IN BRITAIN, 1000-1300

THE IMAGE OF ARISTOCRACY IN BRITAIN, 1000–1300

David Crouch

London and New York

First published 1992
by Routledge
11 New Fetter Lane, London EC4P 4EE

Simultaneously published in the USA and Canada
by Routledge
a division of Routledge, Chapman and Hall Inc.
29 West 35th Street, New York, NY 10001

Typeset in 10/12pt Garamond by
Falcon Typographic Art Ltd, Fife, Scotland
Printed in Great Britain by
TJ Press (Padstow) Ltd, Padstow, Cornwall

British Library Cataloguing in Publication Data
Crouch, David
The Image of Aristocracy in Britain, 1000–1300
I. Title
305.5

Library of Congress Cataloging-in-Publication Data
Crouch, David
The image of aristocracy in Britain, 1000–1300 / David Crouch.
p. cm.
Includes bibliographical references and index.
1. Nobility – Great Britain – History. 2. Great Britain – Social
life and customs – Medieval period, 1066–1485. I. Title.
HT653.G7C76 1993
390′.23′0941 – dc20 92–1052

ISBN 0–415–01911–7

In Memoriam

RICHARD BENJAMIN
1956-1986

CONTENTS

CONTENTS

FIGURES

PREFACE

In writing a book of this nature, a large number of debts are going to be incurred. There were many scholars who very generously contributed views, knowledge, criticisms and ideas which have found their way into the following pages. Amongst these were Adrian Ailes, Robert Babcock, Dr Julia Barrow, Professor Geoffrey Barrow, Dr Paul Brand, Dr David Carpenter, Dr Michael Clanchy, Professor Sam Clark, Tim Copeland, Dr Charles Coulson, Professor Rees Davies, Dr David Davray, Dr Trevor Dean, Richard Eales, Dr Paul Fouracre, Dr Robin Frame, John Gillingham, Dr Lindy Grant, Professor Ralph Griffiths, Sandy Heslop, Professor C. Warren Hollister, Professor Michael Jones, Dr Maurice Keen, Dr Chris Lewis, Dr Graham Loud, Dr Jane Martindale, Vince Moss, Dr Janet Nelson, Ian Pierce, Professor Michael Prestwich, Dr Susan Reynolds, Dr Nigel Saul, Jack Spurgeon, Julia Walworth, Bruce Webster, Dr Ann Williams and Patrick Wormald. So many and so frequent over the years have been the conversations about aspects of this study that there may well have been others who contributed whom I have not mentioned. I ask their forgiveness; and I assure them and those whom I have mentioned and you, the readers, that the obscurities and errors in the resulting book are wholly my own. Dr David Bates must also be absolved from any share of blame for the errors and inadequacies in this book. More than anyone else, he has attempted the difficult task of guarding me from the consequences of my own hasty enthusiasms over the years. I have profited much over the years from the advice and assistance of many librarians and archivists, particularly from the staff of the Institute of Historical Research, where I was based from 1986 to 1990. My assistants during that time, Eric Hemming and Nicholas Vincent, much enhanced the quality of those years, in good fellowship, ideas and research. Recently, North Riding College (now University College), Scarborough, has provided me with a very congenial and supportive academic home. Linda and Simon Crouch help me as ever with their patience and the warmth of a family home.

The following book is the result of an attempt to find some answers to troublesome questions. The questions relate to the background of the main thrust of my work (which is on the limited question of the nature of the power exercised by the English aristocracy on either side of the year 1200). It was important to find some answers to them, even though they were in the background. Aristocracy was defined by power, and that power stemmed from wealth. Wealth was used to traduce and entice men, but it was also used for the purpose of display. Display in turn partly defined the status of the individual. Much of this book is devoted to that latter aspect of aristocracy; its recognised – and exclusive – material attributes. I make no pretence that most of what is within is of any great originality. It is derived from the labours of several generations of scholars. The main claim to originality is that the subject matter is derived from Great Britain; that is, England, Wales and Scotland. Piecemeal studies have been published on many aspects of aristocracy dealt with in this book, but I do not think that they have yet been brought together in one volume, even for England, let alone Wales and Scotland.

If this book has a direct inspiration, then it is a French work published early in this century. This was the *Essai sur l'origine de la noblesse en France au moyen âge* of Paul Guilhiermoz (1902). Guilhiermoz was reluctant to call his work more than an *essai*. He was exploring in it ideas and meanings of ideas in medieval society which had not been given much serious attention before. He knew that he was beginning a debate, not terminating it. The fact that he deployed such a weight of learning in his *essai* may well account for the quality of the debate on medieval aristocracy which followed, and which still continues. Guilhiermoz's is a strange and engaging work, more footnote than text; a gathering and sorting of a remarkable miscellany of facts. The end result is a compelling study of changing attitudes and shifting names over several centuries. The *Essai* has never since lost its value, as indeed it cannot, for it stands so near the basic source material and offers such minimal comment that later writers tend to quarry it, rather than quarrel with it.

Neither England nor Britain has produced a single comparable work to that of Guilhiermoz. Perhaps the nearest English study in terms of aims and later prestige is Sir Frank Stenton's *First Century of English Feudalism, 1066–1166*, published in 1929. However, Stenton's work has a much narrower focus in time and place. Also Stenton was concerned to do rather more than chart developments in the aristocracy; his intention was to offer a coherent portrait of a century of social upheaval following the Norman conquest and colonisation of England (not Britain, of course). Maurice Keen's admirable *Chivalry* (1984) does tackle many questions considered here, but his horizons are much wider than the British Isles and the three centuries considered here.

The British approach to the question of definition of aristocracy in the High Middle Ages has been industrious, but piecemeal, as the bibliography of this guide will make abundantly clear. Such significant subjects as hereditary titles and heraldry have usually been left to the antiquary and amateur, even in this century. There is a lingering belief that heraldry is for Boutell, and titles for Debrett. A British – as opposed to an English – view of the subject of the medieval aristocracy has been lacking until very recently indeed. The national aristocracies of Wales, Scotland and England have found their historians, but only recently (the works of Rees Davies and Robin Frame) has there been any attempt to explore their interrelations.

This is the work of a general political and social historian. It is not the work of an archaeologist, a linguist or a sociologist. Its deductions and ideas on much of what it is dealing with must be treated with an element of caution where it trespasses into such specialist areas. Indeed, so well aware am I of my deficiencies in them, that you will be quick to notice my reluctance to commit myself. Nonetheless I ask indulgence for this. There is something faintly ridiculous about a general historian attempting to be what he lacks the qualifications and years of study to be (with the odd distinguished exception). You must take what you find of value and feel free to discard the rest.

Scarborough
December 1991

INTRODUCTION
Aristocracy and nobility

This introduction is intended to set a context for the book that follows. The book, you should be warned, is about the outward manifestations of aristocracy, and not about such subjects as 'feudalism', aristocratic incomes and aristocratic power. The exterior trappings of aristocracy are a wide enough study, and have seen relatively little academic work. But I begin, at least, on an Olympian height, even if I will soon descend to metalwork, stone and wax; and scrabble about for the meaning of words. It is only right to begin by examining what we mean by 'aristocracy'; dealing with (or at least reviewing) the problems of class, social friction and identity which form the background to the book's thesis. Its thesis too has a history, and it is to be found in observations first framed (I believe) by Leopold Génicot in the 1960s, although implicit in earlier work on both sides of the Channel.

1 There was no means for contemporaries to define their aristocracies in the Early and High Middle Ages; no overt privileges belonged to the dominant social group, either in law or precedence, by which to identify its members.
2 *Nonetheless, the medieval aristocracy was aware of itself.* Recognition depended on wealth and the way it was used for the purposes of display. Note that this latter observation is implicit in Georges Duby's 1968 study of diffusion of ideas and fashion in medieval society (we will be returning again and again to Duby's thesis throughout this book).

These two observations will be pursued throughout the book, but now we must beat some thickets. We must consider the dominant social groups in British society for the three centuries between 1000 and 1300. There is no magic about these dates, and I am not binding

1

myself tightly to them. They do, however, comprehend a period of change in society which has seen much attention in the past three generations: a period of growing wealth and population, of collapse (and then recovery) of royal power, and growing localism. It was indeed a period in which an aristocracy was likely to thrive and grow. Above all it was a period of rising literacy and widening intellectual debate. It was an age in which people's perceptions of the world about them and the society in which they lived were sharpened. More definite meanings were attached to words as observations were collated and compared, even by laymen. It is no surprise that there were keener perceptions of aristocracy and status at the end than at the beginning of the period. We must particularly ask here if the High Middle Ages did in fact think in terms of social groups with distinct qualities.[1]

NOBILITY

At the beginning of the period of this book, and indeed long before, writers recognised that there was a group in the societies of Britain, France, and elsewhere, called by a variety of Latin nouns: *illustres*, *primates, proceres, primores, principes, magnates, maiores, optimates*, and so on. This range of words was a catalogue of synonyms; it meant one thing: the chief men of the realm, those who assumed a right to intervene in its affairs. The perception of this dominant group was universal in society. The group intermarried within itself; it had wealth, power and access to the rulers – where there were such – who had raised themselves to dominance over provinces and kingdoms.[2]

Where this dominant social group was subordinated to a prince, it is seen by modern historians as an 'aristocracy'.[3] Sometimes it is also called a 'nobility'. The two words are occasionally considered to be synonyms. Take for instance H.G. Wells's convenient definition: 'To

---

1 Needing a label for the period 1000–1300, I here conflate English and German ideas of what is to be understood by the 'High Middle Ages', see discussion in H. Fuhrmann, *Germany in the High Middle Ages, c. 1050–1200*, trans. T. Reuter (Cambridge, 1986), 16–17.

2 L. Génicot, 'Recent Research on the Medieval Nobility', in *The Medieval Nobility: Studies on the Ruling Classes of France and Germany from the Sixth to the Twelfth Century*, ed. and trans. T. Reuter (Amsterdam, 1979), 18.

3 For some useful general observations about 'aristocracy' see, J.K. Powis, *Aristocracy* (Oxford, 1984), 6–8.

be noble is to be aristocratic, that is to say a ruler'. It is verging on the simplistic, but it encapsulates some academic as well as lay thinking on the subject.[4] However, according to some writers, aristocracy is not necessarily nobility. The French had a particular reason to draw a line between 'aristocracy' and 'nobility'. It was bound up with the history of their word *noblesse*. 'Aristocracy' was seen as a term fit for the undefined earlier manifestations of a socially dominant group. It became a 'nobility' when the status of a 'noble' became legally defined and subject to grant by the prince. This means that for some French historians, the 'aristocracy' turned into the 'nobility' in the fourteenth century. Unfortunately, the inevitable corollary for an English historian is that there never was an English nobility; it always remained an unreconstructed aristocracy because the practice never grew up of raising Englishmen (or Scots or Welsh) to the status of 'noble'.[5] The distinction is an artificial one and although I will be distinguishing 'aristocracy' from 'nobility', I will not be doing it for that reason.

There are other reasons for using the word 'aristocracy' for the group being considered here, and avoiding 'nobility'. The word 'nobility' encourages ambiguity: it is both a group noun and a nebulous quality, embracing superiority, free birth and good descent. A problem with 'nobility' is that the group noun gets confused with the quality of 'nobility'; and both senses, group and quality, are comprehended by the Latin word *nobilitas*. We find both in Norman ducal acts of the eleventh century. In his dower settlement on his wife, Richard III of Normandy's scribe refers to the 'nobility' of the lady's lineage. An act of Richard's nephew, Duke William, in favour of the abbey of Marmoutier refers to the assembled 'nobility' of Maine who were present; the word is used as a variant of *proceres, maiores,* and so on.[6] The word leads to further confusions. If the 'nobility' is understood to be a group of men possessed of the qualities embraced by the adjective

---

4 H.G. Wells, *The Research Magnificent*, ch. 6.

5 M. Bloch, *Feudal Society*, trans. L.A. Manyon (2nd edn, 1962), 330–1, gives this distinction. Georges Duby also embraces the difference between 'aristocracy' and 'nobility', but puts the point of change around 1200, when (for him) *adoubement* became the definition of aristocracy, G. Duby, 'The Transformation of the Aristocracy', in *The Chivalrous Society*, trans. C. Postan (London, 1977), 178–9. For another perspective, M. Bush, *The English Aristocracy: a Comparative Synthesis* (Manchester, 1984), 5–7.

6 *Recueil des actes des ducs de Normandie (911–1066)*, ed. M. Fauroux (Caen, 1961), 182, 357.

'noble', then we are committing something of an anachronism. In the High Middle Ages, writers complained that the dominant social group contained too many men who were *ignobilis*; a consequence of kings having complete liberty to raise whomever they liked to power and influence. Doubtless men saw 'nobility' as desirable in their leaders, but they did not always get it.

There was perceived to be a quality or qualities of 'nobility' which were desirable and prized. Nobility was undoubtedly important, but what was it? There are some answers to this question, but a number of ambiguities also.[7] The considerable literature on the aristocracies of various provinces of France in the eleventh and twelfth centuries finds that the Latin word *nobilis* is used in different ways at different times in different areas. Sometimes it may mean 'free man', sometimes it marks a member of the higher aristocracy, at other times it is a middling social group. In at least one area (the Mâconnais) the word *nobilis* applied to individuals of moderate resources was supplanted soon after 1000 entirely by the title *miles* (knight), apparently because local scribes fell in love with the word and its implications of honest service. One is left with the conviction that the French of the eleventh and twelfth centuries had no common idea what a noble was, other than that it was a good thing to be one.[8]

However, nobility clearly related to free descent. The eleventh and twelfth centuries seem to have generally understood that a 'noble' man or 'noble' knight had a line of ancestors who were free and in respectable circumstances. It is worth noting that the usual medieval French equivalent for *nobilis* is *gentil*, which is ultimately derived from the Latin word *gens*, which can mean 'family' or 'stock'. In eleventh-century France the abbot of Bourgeil took up a poor boy and educated him into knighthood, 'Because he was a knight's son, descended from a long line of nobles.'[9] In England, Henry of Huntingdon related nobility wholly to distinguished descent. He imagines the speech of Earl Robert of Gloucester in reply to his son-in-law, the earl of Chester, before the battle of Lincoln (1141):

'It is not unbecoming that you seek the honour of the first

---

7 The best survey (though biased towards a later period) is in M. Keen, *Chivalry* (London, 1984), 143–61.
8 See surveys in J-P. Poly and E. Bournazel, *La Mutation féodale, xe–xiie siècle* (Nouvelle Clio, xvi, 1980), 172–7; D. Barthélemy, *L'Ordre seigneurial, xie–xiie siècle* (Paris, 1990), 128–39.
9 Quoted in Keen, *Chivalry*, 143.

blow, whether from the nobility or the virtue in which you excel. But if you argue the point, I, the son of a most noble king [i.e. Henry I], and grandson of the greatest of kings [William the Conqueror], cannot be surpassed in nobility. And if you talk of virtue, there are many choice men here, to whom none living can be preferred in prowess.'[10]

It is rather interesting that Henry divorces 'virtue' (*virtus*) – probably intending to mean in this case 'prowess' – from nobility. His point is that blood makes for nobility: he has to separate virtue from nobility, for in the same speech he describes several men of eminent and even royal descent as faithless, perjured, cowardly and corrupt. Not one of them does he call ignoble, however. He certainly could envisage a nobility with members who could not be called 'noble' in their conduct.[11]

To be ignoble, or rather, non-noble, was generally perceived to mean to be without blood or descent. *Ignobilis* is the adjective applied by Orderic Vitalis to the families of the men whom Henry I raised over the heads of earls and barons to positions of influence and trust. Other writers complained in the same way of such 'new men'; lowly birth – described in a variety of ways – is their main complaint.[12] Since many of the men stigmatised as without descent

10 Henry of Huntingdon, *Historia Anglorum*, ed. T. Arnold (Rolls Series, 1879), 268–9.
11 The chronicler of St Pancras, Lewes, makes the same point about William, son of the count of Eu, in 1095 'more distinguished by ancestry (*genere*) than prowess (*probitate*)', *Chronica monasterii de Hida iuxta Wintoniam*, in *Liber monasterii de Hyda*, ed. E. Edwards (Rolls Series, 1866), 301. Another very clear example of erring nobility is in the account by Gervase of Canterbury of Henry II's failed Welsh campaign of 1157, when the king's banner-bearer, Henry of Essex, found himself surrounded by Welshmen and dropped the royal banner in order to escape, on which Gervase comments: 'From this mishap, Henry experienced shame and perpetual disinheritance, since he was a great nobleman [*nobilissimus*] amongst the English magnates'. This indicates that good courage was expected of the noble, even if he did not show it, *The Historical Works of Gervase of Canterbury*, ed. W. Stubbs (2 vols, Rolls Series, 1879–80), i, 165.
12 Orderic Vitalis, *The Ecclesiastical History*, ed. M. Chibnall (6 vols, Oxford, 1969–80), vi, 16. R.V. Turner, 'Changing Perceptions of the New Administrative Class in Anglo-Norman and Angevin England: the *Curiales* and their Conservative Critics', *Journal of British Studies*, xxix (1990), 93–5, neatly summarises this twelfth-century view. There is however a different view of the officers of princely households expressed by Wace: he portrays the household of Richard II of Normandy as particularly distinguished because all the lay and clerical officers were *gentil*, *Roman de Rou*, ed. A. Holden (3 vols, Société des Anciens Textes Français, 1970–73), ll. 797–808, quoted in P. Contamine, 'Introduction', *La Noblesse au moyen âge, xie–xve siècles: Essais à la mémoire de Robert Boutruche*, ed. P. Contamine (Paris, 1976), 28.

by critical writers were at least well-established landowners (such as the Clintons and Bassets) with several generations on a family fee, we may assume that it was not always enough to be a free landowner to be considered of noble descent in the England and Normandy of the twelfth century.

Otherwise, the quality evoked by the adjective and noun 'noble' is more hazy. 'Nobility' can be confused with dignity; with the decorous and distinguished bearing and conduct which went along with title and high lineage. Gerald of Wales talks of the 'nobility of conduct (*nobilitas morum*)' of Louis of France, when welcoming his arrival in England in 1216.[13] Dignity and nobility cannot be wholly divorced from each other in the medieval (or modern) mind. Hardly so, for the two words cover the common ground of superiority. Yet dignity was separate, and related to high social position, whereas nobility need not.

To be noble, or a noble, was clearly a good thing; it proclaimed superiority and notability, but not just the superiority of the titled magnate. It was so good a thing – and this is the complicating factor – that it was not simply applied to humans. A count might be 'noble', but so might his county.[14] The city of London was 'noble' according to one of its devoted sons in the twelfth century (see below, p. 25). A horse might well have been said to have a 'noble shape', as Gerald of Wales said of the horses of Powys (but these at least were held to have had a distinguished Spanish lineage).[15] A judgement, such as that of Solomon, might be lauded by a poet as 'noble'.[16] All these were superior and admirable in one way or another, but there was nothing specific which made them noble. Geoffrey de Mandeville built a castle at Walden in Essex, and in doing so he was said to have 'ennobled' (*nobilitaverat*) the place, meaning no more than that he had made it more notable or famous.[17] 'Nobility' was indeed a curious quality. It is not always good enough to translate 'noble' as 'high-born', and indeed, it never has been. Before 1000 nobility may perhaps have been regarded simply as the property of a free

13 R. Bartlett, *Gerald of Wales* (Oxford, 1982), 223.
14 The *nobilem consulatum* of Maine is referred to be Orderic Vitalis, *Ecclesiastical History*, ed. Chibnall, v, 246.
15 Gerald of Wales, *Itinerarium Kambriae*, in *Opera*, ed. J.S. Brewer, J.F. Dimock and G.F. Warner (8 vols, Rolls Series, 1861–91), vi, 143.
16 *Song of Lewes*, in *The Political Songs of England from the Reign of John to that of Edward II*, ed. T. Wright (Camden Soc., vi, 1839), 111.
17 *Liber de fundatione abbathiae de Walden*, in *Monasticon Anglicanum*, ed. J. Caley, H. Ellis and B. Bandinel (8 vols, London, 1817–30), iv, 141.

man.[18] We find the same sense of the word well after 1000. To be a 'noble' in thirteenth-century Wales (*bonheddig*, usually the translation of Latin *nobilis*), it was enough to be born of Welsh parents.[19]

It may be that English or Norman writers of the eleventh and twelfth centuries would not lay out such a broad definition of nobility as that to be found in the Welsh Laws. Yet even so there are numerous entries in Norman and English monastic registers (just as in French ones) which speak of this 'noble man' or that 'noble knight' who presented a benefaction to the house. Many of these inspired men are complete unknowns, and certainly not magnates. Their nobility can often have resided only in the pen of the clerk, who had rather his abbey's benefactors were adorned with so much dignity.

Nobility might also be confounded with negative qualities. William of Malmesbury talks of the Breton, Hervey de Lyons, whose nobility (*nobilitas*) was so tainted with pride (*supercilium*) that he withstood even the blandishments of Henry I that he come to his court.[20] Perhaps for this very vagueness of the quality of 'nobility' we find that *nobilis* is a word that will not always do for Latin writers, they needed to make it more positive. Bloch long ago noted that *nobilior* is a comparative which intensifies the quality; *nobiliores* and *nobilissimi* are of that multitude of words encountered in eleventh- and twelfth-century France and England which can be translated as 'magnates' or 'leaders'.[21]

It may be best to conclude with the examples set out by one writer, which come nearest a definition of nobility (at least, in late twelfth-century terms). The intriguing French writer, Andrew the Chaplain, gives us a remarkable insight into one man's view of nobility and social groups. His essay on love was also an essay on interaction between different social levels. The word he uses is *ordines*. Since he tells us in what way he meant these *ordines* to be taken, we know that he was not thinking in terms of function but of social level, for he presents them as the commoner (*plebeius*), the nobleman (*nobilis*), and the magnate (*nobilior*). Judging by his use

18 Bloch, *Feudal Society*, trans. Manyon, 286–8.
19 *Llyfr Blegywryd*, ed. S.J. Williams and J.E. Powell (2nd edn, Cardiff, 1961), 58, commented on by R.R. Davies, *Conquest, Coexistence and Change in Wales 1063–1415* (Oxford, 1987) repr. as *The Age of Conquest* (Oxford, 1991), 16, 115.
20 William of Malmesbury, *Historia Novella*, ed. K.R. Potter (London, 1955), 31.
21 As for instance the English *nobiliores* in *Liber Eliensis*, ed. E.O. Blake (Camden Soc., 3rd ser., xcii, 1962), 186–7, when talking of the rising of 1069.

of synonyms within each passage, he quite clearly meant these three levels to be understood as a bourgeois, a knight, and a count or marquis.

But despite (apparently) excluding the bourgeois from the degree of *nobilis*, Andrew did not mean to imply that the bourgeois was necessarily ignoble, or even non-noble. He had one of his characters, a noblewoman, address a suitor, a merchant, along the lines that the orders (*ordines*) of society had been laid down from the earliest times; that each man should be happy with his lot within the bounds set by nature; nor should affect the manners (*natura*) of his betters. Yet her importunate suitor persisted, saying that his honesty brought him within the confines of nobility: 'a man's nobility should be judged more from his conduct than from his blood'. In doing so he was quoting a view whose pedigree stretched back to Aristotle.[22] In a further imagined encounter between a merchant and a countess, the same arguments are loftily dismissed, yet from her great social height she is willing to concede that the prince who stands above them all might by his prerogative confer 'nobility' on any man of good conduct.[23] The assumption must be here that Andrew is equating the conferring of 'nobility' with the act of knighting, since letters of ennoblement were over a century in the future when he wrote. The implication is that by the time he wrote, the quality of *nobilitas* was beginning to be restricted in its social application. The act of knighting seems to have been then perceived as one way of dropping the bar on those judged socially unworthy. Yet the possession of reputation, wealth and resources still gave a man a claim to be considered *nobilis*, knight or not.

The interrelation of *nobilis* with *miles* has been exhaustively explored by French historians. It is a subject to which we will return in Chapter 4. From Bloch onwards, knighthood was long perceived by them as a force for the transformation of the aristocracy, either by defining it, or by enlarging it. Georges Duby has put the upward transformation of knighthood into nobility as the key development of 'aristocracy' into 'nobility'. When society recognised the act of *adoubement* (knighting) as conferring a superior social degree, then, says Duby, the closed noble class had come into being.[24] Whatever reservations one might have about so sweeping a statement, there can

22 Keen, *Chivalry*, 149.
23 Andrew the Chaplain, *Amoris Tractatum*, ed. P.G. Walsh (London, 1982), 62, 66, 78.
24 Duby, 'The Transformation of the Aristocracy', 178–81.

be no doubt in reading Andrew the Chaplain that his contemporaries were indeed finding the status of knight a useful social indicator by the mid-1180s in northern France. By then, knighthood could be said to include and define *nobilitas*. It is unfortunate that not all writers were as thoughtful and considered in their use of the word 'noble' as Andrew, and that perceptions of 'nobility' were not discussed so intensely that an authoritative consideration was published before the fourteenth century.[25] Regretfully, therefore, we must put the concept of 'nobility' aside, bundled up in a mass of qualifications. Unlike Duby, I shall embrace the more neutral word 'aristocracy' when dealing with the dominant social group throughout the period of this book.

NOBILITY AND GENEALOGY

The eleventh century in France had brought something of a renewed emphasis on descent, and therefore nobility; or at least new ways were found to emphasise it. Studies, particularly by Georges Duby, have noted the concern of the higher aristocracy after 1000 to stress descent from men of power and achievement, leading to a growing number of genealogical treatises and family histories. To this was added a concern to take an hereditary surname, often the name of a family estate. The passing of the estate from generation to generation was then more clearly marked, and a consciousness of family continuity assured. This consciousness of genealogy began with the high aristocracy imitating the way royal families perceived themselves; it passed to the lesser magnates and thence to the knights.[26] Other developments might well be used to complement Duby's conclusions. There can be no doubt that the earliest manifestations of heraldry were designed to proclaim family identity and high descent; and heraldry too passed down through the ranks of society (see Chapter 6). Family religious patronage is yet another example of the reinforcement of genealogy (see Chapter 10).

Duby uses these developments to illustrate a theory of changing perceptions of family. From an aristocracy which lived in the

---

25 Keen, *Chivalry*, 148–9, points particularly to the influential views on *nobilitas* of the fourteenth-century Italian lawyer, Bartolus of Sassoferrato.
26 See in particular G. Duby, 'The Structure of Kinship and Nobility', in *The Chivalrous Society*, trans. C. Postan (London, 1977), 134–48.

present, conscious only of its contemporary kin, we move around 1000 to an aristocracy more conscious of its continuity with the past, with past greatness and past great men. It is in this context that we must view *nobilitas*. As Duby says, if there was more distinction to be gained from stressing descent from the maternal line, that was preferred. Eleventh- and twelfth-century aristocracy was more interested in finding sources of nobility, than stressing male descent. The examples of the great aristocratic houses of Warenne, Mandeville and Percy in England bear him out. In each case the male line of the original family died out in the twelfth century. The heiress of each came to men with less descent: Warenne to Hamelin, a bastard brother of Henry II; Mandeville to Geoffrey fitz Peter, son of a royal forester; Percy to Joscelin, a cadet of the ducal house of Lotharingia, but a stranger in England. The sons of Hamelin, Geoffrey and Joscelin all took the names (and in the case of the first two, the heraldic bearings) of their mothers' families.[27] They were claiming the superior nobility of their maternal descent.

One may have some doubts about Duby's reasoning about families' perceptions of their past in France, particularly when we transfer our gaze to Welsh aristocractic society. Here was a society where family focused on a leading member, a *pencenedl*, and family property was shared out amongst brothers and even cousins;[28] to some extent it fits Duby's model of pre-1000 French society. Yet here in Wales there was also a marked consciousness of the family as a *gens*, descended from kings and great heroes of long ago; and a determination to milk as much nobility from an individual's connections as possible. To take the example of Gruffudd ap Cynan, king of Gwynedd (died 1137); his biographer began by exploring his genealogy, through his father and mother. Through the father he got back to Rhodri Mawr, the great founder of the fortunes of Gruffudd's family, and through him to Brutus, the royal dynasty of Troy and eventually Adam; through the mother he took care to trace back a connection with the dukes of Normandy, and thence the royal dynasty of England.[29] His purpose was to demonstrate as unquestionably as he could how Gruffudd was a *bonheddwr*, a man of nobility (partly because

27 See for Warenne and Mandeville, D. Crouch, 'Strategies of Lordship in Angevin England and the Career of William Marshal', in *The Ideals and Practice of Medieval Knighthood*, ii, ed. C. Harper-Bill and R. Harvey (Woodbridge, 1988), 12–16.
28 W. Davies, *Wales in the Early Middle Ages* (Leicester, 1982), 71–6.
29 *The Life of Gruffudd ap Cynan*, ed. D. Simon Evans (Lampeter, 1990), 23–7.

Gruffudd's title to his kingdom was not so clear-cut as he pretended).

It does not necessarily do to assume, as does Duby, that the horizontal and vertical views of family were necessarily exclusive. Wales had an artistic medium, the praise-poem, which preserved long genealogies, as did pre-Conquest England. France seems to have lost the art of genealogy after the Merovingians, but it may not have lost the consciousness of it. Wales and England harboured long genealogies without the benefit of surnames and heraldry. The enumerated descent from founder-figures was sufficient for a vertical family consciousness. For this reason surnames never really caught on in twelfth- and thirteenth-century Wales, although one or two Welsh magnate families experimented with them (see Chapter 4). The study of heraldry, in default of genealogical poetry, seems to indicate that this mixture of horizontal and vertical views was present in France and England too. The early twelfth-century example of the families of Vermandois, Meulan, Warenne and Warwick indicates a common perception of kinship which began with the marriage around 1100 of Robert I, count of Meulan (and later Leicester) to Elizabeth, daughter of Hugh the Great, count of Vermandois. The high nobility of the ancient line of Vermandois – it was descended from Charlemagne – was behind the resolve of all the Anglo-Norman families which derived from Elizabeth's two marriages to imitate the distinctive device of the Vermandois family: a blue and yellow checky design (see Chapter 6).

ARISTOCRACY, DIGNITY AND SOCIAL DEFINITION

Nobility, that elusive quality, is not going to help us much in our search for the nature of aristocracy. There is another quality, nearly as difficult to evoke, which may help us more. Titles, as we will see, evoked a dignity beyond the men who carried them, and that dignity was part of the image of aristocracy, maybe its most important part. So can we define what such dignity was, apart from nobility? A level of bearing and greatness was long expected of the great earl in England. The epitaph of John Digby, earl of Bristol (died 1698), carved the selfsame sentiment on marble long after many of the other ideas of the Middle Ages had died out:

His distinction from others never made him forget himself

11

or them. He was kind and obliging to his neighbours, generous and condescending to his inferiours, and just to all Mankind.[30]

Such a bearing was what was expected five or six centuries earlier, for Gerald of Wales could talk of 'the levels of dignity (*gradus dignitatis*)' on which princes, dukes and earls stood, and of what he believed to be the qualities that went with each grade of the hierarchy.[31] In 1141, William of Malmesbury tells us of the bearing of his hero, Robert of Gloucester, in captivity: 'such consciousness of his high breeding (*alte nobilitatis*) he breathed that he could not be humbled by the outrage of fortune'.[32] We have already heard Andrew the Chaplain on the subject. He believed that there was a certain 'air' (*natura*) that great men possessed, and lesser men tried to counterfeit.

This *dignitas*, consciousness or air truly belonged only to the great magnate or courtier. Poorer men envied it, and kings could respect it. English kings allowed earls a certain level of deference; indeed, as we will see, they fostered their high position in many ways. Since earls were their most distinguished servants it was expedient as well as polite for kings to do so. French kings were not in such a fortunate situation; their counts were not so tied to them. But in England in the twelfth and thirteenth centuries it was considered suitable for a party of earls to make up the secular side of royal embassies, as when the earl of Warenne and the count of Meulan went to the region of Paris to meet Louis VII on King Stephen's behalf in 1138, or when the same king sent another party of earls to represent him before the Council of Winchester the next year. Henry II in 1164 had the earls of Cornwall and Leicester bear his court's judgement to the erring Thomas Becket. Earls performed the greater offices in the coronation procession of Richard I. Earls went to Germany, to Navarre and even Rome on the king's behalf, for, wrapped in their own dignity, they were more suitable mouthpieces for his wishes and words. The dignity of earls must admit of a certain distance, even from other earls. In 1153, when King Stephen and the young Henry Plantagenet conceded to William, Stephen's son, the county of Norfolk, the lands and rights of other earls were exempted from

---

30 His remarkable tomb is to be found in the south transept of Sherborne Abbey.
31 Gerald of Wales, *De Principis Instructione*, in *Opera*, viii, 103, 106.
32 *Historia Novella*, ed. Potter, 61.

his control, particularly the 'third penny' enjoyed by Hugh Bigod, earl of Norfolk.[33] At the last, when all had abandoned him on the field of Lewes in 1264, Henry III presented his sword in surrender to Gilbert de Clare, earl of Gloucester, 'as the king held him to be the most noble and powerful amongst the magnates', denying the pleasure to the earl of Leicester, to whom 'the better men' surrendered.[34]

Apart from these examples, we can see the dignity of the titled magnate most clearly in the addresses that were concocted for him by his correspondents, and the various ways he would dignify himself in his own written acts. Here there is an abundance of evidence still not systematically explored, as that of early letter collections have been. Letters of the ninth or tenth centuries might address counts as 'the illustrious', 'the glorious', 'most noble', 'most excellent' or 'magnificent and honourable': adaptations from earlier imperial formulas, or newly coined adjectives to express deference before the great. Indeed, one fourth-century formula was still around in the twelfth and thirteenth centuries, being applied to English earls. The formula 'the illustrious (*vir illustris*)' is one frequently applied by the deferential to English earls for some centuries after the Conquest.[35] William of Malmesbury addressed Robert, earl of Gloucester, as 'your Highness'. The English bishop, Gilbert Foliot (died 1187) had a fondness for addressing letters to 'venerable' earls and countesses.

Counts, earls and countesses of the eleventh and twelfth centuries not infrequently invoked divine grace and providence in the styles they gave themselves in their charters. The Norman counts of Meulan and Eu did so, as did the mid-twelfth-century English earls of Chester, Essex, Richmond and Warwick. The practice was known in Carolingian Francia and Lombardy. It is hardly surprising to find that it penetrated England. In Stephen's reign, however, this infrequent practice of appealing to divine sanction for the comital style became a decided vogue. It doubtless reflects

33 *Regesta Regum Anglo-Normannorum*, ed. H.W.C. Davis, C. Johnson, H.A. Cronne and R.H.C. Davis (4 vols, Oxford, 1913–69), iii, no. 272.
34 *Annales de Waverleia*, in *Annales Monastici*, ed. H.R. Luard (5 vols, Rolls Series, 1864–9), ii, 357.
35 As for instance to William Marshal (I) of Pembroke in John's reign, see J.H. Bernard, 'The Charters of the Cistercian Abbey of Duiske', *Proceedings of the Royal Irish Academy*, xxxv (1918–20), 28; Edmund earl of Lancaster in the reign of his brother, Edward I, see Public Record Office (PRO), DL42/2 fo. 103r (who is also called on occasion *nobilis vir* and *inclitus vir*, though these are less frequent).

insecurity about the newness of the dignity to some of the families which had been adorned with it. It is striking that the practice fades out rapidly in the reign of Henry II (1154–89) in England. Only one earl uses it then, as far as I know, and that is William III, earl of Arundel (1173–1221) in a charter for Durford priory.[36] In northern France counts continued to invoke divine grace for their status into the reign of Philip Augustus, as do also viscounts and the odd castellan besides. But that tailed off too as the thirteenth century progressed.

The medieval idea of high aristocratic 'dignity' is one that is not always easy to resurrect, for it was bound in at an early date with the much less restricted idea of 'chivalry'. Professor Stephen Jaeger has recently explored to great effect the quality of 'courtesy' which writers of the twelfth century expected of the courtier and aristocrat, and its origins in earlier expectations of the behaviour of high clerics. In the twelfth-century quality of 'courtesy' (the Latin word *curialitas* first appears around 1100) we find many of the qualities associated in later centuries with 'chivalry': modesty, good humour, mildness of bearing, accomplishment and demure language. Such qualities would eventually be seen as appropriate to knights, transmitted through the pattern heroes of the romance, but only once knights were indubitably aristocratic.[37]

But high aristocratic dignity stood a little apart from these courtier-qualities. We find in earlier centuries a general acceptance that titled magnates were entitled to greater consideration than others, and their state was superior, such as that conceded early in the eleventh century to Count William of Poitou even by his rivals (see Chapter 2). There was some sanction in law for this hedge of dignity, even in twelfth-century England. We find it in other ways. Medieval art and literature reserve certain stylised scenes for the great. Dukes and princes seated (and eventually crowned) on chairs of state, grasping the swords that represented their power to discipline and coerce, was one of these. This was a means of indicating a count or earl too, and we find examples of it as early as the eleventh century (see Chapter 3). By the end of the twelfth

---

36 Cartulary of Durford, Brit. Libr., ms. Cotton Vespasian, E xxiii, fo. 26v.: *Willelmus dei gratia comes Sussex tertius.* Hamelin, earl of Surrey (1164–1202) called himself earl *dei gratia* in two charters of the 1180s, but he did so in charters to the Picard abbey of St-Bertin, *Les Chartes de St-Bertin*, ed. D. Haigneré (4 vols, St-Omer, 1886–90) i, 144, 160.
37 C.S. Jaeger, *The Origins of Courtliness* (Philadelphia, 1985).

century the most elevated of dukes, like Normandy and Aquitaine – and possibly Brittany in the next century – would be installed by prelates in cathedrals with the regalia of their duchies in specially staged benedictions.

Such trappings were imitable, and, since they evoked power, invited imitation, and indeed begged it.[38] They were the ways in which Génicot's *richesse* was transmuted into material measures of status; it was by them that the aristocracy knew itself. Banners, devices, distinctive social titles, luxury clothes, great seals and prestige residences; these marked the magnate in 1100. In 1300 many of them marked the knight too. Between 1100 and 1300 then, the aristocracy had expanded. Knights were admitted into the use of many of the superior patterns of behaviour of the magnates; they became aristocratic according to the perceptions of the time, taken within the picket fence of status, even if at a lower level of status.

The process of enlargement did not cheapen aristocracy, however. It forced, by way of compensation to the magnates, firmer stratification within the aristocracy; recognised levels of status multiplied. This is perhaps the true 'transformation' of the aristocracy caused by the elevation of the knights. It triggered more defined levels of status amongst the aristocracy. Where there had been just earls and barons in 1100, by 1300 there were princes, earls, and knight-bannerets – and soon there would be dukes between the prince and earl (see Chapter 2). The knights too had divided by 1300. The pool of families which were still able to afford the new knighthood had fabricated the rank of squire. This would compensate the son of the knight who did not want the onerous administrative burden of knighthood (see Chapter 5). The process went on into the fifteenth century, in which evolved the new (and non-aristocratic) rank of gentleman to dignify the more prosperous and educated free man.[39]

THE QUESTION OF SOCIAL GROUPS

I have already said (agreeing with Génicot) that there was such a thing as a self-conscious and dominant social group at the head of

38 Such pretension is the substance (although not the whole) of the social mechanism described by G. Duby, 'The Diffusion of Cultural Patterns in Feudal Society', trans. R.H. Hilton, *Past and Present*, xxxix (1968), 3–10.
39 K.B. McFarlane, 'The Stratification of the Nobility and Gentry in the Later Middle Ages', in *The Nobility of Later Medieval England* (Oxford, 1973), 122–5; C. Richmond, 'The Rise of the English Gentry, 1150–1350', *The Historian*, xxvi (1990), 14.

society in England, Normandy and elsewhere in the High Middle Ages.[40] I have also speculated on the way that this group could recognise itself as an aristocracy. 'Group' is a fairly safe word for such a phenomenon, because it is neutral. But did this perception amount to what we would see as social class?

It can be proved with some ease that the people of the eleventh and twelfth centuries could comprehend such notions as groups within society, even if they did not often speak of them consciously. People of the time, and before, were not averse to thinking in groups, possessing group characteristics. The idea of *gentes*, peoples, possessing common features because of common descent and long residence in a distinct part of the world, had come down to the Middle Ages from Rome through Isidore.[41] Common origin and common characteristics; these things made for medieval ideas of group identity. People of the High Middle Ages could understand humanity in the mass, and humanity subdivided; so far so good.

Medieval people perceived groups, so could they then perceive class? Did they visualise a society divided laterally by degrees (or lack of) wealth and descent? McFarlane found talk of 'class' unhelpful in dealing with the medieval aristocracy.[42] I cannot deny that he had a point. People of that remote time had not our experience of self-excoriating social analysts, alert politicians appealing to constituencies, and novelists of social embarrassment, let alone sociologists. But to follow McFarlane's lead and relegate ideas of class to the back of our minds is to dodge a difficult fact. The High Middle Ages did not understand the idea of class as we do, but that is not to say that it did not perceive and experience something like it. Certainly, there was then current an idea of the mass of society, expressed as the whole body of the faithful in Christ, and the mass was subdivided. Many writers saw the faithful as a tripartite group, divided by function. By the eleventh century

40 This is implicit for pre-Conquest England in Dorothy Whitelock's treatment of the nobleman and his way of life in *The Beginnings of English Society* (repr. Harmondsworth, 1979), 85–96; in early Wales the same perception of *optimates*, *meliores* or *nobiles* at the head of society is present, Davies, *Wales in the Early Middle Ages*, 62–3; for Normandy see D.R. Bates, *Normandy before 1066* (London, 1982), 106–7.

41 G.A. Loud, 'The *Gens Normannorum* – Myth or Reality', *Proceedings of the Battle Conference*, ed. R.A. Brown, iv (1981), 104–17; S. Reynolds, 'Medieval *Origines Gentium* and the Community of the Realm', *History*, lxviii (1983), 375–90; idem, *Kingdoms and Communities in Western Europe, 900–1300* (Oxford, 1984), 250–60.

42 McFarlane, *The Nobility of Later Medieval England*, 6.

the three groups were generally seen to be: those who pray, those who fight, those who labour.[43] This was not too far removed from a perception of social class, although medieval thinkers saw these divisions within a religious framework. But when we cast our gaze wider, we do find subtler medieval perceptions of social groups. It is sharpest at the economic book-ends of society, and it is these we will now go on to consider.

In the case of the peasant, there is evidence of an antagonism towards them as inferiors which speaks of a perception of the peasantry as a lower social group. The peasant, whose labour supported the others, was to the upper classes self-evidently inferior, because he was poor. Dives and Lazarus represented an ancient antagonism in society, which the moral of the parable did nothing to heal. By the eleventh century, and doubtless long before, the contempt of those above for the poor below had reinforced the division, and had created a stereotype, an avatar of all that was despicable. In a statement of the grievances of the Poitevin magnate, Hugh de Lusignan, composed in the first quarter of the eleventh century, Hugh gives us what looks like good evidence of this noxious archetype. He tells of the count of Aquitaine insulting him by saying, 'You are so dependent on me that if I had told you to make a peasant (*rusticus*) your lord, you ought to have done it.' For a castellan such as Hugh, such an unlikely demand would have been an intolerable abasement, as the count knew.[44]

The peasantry remained the target of casual vilification over the following centuries; indeed, the French *vilain* (from Lat. *villanus*, from which we get our 'villein') was a term of abuse used against counts and knights in mid-twelfth-century romances. The level of abuse towards the peasant was such that it marks peasants out as the whipping boys of society, the contemptible dregs, both despised and feared. Indeed, the abuse was intellectualised. One twelfth-century writer in the Empire accounted for it by devising an 'origin myth' for the peasantry: it was descended from Ham, the son of Noah, who had cursed Ham's son: 'A servant of servants shall he be unto his brethren'. Free men were consequently descended

---

43 G. Duby, *The Three Orders: Feudal Society Imagined*, trans. A. Goldhammer (Chicago, 1980), 44–55.

44 J. Martindale, '*Conventum inter Guillelmum Aquitanorum comes et Hugonem Chiliarchum*', *English Historical Review*, lxxxiv (1969), 544; Duby, *The Three Orders*, 92–9.

from Shem, whom Noah had blessed and placed over Ham's children.[45]

The twelfth century produces some choice examples of contempt for the peasant. Artists of the later twelfth century began to depict the shepherds of the Nativity as gross beings, with thick lips, leering mouths, and matted hair, setting at nothing theological symbolism, which equated the shepherds with the Doctors of the Church.[46] The hermit, Godric of Finchale (died 1170), whose untutored sanctity was both a marvel and an embarrassment to the religious of northern England, was roundly abused by the Devil (according to his biographer) as a 'stinking old peasant'.[47] He was certainly of peasant origin, but the reference to his standard of hygiene was purely gratuitous, and arose from the mind of an upper-class monk of Durham cathedral. Nor was it the only one of its kind. A literary duel fought between two monks of Peterborough in the late twelfth century culminated in one abusing the other in these terms: 'He who wrote this [attack] had a peasant for a father, who slept in a dung-filled sty'.[48] The literary impostor and bishop of St Asaph, Geoffrey of Monmouth, shared his contempt, but played instead on the dullness of the peasant:

> It is easier for a kite to be made to act like a sparrowhawk than for a wise man to be fashioned at short notice from a peasant. He who offers any depth of wisdom to such a person is acting as though he were throwing a pearl amongst swine.[49]

These clerical outbursts against the weaker of the Church's flock

---

45 Honorius Augustodunensis, *De imagine mundi*, in *Patrologia Latina*, ed. J-P. Migne (221 vols, Paris, 1844–64), clxxii, col. 166; quoted by G. Duby, 'The Nobility in Medieval France', in *The Chivalrous Society*, trans. C. Postan (London, 1977), 107. The use of the words *servus servorum* in the Vulgate gave the myth added force, Gen. x, 25–6.

46 T.A. Heslop, 'Romanesque Painting and Social Distinction: the Magi and the Shepherds', in *England in the Twelfth Century*, ed. D. Williams (Woodbridge, 1990), 147–9. Physical grossness was regarded as an attribute of the lower classes; Andrew the Chaplain depicted the merchant in his dialogues on love as squat, with bandy legs (see below, p. 25).

47 *Libellus de Vita et Miraculis sancti Godrici heremitae de Finchale, auctore Reginaldo monacho Dunelemensi*, ed. J. Stevenson (Surtees Soc., xx, 1847), 93; quoted in M.T. Clanchy, *From Memory to Written Record* (London, 1979), 190.

48 John de St-Omer, *Norfolchiae decriptionis impugnatio*, in *Early Mysteries and other Latin Poems of the Twelfth and Thirteenth Centuries*, ed. T. Wright (London, 1838), 102.

49 Geoffrey of Monmouth, *Historia regum Britanniae*, i, *Bern, Burgerbibliotek ms. 568*, ed. N. Wright (Cambridge, 1985), 59; translation by Lewis Thorpe.

may have much to do with views expressed a generation later by the courtier-cleric, Walter Map. He bemoaned the growing numbers of boys of peasant extraction entering the Church, not to acquire virtue through education, but to make as much money as they could by becoming harsh and grasping civil servants. Map saw clerks from this sort of background as innately corrupt and debased.[50] Laymen had the same fear of self-improvers and social climbers; the sort of men 'raised from the dust' by Henry I and so hated by the established courtiers of the reign. The sinister peasants who rise through the favour of princes to power, which they promptly abuse, is a theme both in contemporary literature and moral treatises.[51] We see it in even more extreme form in Magna Carta (clause 50), where the foreign mercenaries raised by King John to positions of local prominence as castellans and sheriffs were exiled by name at the barons' insistence. Along with them were to go their *sequela*. As F.W. Maitland points out, this word was used of the offspring of both cattle and unfree peasants; these obscure foreigners were being stigmatised and insulted by the high-born barons, their enemies.[52]

Such antagonism and abuse was indiscriminate. It is quite possible that many of the men pilloried and stigmatised as *rustici, nativi* or *servi*, were from humble, but not inconsiderable, agricultural families of free men.[53] But class antagonism (as I think we can call it) had little time for niceties. Orderic Vitalis tells us that Geoffrey de Clinton and Richard Basset were men 'raised from the dust' by royal favour. Yet Geoffrey and Richard both headed families of local prominence in Normandy; the Clintons held lands both in the Cotentin and Oxfordshire before Geoffrey came to royal notice. The Clintons may even have had a castle before their elevation, but that counted for nothing with those who needed to condemn them because of the threat their upward rise posed. The complexities of the levels of status and freedom amongst the agricultural poor were just as irrelevant to social groups of higher status who felt insecure and threatened. It was axiomatic that the

50 Walter Map, *De Nugis Curialium*, trans. M.R. James (revised edn, Oxford, 1983), 12.
51 Duby, *The Chivalrous Society*, 182–3.
52 *The Pleas of the Crown for the County of Gloucester, A.D. 1221*, ed. F.W. Maitland (London, 1884), pp. xiv, xvii; J.C. Holt, *Magna Carta* (Cambridge, 1965), 328–30.
53 For the complexities of divisions amongst the peasantry see R.V. Lennard, *Rural England, 1086–1135: a Study of Social and Agrarian Conditions* (Oxford, 1959), 339ff.

peasant must be filthy and corrupt, cunning but stupid, immune, and even allergic, to the higher things in life. Hence the story of the peasant 'brought up in squalor and stench' who fainted clean away on sniffing the wholesome aromas wafting from an apothecary's shop. He could only be revived by being thrown on a dung-heap.[54]

Such was the despised tail of society, obvious as a category because it was despised; what of the other end of the continuum of wealth? Again, as we have seen, there was a perception, this time that a group of men formed society's head. It was as much of a social group as the peasantry, but it was less easy to define than even the under-class. This was hardly surprising, for it was the natural ambition of anyone with resources to be included within it, or at least to pretend that he was within it. As early as the eleventh century we find mountebanks posturing on the roads of Northern Europe in gaudy clothes and borrowed names to gull the credulous; and crafty merchants in the next century were reputed to masquerade as knights in order to dodge the tolls levied at bridges and town gates.[55] So how do we assess and define this aristocracy, as I think it best to call it? There are no easy answers. In fact, I would be willing to admit that we can only come to an approximation of an understanding of some of its aspects. To take the most obvious question – that of the size of the English aristocracy – working out its numbers, even in well-documented England, is difficult, to say the least.

One practical definition of the magnates is that they were those men whom the king habitually had about him in the conduct of affairs. Before 1066 the king of England had his Witan, while the duke of Normandy had his *conseil* of bishops, counts and barons, of which William de Poitiers says: 'Maintained by the energy and intelligence of these men, he was secure; the Roman Republic, if it had them and had survived to this day, would not have needed its two hundred senators.' William mentions about a dozen men in the ducal council, and charter evidence does not indicate a much bigger group, a clique, as David Bates calls them.[56] The witness lists of particularly solemn Norman royal and ducal diplomas, assizes and

---

54 *A Selection of Latin Stories*, ed. T. Wright (Percy Soc., viii, 1842), 84.
55 Guibert de Nogent, *De Vita Sua*, ed. E.R. Labande (Paris, 1981), 54; Chrétien de Troyes, *Le Conte de Graal*, ed. F. Lecoy (2 vols, Classiques français du moyen âge, 1972–5), i, ll. 5024–58.
56 William of Poitiers, *Gesta Guillelmi ducis Normannorum et regis Anglorum*, ed. R. Foreville (Paris, 1952), 148; Bates, *Normandy before 1066*, 158–60.

charters give us a guide to the numbers of men deemed worthy of associating with a particular prince at a particular time, but only a rough guide. Take the important Easter court of King Stephen, held at Oxford in 1136. The new king had been generally accepted by his aristocracy and had exerted himself to attract all who might be useful to him. The charters issued at that Easter court listed as present 'in common counsel' two archbishops, twelve bishops, four earls, ten baronial office-holders and eight others (a total of thirty-six). In 1164 the Constitutions of Clarendon were enacted before two archbishops, twelve bishops, ten earls or counts, and thirty barons and office-holders (a total of fifty-four).[57] In 1215 at Runnymede King John was attended by two archbishops, seven bishops, a cardinal, the Master of the Temple in England, four earls and twelve barons and office-holders (a total of twenty-seven).

But such figures are next to meaningless, for they were not intended to be comprehensive lists of people present. They only listed the most prominent men present. As the list of those at Clarendon puts it, it omitted: 'many others, magnates (*proceres*) and nobles of the realm, clergy and laity'. Magna Carta also mentions 'others' who were present, and we may assume the same for 1136. How many were really there? We cannot know for sure. It might be assumed that earls and greater barons – who must be aristocratic by whatever definition you use – would always be rated among them, but would they? Even here, kings could be quirky about whom they would summon to their councils. Henry II deliberately excluded several earls and counts from his confidence and court, notably William of Gloucester, Richard Strongbow of Striguil and Robert III of Leicester. In 1183 when the king was once again involved in warfare with his sons he ordered a round-up of men he regarded as suspect and his justiciar arrested Gloucester and Leicester, their wives 'and many others of the most powerful and wealthy men of the realm and imprisoned them'.[58] If we try to make closeness to the prince, and regular attendance at court, a definition of aristocracy, then many great men would be left out. There is no way of making a realistic assessment of the numbers and personnel of the upper class by this method.

---

57 The meeting at Clarendon in 1164 provides one of the biggest witness lists of the reign; for an assessment of magnates attesting Henry II's acts see T.K. Keefe, *Feudal Assessments and the Political Community under Henry II and his Sons* (Berkeley, 1983), 102–12.
58 *Gesta Henrici Secundi*, ed. W. Stubbs (2 vols, Rolls Series, 1867), i, 294.

At first sight, a definition of the aristocracy of England as those who held baronies from the king is very seductive as an alternative.[59] We know what these baronies were, their number (more or less), and who held them. Dr Ivor Sanders's much used and abused study of them calculated that there were 210 baronies established in the reigns of the Norman kings. The holders had a status which can be defined. After the process was regularised by Magna Carta (clause 2), these barons paid £100 to succeed to their lands, while common knights paid only 100 shillings. Unfortunately the semblance of regularity is an illusion. Part of the reason for that is to be found in a royal decree made at some time around 1135. The king agreed that baronies could be divided up between the daughters of a defunct baron, if he had no son. Before that, the inheritance generally went intact to the eldest daughter.[60] As a result of the decree there was an increasing fragmentation of baronies. By 1250 approaching a third of baronies (sixty-three) had been broken up because of divisions between heirs; all but a few, female heirs. One or two baronies had degenerated into six parts; and of course many had not been all that large in the first place.[61] Holders of some of these fragments could not be considered magnates by any stretch of the imagination. Headington, the barony of Thomas Basset, had never been more than one manor and the control of an Oxfordshire hundred court; yet it was used as the excuse to levy a baronial relief on him. When he died, leaving three daughters in 1220, Headington itself was too small to be divided, and formed the share of but one daughter. The other two were left with a share of Thomas's estates held as knights' fees.

Final totals will always elude the student of the various levels of the medieval aristocracy. It should be sufficient for us, perhaps, to know that contemporaries *did* at least see a controlling, powerful group at the head of society besides the king. The aristocracy knew itself too. The barons, Richard Marshal and Gilbert Basset demanded trial by their peers in 1231, meaning their equals in nobility. The denial by Peter des Roches that there were such 'peers' in England was part of the reason for the subsequent rebellion. By the 1240s, as a declaration of the baron, William de Beauchamp of Bedford tells us, the idea that there were 'peers' in England

59 This question is the subject of some interesting observations by C. Given-Wilson, *The English Nobility in the Later Middle Ages* (London, 1987), 11–12.
60 F.M. Stenton, *The First Century of English Feudalism, 1066–1166* (2nd edn, Oxford, 1961), 38–40.
61 Figures derived from I.J. Sanders, *English Baronies* (Oxford, 1960).

INTRODUCTION

including earls and barons, was a commonplace.[62] England was not
France, where the Twelve Peers had already become established as
the highest group within the aristocracy. To put an exact number on
the aristocracy in England is to ask too much. It shifted and changed
from year to year with the vagaries of inheritance and royal favour.
Royal favour became more important after 1215. Magna Carta
(clause 14) recognised a group of great barons (*maiores barones*)
who, along with the earls and prelates, had a right to be consulted
on so great an affair of the realm as the granting of an aid to the
king. Such men were to be summoned individually by royal writ
to attend the council or parliament which would consent to the tax.
The king therefore might be said, after 1215, to have had a way of
deciding who was or was not a great baron: he was a man worthy
of a separate summons to a council. Unfortunately, we are not privy
to the king's ideas on this subject until the end of the thirteenth
century. We are left with generalities. The earls and counts (a group
veering from seven to thirty in the twelfth century) and a number of
exalted families which never achieved earldoms were undoubtedly
to be rated as great barons (like Briouze, Stafford, Montfichet,
Monmouth, fitz Alan, fitz Walter or Mortemer). Glover's Roll of
Arms of *c*.1250 lists about a hundred such great families before it
proceeds down to the level of the county knights. I, for one, am
happy to stick with that approximate number.

THE MIDDLE GROUND IN SOCIETY

We have looked at the extremes of wealth and poverty in medieval
society and found there recognisable, recognised and self-conscious
social groups. Although I have thrown around the term 'class
antagonism' in a rather Marxist way, I have generally refrained
from calling these groups 'classes' for a number of reasons. In
part this is because of uncertainty as to how I could categorise
the rest of society between the extremes. Associated with the high
aristocracy were groups which had local and economic weight, but
rather less status. To an extent, this is true of the eleventh century,
and by the thirteenth century the claims of the middling groups for
consideration become even more insistent. To talk of a 'knightly

62 Matthew Paris, *Chronica Majora*, ed. H.R. Luard (7 vols, Rolls Series, 1884–9),
vi, 252. For William de Beauchamp see below, p. 105.

23

class' below the 'magnate class' - although it is frequently done[63] – would be confusing, since both groups shared aspirations and badges of status throughout our period. Knights became closer in their behaviour and their use of trappings to magnates during the twelfth century; treating them as separate 'classes' therefore has its dangers when we often mean that they occupied different levels of status in the same social group. Another reason for avoiding too much free talk of 'class' is to avoid an anachronistic debate. It is not within me to relate these ideas to the wider debate on the meaning of the sociological models of class and their applicability to the pre-industrial era. The English reader would do best to refer to the writings of Rodney Hilton, his pupils and colleagues.[64]

But we cannot abandon the middle ground between Dives and Lazarus. Between the agricultural poor and the glittering great was a fragmented group so worthy of a category that historians have invented several terms to describe it. Sections of it have been variously called 'the lesser nobility', 'the knightly class', the 'gentry' or (at the lower end) the 'bourgeoisie' and 'parish gentry'. Of these terms those relating to knights and the bourgeoisie have the best claims to attention. Knights were perceived very early on as an *ordo*; a term which at least comprehends ideas of function. In the eleventh century we hear of families distinguished as being 'knightly' (see p. 123). Problems begin when we look to knights and the bourgeoisie for the sort of common characteristics of behaviour and dress which we find attributed to the magnates. In the early period (apart from their military function and licentiousness) they are lacking for the knight, and in the later part of our period they are usually modifications of what were expected of the magnate. There are indications of solidarity amongst knights in the eleventh century, but the questions of general awareness of the knight in society and self-consciousness amongst knights leads us into realms

63 See P.R. Coss, *Lordship, Knighthood and Locality: a Study in English Society, c.1180–c.1280* (Cambridge, 1991), particularly chs 7–8.
64 Not surprisingly, much of the debate about 'class' in the Middle Ages revolves around the peasantry, see observations in R.H. Hilton, *The English Peasantry in the Late Middle Ages* (Oxford, 1975), 3–13; R. Brenner, 'Agrarian Class Structure and Economic Development in Pre-Industrial Europe', *Past and Present*, lxx (1976), 30–75; R.H. Hilton, 'Agrarian Class Structure and Economic Development', *Past and Present*, lxxx (1978), 3–19. For wider observations about class, estates and caste in medieval society see R. Mousnier, *Les Hiérarchies sociales de 1450 à nos jours* (Paris, 1969), 17–35.

of vagueness and nebulosity which are often frankly impenetrable (see Chapter 4).

As we have seen with the writings of Andrew the Chaplain, there was in the twelfth century a clear consciousness of the bourgeois as an inelegant and ill-formed person, who did not share the aspirations of the aristocrat, despite the claims of wealth. The *marcheant* or *changeor* was perceived as below the salt in social terms, but this does not alter the fact that merchants were wealthy men who could afford as much in the way of luxury as an aristocrat, and in reality might well aspire to their habits. So Andrew the Chaplain has a bourgeois who attempts to seduce noblewomen and countesses, and who argues that his status might be noble, or at least open to ennoblement. The leading members of the populace of London, (called *nobiles*) were praised in the 1170s by one of the city's writers thus:

> This City wins honour by its men and glory by its arms and has a multitude of inhabitants, so that at the time of the calamitous wars of King Stephen's reign the men going forth from it to be mustered were reckoned twenty thousand armed horsemen and sixty thousand foot-soldiers. The citizens of London are everywhere regarded as illustrious and renowned beyond those of all other cities for the elegance of their fine manners, raiment and table. The inhabitants of other towns are called citizens, but of this they are called barons.[65]

Nobility, martial prowess, egregious manners and dress were by the 1170s aristocratic attributes. According to this one partial writer, the leaders of London society had them then. What is more, a number of Londoners (notably members of the Cornhill, Tolosan and Blunt families) attained knighthood in the thirteenth century. The odd example can be offered from other English, and one or two Norman, towns.

There were differing opinions about the social position of these two discernible groups. The clearest conclusion that can be made regarding them is that the richest and most distinguished of the bourgeoisie and knights, by being rich and distinguished, found an entry into the aristocracy in the course of the twelfth century. This was a transition that was made more easy because richer

65 William fitz Stephen, 'A Description of the Most Noble City of London', trans. H.E. Butler in F.M. Stenton, *Norman London: an Essay* (London, 1934), 27.

merchants (especially, but not exclusively, from London) tended to invest some of their wealth in land, which naturally brought them into local aristocratic society.[66] Although the bourgeoisie and knights were distinguishable groups in society between 1000 and 1200 they did not themselves occupy a specific social level. They were distinguished by their functions: trade and war.[67] When it came to considering them as groups with a discrete status they fragment as we grasp at them. If we look at the whole range of status between magnate and peasant, it is difficult until the thirteenth century to find much consciousness of it beyond the uninformative catch-all, 'freemen'. Certainly we find no consistent consciousness of a middling group in society, compared to the level of consciousness of magnates and peasants. To that extent, we can only conclude that post-Conquest lay society in England had only a rudimentary conception of hierarchy, when applied to itself.

We have to look late in our period to find in England a clear awareness of a level of status below the magnate. Clause 14 of Magna Carta has something to say about them. Apart from the 'great barons', lesser men who held land directly from the king were also to be summoned to grant an aid. But it says that they were only to be called on in a general way through the sheriffs, not individually like their betters. Besides these, in 1212 and 1213, the king was willing to call to him representatives of the county knights to consult and harangue about national affairs.[68] This more than hints that by the end of the twelfth century the king was aware that there was a lesser social group to whom it was to his advantage to talk. Another document of the time of Magna Carta has something similar to say. This is the 'Magna Carta of Cheshire' issued in the months after the events of Runnymede by Earl Ranulf III in response to the complaints of the men of his great earldom. It was done 'at the petition of my barons of Cheshire', a dominant group in the shire distinct from the 'common knights' who were their tenants (presumably the barons of Cheshire were themselves

66 Coss, *Lordship, Knighthood and Locality*, 92, from his study of twelfth- and thirteenth-century Coventry, cautions against seeing this tendency as common in the provinces, although he can point to one or two instances of it.
67 Note the surprised comment of Jordan Fantosme on the burghers of Dunwich who went to war in 1173, that 'that day you would see *burgeis* as full valiant as knights', *Jordan Fantosme's Chronicle*, ed. R.C. Johnston (Oxford, 1981), 64.
68 J.C. Holt, 'The Prehistory of Parliament', in *The English Parliament in the Middle Ages*, ed. R.G. Davies and J.H. Denton (Manchester, 1981), 5–8.

knights who were more than common).[69] Here were men of local influence; influential enough to oblige their immediate lord to come to terms with them. Every shire could boast a similar group, leading knights who guided the affairs of the court and who had since 1176 been recognised by the king as having a right to do so.

Were these men a group within society? Were they part of a greater aristocracy? If it is difficult to define the magnates, it is frankly impossible to define this lesser group at all closely. Then there is the question of whether we ought to bother to do it at all. The term 'knightly class' is often used to comprehend this group. At least one attempt has been made to wrestle some sociological meaning out of it.[70] But in my view this is a blind alley. Since twelfth-century knights affected the manners of greater men they can hardly be regarded as a discrete 'class' as such, as they had ambitions to be included within a higher social level. The term 'gentry', despite being both anachronistic and shapeless, is a better bet than 'knightly class'; better for being shapeless maybe: a loose garment to envelop a flabby body.[71]

IDEAS OF INDIVIDUAL RANK AND STATUS

A final question relates to medieval ideas of individual status. To some extent this concern stands outside (as well as complementing) a discussion of social groupings. For, as I have said, late eleventh- and twelfth-century English society seems not to have been perceived by contemporaries as hierarchic. The artificial hierarchies of jurisdiction and tenure caused by the obligations relating to grants of fees do not amount to a social hierarchy. It was perfectly possible – and in fact happened – that an earl could hold a fee of a simple freeman. But it is possible for a society to have loose ideas about hierarchies of groups, but still be alert to differences of individual status.

The Middle Ages inherited a regard for status from Antiquity. The Church was a constant reminder to men to think in terms of relative

---

69 *Charters of the Anglo-Norman Earls of Chester, c. 1071–1237*, ed. G. Barraclough (Record Society of Lancashire and Cheshire, cxxvi, 1988), 388–91.
70 For a well-intentioned attempt by a historian to argue the toss with a sociologist see the questioning of Georges Gurvitch's model of class in a medieval context by J.M. van Winter, 'The Knightly Aristocracy of the Middle Ages as a "Social Class"', in *The Medieval Nobility*, ed. T. Reuter (Amsterdam, 1979), 313–29, particularly p. 329.
71 For a review of the terms 'gentry' and 'parish gentry' as used by later medieval historians, see Given-Wilson, *The English Nobility in the Later Middle Ages*, 69ff.

importance and titles. In the earlier period the throne and ranked bench around the cathedral apse was a practical demonstration of the descending orders of bishop, priest and deacon. In the later period the stepped seats of the sedilia in the chancel of every large church was a continuing exercise of degree observable to all through clouds of incense and chancel screens. The Church was not alone in thinking in terms of order and degree, as I mean to go on to consider. But it is as well to consider the Church first, because it was members of the clergy whose deliberations on questions of degree were formalised in writing.

The writer on medieval society is often drawn back to Isidore of Seville, the Spanish bishop (died 636) whose *Etymologiae* were the foundation of many a medieval education. In Chapter 3 of Book 9 of this work Isidore collected together all the titles he had trawled from his reading of Roman histories. His catalogue rests on Livy in part: kings give way to consuls and the whole range of Republican dignitaries: proconsuls, exconsuls and dictators. He moves on to lustrous words like caesar, emperor and Augustus; the men who brought the Republic low. But the succeeding section deals with the dignities of Hellenic Palestine and the Late Empire. We find now kings once more at the head of what seems to be meant as a hierarchy of titles: prince (*princeps*), duke (*dux*), and on into less relevant, defunct titles, tetrarch, tribune and chiliarch.

Isidore's encyclopaedic approach was (and to an extent still is) seductive. Echoes of his reasonings and explanations continually recur in High Medieval sources. To give one example, a creature often met with in the late eleventh and early twelfth centuries is the *miles gregarius* (translated as the 'common knight'). The association of that particular adjective to the noun *miles* (which signifies 'knight' by then) is odd, and much has been made of it in explaining early divisions within the knightly class.[72] But if you look at Isidore, you find at least a clue to the origins of its use, for he writes:

> A *miles* is either an *ordinarius* or an *extraordinarius*. An *ordinarius* fights in the ranks, and no degree of honour attaches to him, for he is a common (*gregarius*) or humble (*humilis*) soldier. But an *extraordinarius* is he who is promoted from the ranks because of his abilities.[73]

72 S. Harvey, 'The Knight and the Knight's Fee in England', *Past and Present*, xlix (1970), 28–9.
73 *Etymologiae*, in *Patrologia Latina*, lxxxiv, col. 345.

Early in the eleventh century, the clerk who drew up the statement of grievances his lord, Hugh de Lusignan, had against the count of Aquitaine must have trawled Isidore to find the title 'chiliarch', with which he equipped Hugh to bolster his dignity against the count (doubtless as a literary alternative to 'castellan').[74] Isidore says 'Chiliarchs are they who rule over a thousand, we (in Latin) call them *millenarii*; chiliarch is a Greek word'. The later use of the title 'prince' in Britain may have a lot to do with Isidore's placing of it in his list (after the king, but before the duke). Echoes of his explanations for other titles reach us from as late as Gerald of Wales and Bracton when they turn to look at the ranks of the aristocracies of their days.

Isidore's method was as influential as his explanations. A number of ninth-century (and perhaps earlier) texts on ranks (*gradus*) survive. The earliest quotes directly from Isidore (on consuls) and its origin has been recently ascribed to England.[75] The most effective of such essays is that by the ninth-century author, and imperial tutor, Walafrid Strabo (who studied at Aachen under Alcuin of Northumbria). Walafrid launches into an explanation of the ranks of the Church of his day, and excels Isidore by comparing the ranks of the Church with those of contemporary lay society. He gives us a singularly cogent view of the dual structure of his world. The pope related to the emperor in degree, a patriarch with a patrician (still a rank of honour in use in Carolingian times), he compared an archbishop with a king, metropolitan bishops with dukes, bishops with counts, commanders of armies with abbots, imperial arch-chaplains with counts of the imperial palace, imperial chaplains with imperial vassals, and so on down the ranks of local government. Walafrid called the lay ranks he was describing *ordinationes*, which recalled the ordained orders of the church, but which might be legitimately translated as 'ranks' or 'degrees'.[76]

In looking to classify and expound upon these degrees, Walafrid

---

74 Martindale, '*Conventum inter Guillelmum Aquitanorum comes et Hugonem Chiliarchum*', 528n, 541. Other vocabulary in the same document recalls Isidore and later tracts on status; an official is called a '*tribunus*'.

75 P.A. Barnwell, '*Epistula Hieronimi de gradus Romanorum*': an English School Book', *Historical Research*, lxiv (1991), 77–86.

76 *De exordiis et incrementis quarundam in observationibus ecclesiasticis rerum*, in M[onumenta] G[ermanicae] H[istoriae], *Capitularia regnum Francorum*, ed. A. Boretius and V. Krause, ii (Hanover, 1897), 515. I must thank Dr Janet Nelson for drawing this example to my attention.

was demonstrating not merely the compulsive tidiness of the encyclopaedist, but the mind of the courtier acquainted with government. The vocabulary existed in his circles with which to describe a hierarchic lay society, and it is clear enough that he and many others both saw it that way, and were instructed by Isidorean tracts to see it that way. The word *ordo* was already being deployed, as the Romans and Fathers had deployed it, to mark out identifiable groups within society, particularly in the trifunctional scheme of those who pray (*oratores*), those who fight (*bellatores*) and those who work (*laboratores*).[77] Another word that filled a similar need was *gradus*, used frequently in the tracts which describe the ranks of the lay aristocracy. *Ordinationes, ordines* and *gradus*: the use of these words by itself tells us that European writers were grappling with ideas of rank, function and status long before the period with which this study deals. Such words did not comprehend any idea of class, of course, but it was perhaps the nearest that medieval society got to the idea.

But these were churchmen and intellectuals. What of the ordinary folk, those who did not normally commit their thoughts to writing? This is a question that plagues the historian. We look at early society through the distorting lens of Latin vocabulary, and through the eyes of a particular group which had prejudices and idiosyncratic interests. How are we to say whether a perception of rank was general in society, and if so, what was it? Without attempting amateur sociology, it is at least possible to say that there is evidence that commoner people had a lively sense of individual status in early medieval society too. The lawbooks are a useful indicator here, because law involved communal thinking and discussion; it was not a solitary intellectual exercise conceived in a monastic cell. From legal collections we find that the English and Welsh from the earliest times were absorbed by questions of status. Early on, they distinguished the ceorl (the freeman) from the eorl (the well-born freeman); the 'dearly-born' from the 'cheaply born'. Later lawbooks put forward a hierarchy of ranks within society when defining the amount of the *wer* and *manbót* owed at the death of a man. Such a system must create and reinforce a graduated scale of status amongst men, from slave to ealdorman (although different regions might express the divisions differently).[78]

77 Duby, *The Three Orders*, 73–5.
78 Whitelock, *Beginnings of English Society*, 83–4.

Wulfstan of York, in the first quarter of the eleventh century, felt moved to compile the various systems of ranking by wergild that he had encountered: those of Wessex, Northumbria and Mercia. Here we find a distinct emphasis on wealth and royal service in categorising men. A ceorl with a hall, gatehouse and chapel and five hides of land, might claim the status of thegn; a thegn who prospered and was attended before the king with lesser thegns could be considered an eorl (that is, a noble). Rather like Walafrid Strabo, he compared ecclesiastical and secular dignities: archbishops to athelings (designated royal heirs); bishops to ealdormen; heads of minsters to thegns. These classifications were still understood – and perhaps operated – in the England of Henry I, where the lawbook known as the *Leges Henrici Primi* (Laws of Henry I) still classified men in an ascending order: slave, 200-man, 600-man, or thegn (1,200-man). In the case of the last we are told that 'he is a man fully noble' and his *bót* was a considerable sum.[79]

This system of classifying men was in decay in England in the early twelfth century, but in Wales and Scotland it continued to develop into the next century. There is the evidence of a tenth-century text that the Welsh had copies of the tracts on the Roman dignities, and were fully in tune with English and Continental ideas at an early date. An eleventh-century text from South Wales can use words such as *rex*, *dux*, *satraps*, *princeps* or *prepotens*, given in that order, for the powers that rule the world.[80] Welsh legal texts show the same lively appreciation of difference between degrees of men as do the English. Thirteenth-century redactions of the Welsh laws (which derive from twelfth-century exemplars, and they from more ancient custom) talk of the degrees of status (*braint*) which belong to various ranks of court and society, and the compensation (*sarhad*) owed for offences against their dignity, and the wer (*galanas*) for offences against their person. Welsh society, even the Church, was obsessed with individual status, and remained so into the thirteenth

79 'A Compilation on Status', translated in *English Historical Documents*, i, c. 500 *AD–1042*, ed. D. Whitelock (London, 1955), 431–4; F. Pollock and F.W. Maitland, *The History of English Law* (2 vols, 2nd edn, Cambridge, 1898) ii, 458–60; *Leges Henrici Primi*, ed. L.J. Downer (Cambridge, 1972), c.76. Confirmation that there was some reality in this categorisation in the early twelfth century can be found for the north of England, where thegns, drengs and smallemen appear as free tenants between Tyne and Tees in *Pipe Roll of 31 Henry I*, ed. J. Hunter (Record Commission, 1833), 132.
80 Barnwell, '*Epistula Hieronimi de gradus Romanorum*', 85–6; *The Text of the Book of Llan Dâv*, ed. J. Gwenogvryn Evans (Oxford, 1893), 266; quoted in W. Davies, *Patterns of Power in Early Wales* (Oxford, 1990), 12.

century.[81] Welsh poetry of the twelfth century gives more evidence of popular perceptions. Thomas Charles-Edwards has demonstrated (principally from the *Mabinogion*) how twelfth-century Welsh literature shows a society well attuned to degrees of status amongst its rulers, even though there was no formal distinction of title; there is evidence that this was so in earlier centuries in Wales too.[82]

The legal tract known as *Regiam Majestatem* presents a graduated picture of medieval Scottish society which is similar in its regularity to those of England and Wales. The king was at the top, of course; the son of the king, in the next level beneath, ranked with an earl, and an earl's son ranked with a thain. This Scottish source is late, but I think it reflects earlier attitudes of Scottish society. It reveals that the Scots had a singularly coherent view of themselves by the end of the eleventh century: kings presiding over *mormaer*-earls, and *toiseach*-thanes ranking beneath them. How did the English, Welsh and Scottish perceptions of status interrelate? That there was some cross-fertilisation of ideas is certain, especially between England and English-speaking Scotland. The English may have influenced Wales too; and the English source 'the Ordinance of the Dunsaete' can refer to Welshmen as of the rank of ceorl or thegn, and English diplomata impose the ranks of *reguli* or *subreguli* on Welsh kings (as if they were ealdormen). It is as likely, however, that independent traditions of organising society were involved.

We have a number of scattered indications of the sharp appreciation of lay status in Anglo-Norman society, outside the lawbooks. The most formidable, but profitable, body of evidence is to be found in charters. Taking a charter which derives from Chester abbey around 1100, we find that it talks of a variety of grades of followers of the earl of Chester: his principal barons, other barons, knights, burgesses and 'other free men'.[83] The separation of burgesses from other free men, after the knights, is a significant one, for it implies status of a sort attaching to their economic weight. A century and more later, the poet who compiled the historical romance called *The*

---

81 W. Davies, *Wales in the Early Middle Ages*, 61–2; R.R. Davies, *The Age of Conquest*, 115–19.

82 T.M. Charles-Edwards, 'Honour and Status in some Irish and Welsh Prose Tales', *Ériu*, xxix (1978), 123–41; see also Davies, *Patterns of Power in Early Wales*, 12–13.

83 *The Charters of the Anglo-Norman Earls of Chester*, ed. Barraclough, 4. The act in question appears to date from the mid-1090s and may derive from a pancarte of the abbey; it was incorporated in a spurious charter of Earl Hugh I concocted in the mid-twelfth century.

Song of Dermot and the Earl has King Diarmait of Leinster writing generally to the March of Wales, asking for assistance. The address of the letter (which has no parallel in surviving letters of the time) again attempts to categorise military society comprehensively; he wrote to 'earls, barons, knights, squires (*vallez*), serjeants (*serianz*) and common soldiers, on horse or foot'.[84] These divisions should not be taken as hard and fast; they represent but one man's view, and a poet at that. The meaning of certain of the terms he uses is disputable. *Valet* and *seriant* were terms whose use was not always clear. Here they are obviously meant to be taken as having different meanings (despite both being often translated today as 'squire'). Other writers of the twelfth century forgot about the *valet*, and meant *seriant* to be taken as the rank below knight. Chrétien de Troyes did as much; he has King Arthur offering a gold cup to the man responsible for taking Windsor castle if he were a *sergenz*, but if he were a knight, he would have the cup and any other reward he named.[85] So, qualification aside, we have good indications of a vigorous appreciation of status in lay society in the High Middle Ages. It is not a clear appreciation with a standardised vocabulary, but that does not detract from the evidence of an underlying need to categorise at the time.

To get the full savour of this medieval desire to categorise people, we need to turn to the evidence of the witness lists of diplomats and charters. This provides a solid grounding of material with which to assess ideas of status in medieval society, the problem only being that as the twelfth century progresses, there becomes too much of it even for computers to handle. The lists of witnesses that conclude these documents were drawn up by clerks, who must have been churchmen in the early period, but like tracts on law, they had to echo lay perceptions. English royal acts of the early eleventh century, just as much as Norman ducal acts, demonstrate a powerful sense of order in this respect. English clerks ranked witnesses in order: first the royal family, then the bishops, earls (*duces*) and thegns (*ministri*) present. Norman acts will similarly list first archbishops and bishops, then counts (*comites*), viscounts (*vicecomites*) and ducal household officers, before getting down to the common or garden landholders. A common process was at work here. Clerks would not list men at random, as they caught their eye.

84 *The Song of Dermot and the Earl*, ed. G.H. Orpen (Oxford, 1892), 32: *cuntes, baruns, chevalers, vallez, serianz, lue devers, gent a cheval e a pe.*
85 *Cligès*, ed. A. Micha (Classiques français du moyen âge, 1957), ll. 1529–33.

They felt obliged to record them by some generally acknowledged (and doubtless continually revised) scheme.

In the twelfth century, the rapidly multiplying number of charters shows us how widespread were ideas of ranking in witness lists; the Channel was no boundary marking different practices. An early example, indeed one of the earliest private charters surviving from England, which has the advantage of being dated, is worth looking at in this regard. It is the charter by which Robert Losinga, bishop of Hereford, came to an agreement about knight service with his tenant, Roger son of Walter, in 1085.[86] The charter has two witness lists, one for the bishop's side, the other for Roger. Roger brought forward several great men on his behalf. The list runs as follows:

Earl (*comes*) Roger (of Shrewsbury)
Hugh, the earl's son
Everard, another son
The countess (Mabel) his wife
Warin the sheriff (*vicecomes*)
Osbern fitz Richard (lord of Richards Castle)
Dreux fitz Pons (lord of Clifford)
Gerard de Tournai
William Malbedan
Gilbert the earl's constable

The earl naturally came first, and naturally too his sons were listed next, being seen as closest in dignity to him (eldest first, for Hugh succeeded to the earldom of Shrewsbury in 1094). The countess was listed last in the family group, but before the sheriff and barons present. Women, especially titled women, always caused a problem when they featured in a witness list, and their position when they do appear is difficult to predict. Warin the sheriff of Shropshire, being regarded here as truly *vicecomes*, was ranked after the comital family. Two substantial Marcher castellans then follow him, and two unidentifiable comital followers, the rear being brought up by a household officer of the earl, his constable.

A charter of the next generation shows some of the problems when a large family group (including an unusually large number of women) was assembled for a particularly solemn transaction: the foundation of a priory. This was the foundation of the priory

---

86 PRO, C115 G/31/4095 (Duchess of Norfolk Deeds); printed in V.H. Galbraith 'An Episcopal Land-Grant of 1085', *English Historical Review*, xliv (1929), 372.

of Le Désert by Earl Robert II of Leicester, which was transacted
in the forest of Breteuil in Normandy at Lême on 28 April 1125.[87]
It runs as follows:

Ouen, bishop of Evreux
Ralph, archdeacon
William de Glos, archdeacon
William dean (of the collegiate church) of Breteuil
Goscelin chaplain of L'Aigle
Vitalis the chaplain
Arnold du Bois
William Fresnel } barons of Breteuil
Baldwin de Grandvilliers
Reginald Boffey
Baldwin de Charnelles
William clerk of Glos
Amice, countess of Leicester
Margaret, countess of Warwick (the earl's widowed aunt)
Rotrou, her son
Henry, another son
Juliana de l'Aigle (Countess Margaret's sister)

This particular list has the clerical witnesses listed before the lay,
as is common in the post-Gregorian age. The clergy present are
strictly ranked, bishop followed by archdeacons, by a dean of a
secular college, and by two chaplains. A humble clerk finds his
way into the lay section of the list, after the men, just before the
women and children. This *clericus* might not have been classed as
worthy of joining the prelates and chaplains present, disqualified
by lack of office, or by belonging to minor orders. The laymen
present can be identified from other sources as having been listed
in order of wealth and confidence in which the earl held them; the
first of them, Arnold du Bois, appears a decade later as the earl's
seneschal of Breteuil.[88] All the women are in a sump at the bottom
of the list, countesses or not. There are two countesses present; the
earl's wife is first, and his widowed aunt comes second. Two males
then follow, Rotrou and Henry, third and fifth sons of the late Earl

87 Cartulary of Le Désert, Archives départementales de l'Eure, G 165, fos
1r–2v; printed in A-J. Devoisins, *Histoire de Notre-Dame du Désert* (Paris,
1901), 103–7.
88 For the laymen present see D. Crouch, *The Beaumont Twins* (Cambridge,
1986), 102–13.

Henry of Warwick. But since the earl died in 1119, it is clear that these two are still minors in their mother's care. Even they precede the last-named woman present, Juliana de l'Aigle, who although the wife of a great Anglo-Norman baron and daughter of the count of Perche, must follow even the boys.

Both the early lists we have looked at have a clear internal logic. In terms of laymen, titles counted for most, it seems, then came economic weight, then lesser office in household, and lastly the women. It is even possible to distinguish some logic behind the ranking of people who are roughly equals. Thus the young Countess Amice who was the wife of Earl Robert preceded the older Countess Margaret who was his aunt; closeness to the earl was what counted here. Of the three barons of Breteuil listed (although their estates were roughly equal in size) the first, Du Bois, was first because he was the earl's confidant and the last, De Grandvilliers, was a newcomer to the lordship, who had recently inherited his lands there by marriage. The clerk who drew up the list was demonstrating a fine sensitivity to the kin, history and economic positions of individuals present. Was he assisted in this? It is possible to imagine the scene at the commissioning of the charter, perhaps in the church of Le Désert at Lême. The clergy present would have been assembled in a party at one side of the earl (as we see in contemporary illustrations), the most prestigious amongst them nearest their host. The laymen would have been in another party; again, those closest to their master being those who had been longest in his service and who had the most wealth. The women and children would have been to one side, perhaps seated and looking on. The countesses and the lady of L'Aigle would have been a richly dressed group, the boys standing around their distinguished mother. The clerk would naturally have included them, even though they were disabled from an active part in the proceedings. The boys, at least, would have been useful to include, as they would probably live longer than the adults present, and their *recordatio* of the proceedings was the more valuable. What we may be seeing in the concluding witnesses of the charter transacted at Lême in 1125 was the translation of a physical grouping around the earl into writing. It reminds me irresistibly of nineteenth-century posed portraits, taken in oils or by photographic plate, of solemn occasions: the signing of a treaty, a royal visit to a municipality, or the opening of a bridge.

These two Anglo-Norman charters are representative of the long witness list attached to the more elaborate written act. The principles

they demonstrate are evident for the succeeding centuries in England
(witness lists do not generally feature in northern French charters
after about 1230). There are some significant changes. The witness
list got more formalised towards the end of the twelfth century
as it became customary to designate laymen in them by the
title of 'knight' and corral them at the beginning.[89] The position
of aristocratic women in their families' charters becomes more
formalised and prominent – although they did not in general
appear in many public acts. Increasingly the wife of an earl (if
she featured at all) is to be found heading the list, preceding her
children and in-laws. In the thirty-one charters of Roger earl of
Warwick (died 1153) twelve feature his wife, Countess Gundreda.
She is first witness in all but one, where she is displaced by the earl's
three brothers. Since Gundreda lived at a time before deference to
women became general in society, this may be a tribute to her
personality. She was notorious as a strong-willed woman: her
husband is said to have died of a heart attack when he heard
she had welcomed the king's enemies into Warwick castle, while
he was himself in the king's army.[90] On a more practical point, her
prominence may have much to do with an increasing perception
that her eventual dower rights in her husband's lands made her
appearance in their disposition desirable. Women otherwise are
not much in evidence in charters of the later twelfth and thirteenth
centuries. Even the women who issued great numbers of them (such
as Mathilda countess of Warwick, Alice countess of Eu, Ela countess
of Salisbury and Isabel de Forz countess of Aumale and Devon)
do not include their female friends in their acts. Instead they are
attended by their knights, seneschals and male household.

Reviewing what evidence there is, it is fair to conclude that
the eleventh, twelfth and thirteenth centuries had a good idea of
individual status. It was not a closed notion, circulating amongst
intellectuals and commentators. The idea of status and hierarchy
was common to all, and was already sophisticated by the eleventh
century. Status was founded in a variety of sources: titles, occupation,
kinship and wealth. It was more or less automatic for any medieval
clerk to attempt to categorise lists of people in this way. We have

89 A useful numerical study of this process is in D.F. Fleming, '*Milites* as Attestors
to Charters in England, 1101–1300', *Albion*, xxxii (1990), 185–98.
90 *Gesta Stephani*, ed. K. Potter and R.H.C. Davis (Oxford, 1976), 234; Robert
de Torigny, *Chronica*, in *Chronicles of the Reigns of Stephen, Henry II and Richard*,
ed. R. Howlett (4 vols, Rolls Series, 1884–89), iv, 172.

examined charter witness lists, but other forms of list tell exactly the same story. In the English *Cartae Baronum* of 1166, which list the amounts of knight service owed by individual tenants to their lords, under the king, the first names are usually those who owed most, even if they are not in numerical order. In the later thirteenth century there is an even more sophisticated example in the early rolls of arms compiled to record the armorial devices of the kingdom. Take the roll known as Glover's Roll, which dates from the 1250s and has 215 entries. First is the king and then a procession of earls, followed by the barons and then (after entry 105) the significant county knights. Even the earls are ranked in a discernible order. The first after the king is his brother, Cornwall, the next Leicester, his brother-in-law. Then follows the wealthiest earl, the Clare earl of Gloucester and Hertford. A collection of the arms of defunct earldoms brings up the rear, followed by the king's foreign favourites: Lusignan and Plessis. After them come a procession of barons in no particular order, and finally the armigerous major knights of the shires, beginning with Du Bois of Leicestershire, Sandford, Montfort of Beaudesert; all major actors in the events of the reign, but not holders of baronies.[91]

The touchiness of earls with regard to their status is registered as early as Stephen's reign, and one example will do as an endpiece to this Introduction. Geoffrey Gaimar's (largely imaginary) description of the opening of William Rufus's new hall at Westminster has four English earls seizing the swords of state, which were to go before Rufus, from the Welsh kings who had claimed the privilege of carrying them. One earl stood aloof even from that. Gaimar has Hugh of Chester spurn such an office: 'I will be no servant (*sergant*)'. The king laughed and recognised the fat earl's claims to pre-eminence by giving him his gold sceptre to carry.[92] Perched on the apex of society, the king who was beyond status could be amused by the game his people played, for the pack was his to shuffle. That kings were alert to the possibilities that the scrabbling for status gave them for patronage and control is enough to tell us of its importance.

91 *Rolls of Arms: Henry III*, ed. T.D. Tremlett (Harleian Soc., 1967), 91–159.
92 *L'Estoire des Engles*, ed. A. Bell (Anglo-Norman Text Soc., xiv–xvi, 1960), ll. 5975–6020. In Richard I's coronation in 1189, the office of the sceptre went to William Marshal; in the coronation of Queen Eleanor in 1236, it went to Richard Siward; both men were eminent warriors and royal counsellors.

Part I

HEREDITARY TITLES AND SOCIAL DIGNITIES

1

THE EARL AND THE COUNT

Aristocracies are particularly fond of titles. Where the possession of political and economic power is hereditary, hereditary titles advertise the ascendancy of one class over the others in a most satisfactory way, and neatly define social divisions. In this and the next chapter I will chart the slow elaboration of the use of titles over several centuries in the societies of England and its neighbours as a means of identifying its aristocracy to itself (and to us).

The essential theme is regulation, as will soon become apparent. I have long considered the use of titles to be at the direction or pleasure of the monarch, or, latterly, the monarch's government. This is a habit of thought that is difficult to shake off. It was impossible to shake off for earlier generations of historians. Round, Ellis and the peerage lawyers of the nineteenth century cultivated a number of myths, but none was more long-lasting than their unconscious assumption that what was the case with the titles of the English peerage of their day applied equally to the aristocracy of the days before the reign of Edward III. But in the years 1000–1300 there is an abundance of evidence that the aspirations of individuals and the easy conscience of general society tolerated a far looser use of titles, even the greater titles, than has ever been allowed for in this period. At the beginning of the period the king had no ambitions to monitor and control the life of his realm, merely to make money out of it and attain security. That this attitude changed in the fourteenth century is one of the least explored movements of the mind in medieval society. Before 1300 the king's role in the use and assumption of titles was limited and unambitious. As we will see, the first firm and general pronouncement of a king on a matter of social dignity did not come until 1292 in England.

The hereditary titles we find in 1000 were almost all at one time the names of offices, held at a monarch's pleasure. But once obtained, a great man would be reluctant to relinquish a title he had been given, and if the sovereign who granted it was willing, the office might stay in his family's hands and become what has been called, and was called in the eleventh century, a 'title of honour': a hereditary dignity which might or might not have real attributes of power about it, but which was infinitely desirable to those who did not have it.[1] The idea of hereditary titles in Western society is a very ancient one. To the Romans, and those who came after them, an office was a 'dignity', an 'honour', one of life's prizes. With that sort of attitude, it is hardly to be wondered at that the acquisition of office was followed almost naturally by the desire amongst fathers to transmit it as a privilege to their sons. As early as the time of the Roman emperor Theodosius, fathers were petitioning hard for their sons to enjoy their office. After the Empire's fall, in England and on the Continent, it seems to be a universal phenomenon that lay offices of state tended to fall into the hands of great families. When they did so, these families regarded the offices as their natural entitlement. Titles passing from generation to generation in such families may not have done so out of hereditary right, but it is easy to see how these families would soon have regarded their titles as their right.

The titles of honour that great men used and sought in the year 1000 were already established in some sort of hierarchy. The word is an apt one because men had already by then compared the order of ranks in lay society with the elaborate hierarchy of the Church. The Church was, and long had been, in love with proper order and obedience. It was thought in the early Church that order and hierarchy sprang from men's souls, where good and evil were unequally mixed; in short, some men were better than others and as a consequence, worthier than others. As a result Christian society must be led by a hierarchy ranked by goodness, with Christ at the summit. Lay society as well as the Church must observe the established ranks. And those ranks were borrowed from the society in which the Church had grown up: the stratified bureaucracy of the Late Roman Empire. Gregory the Great regarded with alarm a society where due order and what was left of the secular hierarchy was not observed. 'No kings, no dukes,

---

1 Orderic Vitalis, *The Ecclesiastical History*, ed. M. Chibnall, (6 vols, Oxford, 1969–80), v, 246–8: Count Elias of Maine is made by Orderic to refer to the *nominis et honoris titulo* (which might be translated 'title of distinction and of dignity') which he had lost when Maine was conquered.

no counts!' he said of the Lombard kingdom in a letter to his envoy in Constantinople in AD 594, 'It is fallen into the most profound confusion!'[2]

There had been a great regard for the use of titles during the Roman Empire, which possessed from the time of Diocletian a rigid bureaucracy inspired by the organisation of its formidable army. In due course, the Roman army and bureaucracy provided many of the titles used by later medieval Europe. Its influence lingered in the Gothic, Lombard and Frankish kingdoms which succeeded the Western Empire, ever anxious to dignify themselves with the rags of power left over from Rome's heyday. It was in this period, not long after Gregory the Great's pontificate, that the single work most influential on the later use of lay titles was written. I have already had cause to mention the 'Etymologies', written by Isidore of Seville in Gothic Spain in the early seventh century (see pp. 28–9). Isidore set out an encyclopeadic list of all the ranks he had trawled from his extensive reading. In the ninth book is a list of, and commentary on, the lay dignities he had noted down. Isidore made an effort to put them in an order of importance, for this was essential if the principle of order and hierarchy was to be observed. Isidore's little list was influential. It inspired later treatises on ranks, and provided a good deal of the material contained within them. A later reader might well find in Isidore much to explain his world. If (like Bracton) one read 'count' instead of 'consul' (and the two words were often used as equivalents) then one could find in Isidore the basic list of titles in use in Europe in 1000: kings, princes, dukes and counts. The making of a list also provided the foundation of a hierarchy, for it is clear that Isidore intended his list to reflect relative importance. Political writers of thirteenth-century England, Gerald of Wales and Bracton, still quoted Isidore as the ultimate authority on titles. His influence is all-pervasive and startling; the later rank of prince, and its placing in the hierarchy ahead of duke, is partly Isidore's doing, because in his brief description of the title he was firm in declaring 'prince' to be 'a dignity and an order'.

The theme broached by Isidore was to be part of the intellectual life of the West. It was cherished by Hincmar and Walafrid Strabo, and its vitality persisted after 1000. Ralph Glaber in the early 1030s could talk of 'the ranks of men' of which kingship was the highest.[3]

2 *Monumenta Germaniae Historica: Epistolae* i, 286.
3 *Vita Domni Willelmi abbatis*, ed. N. Bulst and P. Reynolds (Oxford, 1989), 284.

A passage written about 1100 in a posthumous panegyric of William of Normandy tells us much the same:

> He moved through the successive ranks, beginning with
> consul,
> Soon he will be beyond the ranks, to emperor from
> duke.[4]

These recognised 'ranks of men' formed a group of men at the top of society small in number. They were a minority even within the tiny social group represented by the magnates. At most, there were only ever twenty-five men bearing the title of earl at any one time in England between 1000 and 1300. Often the title was confined to far fewer men, seven in the reign of Henry I (1100–35); in 1300 there were eleven. In Normandy the maximum number of counts was five, in the time of Robert II (1087–1106). They undoubtedly formed an élite within an élite. Counts and earls headed all lists of those attending on the king, or owing military service to him. Their 'high nobility' was noted by writers of the twelfth century. They were the highest social level of the country, sharing their rank with the king's sons.

The repertoire of titles in use in 1000 in northern France, under the king, had resolved into a hierarchy headed by the **duke** (Lat. *dux*; Fr. *duc*; Ger. *Herzog*) with its occasional equivalent of **prince** (Lat. *princeps*; Ger. *Fürst*). These two were in an unresolved bunch at the top, competing for dignity, one might say. Below them was a relative newcomer, the **marquis** (Lat. *marchio*; Ger. *Margraf*), who was acknowledged to be a step above the universal and undifferentiated **count** (Lat. *comes* or occasionally *consul*; Fr. *comte*; MFr. *cuens*, *contor*; Ger. *Graf*). A hereditary rank of **viscount** was beginning to be observed below the count in France (Lat. *vicecomes*; Fr. *vicomte*). Other lesser ranks, like vidame (Lat. *vicedominus*) or advocate, had appeared in northern France, but are omitted here as they found no lasting place amongst the others. In England in 1000, of course, things were different, although here too there are traces of hierarchical thinking, but more of England later. The rest of this chapter will be devoted to a consideration of the changing meanings and status of these ranks in the period into the fourteenth century, and their fate after their importation into England. This concerns,

---

4 Baudrey de Bourgeuil, *Adelae Comitissae*, trans. M.W. Herren, in, S.A. Brown, *The Bayeux Tapestry: History and Bibliography* (London, 1988), 168, ll. 241–2.

in particular, the earl, with whom I will start, because for most of this period the earldom was the only recognised title of honour in England, Scotland and Wales, until the title 'prince' made its entry in the later twelfth century.

Earls and counts are distinguished in England today by separate words, as if they were separate ranks. The 'earl' is seen to be a specifically English rank; the 'count' belongs to the Continent (Scandinavia apart). But this is a relatively new way of looking at it, which only begins to crop up in the sixteenth century in England. In medieval England after the Conquest no difference was seen between French counts and English earls. Latin-speakers called them both *comites*, English speakers *eorlas*, and French speakers *contes*; for that matter Welshmen called them both *ieirll*. Whether in France or England the title was regarded as the same. The Anglo-Saxon Chronicle in 1120 talked about the 'eorl of Ceastre' (Chester) and a few lines later the 'eorl of Flandran' (Flanders), and saw no incongruity in relating the two.[5] Alan, a count of the Breton ruling family who was also earl of Richmond, could issue charters in the mid-twelfth century describing himself as 'a count of Brittany and England' (*comes Britannie et Anglie*).[6] A century later, Richard, brother of King Henry III, styled himself 'count of Poitou and Cornwall (*comes Pictavie et Cornubie*)' because, to him as to Alan, a count was an earl was a count. After the fall of Normandy in 1204, the Norman count of Aumale was able to decamp to his Yorkshire estates and he and his successors lived on there for generations as titular 'counts of Aumale' with no feeling of being somehow in the wrong place. The ranks related absolutely in whatever language you used.

The divergence in the use of the titles was a wholly English business, maybe a projection of growing insularity in Tudor England after the Reformation. Certainly by the nineteenth century it was general amongst English writers to separate earls and counts; counts were foreign and different, earls were familiar and English. Modern French writers still do not differentiate. To a Frenchman, the earl of Snowdon is *le comte de Snowdon*. This causes me some difficulty; how do I proceed? It seems best, however, to stick to modern English usage to avoid confusion. The reader must simply take this

5 *The Peterborough Chronicle*, ed. C. Clark (Oxford, 1970), p. 40, *s.a.* 1120.
6 Durham Dean & Chapter archives, charter no. 1.3 Ebor. 12.

as a warning that the modern English use can distort the medieval attitude that preceded it: from the 1070s onwards 'count' and 'earl' indicated the same rank.

ANGLO-SAXON EALDORMEN AND EARLS

The word 'eorl', from which we get the modern 'earl', first acquired the cachet of rank in English society in the course of the tenth century. It was eventually to replace an older, and long-established rank, the 'ealdorman'. The rank of ealdorman was still surviving, indeed flourishing, in England in 1000. The influence and authority of ealdormen varied at the time. Under Aethelred II (978–1016) ealdormen might preside over regions as varied in size as Northumbria and Essex; groupings of shires or single shires. However, not all shires had ealdormen under Aethelred. He was often reluctant to replace ealdormen who died or went into exile: the first known English king consciously to adopt this strategy of limiting access to rank; an oblique acknowledgement of its importance. The ealdormanic office had two known responsibilities: to assist in maintaining justice in their shires, and to lead the armies that defended them. The office was not hereditary, but in practice ealdormen were appointed from families with a history of possessing the office. The title was generally attached to the region of its responsibility ('ealdorman of East Anglia', or whatever), but ealdormen might be moved, or their region of authority adjusted.[7]

'Eorl' itself was an old word by 1000, generally used in earlier centuries in poetry. It was a cognate of the Scandinavian *jarl*, but before the tenth century an 'eorl' meant no more (or no less) than a man of high birth. Unlike the word 'eorl' in English society, *jarl* was a word in practical use amongst the Scandinavian peoples to mean a leader of an army or a governor. The appearance of Scandinavian 'jarls' in England gave a new meaning to the word 'eorl' and in time it was used to mean a rank in society. The idea of an earl seems to have been gaining currency in English circles steadily during the tenth century. Several Scandinavian leaders were recorded as the *suffragenei* (or under officers) of Ealdorman Athelstan 'Half King' during his rule of recently reconquered East Anglia in the

7 See generally for this, S. Keynes, *The Diplomas of King Aethelred 'the Unready'*, *978–1016: A Study in their Use as Historical Evidence* (Cambridge, 1980), 197–8, 197n, 206–7n.

middle of the tenth century; one, Thurferth, seems to have had responsibility for the Northamptonshire area, and he and they were doubtless called *eorlas* in the vernacular, to differentiate from the ealdorman, their chief.[8] In 959 King Edgar was said by the Anglo-Saxon Chronicle to have subdued both kings and *eorlas* to his rule.[9] This probably indicates that 'earl' was not yet accepted as a title proper to Englishmen as such, for the passage refers to the recognition of the new king's *imperium* by marginal folk, British and Scandinavian. But 'earl' began to become popular as an indigenous title in the reign of Cnut (1016–35), himself, of course, a Dane.

Cnut's imposition of provincial governors on the three regions of Northumbria, Mercia and East Anglia in 1017 might well be taken as the point where the story of the English earl began. These governors differed in their wide responsibilities from the ealdorman and his ealdordom of one or more shires.[10] These three men were doubtless called earls, although a version of the Anglo-Saxon Chronicle still uses the title ealdorman for Aethelweard, banished in 1020. But the next year we find mentioned in the *Chronicle* one of the three provincial governors, Cnut's friend, Thurkil (to whom he had committed East Anglia) called an 'eorl'. After that Scandinavians and English alike are *eorlas*, and so indeed is Robert, count or duke of Normandy.[11] Both the ealdorman and his successor the earl were generally translated into Latin as *dux*.[12] This tells us in effect that society saw them as the same men, with the same duties; the earl was the continuation of the ealdorman by another vernacular name. In practice also there does not seem to have been anything to distinguish the ealdorman from the earl, his successor, other than a reluctance to attach a territorial responsibility to the earl's title.

The Mercian and West Saxon dynasties which dominated England

---

8 C. Hart 'Athelstan "Half-King" and his Family', in *Anglo-Saxon England*, ii, ed. P. Clemoes *et al.* (Cambridge, 1973), 122–3.
9 *Anglo-Saxon Chronicle*, s.a., 959.
10 E. John, 'The Age of Edgar', in *The Anglo-Saxons*, ed. J. Campbell (London, 1982), 172; idem, 'The Return of the Vikings', ibid., 209.
11 *Anglo-Saxon Chronicle*, s.a., 1031.
12 *Princeps* was the word favoured by Bede for the lesser kings or ealdormen of his day, J. Campbell 'Bede's *Reges* and *Principes*', in *Essays in Anglo-Saxon History* (London, 1986), 88–92. *Dux* became increasingly popular after the eighth century. The Latin word *comes* as an equivalent of 'earl' makes some early appearances in the England of the Confessor, a king given to admiration of Continental practices, and, one assumes, titles, see C.P. Lewis, 'The Early Earls of Norman England', in *Anglo-Norman Studies*, xiii (1990), ed. M.M. Chibnall, 213.

from the eighth century onwards were very much alive to how the Carolingian kings on the Continent ruled their kingdoms, and when they and their clerks were looking for Latin words to describe the provincial governors of their expanding kingdoms, it was often to *dux* they turned. The status of the pre-Conquest English ealdorman/earl was therefore truly ducal, and we find it on one occasion explicitly recognised. The Flemish author of a 'Life' of the Confessor distinguishes English *duces* from Continental *comites*.[13] *Duces* were, besides, often men of royal blood, cadets of the Mercian, Northumbrian and West Saxon royal houses. The establishment of *duces* as removable agents of royal government in the new English kingdom was the point at which sub-kingship became aristocracy. This makes their equation with the Carolingian *duces* all the more appropriate.

Rather more than their colleagues on the Continent, the English earls remained removable officers. To that extent the Carolingian Empire lived on in England. In early eleventh-century England, as in eighth-century Francia, the 'duke' was an officer of government; his appointment and removal, and even the area of his jurisdiction, lay at the king's whim, if he was a strong king. But, as in eighth-century Francia, sons of a *dux* might well expect to achieve their father's status, even if not the exact area he had presided over. In the tenth century the ealdormanic dignity ran in the house of Aethelfrith, ealdorman of south-eastern Mercia, many of whose sons and grandsons held office.[14] Earl Godwin of Wessex was eventually succeeded in most of his territory by his son Harold, and other sons of his, Beorn, Gyrth, Leofwine and Tostig were in time granted earldoms of their own as they came of age. The three families which dominated the earldoms of Mercia and Northumbria at various times also managed to do quite as well for their issue. This may not have amounted to a strict hereditary principle, but the practicalities of power were forcing the earldoms that way. Before the Normans arrived earldoms were confined to but four families in England.[15]

It is true that England was divorced from the Continent in its approach to titles before 1066, but not that far divorced, in fact only a little more divorced than Normandy was from the Ile de

---

13 *Vita Eadwardi Regis*, ed. F. Barlow (Oxford, 1962), *passim*, quoted with references in Lewis, 'Early Earls of Norman England', 212 and n.
14 Hart 'Athelstan "Half-King"', 116ff.
15 Lewis, 'Early Earls of Norman England', 210.

France. A common tradition linked England and the Continent and a curious example illustrates this. Ralph, a younger son of the count of Amiens-Vexin, a noble of the region around Paris, came to England to make his fortune in about 1050, as quite a number of Frenchmen and Lorrainers did. He had the useful asset of being King Edward the Confessor's nephew. His sympathetic uncle, much given to things French, made Ralph earl with authority in the East Midlands, adding later the shire of Hereford. Ralph's career was short, for he died in 1057 and was laid to rest at Peterborough abbey, but it was nonetheless intriguing. Ralph does not seem to have had much difficulty comprehending English political life and social organisation, even though its military habits may have infuriated him. A contemporary source records the failure of his attempt in 1055 to get his English levies in the Marches to fight and ride like the Continental knights.[16]

The earl retained in England functions that his Continental counterparts had lost, or were losing. The earl had public duties as the king's viceroy in the provinces. First, and perhaps foremost, he was a military leader, prominent in the defence of the particular province with which the king had entrusted him. There was also one particular political duty with which he was charged: his joint presidency over the shire court with the local bishop. Continental counts of northern Europe had a similar duty in Carolingian times, to preside over the *mallus* (the court of the *pagus*, or county) of their territories, but before the eleventh century the *mallus* was nearing extinction as a public court of all free men (see p. 51). Not so the shire court, for the English kings remained sufficiently powerful to have their interest still represented in the vigorous communal courts of shire and hundred. Contemporary English law codes and royal writs show that the earl and the bishop, in whatever shire they presided, were expected to attend these assemblies. In one eleventh-century shire, Hereford, an earl is known to have done so.[17] A political tract by Archbishop Wulfstan of York, written in the early eleventh century, specifically tells us that society looked to the earl to do justice to the poor and unfortunate, and to curb and condemn the criminal; though since Wulfstan also charges earls not to play favourites for reasons of money or patronage, we may

16 A. Williams 'The King's Nephew: the Family and Career of Ralph, Earl of Hereford', in *Studies in Medieval History presented to R. Allen Brown*, ed. C. Harper-Bill *et al.* (Woodbridge, 1989), 327–40.
17 Lewis, 'Early Earls of Norman England', 209.

suspect that they were not living up to the ideal he expected of them.[18]

Yorkshire provides more confirmation of what its archbishop tells us about an earl's status. When Orm son of Gamel bought the ruined minster of Kirkdale (in the North Riding) and had it restored around 1060, his commemorative inscription tells us that it was done 'in the days of King Edward *and Tostig the earl*' (emphasis added). Here are remote echoes from Kirkdale of the consular dating of the Roman Empire. Here too is the same attitude of mind as we find in legal sources: the earl as presiding force in his province, his term of office acknowledged and marked; indeed half a century later a Durham writer could compose a catalogue of earls of Northumbria, comprehending the two centuries before he wrote, and reflecting on the area of the earls' responsibility, their comitatus.[19] This is an instance, valuable in its early date, of awareness of the link between earls and the region whose name they bore; they had an informal, but acknowledged, claim on local pre-eminence. As an additional local recognition of his favour the king generally awarded to earls, just as the Carolingian kings had to their counts, a share of the profits of justice in their regions. In England an earl could expect a third of the fines and forfeits of the shire court, as well as a third of the profits of the king's rents in the royal borough or boroughs of his shire. From this we can see that when the Normans came to England they would have found a situation recognisable to the more instructed among them, though antiquated according to their own ideas.

THE CONTINENTAL EXPERIENCE

What were the Normans' corresponding ideas about their counts? At this point, to penetrate the matter further it is necessary to look back well into the past. The title or office of count (*comes*, plural: *comites*) has a distinct beginning in the early years of the

18 *Die 'Institutes of Polity, Civil and Ecclesiastical': Ein Werk Erzbischof Wulfstans von York*, ed. K. Jost (Schweizer Anglisische Arbeiten, 47, 1959), 78–93, translated in *Ancient Laws and Institutes of England*, ed. B. Thorpe (2 vols, Record Commission, 1840), i, 318–21.
19 *De Northymbrorum Comitibus*, in Simeon of Durham, *Opera omnia*, ed. T. Arnold (2 vols, Rolls Series, 1882–5), ii, 382–4.

Emperor Constantine (AD 312–337). Constantine was a man who rejoiced in elaborate and grandiloquent titles, and early in his reign he erected the informal description of his resident courtiers (*comites* = 'companions' in its original meaning) into an office, granted by imperial codicil, or letter. The new imperial counts were divided within the palace into three grades of honour. Later some were dispatched to the provinces to serve as trouble-shooters, governors of high status to deal with corruption. Others besides were given military responsibilities. The Roman imperial tradition therefore spawned two types of count: those within the palace (companions and intimates), and those outside it (imperial governors and generals).

The Gothic and Frankish kings who assumed power in Western Europe as successors to the emperors also had counts as a matter of course. The Goths in Italy, at least, continued the practice of granting the office by codicil. These early counts remained removable officers, although there is evidence from the time of Theodosius that the dignity was finding its way into the hands of certain exalted families. The Frankish kings even perpetuated the division of counts within and outside the palace, although the 'counts of the palace' of the eighth century were lesser creatures than the counts who governed the provinces (the *pagi*; Fr., *pays*). By 1000 however, the structure of the old Frankish kingdom had long collapsed. Royal authority had retreated in France (the Western Frankish lands) to the region around Paris where the new Capetian dynasty had its ancestral lands. Real power in most of France was wielded by the descendants of the former Carolingian aristocracy, who acknowledged less and less the overlordship of the king in Paris.

The new rulers of France were often the descendants of the greater Carolingian counts, who had taken their title in heredity, with or without royal permission. The powerful counts of Vermandois in Picardy were, indeed, direct descendants of Charlemagne himself, while the counts of Flanders derived from a forced marriage between an ambitious ninth-century Flemish notable and a Carolingian woman. Comital rights were conceded to bishops by the king as an indirect way of maintaining control: so came about in northern France the count-bishops of Beauvais, Noyon, Laon and Reims. But most of the French counts of 1000 were relative newcomers, many of them self-made men. A good example is that of Mâcon. At the end of the tenth century two men were governing this region of the Upper Rhone as representatives (*missi*) of the duke of Aquitaine, and later took the name 'counts' quite on their own initiative. Successive members of their families followed them, and took the same title. There was no one to gainsay them; neither king nor duke was in a position to persuade them otherwise. Literally dozens of such personages, to be followed by their dynasties, sprang up in the years before and around 1000, often within what had been the preserve of greater rulers, whether dukes or even other counts. Lesser counts appeared at Boulogne, Guînes and St-Pol within the part of northern France which was the sphere of the counts (or marquises) of Flanders. The greater count had to recognise them as *faits-accomplis*, and be content with their allegiance. Even within the Ile de France where the Capetian king still held sway, his power was not strong enough to prevent local castellans assuming the title of count, and so appeared the counts of Beaumont-sur-Oise, Clermont, Corbeil, Dammartin and Ponthieu.

A direct comment on the changing nature of men's attitudes to the dignity of count is preserved by St Odo of Cluny (died 947) in his 'Life' of St Gerald of Aurillac (died 909). Gerald was a powerful castellan and royal vassal. Odo pictured him on one occasion in Venetia, returning from Rome. He and his men fell in with a party of merchants. The merchants and his servants talked about Gerald and referred to him amongst themselves as 'the lord count: for such all called him'.[20] Gerald was called a count in society, not because a king had made him one, but because he was a man powerful and important enough for it to seem natural that he should be one.

The unregulated rise of comital families in France before 1000 is but one symptom of greater changes. On the Continent, and in England too, attitudes to the exercise of power were shifting, and local potentates were acquiring jurisdiction at the king's expense. The king was by no means powerless in the face of it, for he still possessed powers of patronage and moral authority. These new, posturing underlings might be domiciled into an obedient pack, and if so royal power was actually enhanced; but if the king lost

---

20 *Patrologia Latina*, ed. J.P. Migne (221 vols, Paris, 1844–64), ciii, col. 658. Odo's loose application of the title has been commented upon by J. Dunbabin, *France in the Making, 843–1180* (Oxford, 1985), 11. Geoffrey, viscount of Turenne, is alloted the title *comes* by Odo. Dr Dunbabin sees in this a later manifestation of the vague status of courtier and 'companion'.

control of them they could, and quite often did, turn and rend him. In England and Germany the king was able to do the former, in France for many years the latter case applied. The sanction of titles remained with the king therefore in England, but in much of France the new class of local potentates was out of royal control, and the old Frankish official hierarchy was given a wholly new meaning by them: it became an expression of their aristocratic aspirations and solidarity.

However, the progress of this phenomenon was by no means even or standard throughout France. Normandy is a good case in point. In 911 it had been conceded to a party of colonising Vikings led by one Rollo. Rollo and his successors assumed the powers of a Carolingian count and based themselves at Rouen, controlling most of the area formerly known as Neustria, and renamed after them and their people as *Normannia* (the land of the Northmen). By 1000 the Norman dynasty of counts had become almost entirely Frenchified; only the memory of their origins made them any different. They ruled a powerful and stable principality with an administration and society broadly similar to the rest of northern France, including its aristocracy. Their Scandinavian language and customs, beyond the odd relic and some persistent Northern family names, had evaporated within a few generations.

The most usual title for the ruler of Normandy until after 1066 was 'count of Normandy' or 'count of the Normans', not duke. Indeed the king of France hardly ever admitted that the ruler of Normandy was a duke until after 1204, when independent Normandy was extinct and the duchy bestowed on his heir. But by 1006 Richard II of Normandy, the great-grandson of Rollo, was experimenting with rather more grandiose titles than count. In that year he appeared in an original charter for Fécamp abbey as 'duke'. A little later however he was 'marquis'. His grandson, William, the conqueror of England, was adorned before 1066 in a charter of the abbey of Jumièges with a rich cocktail of titles that leaves the reader a bit bemused but in no doubt of the importance of the benefactor: he was 'prince and duke, count of Normandy'. In general however, after Richard II, there was a distinct enough preference for 'duke' in charters and histories for the reader to believe that it was the ruling dynasty's chosen title. The abbey of Fécamp in the twelfth century cherished a legend that Richard II had been awarded the ducal style by no less an authority than Pope Benedict VIII (1012-24): perhaps a necessary fiction when the king himself had not been consulted in the process.[21]

There was at least one pressing reason why the count of Normandy should suddenly begin experimenting with grander titles in the early eleventh century, apart from the unrestrained egotism that seems to have been the spirit of the times. This was because the ducal house began to award the title 'count' to its younger members, very much in the same way as the title was spread amongst the ruling house of Brittany or the cadets of the surviving Carolingian counts of Amiens–Valois–Vexin. The ruling counts of both Brittany and Normandy began to experiment with enhanced titles early in the eleventh century. If there was then a flock of relatives bearing the same title there is every reason to see this as the reason why they needed to aggrandise themselves. All the five counts who appear in the reign of Richard II (996–1026) were his close blood relations. They were settled at castles, mostly in border regions (Brionne being the exception) and they undoubtedly at this time had a military function. Their appearance has been seen as an initiative to strengthen the border defences of Normandy against neighbouring principalities. The ducal family's monopoly on the dignity of count was no short-lived thing. All the sons of the Conqueror are described at various times as counts; Robert and William Rufus, the two eldest, are called counts in the Conqueror's own lifetime, the youngest, Henry, soon after.[22] It was not until Henry I created Elias de St-Saens count of Arques in 1106 that a Norman count came into being who was not a close blood relation of the duke.

The first generation of lesser counts in Normandy owed something to earlier practice. Duke Richard moved his brother Count William from Exmes to Eu, and we can see in this a relic of earlier attitudes: the count as removable officer. But in other ways the new Norman counts were quite different to the counts of the rest of France. They were, to begin with, licensed creations, acts of patronage within the ducal family, not usurpations, as in Picardy or the Ile de France. Count Richard of Evreux in the years immediately before Hastings, traced his 'election and establishment' as count to a distinct act of will by his grandfather,

21 Bates, *Normandy before 1066* (London, 1982), 148–50.
22 D.C. Douglas, 'The Earliest Norman Counts', *English Historical Review*, lxi (1946), 129–55.

Duke Richard II, in favour of his father, Robert.[23] There also seems to have been little doubt that the new Norman counties were to be hereditary styles, although, as we will see time and again in this chapter, the hereditary principle conflicted at that level in society with ducal pragmatism. Several members of the ducal family were deprived of their titles and honours and banished because of their political miscalculations: in this way the counties of Brionne, Arques and Mortain all lapsed before 1066, not because the duke was against the hereditary principle, but because he was not in agreement with his counts' political activities. Unlicensed creations of counties came late to Normandy (rather the reverse to the rest of northern France). Earl Ranulf II of Chester aspired to be count of Avranches at some point in Stephen's reign (1135–54), and the cadets of the Norman, William Talvas, count of Ponthieu (died 1171), appear to have created for themselves a 'county of Alençon' or 'Séez' on the southern frontier of late twelfth-century Normandy.[24]

It is not safe to see the French who came to England in 1066 as possessing any common idea of what a count should be. Doubtless they would all have agreed by then that counts were hereditary dignitaries. A Breton and Norman would see a count as a member of his ruling house, and the Norman would see the count as a less impressive figure, subject to removal by his duke. Angevins, French, Poitevins, Picards and Flemings in the invasion force would have had a different experience. For them a count was a local potentate of non-royal or non-princely origins, his title self-assumed and often a recent phenomenon, depending on no exterior authority or consent. No wonder, perhaps, that ideas about English earls after 1066 were so confused.

If ideas were confused about the title of count, they were just as confused about the count's powers. Norman counts had no known formal powers; they did not even exert the untrammelled lordship of French barons outside Normandy. They were no more than barons who happened to have a hereditary and prestigious title and who had control over a *civitas* or major fortress, which

23 *Recueil des actes des ducs de Normandie* (911–1066), ed. M. Fauroux, (Caen, 1961), 396.
24 For the 'county of Avranches', see *Regesta regum Anglo-Normannorum*, ed. H.W.C. Davis, C. Johnson, H.A. Cronne and R.H.C. Davis (4 vols, Oxford, 1913–69), iii, no. 180; the example of Alençon was brought to my attention by Mrs Kathleen Thompson.

gave them something of an antique air of quasi-public authority. Elsewhere in northern France there were counts who possessed a whole range of powers: counts like those of Anjou, Vermandois, Boulogne and Flanders, for example, who occupied a position little less than sovereign, and whose realms were marked by distinct ambitions, customs and coinage. Other counts occupied a middle ground, like Meulan and Beauvais: obedient (occasionally) to the king but levying tolls, holding courts and issuing coinage in their own name. They did this partly because they claimed the delegation of royal rights; partly because of surviving memories of the public authority of Carolingian counts; and partly because of a new but nebulous concept of high justice and dignity which went along with the title (see Introduction).[25] Again, we can only note the wide range of ideas which the French invaders brought to England with them in 1066.

THE POST-CONQUEST ENGLISH EARL

The French conquerors of England in 1066 did not immediately dismantle the apparatus of the English state which had fallen into their hands. This included the office of earl. Recent important work by Dr Christopher Lewis has reached the persuasive conclusion that the old structure of earldoms in place in 1066 was continued into 1071, with the Conqueror's friend and steward, William fitz Osbern, placed in Harold's late earldom of Wessex; Odo of Bayeux, the Conqueror's half-brother, replacing Leofwine, Harold's brother, in Kent and the south-east; and Ralph de Gael, a Breton, replacing Earl Gyrth, another brother, in East Anglia. During this period several pre-Conquest English earls survived in Northumbria, Mercia and Huntingdon. But the persistence of English resistance, and the death of fitz Osbern undermined this experiment. The next decade saw a gradual infiltration of Continental ideas. Charters of 1067 and 1068 still record the use of the title *dux* for earl, whether the earl was an English survivor, like Waltheof of Huntingdon, or a Norman, like William fitz Osbern. When the Bayeux 'tapestry' was embroidered,

---

25 For comments on the powers inherent in an eleventh- and twelfth-century French *comté*, see O. Guyotjeannin, *Episcopus et Comes: affirmation et déclin de la seigneurie épiscopale au nord du royaume de France* (Geneva, 1987), 234–8, particularly his observation about the rarity of the word *comitatus* in contemporary documents.

probably in Kent in the 1070s, its designer still thought fit to dignify Earl Harold as *Harold dux Anglorum* ('Harold the English earl' is a possible translation). However, another product of Kent in the 1070s tells us of a different idea in play. A bilingual writ of Odo of Bayeux to Canterbury cathedral has him in English as *Odo biscof Baius and eorl of Coent*, but in the corresponding Latin text as *Odo Baiocensis episcopus et* comes *Cantie*.[26] The decade or so after 1066 saw the all-important Latin title in a flux, with the new idea that an 'earl' was equivalent to a French count gaining ground. In a charter of the Conqueror of 1069 to Exeter cathedral, for instance, all the earls and counts present were *comites*, including the English survivors, Edwin and Morcar.[27] In Domesday Book in 1086, where deceased English earls of the period before 1066 are mentioned, it is as *comites*, and their wives, such as Godiva, widow of Leofric of Mercia, or Gytha, widow of Earl Ralph, are even called 'countesses', even though the English knew of no such dignity.

There is sufficient evidence to prove that this stemmed from a conscious decision of the Conqueror and his literate counsellors. This must have been so because the phrasing of his royal acts had to be agreed in advance of their issue, and his Latin writs from the late 1060s onwards employ the word *comites* for earls. This demotion may have satisfied William's doubts about the old order, which he swept away in 1071. He wanted after that no Godwins and Godwinsons in his kingdom; no ducal figures wielding power over the provinces backed by retinues of thegns and huscarls, however theoretically removable. The earldoms created after 1071 were of a different order. Most of the new earls had responsibilities (however vestigial) for only one shire: Chester, Cornwall, Hereford, Huntingdon, Norfolk and Shrewsbury. Many of the new earls' titles, like those of the Norman counts, referred to the city and castle in which they were based.

Sometimes the title *comes* was even distanced from place. In England in the reigns of the two Williams there were for a time men with the title *comes* whose counties were barely more than titular. One of these was the Odo *comes* of Champagne, who had married the Conqueror's daughter and obtained Holderness; similarly there was Roger *comes* 'of Poitou', a younger son of Roger

---

26 *Sir Christopher Hatton's Book of Seals*, ed. L.C. Loyd and D.M. Stenton (Oxford, 1950), no. 431; Cartulary of Christ Church, Canterbury, Canterbury D & C Register B fo 398r–v.
27 See in general, Lewis, 'The Early Earls of Norman England', 211–22.

de Montgomery who had married the heiress to the county of La Marche. Count Roger enjoyed a substantial lordship in England including the honor of Eye and the district between Ribble and Mersey.[28] In a different development, several Anglo-Norman earls attached their title, or found their title attached, to their family name rather than area of responsibility. This was the case with the earldom of Surrey created in 1088 for William de Warenne. Holders of the title were usually known as 'earls Warenne' from an early date, rather than 'earls of Surrey'.[29] The Giffards, who had the title of earl of Buckingham in 1088, are usually 'earls Giffard' in the same way. The antiquity of the surname was clearly important here; the surname was the way these families had been known, and their prestige was vested in it rather than in the newer territorial style.

The new earls recalled in name and status the counts of the French *pays*, and in their alignment along border areas or in exposed coastal districts (saving Huntingdon, the continuation of a minor pre-Conquest entity) the Norman counts of Richard II. On the other hand, there was no attempt to confine the dignity to the ducal family, which did not in any case have sufficient members for the purpose. Odo of Bayeux and Robert of Mortain, the Conqueror's half-brothers, each received earldoms in England, to add to their Norman dignities, but the rest had only remote connections, if any, with the ducal house. Bretons had Norfolk, and briefly Cornwall; a Frenchman from the region of Paris had Northampton; Normans were settled in Hereford, Shrewsbury and Northumbria; and a Fleming for a short while was (perhaps) earl at Chester: a miscellaneous collection familiar with a wide range of traditions.

We must not therefore expect too much consistency in assumptions by contemporaries about the status of earls and counts. Ideas about

28 For Count Odo, see B. English, *The Lords of Holderness, 1086–1260* (Oxford, 1979), 9–13; for Count Roger, see J.F.A. Mason, 'Roger of Montgomery and his Sons', *Transactions of the Royal Historical Society*, 5th ser., xiii (1963), 14–15; V. Chandler, 'The Last of the Montgomerys: Roger the Poitevin and Arnulf', *Historical Research*, lxii (1989), 1–14; C.P. Lewis, 'The King and Eye: A Study in Anglo-Norman Politics', *English Historical Review*, civ (1989), 571–84.

29 Earl William de Warenne II (1088–1137) appears most frequently in acts of William Rufus, Robert Curthose and Henry I as *Willelmus comes Warenne*, or *Willelmus comes de Warenna*. Occasionally he is simply *Willelmus de Warenna* with no title; on only seven out of seventy-three occasions does he appear as *comes de Suthreia*. He is *comes de Suthreia* in nineteen out of the fifty-seven charters of his which I have, which indicates William's own partiality for the style.

title in France and England in the Early and High Middle Ages were not hard and fast. Individual writers were prey to a number of notions on the subject, and it would be as well at this point to get some measure of quite how unresolved were medieval ideas on the meaning of titles and the status of their holders. The flourishing generation of writers of the Anglo-Norman realm in the early twelfth century had a wide range of ideas about earldoms or counties. Orderic Vitalis on one occasion came out with the view that in losing his county, a count lost his right to be called by the title, although the title might be conceded to him by royal sufferance.[30] Yet the loss of the lands of Arnulf de Montgomery did not prevent Eadmer and the chronicler of Lewes priory (Orderic's contemporaries) from referring to Arnulf on several occasions after 1102 as *comes*.[31] Simeon of Durham, another contemporary, believed with Orderic that the award of an earldom depended on the king's will. So the Conqueror had made Gospatric son of Maldred earl of Northumbria, and Gospatric paid heavily for the privilege. On the other hand, Simeon said of the same Gospatric that 'the dignity of that earldom was his right from his mother's blood, for she was Algitha, daughter of Earl Uthred'.[32] This contrasts rather with his earlier observation. Is he saying (as earlier English practice hints) that some men had by blood – and female lineage at that – a better right to attain earldoms than others? He gives the king the prerogative of granting and retracting an earldom, for to him the Conqueror had both conferred the honour, and then deprived Gospatric of it. Yet he then implies that Gospatric was able to maintain his status after his deprivation by the Conqueror, basing himself and his men at Dunbar in Lothian with the support of King Malcolm III. As is well known, Gospatric and his descendants continued to use the style of earl, eventually attaching it to their fortress of Dunbar.

These Anglo-Norman writers had contradictory beliefs about the status of earl or count. That the king-duke had the decisive say in who was to hold an earldom comes from both Orderic and Simeon, and indeed from elsewhere. Since the earl needed the support of

30 Orderic Vitalis, *The Ecclesiastical History*, ed. M. Chibnall, (6 vols, Oxford, 1969–80), v, 246–8: referring to Elias of Maine.
31 Eadmer, *Life of St Anselm*, ed. R.W. Southern (Oxford, 1962), 146, 153–4; *Chronica monasterii de Hida iuxta Wintoniam*, in *Liber monasterii de Hyda*, ed. E. Edwards (Rolls Series, 1866), 306.
32 Simeon of Durham, *Historia Regum*, in *Opera Omnia*, ed. T. Arnold (2 vols, Rolls Series, 1882–5), 199.

considerable estates, that is not surprising. The king was the arbiter on questions of landholding. Yet all these writers were also willing to consider the idea that comital status (or candidacy for it) depended on innate qualities, and blood and previous possession had a part to play. There is also the clear belief that men who had once been earls remained earls, even after they lost their estates. In the minds of these writers there seems to have been a personal dignity of 'earl' which stood apart from possession of an earldom, and which survived the loss of it. Did they see a conflict here? It seems not, I think. Comital status was simply not then closely defined, as it has been since the fourteenth century, by royal countenance. The matter of status was a matter for general society to arbitrate in the High Middle Ages.

The military nature of the earliest Norman earldoms in England seems clear, but their fate reveals how short-lived was the emergency. Cornwall, Hereford, Kent, Norfolk and Shrewsbury lapsed before the Conqueror's death. New creations only partly compensated for the drop in numbers: Buckingham, Warwick and Surrey (1088), and Leicester (1107). When Henry I died in 1135 there were fewer earls than when the Conqueror died in 1087, a mere seven. Many earldoms, as with the Norman counties, were political casualties, but that does not really explain why their numbers were not made up. There is a clear reluctance amongst the majority of medieval kings to multiply titles amongst the aristocracy; earlier I suggested we might look back as far as the reign of Aethelred II to see this. To say why kings were chary of making new earls is no easy matter, but to my mind it must have something to do with the stream of thought in medieval treatises on law and government which sprang from the etymological meaning of the title *comes* (companion).

In the later twelfth century, Richard fitz Nigel saw earls as 'associated' with the king's interests (*fiscum*) and a 'partner' in receiving revenue (i.e. the third penny).[33] In the next century the legal treatise called Bracton talks at greater length but in a similar strain (quoting Isidore in part):

> In temporal matters there are emperors, kings and princes in those matters which pertain to the realm, and under them dukes, counts, barons, magnates or vavassors, and knights,

---

33 *Dialogus de Scaccario*, ed. C. Johnson *et al.* (Oxford, 1983), 64–5.

and also freemen and villeins, and different powers established under a king. Counts (*comites*), for instance, because they have derived their name from companionship (*comitatu*) or association (*societate*), who may also be called *consuls* from consulting (*consulendo*); for kings associate with themselves such persons for consultation and to govern the people of God, ordaining them in great honour and power and name, when they gird them with swords, that is, with sword belts.[34]

In this awkwardly phrased passage we can find an abundance of reasons for English kings to be cagey about their nearest neighbours in dignity. A sovereign with high ideas of his place in the order of things might take exception to this view of his proper 'companions' – the *de facto* stake in government which the great magnates already had could do without such an ideology to back it up. Francis Bacon, reflecting on nobility in the reign of a king who bestowed titles with a profligacy and originality previously unequalled, put the royal dilemma succinctly:

> It is well when nobles are not too great for sovereignty, nor for justice, and yet maintained in that height as the insolency of inferiors may be broken upon them before it come on too fast upon the majesty of kings.

Their 'great honour, power and name' may have been whittled down after 1066, but earls, being (except for the earl of Oxford) men of great wealth were naturally dangerous men and more dangerous still with the prestige of a title, hence the stress the passage lays on the English royal right to invest earls with sword and belt before they might assume the title. This was a royal prerogative unknown in France or (probably) Scotland, but in England the Crown was able to assert at least this one method of supervision of its titled aristocracy.

It was not until the second half of the twelfth century that English earls lost the formal attributes of power that went with their titles. Royal writs continued to address the earl and bishop of the relevant shires, as well as the sheriff, the more obvious executive officer, for many decades after 1066. A law treatise of the 1110s, the *Leges Henrici Primi*, seems still to expect that the earl of a shire, if there

---

34 Translation from *Henrici de Bracton de Legibus at Consuetudinibus Angliae*, ed. T. Twiss (6 vols, Rolls Series, 1878–83), i, 37.

is one, should be present at the greater sessions of its public court. Though there is antiquarian dross in this treatise, its view does correspond with the evidence of the writs of the Norman kings. The *Leges* also contains a fleeting reference to an area of the 'earl's peace' which lay about his house, giving him immediate jurisdiction over homicides there; a privilege he shared with bishops, and which also appears in a Scottish law code of the early fourteenth century. It would be wonderful to know whether this privilege was really in operation in the England of Henry I, as it betokens a high idea of the earl's dignity at that time, but there seems to be no subsequent mention of it in England.[35]

The degree of real power – as opposed to theoretical rights of jurisdiction and supervision – exercised by earls is difficult to assess. 'Real power' rested on wealth and control of resources, and these could be translated into political power through the mechanism of patronage. Earls were usually lords of great honors too, and it was from these that their power really came. Their titles were usually an aid and a prop only. Just as with any baron, the more concentrated were an earl's honor and resources, the more potentially powerful he was in a region. In the Anglo-Norman period we have at least the two extremes of comital power marked. The most powerful earl (in terms of the concentration of land in the county of his title) was undoubtedly Chester. Chester was a product of the second wave of creations of earls in the reign of the Conqueror. Cheshire had a unique pre-Conquest pattern of landholding: apart from those of the Church, the manors of the county had all answered to the earl of Mercia. Earl Hugh of Chester succeeded to that position. His landed hegemony gave rise to a unique position of authority and power. By the late twelfth century, a Cheshire cleric called Lucian could write that in his county the earl occupied the position the king did elsewhere in England. By the mid-thirteenth century, the

---

35 *Leges Henrici Primi*, ed. L.J. Downer (Cambridge, 1972), c. 7.2, c. 80.8. For the Scottish 'earl's peace' see *Liber qui dicitur Regiam Maiestatem* c. 56, in *The Acts of the Parliaments of Scotland* (12 vols, London, 1845–75) i pt 2, 276. The earl's peace in Scotland was one of a number of jurisdictions relating to Scottish magnates recorded in this thirteenth-century tract. The earl and the king's son were equated in this work, as was the son of an earl and a thane. It is very likely that this passage in the tract and the passage in the *Leges Henrici Primi* derive from a common tradition of Anglo-Saxon law; both probably are survivals of the known fineable offences of fighting in the houses or presence of ealdormen or their officers or members of the Witan mentioned in the law codes of Ine and Alfred, *The Laws of the Earliest English Kings*, ed. F.L. Attenborough (Cambridge, 1922), Ine c. 6.2 (p. 39), Alfred c. 15 (p. 73), c. 38.1–2 (p. 81).

word 'palatine' had come to attach itself to the earls of Chester, as a means of distinguishing them from other earls.[36]

But the power of the earl in Cheshire did not arise from his title, it arose from the fact that the shire court and the honor court of Cheshire were one and the same, and that the sheriff of Cheshire was a baronial officer. Baronial and public power in Cheshire were united in one magnate. The opposite pole in terms of power was the earldom of Oxford, created for Aubrey de Vere in 1140. The earl of Oxford did not possess so much as an acre of land in the county of his title. His lands were mostly in Essex, where he played second fiddle to the Mandeville earl of the county. In between the extremes of Chester and Oxford were earls like Leicester. The earl of Leicester was indeed a dominant figure in the shire of his title, particularly strong in its south and west, with almost exclusive control of the town of Leicester. But he was not the only magnate of influence in the county. The earl of Chester dominated one corner of it, and the lord of Belvoir another. That the earl was keen to gain more control over the shire is evident from his activities. Throughout the reigns of Henry I and Stephen, Earl Robert II (1118–68) waged campaigns of intimidation against local rivals (the earl of Chester and the bishop of Lincoln) in order to increase his control over Charnwood, the Soar valley and the town of Leicester.[37]

In the reign of Stephen (1135–54) the earl had a sudden and remarkable Indian summer of formal power. In 1138, the king – apparently disenchanted with his predecessors' ministers – decided on a reform in local government which established an earl as his intermediary in each shire (almost a prototype Tudor lord-lieutenant). The sheriff became the earl's underling, not the king's direct representative. Between 1138 and 1141 the king joyfully

36 See for this, *The Earldom of Cheshire and its Charters: a Tribute to Geoffrey Barraclough*, ed. A.T. Thacker (Chester Arch. Soc., lxxi, 1991), *passim*. P. Latimer, 'Grants of "Totus Comitatus" in Twelfth-Century England: their Origins and Meaning', *Bulletin of the Institute of Historical Research*, lix (1986), 137, likewise distinguishes the power of the earl of Chester, but is wrong to see Chester as the continuation of a pre-Conquest earldom: Cheshire was part of the earl of Mercia's estates, and English earls in general had estates as scattered as their Norman successors. Neither Shrewsbury, Cornwall, Richmond nor Northumbria were earldoms which approximated the 'Chester-type' as closely as he suggests.
37 E. King, 'Mountsorrel and its Region in King Stephen's Reign', *Huntington Library Quarterly*, xliv (1980), 8; D. Crouch, *The Beaumont Twins: the Roots and Branches of Power in the Twelfth Century* (Cambridge, 1986), 80–4; D. Crouch, 'The Foundation of Leicester Abbey and other Problems', *Midland History*, xi (1987), 4–7.

multiplied the number of earls until they reached a total of twenty-three. Stephen seems to have been drawing, if anything, on the Carolingian tradition which stood behind both the French and English experience. But his earls were to be hereditary, as the surviving creation charters make perfectly plain, not removable officers. This was a large-scale experiment quite unprecedented in England, or on the Continent. It has been partly blamed for the catastrophe of his reign, or at least its intensification. The other party in the civil war of the reign was equally profligate in its creations, and added another seven earls to the total. Whatever the consequences, there is one immediately noticeable fact about this experiment. No earldom was created for any mean men: they all went to men of substance and family, that is, men of nobility. This may point to an underlying and undervalued imperative for this action: the need for titles in an aristocracy which had been long starved of them; a necessary aristocratic catharsis. This would explain the otherwise surprising fact that Stephen's rivals fell in with his experiment: they too felt the pressing need to answer the clamour for patronage.

When Henry II succeeded to the throne in 1154 the earls reverted to their status of 1135, and what Stephen had done was forgotten so utterly that it has only been reconstructed in our generation from rigorous charter analysis by the late Professor R.H.C. Davis. After 1154 certain earldoms were suppressed: for example York, Hereford, Northampton, Somerset and Worcester. Pembroke was drastically curtailed and its seat removed to Chepstow (anciently called Striguil). Here is evidence that the king was still free enough to control or even eradicate his *comites* should the need be on him. Where there were rival claims to the same counties from both sides (Cornwall, Lincoln and Norfolk) the earl created by Henry II's party was preferred over his rival. But even so, many of Stephen's earls continued in their titles, and so after 1154 the number remained boosted to twenty-two, declining by natural wastage and political forfeiture until by 1327 there were only eight earls.

The particular case of the earldom of Huntingdon-Northampton is exceptional, but adds some intriguing sidelights to the process. The Scottish royal family and the Senlis family both claimed the same earldom by descent from Earl Waltheof and his daughter Mathilda. The Scots called it Huntingdon, the Senlis called it Northampton. In Stephen's reign Simon II de Senlis was preferred by the king over the Scots, who in any case supported the Empress Mathilda. Simon conveniently died in 1153, allowing Henry II to restore the earldom to King Malcolm IV of Scotland, his ally. But Simon left a young son, Simon III. This boy was well connected; his grandfather was the earl of Leicester, the new king's chief minister. So the king compromised or at least turned a blind eye, for Simon called himself 'earl' and was given a wife who brought him a Lincolnshire estate big enough to support an earl's dignity. But in his charters he never says of what place he was earl, he is only 'Earl Simon'. In this compromise is a remarkable insight into changing views of comital status; the dignity for once cut loose from land and authority. Here is evidence that in the new reign the title was to be little more than honorific, and could survive happily when severed from the old roots of its power. Despite the opinion of John Horace Round, the idea of an earl without a county had long been conceivable. But with Earl Simon III de Senlis, as later with Earl Richard of Striguil, the idea of personal comital status had reached the stage when it had apparent royal sufferance.

After 1154 the earls no longer had any innate political function. For the most part they continued to receive the third penny of their shires (a right tempered by royal parsimony), or compounded with the king to exchange it for a settled rent charge on a royal estate.[38] This was the only thing that set the English earl apart from the French count after 1154, and indeed, apart from the vernacular title, the only relic of the pre-Conquest status of the earl in England. This should not, however, lead us to suppose too readily that earldoms were subsiding in importance. An earl remained great in dignity still, even if sapped in the formal exercise of power. The political oversight of the succession to earldoms maintained by the king through his use of the ceremony of investiture is some evidence that the title had a long way to go before it faded into a political never-never land. The king did not relax the necessity for royal investiture of a hereditary earl until the fourteenth century. Moreover, there is the contemporary testimony of Ralph de Diceto on another way the king could regulate titles. He states, when talking of William de Mandeville's assumption of the title of Aumale in 1180, that magnates entering the royal presence were announced by their titles, and that the king had to approve any such title by which they were to be

38 For the third penny, see studies in J.H. Round, *Geoffrey de Mandeville* (London, 1892), 287–96; G.E. Cockayne, *The Complete Peerage*, ed. V. Gibbs *et al.* (13 vols in 14, London, 1910–59), iv, 658–9; G. Ellis, *Earldoms in Fee* (London, 1963), 80–4.

announced to him.[39] A magnate of great lineage and estates might be called 'earl' by his men and even by his country, but when he was before the king he would find that the status needed 'official' sanction. One is entitled to ask what special dangers the king saw in the earls as opposed to the rest of the aristocracy, for there certainly is evidence of a particular royal insecurity with regard to them, rather than to the untitled section of his aristocracy, which appears in more than just the reluctance to create new earls.

For me, the key to the volatility in relations between the English king and his earls lies in the Continental experience. Some elements of the unregulated aristocratic attitude to the title did pass into England with the French colonists. The titled aristocracy throughout the twelfth and into the thirteenth century can be glimpsed again and again marching to a pace different to Bracton's solemn royal march, a much livelier French air. Both the Norman and the English experience of titles was that they were created as acts of patronage by the duke or king. That remained the case in both countries after 1066. However, the Norman experience was that counties were hereditary, and this led to complications. It happened now and then that as an act of political control the king-duke banished and imprisoned earls and confiscated their lands and titles. Society in general was less than clear how that decision affected the rights of the heirs of the deprived earl, however merited his disgrace.

There was a grey area around the transmission and use of title that occasionally manifested itself and showed that royal control was by no means as assured as it appears at first. The very idea of kingship itself was a mass of unresolved theories. From where did the king draw his authority? A writer like Bracton could quite cheerfully discuss ideas of royal power deriving from the Caesars and communal restraints on kingship arising from more recent history in the same tract, and see no apparent contradiction.[40] How much less clear was thinking likely to be on the subject of earls? The king when he created a title was very much in the position of a man who throws a seed into his garden. If it struck root it would grow as it, rather

39 Ralph de Diceto, *Ymagines Historiarum*, in *Opera Historica*, ed. W. Stubbs (2 vols, Rolls Series, 1876), ii, 3.
40 R. Frame, *The Political Development of the British Isles* (Oxford, 1990), 101–2.

than he, wanted, and might be the devil to get rid of if the need arose.

A case in point was the earldom of Hereford that had been deemed to be created for William fitz Osbern in 1067 (although in fact the earldom as held by William carried much wider responsibilities). After William's death in 1071 his younger son Roger succeeded at least to the Herefordshire and Marcher part of his father's estate. A rebellion in 1075 led to his deprivation. He had descendants who survived as minor barons in England in the twelfth century, but who never, so far as we know, asserted a claim to the earldom. On the other hand, the Norman branch of his family represented by fitz Osbern's elder son William de Breteuil thought that they did preserve a rightful claim to it. In 1140 Robert II, earl of Leicester, then high in favour with King Stephen, secured a grant in general terms of the county of Hereford 'as well and freely as William fitz Osbern held it'.[41] Robert's claim was that he had married in 1121 the daughter of the sister of William de Breteuil (who had no legitimate heirs).

Another most interesting example also occurs in 1140, a year in which the king's ornamental garden of titles had very much run riot. Alan, a count of Brittany, was sent by King Stephen to take Cornwall back from his enemy, Reginald, a bastard of Henry I, whom the Empress Mathilda had elevated to earl there. Count Alan had a startling but short-lived success. The king rewarded him, we are told, with the earldom of Cornwall he had taken from Reginald. But we know that Alan himself saw it differently. To celebrate his conquest he summoned the county court of Cornwall to Bodmin, and amongst other things, made a grant to the priory of St Michael's Mount for the soul of his late uncle Brian, 'of whose inheritance', he said, 'I have the land of Cornwall'. What was more he described himself as earl (as many of his contemporaries did) 'by the grace of God'.[42] Alan was earl, firstly because of divine providence, and secondly because his uncle Brian had previously had Cornwall (which he could only have done briefly, in the initial stages of the Conquest).[43] No mention at all of the king.

There is another example of the same period in which sources

---

41 *Regesta regum Anglo-Normannorum*, iii, no. 437.
42 *The Cartulary of St Michael's Mount*, ed. P.L. Hull (Devon and Cornwall Record Soc., new ser., v, 1962), 6.
43 The evidence for Brian's earldom is discussed by J.E. Powell and K. Wallis, *The House of Lords in the Middle Ages* (London, 1968), 28.

of power other than the king are evoked by an earl. In 1138 King
Stephen created Gilbert fitz Gilbert earl, and gave him the royal
estate of Pembroke in Wales. Earl Gilbert's view of his position
did not correspond to the king's, however. He later wrote to the
archbishop of Canterbury saying that 'there is a place in Wales called
Daugleddau, in those parts which divine goodness has annexed to
my authority'.[44] It is a remarkable fact that the part that royal
goodness played in Alan and Gilbert's acquisitions is forgotten.
This was not because either of them had changed their allegiance at
the time of the charters quoted. They felt justified in looking to God
for the source of their power and fortune, rather than the king.

The persistence of hereditary claims in the face of hostile royal
power was by no means confined to Stephen's reign, although the
political chaos of that era undoubtedly intensified the problem. Men
might be called, and call themselves, earls with no royal sanction at
all, simply by right of holding the estates and heiress of a dead earl,
or on even more visceral or tenuous grounds. An early example
is Morcar, earl of Northumbria, who was captured in rebellion in
1070, and spent much of the rest of his life in honourable captivity
in a castle on the banks of the Seine estuary in Normandy. But it is
interesting to find that in 1086 he witnessed a charter of his gaoler,
Roger de Beaumont, as Morcar *comes*.[45]

There is also the startling evidence that Philip, a younger son of
Earl Robert of Gloucester, was credited generally with the title of
earl in the 1140s, on what can be no other grounds than that he
was a great man and a grandson of a king.[46] This we may ascribe
to relics of older practices perhaps: the custom of the Norman
ducal house of awarding the title generally to its cadets, as well
as the general idea that a great man near to the ruler might be a
comes simply because he was great and close to the centre of power.
There is some contemporary evidence from France that powerful
counts there might concede their dignity to their sons in their own

44 *Cartulary of Worcester Cathedral Priory*, ed. R.R. Darlington (Pipe Roll Soc.,
lxxvi, 1968), 134.
45 F. Lot, *Etudes critiques sur l'abbaye de St-Wandrille* (Paris, 1913), 95–6.
46 Cartulary of Tewkesbury, Brit. Libr. ms Cotton Cleopatra A vii, fo 78v. A grant
was said to have been made by Odo le Sor, a Gloucester tenant, 'a considerable
time before Earl Philip held the castles of Cricklade and Cirencester' (viz. before
1145). 'Earl' Philip's activities were in Wiltshire, which already had an earl of his
father's party. He could not have received that county. Therefore one is driven
to the conclusion that he held a personal dignity, conceded him by his followers,
like Odo le Sor.

lifetime; thus Matthew II de Beaumont-sur-Oise is 'count' in 1154, in the lifetime of Count Matthew I, his father. A near-contemporary French example of the partition of dignity amongst sons is the way that the sons of Count Theobald IV of Blois–Chartres–Champagne (brother of King Stephen of England) behaved. After their father's death, all three took the title count. The two eldest, counts of Blois and Champagne, had some reason to do so. But Stephen, the youngest, had from his father the lordship of Sancerre, in Berry, which had never been a county. Stephen nevertheless took the personal dignity of count. His sons after him also took the title, and so was 'created' the county of Sancerre, with no mandate other than a man's desire to share in his family's comital dignity.[47]

In assuming the title of count, Philip son of Earl Robert was taking to himself no more than what the generation of his grandfather, the Conqueror, might have expected. Society in England as in France was long prepared to put up with the informal use of the comital dignity. William Marshal in 1189 married the daughter and heir of Earl Richard Strongbow. In the 1190s he appears credited on at least two occasions as 'earl' or 'earl of Striguil'. Yet in his charters of the 1190s he never claimed the title for himself, insisting only that his wife was a countess in her own right.[48] When he was finally invested as earl in 1199 Howden remarks that he had long been called earl by many. What was more, on at least two occasions before his death, Exchequer records absent-mindedly called his son and heir, William, the 'young earl Marshal'.[49] Much the same thing happened to Ralph d'Issoudun the younger (died 1243) who was kept from the title of count of Eu by the survival of his mother, the heiress of Eu. Yet the family abbeys of Le Tréport and Eu both remembered him as 'Count Ralph' or 'the young Count Ralph'.[50] Henry, the

---

47 *Cartulaire du prieuré de St-Leu d'Esserent, 1080–1538*, ed. E. Müller (Pontoise, 1901), 67; G. Devailly, *Le Berry du xe siècle au milieu du xiiie siècle* (Paris, 1973), 360. In the early 1180s Count Robert I of Dreux associated with him in a charter to the abbey of L'Estrée 'Robert my son, to be count in due course after me, by God's grace' (*comes per dei gratiam post me futurus*), which is a step down in association of rank, A.W. Lewis, 'Fourteen Charters of Robert I Count of Dreux (1152–88)', *Traditio*, (1985), 170–1

48 See charters in Cartulary of Ely, Brit. Libr. ms Egerton 3047 fo 4r; Westminster Abbey Muniments no 3137; *Calendar of Charter Rolls preserved in the Public Record Office* (6 vols, P.R.O., 1903–27), ii, 164.

49 *Pipe Roll of 17 John*, 40, 43.

50 *Recueil des historiens des Gaules et de la France*, ed. M. Bouquet et al. (24 vols, Paris, 1869–1904), xxiii, 445–6.

bastard of Earl Reginald of Cornwall, after his father's death long sought to secure his father's lands and title, despite having legitimate sisters with whom the earldom would have properly rested, had not Henry II refused to allow the earldom to continue.[51] Eventually, in the reign of John, Henry had the lands committed to him, but no more. In the short period that he controlled Cornwall, with no royal sanction at all, he triumphantly issued charters describing himself as earl.[52] That the title of 'earl' used by both William Marshal II in his father's lifetime, and by Henry of Cornwall on his own authority, had a wider currency is proved by the writings of Matthew Paris. He too refers to 'the young earl Marshal', when he lists him among the Twenty-Five in 1215, and to him Henry was 'earl of Cornwall' that same year.[53]

In these references we find a more complicated world than we would expect from what has been written by earlier generations of historians of the peerage, all tutored in Stubbs's *Constitutional History*; king's friends to a man. It was a world where political disgrace and imprisonment did not deprive a man of the dignity of his title once given, and where men and their neighbours could be more important arbiters of who was entitled to be called earl than the king himself. The deference to royal intentions about titles that we assume to have existed in this early period, because it existed in the later Middle Ages, was not in fact there, nor would be until at least the fourteenth century. How else than in such a world could the ex-Empress Mathilda, daughter of Henry I – a woman no more in real dignity than the wife of the count of Anjou – go to England to fight for her father's crown and in the process create with her half-brother numerous earls, although never herself so much as anointed queen, let alone crowned!

Another example we have states bluntly the private views of an early thirteenth-century earl on his right to his dignity. Henry de Bohun had the earldom of Hereford revived for him by King John in 1200. He derived his claim to it from his grandmother, Margaret,

---

51 Since Earl Reginald was a bastard his family was in a weak position when he died. Lands held by bastards could be held to be escheats at their death.
52 Cartulary of Launceston, Lambeth Palace Library ms 719 fo 199r–v: *Henricus filius comitis Raginaldi comes Cornubie.*
53 Matthew Paris, *Chronica Majora*, ed. H.R. Luard (7 vols, Rolls series, 1872–83), ii, 587, 605.

sister of the Earl Roger who had held it until his ill-timed rebellion in 1155. Earl Roger had three younger brothers who were allowed to succeed in turn to much of Roger's land and to the family's lesser title of royal constable, by which they were dignified in their charters. All three brothers died without children, leaving their sister as heir. But, looking back to the roots of his family tree from the thirteenth century, Earl Henry de Bohun made good this deficiency for his own satisfaction. In a charter drawn up before 1220 he had his clerk recall the generations of his predecessors. Earl Roger is there, but so also are his brothers, not constables, according to Henry de Bohun, but *Earl* Walter, *Earl* Henry and *Earl* Mahel.[54]

If we move into the thirteenth century some of the same persistence in titles is found. Simon de Montfort, the infamous crusader against the Albigensian heretics, married one of the heiresses of the last Norman earl of Leicester. Through her he claimed and received the title and a share of the late earl's great estates for a while, but they were later withdrawn. His son Aumary de Montfort never went to England, nor argued for his rights to be recognised, but nonetheless in 1222, in a charter, he had himself carefully styled as 'Amaury, by God's providence, duke of Narbonne, count of Toulouse and *Leicester*, and lord of Montfort'.[55] Distance apparently lent an unlikely enchantment to the earldom in question. But such presumption was to be found nearer to home. Earl William Longespée enjoyed the earldom of Salisbury in right of his wife, Ela, until his death in 1226. He left a son who petitioned for the title when his mother announced her intention of entering a nunnery in 1237. But the Crown did not allow his claim in 1238, nor when he renewed it in 1240. He was killed in February 1250 never having been formally invested, but still generally known as 'earl'. His own son died in 1256, ending the male line of the Longspée family before Countess Ela, by then

---

54 Bodleian Library, ms Dugdale 17 p. 71, from an original in the possession of Sir Edward Raleigh of Farnborough in 1638. Earl Henry's sensitivity to his family's history and claims also appears from a charter he produced from the family's archive. It was a grant by Henry II to Earl Roger in 1155 before his disgrace, confirming many of the earl's gains in Stephen's reign. Earl Henry was plainly attempting to assert his right to these grants for his own profit, and King John persuaded him to drop his claims for the time being, *Rotuli Chartarum*, ed. T.D. Hardy (Record Commission, 1837), 61.

55 *Cartulaire de l'abbaye de Notre-Dame des Vaux de Cernay de l'ordre de Cîteaux au diocèse de Paris*, ed. L. Merlet and A. Moutié (2 vols, Paris, 1857), i, 225.

abbess of Lacock, herself died in 1261.[56] Perhaps if her grandson had survived her, he would have then been invested; certainly the case of Roger de Quincy indicates that this might have been done. His father had been earl of Winchester in right of his wife, who survived him. It was not until her death in 1236 that Roger was allowed the title of Winchester; it was then confirmed to him without delay. But the Longespée claim to the earldom of Salisbury was not forgotten and the female line of the family was credited with the title into the fourteenth century in a notably persistent way, although the Crown never recognised it.

The briefest touch of the dignity of earl was still enough to transform a man's status in the mid-thirteenth century. In 1242 John Marshal, a Norfolk knight and kinsman of the earls of Pembroke, married Margaret, sister and heir of Thomas, earl of Warwick. Within months Earl Thomas died and John's wife became countess in her own right. Sadly, John did not live long in the reflected glory of his wife's title. Before the end of 1242 he too was in his grave; he could not even have had time to receive investiture. Yet a dozen years later a Norfolk jury could still look back and recall him as 'John, earl of Warwick', and it is as earl of Warwick that he is depicted in the fifteenth-century history of the earls by John Rous.[57]

THE SIGNIFICANCE OF INVESTITURE OF THE EARL

There is a distinct relaxation of royal attitudes towards the title of earl in the fourteenth century. This may be attributable in part to the rather more composed views of Edward III (1327–77), but perhaps by now the country was conforming more to Stubbs's and Round's view of things. When he assumed power in a *coup d'état* in 1330, the young king found that the titled members of his aristocracy numbered then a mere eight, and, apart from the youthful earls of Arundel and Warwick, they were not men who

---

56 William Longespée II is many times 'Earl William' or 'the Earl Longespée' in a poem composed to celebrate his death (and consequently martyrdom) at the hand of the Saracens at Masoura in 1250, 'The Assault of Masoura', in *Excerpta Historica*, ed. S. Bentley (London, 1833), 70, 72 (*passim*), 76, 78. A parallel is to be found in the case of the county of Eu, where Countess Alice (died 1245), the heir of Count Henry II and wife of Count Ralph, survived her only son Ralph (II) who was never allowed the title of count, *Chronique des comtes d'Eu*, in *Recueil des historiens des Gaules et de la France*, xxiii, 443.

57 *The Rous Roll*, ed. C. Ross (Gloucester, 1980), no. 38.

could be expected to be of much use to him. Edward III belonged to a newer generation, and the fear of titled magnates was not on him. In 1337 the king lectured parliament in terms reminiscent of Bracton on the desirability of hereditary dignities to 'fortify' and 'buttress' his own powers. He deplored the decline in earldoms and concluded that 'this realm has long suffered a serious decline in names, honours and ranks of dignity'.[58] At considerable personal expense he then rectified this situation by raising six of his companions to the rank of earl in one sitting: Salisbury, Huntingdon, Suffolk, Northampton, Derby and Gloucester. England had not seen such a mass elevation of earls since Stephen's reign. Edward III in his long reign created in all eleven new earls; his grandson, Richard II (1377–99) created another ten. As with earlier reigns, these new titles went to members of the royal family, or to royal favourites. The peculiar volatility of fourteenth-century politics, as Christopher Given-Wilson has pointed out, meant that these titles had no very long life: most of their recipients held them for less than five years. But, however this may be, the willingness to create earls and, as we will see, to multiply the types of title in the fourteenth century was something new.

A symptom of the new attitude can be seen in the failure to enforce any longer the king's right to invest an earl who had succeeded his father in his dignity, as opposed to investing a newly-created earl. The investiture of an earl with sword and belt is first mentioned in the later twelfth century, when King Richard belted Hugh de Puiset, bishop of Durham, as earl of Northumbria in 1189, calling on everyone, with a rather inappropriate humour, to see how he had made a new earl out of an old bishop. There is a confusion about which of the trappings was the key one: charters insist on the 'belting', but Roger of Howden talks of the swords symbolising the county. In the ceremony, contemporaries could not discriminate much between sword and belt, as one could not be attached by the king to a new earl without the other. Once the ceremony was over, iconography demonstrates that people associated unsheathed swords with earls and other lay magnates as symbols of power. They had been making this connection since the eleventh century, so it may well be that what we are getting in 1189 is the first description of a much older ceremony associated with the making of an earl, which simply was not mentioned by chroniclers (as indeed the

---

58 This is a view which is found in his father's reign, T.F. Tout, 'The Earldoms under Edward I', *Transactions of the Royal Historical Society*, new ser., viii (1894), 132.

rituals of royal coronations were not mentioned) because the habit of describing lavish ceremonial for its own sake was a new one, made fashionable by a different literary genre. It is a remarkable fact in this light that it is the romancers of the twelfth century (beginning in England with Geoffrey of Monmouth and Geoffrey Gaimar) who precede the English chroniclers by half a century in celebrating the pomp of kings and luxury of festivals; but they were writing for a different audience.

It would seem likely on this evidence, then, that kings had been belting earls (at least on the first creation) from the early Norman period. Moreover, when the king knighted a young earl who had come of age and out of wardship, he might have been taken to have repeated the original act of creation. In this way the knighting by Henry I of Robert II, earl of Leicester, along with his twin brother, Waleran, count of Meulan, when they came of age in 1120, might also have been taken by bystanders as the belting of the new earl. In the late twelfth century it certainly appears that it was customary to belt earls on their succession to their fathers. Robert III, earl of Leicester, died in the Balkans in 1190 on his way to the Holy Land. His son, Robert IV, was in the retinue of King Richard in Sicily, and early in 1191 the king took the opportunity of belting him earl there as successor to his father.

The word 'belting' appears in many of the charters recording creations and confirmations of earldoms, the first being the charter of King John dated 1199, recording the investiture of William de Ferrers as earl of Derby. Belting continued to happen on a hereditary succession to an earldom well into the thirteenth century, as with Devon in 1239 and both Cornwall and Lincoln in 1272. But thereafter, no further such case is recorded, and it seems that in Edward I's reign the practice must have lapsed and never been revived. This may have been just a practical consequence of the shrivelling away in that reign of the numbers of earls; there were so few successions at such long distances between 1272 and 1307 that people just forgot about it (six happened in Edward's reign, and none at all between 1275 and 1296). But its disappearance would certainly seem to indicate that the king no longer felt the need to sanction the use of titles as he had done before 1272. This may be because society's attitudes had changed: it is certainly difficult to find any instance of a man assuming to himself the rank of earl after the first half of Henry III's reign (1216–72), although there may be one exception in the earldom of Pembroke assumed by William de Valence (died 1296), the king's half-brother, towards the end of his life, when he had become something of an elder statesman. In general, the Longespée case must have been the precedent that established once and for all that the use of title, if it was in doubt, might be sought and argued for in the royal court, rather than stealthily assumed or left to public acclamation. Earldoms taken by local acclamation or the wilfulness of men pursuing hereditary claims evaporated. After this the necessity to impose investiture on hereditary earls could be more safely left to lapse.

THE COUNTESS

The 'countess' was a title which had no precedent in England before 1066. This may well reflect the still-dominant official status of the pre-Conquest earl. The English got by on the deferential 'lady' (Lat. *domina*). Alfred the Great's daughter, Aethelflaed, wife of the ealdorman of Mercia, was *hlaefdige Myrcena* (lady of the Mercians). Women might be credited in literature with noble qualities; they might, for instance, be credited as behaving *eorlic*: like an *eorl*, a free man of status. But this does not mean any more than that they acted nobly. *Eorl*, when the word came to be a title of honour, did not apply to women.[59]

On the Continent it had long been the custom by 1000 to dignify the wife of the count by the title 'countess' (Lat. *comitissa*), just as the wife of a king or an emperor had her equivalent title. There appears to have been a belief that counts had an innate dignity in which their women shared, or which they conferred on their wives; a dignity that led them often to describe themselves along with their husbands, the counts, as countesses 'by God's grace' or 'by God's providence'. Examples are certainly known in the ninth and tenth centuries, such as the Italian countess Ingelhard, daughter of Apaldi, a count palatine of the king of Italy, or Adelheid wife of Richard of Burgundy, both of whom were calling themselves countesses 'by the grace of God' around AD 900. It is notable that when she was a widow Adelheid slightly modified her views on her dignity, taking the title 'lately (*quondam*) countess',[60] and this surely reveals what

59 C. Fell, *Women in Anglo-Saxon England* (Oxford, 1986), 15, 91.
60 L.A. Muratori, *Antiquitates Italicae medii aevi* (6 vols, Milan, 1738–42), i, 154–5; K. Brunner, 'Fränkische Fürstentitel: Systematik', in *Intitulatio*, ii, *Lateinische Herrscher und Fürstentitel im neunten und zehnten Jahrhundert*, ed. H. Wolfram (Mitteilungen des Instituts für österreichische Geschichtsforschung, xxiv, 1973), 256–7n.

was then the nub of the dignity of the countess: it was thought by many to depend on the husband. It was the count's decision to marry a woman that brought her the title. The twelfth-century romance '*Erec and Enide*' gives us a rare, explicit glimpse of medieval attitudes to female titles. The count of Limors abducts Enide and forcibly marries her, but attempts to win her over to acquiescence by reminding her that this will make her 'a countess and a lady'.[61] She remained unimpressed.

In Normandy both the wives of the ruler and of the lesser counts were being called countesses in the eleventh century. Gunnora, widow of Richard I and Judith, wife of Richard II appear as 'countesses' in an original deed of Richard II to the abbey of St-Ouen, Rouen, in 1015 x 17. As well as these countesses, there are references to Godhild, countess of Eu, and to two countesses of Eu, Beatrice and Lescelina, before 1066. As the status of count was amalgamated with that of earl in England after 1066, it was natural to institute the feminine form of the title with it. The English language had absorbed the new French word by 1140, when it appears as *cuntesse* in the Peterborough chronicle, applied to the wife of the count (*eorl*) of Anjou.

The Latin title *comitissa* is found in Domesday Book, where we find Countess Judith, the Norman widow of the English earl, Waltheof of Huntingdon (executed 1076), as a major landowner in the Midlands. The famous Englishwoman, Godiva, widow of Earl Leofric of Mercia, was given the title of countess by the Norman Domesday clerks in 1086. This is in itself something interesting. Like Gunnora, widow of Richard I of Normandy, there is no inkling here, as with the Countess Adelheid of the tenth century, that Godiva's full dignity terminated with her husband's death. This is reflected elsewhere in Norman practice, for Lescelina, widow of Count William I of Eu, was called countess after his death. The same applies to the other widowed countesses of Domesday Book: Judith, widow of Earl Waltheof and Gytha, widow of Earl Ralph. Apart from earlier Norman practice, this continuity in female dignity may well derive from views later expressed about the earldom of Northampton-Huntingdon. Later sources make Simon de Senlis say before marrying the daughter of Waltheof and Judith that he did so because, if the Normans were ever ousted from England, he could

---

61 *Erec et Enide*, ed. M. Roquez (Classiques français du moyen âge, 1952), ll. 4665–6.

still hang on to the earldom by right of his half-English wife.[62] So many Frenchmen married into estates in England that it was in the Norman interest to enforce the privileges of English women to the full. In this way there rapidly grew up here the idea of a countess 'in her own right', the first recorded English instance being the Mathilda who carried her own comital status to her two successive husbands, Simon de Senlis and David of Scotland.[63]

Countesses continued to enjoy a high dignity in England as the twelfth century progressed. Margaret, countess of Warwick, whose husband died in 1119 and who never remarried, went to live with a son in Normandy, and was still being called 'countess of Warwick' in her extreme old age in 1156. By this time, if a widowed countess remarried to a man who was not an earl, she might still retain her title, as is apparent from the case of Countess Gundreda, whose husband Earl Roger of Warwick died in 1153. She married again to a baron of English descent, William of Lancaster, lord of Kendal, but after his death resumed the title of 'countess of Warwick', if, that is, she had ever laid it aside. Rohese, countess of Essex, did not abandon her title after her husband's death in 1143, indeed she was 'countess' for the rest of her life, even when she married the baron, Payn de Beauchamp, lord of Bedford. He still made sure that he was named first in their joint charters, however.[64] Some ladies even found themselves in the position of title collectors. Mathilda Marshal, daughter of William Marshal (I) of Pembroke, was successively a countess of Warenne (Surrey) and Norfolk, and when her last brother died in 1245 she acquired the honorific title, 'marshal of England'; all of these accumulated titles were attached to her name in a mid-thirteenth century charter.[65] Isabel, the daughter and sole heir of Earl Richard of Striguil after 1185, shows how a woman might use the title 'countess' in her own right with no form of investiture (belting a countess with a sword would hardly have

---

62 *Vita Waldevi comitis*, in *Chroniques Anglo-Normandes*, ed. F. Michel (3 vols, Paris, 1839–40), i, 125.
63 The case of the English noblewoman, Lucia countess of Chester (died 1138), who successively married Ivo Taillebois, Roger fitz Gerold and Ranulf I, earl of Chester, is comparable in point of succession to an English estate, but she derived her title from her last Norman husband, *Charters of the Anglo-Norman Earls of Chester, c. 1071–1237*, ed. G. Barraclough (Record Soc. of Lancashire and Cheshire, cxxvi, 1988), nos 14–19.
64 Brit. Libr. ms Lansdowne 203 fo 16r.
65 Cartulary of Thorney, Cambridge University Library ms Additional 3021 fo 237r; PRO E40/315; Bernard, 'The Charters of the Cistercian Abbey of Duiske', *Proceedings of the Royal Irish Academy*, xxxv (1918–20), 79.

been appropriate), even after her marriage to a man who was not invested as an earl and therefore did not use the title (see p. 69).

There is no case in England, however, which directly compares in the extremity of deference to female claims to that found in a couple of French cases. In Northern France, once a woman had been raised by her husband to be a countess, it seems that she might later transmit the title to another man. Such was the case in 1043 when the historian Hariulf noted that Enguerrand, advocate of St-Riquier in Ponthieu, killed the count of Boulogne in battle. Enguerrand married the count's widow 'and he took the title of count, because his wife was a countess'.[66] This is not an isolated example. A century later, on the death of her husband, Count Rotrou II of Perche, in 1144, Countess Hawise was remarried to her late husband's neighbour, Robert of Dreux, brother of King Louis VII. Along with Hawise went her under-age son, Rotrou. Robert of Dreux took the occasion of the marriage to the late count's widow, and wardship of his son, to appropriate his former titles, count of Perche and lord of Belleme. This remarkable case may have arisen out of the special circumstances of Capetian ambitions on the Norman March, but it at least has some relevance to England, for Countess Hawise came from the family of the hereditary sheriffs of Salisbury.[67]

However, I have observed some exceptions to this female tenacity to dignity, which rather recall the case of Adelheid of Burgundy some centuries previously. A French countess, Adeliza de Luzarches, described herself in 1186 after the death of her first husband, Matthew II, count of Beaumont-sur-Oise, and marriage to Aumary de Meulan, lord of Gournay, as 'Adeliza once (*quondam*) countess of Beaumont, and now (*nunc*) lady of Gournay'. However, once her untitled husband was dead, she had second thoughts about her status and appears in 1190 as 'countess of Luzarches'.[68] For her, unlike Countess Rohese of Essex, it seems that the dignity of her first husband was extinguished by the second marriage, but, on the other hand, it might be revived once she was a widow again. Loretta de Briouze, the widow of Earl Robert IV of Leicester, took up on

---

66 R. Fossier, *La terre et les hommes en Picardie jusqu'à la fin du xiiie siècle* (2 vols, Paris, 1968), ii, 485–6. Nonetheless, the title originated with her first husband, and not with herself.

67 *Cartulaire de Marmoutier pour le Perche*, ed. L'abbé Barret (Mortagne, 1894), 44–5, 45n; *Géographie du Perche et chronologie de ses comtes* (2 vols, Mortagne, 1890–1902), i, 50.

68 *Recueil de chartes et documents de St-Martin-des-Champs, monastère Parisien*, ed. J. Depoin (5 vols, Paris, 1912–21), iii, 96–7.

one occasion the style 'once (*quondam*) countess of Leicester'.[69] It is not easy to say why she did this, for in others of her charters as a widow she does not qualify the title, and indeed remained 'countess' to her friends the Franciscans even when she had retired to an eremitical life. In the cases of both countesses there may have been an element of what they may have considered to be courtly demureness about this.

With this background of deference to female claims, it is not surprising that a great age of dowager countesses had dawned long before the fourteenth century. Protected from the early twelfth century by written marriage settlements, and after 1215 by courts primed to enforce dower more rigidly than any other form of plea, long-lived aristocratic women began to dominate their class. The reign of Henry I provides the first of them, for in 1100 Henry had conceded control over the remarriage of widowed aristocratic women to their families, and stood by his promise. Agnes, countess of Buckingham, was able to avoid remarriage and for many years control her late husband's earldom because she was allowed the wardship of her under-age son. Countess Margaret of Warwick was left with so generous a dower that she had estates in four English counties and her late husband's Marcher lordship of Gower, over which she maintained some control for nearly forty years after her husband died. Later reigns saw some decline in female power as the king made more pressing efforts to control aristocratic marriage, but powerful countesses, whether dowager or heiress, were by no means absent, even in the reign of the rapacious John (1199–1216). The formidable countesses, Petronilla of Leicester and Alice of Eu, both struck bargains with the king to hold on to their estates. In the thirteenth century we find growing numbers of powerful dowagers, like Countess Ela of Salisbury, Countess Philippa Basset of Warwick, Countess Margaret de Quincy of Winchester, and the most formidable of all, Isabel de Forz, countess of Aumale and Devon, whom only K.B. McFarlane's notorious Margaret Marshal, duchess of Norfolk at the end of the fourteenth century, could rival in wealth and calculating power. All these women were themselves great heiresses, and by marrying and remarrying and then taking dower settlements from their late husbands' families, they built up remarkable concentrations of lands and wealth. It is no exaggeration to say that unlucky marriage settlements and several long-lived

69 Archives départementales de l'Eure, Evreux, H 561.

dowagers helped to destroy the wealth and power of the earldom of Warwick after 1204.[70] At one point in the thirteenth century there were no less than four women calling themselves countess of Warwick, and taking a cut from the estates of the earldom. The luckless Earl Thomas (1229–42) controlled little more than the town from which he took his title. The position of women was in general unenviable in the Middle Ages, but for some at least longevity brought its compensations.

THE EARL IN SCOTLAND

The title of earl in the British Isles was not confined to England. English kings before 1400 created earls of Pembroke and March in Wales, and earls of Cork, Desmond, Kildare, Louth, Ormond and Ulster in Ireland. None of these dignities were created for the benefit of native aristocrats, and there does not seem to have been any idea at the time that these outland earls were lesser men in dignity than their English counterparts, whatever their status in terms of wealth. The earls of Ulster and Pembroke, it should be remembered, had large estates in England, as well as on the Celtic fringe. But Scotland was an entirely different case. Scotland was unique in Celtic Britain in having (before 1066) hereditary titled magnates bearing a rank inferior to that of king. These were the mormaers (Gaelic: 'great officers'). They first appear in the tenth century in the Gaelic kingdom of Scotia north of the Forth. By 1000 they can be seen to have been hereditary officials exerting royal authority and acting as military leaders in distinct provinces: Angus, Buchan, Mar, Mearns, Moray, Ross, Strathern. They were unknown in the Lowlands of Scotland at this time (Lothian was in any case part of English Northumbria till the second quarter of the eleventh century). There could be found south of the Forth in the eleventh century hereditary magnates of great power ruling Galloway and Cumbria, but they used or were credited with vaguer titles: 'lord', 'prince' or even 'king'. Earls were not to be found south of the Forth until the twelfth century, at Dunbar and Lennox. In the farthest north of Scotland, in Caithness and Orkney, were Scandinavian jarls, Orkney, being still theoretically subject to the king of Norway until the twelfth century.

70 E. Mason, 'The Resources of the Earldom of Warwick in the Thirteenth Century', *Midland History*, iii (1975–6), 67–75.

The rise of the mormaers in Scotland is difficult to account for, and the evidence for them is thin enough. It might be that they were conscious imitations by the kings of Scotia of the ealdormen of contemporary England (both mormaers and ealdormen were war-leaders in their provinces), but it is just as likely that they were a purely local response to the military problems posed by the Vikings. Be that as it may, at some time in the eleventh or twelfth century, mormaers were related by Scotsmen to the English earls. The lowlands of Lothian show evidence that the Scottish kings had been brought into contact with terms like 'thegn' and 'shire' by the end of the eleventh century. It is not beyond the bounds of possibility that the English-speaking subjects of the kings of Scotland were equating the Gaelic mormaers with earls as early as this, but there is no direct evidence, and the non-appearance of the title 'earl' until later centuries in Lothian, Galloway and Strathclyde tells against it: if there was to be a direct borrowing of the title from England, it should have happened first in the Lowlands and been applied to the *principes* there.

There is no doubt that the titles 'mormaer' and *comes* were regarded as equivalent by the end of the reign of Alexander I (1107–24). Two Gaelic mormaers, Beth and Malise, attest a late charter of the king as *comites*.[71] We can assume with some assurance that by then English-speakers were equating earl and mormaer. In or around 1174 the English writer, Jordan Fantosme, a habitué of the Scottish court, wrote in his French-language chronicle of the *contes* of Buchan and Angus, the same way as he wrote of the *contes* of Leicester and Norfolk. This is fairly conclusive evidence that there was then a generally acceptable equation: mormaer = count = earl. For Gaelic-speakers earls were mormaers well into the fourteenth century. The Gaelic annals of Connacht refer in 1316 to Edward Bruce, earl of Carrick, as *mormaer Cargi*. It was not until the late Middle Ages that mormaer lost this meaning in Gaelic to the Scandinavian loan-word *iarla*.[72]

The twelfth-century Scottish mormaer-earl had some distinct resemblances to his English counterpart. The dignity was hereditary and might be inherited by women, but as in England there still clung to it some elements of public office; if anything these were stronger

71 *Early Scottish Charters, prior to AD 1153*, ed. A.C. Lawrie (Glasgow, 1905), 42–4.
72 For Gaelic ideas of titles see generally, *The Gaelic Notes in the Book of Deer*, ed. K. Jackson (Cambridge, 1972).

in Scotland. The legal jurisdiction of the earl over homicides carried out within the area of his peace survived into the thirteenth century in Scotland (see p. 62). The dignity of the Scottish earl was rarely bolstered by claims to divine sanction in their styles. Although I do know of at least one example of it, when Earl Gilbert of Strathern claimed God's indulgence for his title in a particularly solemn act dated 1200.[73] Few English earls had done so at that date for nearly half a century, but it was still a practice to be found amongst French counts (see pp. 13–14).

Until the fourteenth century the Scottish earl was responsible for the defence of his province and was head of its general levy of freemen.[74] We know that very early in the twelfth century the Scottish king, like the king of England, had taken to creating earls by charter. There is an unambiguous reference to King David I (1124–53) creating his kinsman, Duncan, earl of Fife by charter, and since this could only have happened during the period 1136 x 39, this reference predates the earliest actual surviving charter of creation of an English earldom.[75] This is unlikely to mean, however, that the Scots were the first to use charters in the creations of earls; it is more likely to indicate that King David (made earl of Huntingdon in England in 1113) and his clerks had previously met the practice in England. On the other hand, there does not seem to be any trace of the insignia of belt and sword being applied to Scottish earls in the early period. It is not until 1398 that we hear of a Scottish earl being girded by the king, when David Lindsay was belted earl of Crawford in a parliament at Perth.[76] The only early symbol that seems to be mentioned in connection with the Scottish earl occurs in 1312 when King Robert Bruce (1306–29) mentioned the 'banner' of the earldom of Moray when he granted it to Thomas Randolf: an appropriate symbol for what was still a military rank if the

73 *Liber Insule Missarum*, ed. H. Drummond (Bannatyne Club, 1847), 1, *Gilbertus filius Ferthet dei indulgentia comes de Stratheryn . . .*
74 There are examples of seneschals of Scottish earls being identified by their province, rather than their master, for instance Gillenef, seneschal of Strathern, and Gillemur, seneschal of Athol, appear in a charter of the early thirteenth century in which their masters appear, *Registrum de Dunfermlyn*, ed. Anon. (Bannatyne Club, 1842), 85–6. This indicates a more territorial attitude to their masters' lordships.
75 *Facsimiles of the National Manuscripts of Scotland* (London, 1867–71), i, no. 50.
76 *Complete Peerage*, iii, 508–9. When Patrick, Lord Hailes, was belted earl of Bothwell in 1488, it was said to have been carried out 'according to custom', but how old the custom could have been in 1398 is unclear, *Acts of the Parliaments of Scotland* ii, 206.

banner referred to his status as earl, but perhaps it owed more to Anglo-French ideas of the attributes of a magnate and banneret.

It does not seem that the Scottish king ever had any great ambitions to control the succession to his earldoms. In the case of Buchan there is evidence of Gaelic practices long surviving in the tradition of the investiture of the earl. The investiture (in whatever form it took place) was carried out before his people on a low mound called later the 'Earlsmount' (*super montem de Ellone*) at Ellon, Co. Aberdeen, in the fifteenth century. Ellon was the place where we know that the chief court of the earldom of Buchan was being held in the twelfth century, and this would indicate that the Earlsmount was integral to the earl's authority at least that far back, if not much earlier.[77] This was a ceremony which recalls the investiture of Celtic kinglets in Scotland, Man and Ireland, and particularly the Scottish king himself on the mound of Scone. The example of Buchan speaks volumes about the position of the Scottish earl in regard to his king.

77 *The New Statistical Account of Scotland*, xii, Aberdeen (Edinburgh, 1845), 903.

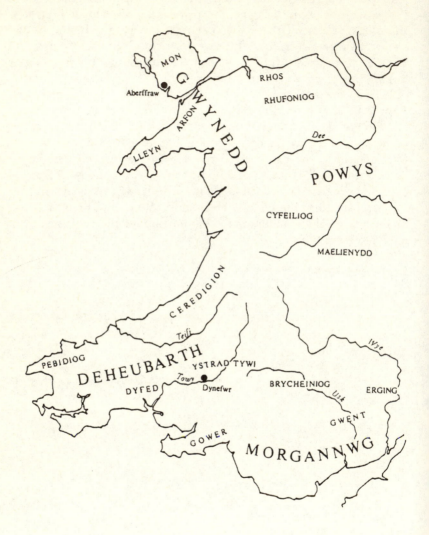

Figure 1 Wales: names of kingdoms and regions.

2

WELSH PRINCES AND THE PREHISTORY OF THE PEERAGE

THE PRINCE

The second hereditary title below that of king to penetrate England came by a very curious route. The title 'prince' (Lat. *princeps*; Wel. *tywysog*) was the particular contribution of the Welsh to the English hierarchy of ranks. Wales in the eleventh and early twelfth centuries was ruled over by a collection of kings called in Latin *rex*, and in regular Welsh usage from the twelfth century onwards *brenin, rhi*. The nature of Welsh kingship need not concern us here, except for the observation that Welsh kingship was intended by its holders to be real kingship (they used the same Latin title as the English king, *rex*, and affected some regal trappings, though not a crown or sceptre). A native Welsh sensitivity to status was evident at an early period. The vernacular had a host of words for 'ruler'. The greatest rulers might be hailed as *gwledig, mynawg* or *rhwyfadur*; these would be the *reges* over the greater realms, rulers of lesser kings who would be called *teyrn, rhi, brenin* or *unben*.[1] But all would be converted in Latin to *reges*, or more rarely *reguli*. In the middle of the twelfth century, however, all degrees of kingship were slowly dropped by Welsh rulers (if not their poets), and the title of 'prince' taken up instead.

The appearance of Welsh princes happened rather abruptly. The numerous Welsh chronicles in both Latin and the vernacular stop referring to Welsh kings in the late 1150s, with but one exception made for the potent North Welsh ruler, Owain Gwynedd, in

---

1 W. Davies, *Patterns of Power in Early Wales* (Oxford, 1990), 10–15, gives an analysis of the early Welsh vocabulary of kingship.

1170.[2] In their own charters Welsh rulers still call themselves kings after the 1150s but not consistently and not at all after the reign of Henry II of England (1154–89). An odd and revealing fact is that English sources continue to call the Welsh rulers 'kings' for some time after the Welsh themselves have dropped the title. As late as 1198 on a document produced in the Chancery, Dafydd son of Owain Gwynedd is described as king. Clearly the English had got used to the idea that the Welsh were ruled by kings, and when the Welsh changed their minds the English did not notice and kept on referring to Welsh kings; literary conservatism, and a general ignorance of what the Welsh were doing is sufficient to account for it. Indeed, the Welsh king had passed into the realm of common cliché; a saying to the effect that certain men were 'as proud as Welsh kings' surfaces in the work of Jordan Fantosme in the mid 1170s.[3] In the 1190s Richard of Devizes could still talk disdainfully of Welsh 'kinglets' on the fringes of the realm of England, though the next generation of writers were more apt to talk of Welsh barons or, at the last, princes.[4]

The abandonment of kingship was therefore a native decision. The Welsh were not forced to it, as has been claimed.[5] At the time when it happened the Welsh were ruled by three particularly potent men (Madog ap Maredudd of Powys, Owain Gwynedd of Gwynedd and Rhys ap Gruffudd of Deheubarth), and native rule was stronger than it had been since the time of William the Conqueror. It is difficult to see any such decision being forced on an unwilling Wales by English power at such a time. But this does not mean that the abandonment of kingship had nothing to do with England. A long period, going back to the ninth century, had seen Welsh kings accept a position subordinate to the English king. English documents before 1066 described them as *reguli* or *subreguli* (kinglets or under-kings). When the Normans arrived things got worse, and under Henry I

---

2 Welsh court poetry, however, continues to use words that betoken kingship, or high rank, long after the twelfth century: *gwledig, rhi, brenhin, teyrn* and others. We may ascribe this to literary conservatism in a language which did not have to accommodate alien notions of rank. My thanks to Mr Robert Babcock for discussing this with me.

3 *Jordan Fantosme's Chronicle*, ed. R.C. Johnston (Oxford, 1981), 14.

4 The Annals of Dunstable in 1220 could also talk of Llywelyn the Great of Gwynedd as 'a Welsh kinglet' meaning to be insulting, see *Annales Monastici*, ed. H.R. Luard (5 vols, Rolls Series, 1864–9), iii, 61.

5 T. Jones Pierce, 'The Age of the Princes', in *Medieval Wales: Selected Essays*, ed. J. Beverley Smith (Cardiff, 1972), 28–9.

(1100–35) there was a time when only the fragmented kingdom of Powys remained a precarious reality in Wales. Only two Welshmen are described as 'kings' by contemporary documents in all of Henry's reign: Hywel ap Gronw who ruled a client state in the region of Carmarthen between 1102 and 1106 was called 'greatest of the kings of the West as far as London' by his court poet (putting him near the level of the *rex Anglorum*); and Gruffudd ap Cynan, who ruled Gwynedd as the obsequious client of the English in the latter half of the reign was described in Latin as king by a Welsh bishop indebted to him for some important relics.[6] It was at this time that the Worcester chronicler talks dismissively of there being no kings in Wales after the defeats of 1093. There was a recovery in Stephen's reign, when all the ancient kingdoms resurfaced, but there can be no doubt that traditional kingship in Wales had suffered a severe shock. Moreover, the leading families were dislocated through murder, dispossession and kin-strife, and over all there could be no doubt in the remotest corner of Wales what considerable power was wielded by the king of England. A king of Glamorgan or Gwynedd would seem piffling by comparison.

The English and Normans undoubtedly considered the Welsh claims to kingship piffling. Geoffrey Gaimar, who composed his French *Estoire des Engles* (History of the English) in Lincolnshire in the late 1130s, recalled an incident which supposedly happened at the 1099 court of William Rufus. The Welsh kings present claimed as theirs the right to bear swords of state before the king at his crown-wearing. But the Norman earls present loudly opposed them, and four of them seized the swords from the Welsh, marching off doggedly before their king.[7] The incident may never have happened, and even if it had the court of Henry I would be a more likely setting – he usually had a tail of Welsh royalty in attendance. But fiction or not, the story indicates that some equation was being made at the time between Welsh kings and English earls, which the Welsh were resisting (rather like the more appropriate contemporary equation between earls and mormaers). A quite explicit statement of such a position on Celtic kingship comes from the Anglo-Norman invaders of Ireland. An anonymous French

---

6 J. Vendryes, 'Le Poème du livre noir sur Hywel ab Gronw', *Etudes Celtiques*, iv (1948), 276; *The Text of the Book of Llan Dâv*, ed. J. Gwenogvryn Evans (Oxford, 1893), 85.
7 *L'Estoire des Engles*, ed. A. Bell (Anglo-Norman Text Soc., xiv–xvi, 1960), ll. 5975–6020.

poem written around 1200 in Ireland (another land well populated by kings) explains to those who were unclear about it, that 'In Ireland there were several kings (*reis*), as elsewhere there are earls (*cunturs*)'.[8]

The Welsh choice of an alternative title to king reveals a new Welsh aristocratic order in the making. The change in the vernacular title must have come first, and may have predated by some years the change observed in the chronicles: *brenhinedd* became *tywysogyon*. Indeed the Welsh chronicles cannot be entirely trusted as a guide to the process; the most important of them had been revised and translated from the original Latin to Welsh in the late thirteenth and fourteenth centuries. It was in the Welsh ruler's charters that the choice of a Latin title reveals most about changing attitudes in twelfth-century Wales. In using a Latin title the Welsh rulers had to fit their new style into an order that was European.

The use of the word 'lord' (Lat. *dominus*; Wel. *arglwydd*) has been noted as one alternative for king in Welsh sources. The dynasty of Deheubarth seems to have adopted it early on as an alternative to 'king'. Successive rulers of Deheubarth, Cadell ap Gruffudd (retired 1154) and Rhys ap Gruffudd (died 1197), are *dominus* in charters and chronicles, and Cadell at least is noted elsewhere as *rex*.[9] Rhys's preference for the style has led to him being known to us today as 'the Lord Rhys'. The Welsh were experimenting in the mid-twelfth century with styles; the way in which the title *dominus* was used in the Welsh sources encourages the idea that it was one such alternative to *rex*. The multiplicity of its uses in England and France (anything from the owner of a hamlet to the holder of a great honor like Breteuil) probably accounts for its failure to catch on in charter styles of Welsh rulers. It seems to have found at least one specific application, however. Welsh legal codes of the thirteenth century use *arglwydd* to mean the holder of a legal franchise, which was its general application in Western Europe, and shows that the Welsh appreciated why it would not do as a style.[10]

---

8 *The Song of Dermot and the Earl*, ed. G.H. Orpen (Oxford, 1892), 160.
9 D. Crouch, 'The Earliest Charter of a Welsh King', *Bulletin of the Board of Celtic Studies*, xxvi (1989), 127n.
10 In this I follow Pierce, 'The Age of the Princes', 27–8, modified by D. Jenkins, 'Kings, Lords, and Princes: the Nomenclature of Authority in Thirteenth-Century Wales', *Bulletin of the Board of Celtic Studies*, xxvi (1974–6), 451–61.

The Welsh found other alternatives to king than 'lord'. *Tywysog*, like duke (*dux*), had an original meaning of 'leader', and it was still being used in that sense, as for instance to describe the chief of a religious community. Its Gaelic cognate word *toiseach* (the same word that is now used as the Gaelic title of the Prime Minister of Eire: the *taioseach*) had, however, long acquired a social meaning, being applied to wealthy freemen in Scotland, where it was used as equivalent of the English rank of 'thane'. But neither 'duke' nor the distinctly inferior 'thegn' was in the minds of the Welsh rulers and their clerks. The Welsh opted in a body for the Latin title *princeps* (prince) in their charters and Latin chronicles.

Twelfth-century charters are our best source here. Unlike chronicles they were not revised by men of later days with different ideas of nomenclature; unlike foreign sources, they did not have preconceptions of the Celtic world. The writers of the charters were men attentive to the pretensions of those for whom they wrote. The style of the issuer of the charter carried a message to its reader or auditor, it stated his dignity and pretensions. The same applied when Welsh magnates were witnesses to other people's charters; their placing and the title given to them were matters of some sensitivity. Charters tell us that in the first half of the century 'king' remained the usual style. In Glamorgan, the dominant Welshman, Morgan ab Owain of Caerleon, was credited as *rex* in a charter of his neighbour, Earl Roger of Hereford, dating to the late 1140s. In Deheubarth, Cadell ap Gruffudd ap Rhys alluded to his father's kingship in a charter of his of the same period and perhaps also on his seal. Elsewhere, he attests as *Catel rex Sudgualliae*. In Powys, its last great ruler, Madog ap Maredudd is *rex Powissensium* in a charter to Haughmond abbey, in which Madog also claims divine sanction for his rule. Indeed, even Madog's underling, Hywel of Arwystli, was claiming the status of *rex* early in the 1140s. Gwynedd too has its contemporary rulers affecting the style *rex*. Owain Gwynedd, indeed, is twice credited with the style *rex Walliae*, once in a charter of his own dating to 1139 x 43, and again in a letter he sent to Louis VII of France in 1165 (did Owain intend the deliberate ambiguity of translation: 'king of Wales' or 'a king of Wales'?). Some few years later Thomas Becket wrote to him under the same style, when seeking his support. Owain's turbulent brother, Cadwaladr, in exile at the court of Ranulf II of Chester in 1147 x 48, is credited with a similar style, *rex Waliarum*, although here the less flattering translation ('a king of the Welsh') is possible.[11]

Owain Gwynedd's later correspondence shows no steady attachment to *rex* as a style. Both in his own letters and those addressed to him, he is *Walliarum princeps* (in 1165) or *Wallensium princeps* (in 1168 x 70).[12] This tallies well with the broad developments that can be gathered from the chronicles, as I have said. There are other indicators besides. Gerald of Wales (well read in Isidore) uses the word 'prince' for Welsh rulers from the time of his earliest writings in the 1180s; he would have picked up the practice when he learned the first elements of Latin and political reality in west Wales in the 1150s or 1160s. The only Welshman Gerald ever called 'king' was Arthur. 'King' did not go abruptly out of use in the time of Owain Gwynedd, or even after it. Owain's son, Dafydd, was *rex* or *rex Norwallie* in two of his charters late in the reign of Henry II, but at the same time he was also *princeps Norwallie*.[13] English chroniclers too were reluctant to dispense with the style *rex* for Welsh rulers, and they refer to Rhys ap Gruffudd (prince of Deheubarth in his charters) as 'king'. Nonetheless, we can see a broad shift under way from 'king' to 'prince' in the mid-century. Examples of 'king' applied to Welshmen after 1160 are increasingly rare, and (as I have said above) can be put down simply to the slow diffusion of the new alternative style: people had got used to the idea that the Welsh had kings of a sort, and were slow to adjust to the new fashion.[14]

Princeps remained a distinctly ambiguous title in Europe until the twelfth century. Bede had used the word to comprehend a whole range of rulers: kings, kinglets or lesser men. For him it

11 For King Morgan see D. Crouch, 'The Slow Death of Kingship in Glamorgan, 1067–1158', *Morgannwg*, xxix (1985), 35–6; *Liber Eliensis*, ed. E.O. Blake (Camden Soc., 3rd ser., xcii, 1962), 320–1. For King Cadell see Crouch, 'The Earliest Original Charter of a Welsh King', 127; *The Cartulary of Haughmond Abbey*, ed. U. Rees (Cardiff, 1985), 222–3. For Kings Madog and Hywel, ibid., 221, 222. For King Owain Gwynedd, Gerald of Wales, 'De ecclesia Menevensi', in *Omnia Opera*, iii, 59; *Recueil des Historiens des Gaules et de la France*, ed. M. Bouquet et al. (24 vols, Paris, 1869–1904), xvi, 116; *Materials for the History of Thomas Becket, archbishop of Canterbury*, ed. J.C. Robertson and J.B. Sheppard (7 vols, Rolls Series, 1875–85), v, 229, 230. For King Cadwaladr, *Charters of the Anglo-Norman Earls of Chester c. 1071–1237*, ed. G. Barraclough (Record Soc. of Lancashire and Cheshire, cxxvi, 1988), 77, 96–7.
12 *Recueil des Historiens de France*, xvi, 117; *Materials for the History of Thomas Becket*, v, 232–8.
13 *Cartulary of Haughmond*, 68–9, 216.
14 *Brenin* still appears in the Welsh law codes of the thirteenth century, but jurists can be as conservative as poets.

was a vague status word that glossed over insoluble problems of hierarchy and dependence.[15] It was long in common use amongst Latin writers, Bede amongst them, to denote the principal magnates of a particular kingdom or region (one of a herd of other Latin words used for the same purpose: see the list in the introduction). It was a popular word in this context because the Vulgate applied it freely to describe the 'leaders' or 'elders' of the Jews and their tribes. In England in the mid-twelfth century Earl Richard of Pembroke could pledge to defend a grant of land 'before the king and princes (*coram rege et principibus*) in every manner of court', and he was not including Welshmen in the guarantee.[16] But alongside this was another ancient and more particular use to signify a sovereign lord (*princeps terrae*) within a particular realm (*regnum*), whether he was a king or held some other title. Thus John of Salisbury and Gerald of Wales (and eventually Machiavelli) addressed their pens to produce political manuals describing the ideal conduct of 'princes'. Letters to King Henry III (1216–72) would address him as 'the magnificent and most excellent prince, the lord Henry by God's grace king of England . . .'.

This mixture of uses may well reflect the fact that *princeps* was not a word that had any firm place in the imperial Roman civil or military order, unlike the duke or count. Its first occurrence as anything resembling a title was when the Roman senate awarded the distinction *princeps Senatus* to the Emperor Augustus. But this was not so much a title as a privilege; the right to speak first in any debate, reflecting its basic etymological meaning of 'chief'. Still, the word's association with the emperors of Antiquity invested it with dignity, and Isidore of Seville included it with a certain deliberation amongst his list of titles, preceding that of duke. Gerald of Wales found it in Isidore's 'Etymologies' and took 'prince' to be a title, like 'king' which it followed, and 'duke' which it preceded. To him it was a 'level of dignity', as he put it.[17]

It would not be surprising if Isidore had directly influenced the Welsh clerical households when they advised their lords as they were shopping for titles; Isidore's 'Etymologies' had been well known in Wales since the eighth century, and was part of every good clerical education. The literate could point to Isidore and say that there

---

15 Campbell, 'Bede's *Reges* and *Principes*', in *Essays in Anglo-Saxon History* (London, 1986), 85–98.
16 Cartulary of Biddlesden, Brit. Libr., ms Harley 4714 fo. 176r–v.
17 Gerald of Wales, 'De Principis Instructione', in *Omnia Opera*, viii, 105, 106.

could be found a warrant for 'prince' as a title which came in rank before that of 'duke' and 'count' (if we take that as a translation for Isidore's *consul*, which by then was frequently done). But it is quite as likely that there were more modern influences at work. On the Continent, and in Britain (particularly England and Scotland), 'prince' had made some headway as a specific title by 1100. It was used vaguely to denote great potentates whether or not they were earls: David, son of Malcolm III of Scotland, was called both *princeps* and *dux et princeps* of the men of Cumbria in the reign of his brother Alexander I; Fergus, ruler of Galloway, was called *princeps* of the Galwegians. Robert fitz Hamo, lord of Gloucester and Glamorgan was a *princeps* to a clerk resident in his Welsh lordship in the generation after his death, but in Norman terms he was no more than a baron.[18] In England before 1066 it had been an occasional synonym for an earl in Latin charters, and immediately after the Conquest it was applied to the great Norman barons, Roger de Montgomery (not then an earl) and Richard de Clare. On the Continent, *princeps* was associated with the greater magnates of the Frankish realm from a very early period, where the words '*dux et princeps*' went in tandem from the eighth century onwards to distinguish the sub-royal rulers of places like Aquitaine, Bavaria and Brittany. We have already seen how a Norman clerk used the formula to boost Duke William's dignity in a document dating to before 1066, and how a clerk of the church of Glasgow used it to exalt the dignity of David of Scotland (although his proper rank, like William's, was a *comes*, and the same document calls his wife a countess).[19]

Outside Wales the title had begun to be used by itself, as a title of honour, consistently in the twelfth century. There had been some earlier, local experimentation, notably the Lombard dukes of southern Italy, who dropped the title 'duke' for 'prince' on the fall of the Lombard kingdom in northern Italy, on which they had previously depended. But its methodical use came later. The title 'prince' was inherited by the Normans when they took over the Lombard principalities. The principality of Capua became an important Norman state, until it was swallowed up in 1135 by

---

18 *Vitae Sanctorum Britanniae et Genealogiae*, ed. A.W. Wade-Evans (Cardiff, 1944), 232: *rege Anglorum Willelmo regnante per Britanniam et Roberto principe Haimonis filio regente Gulatmorcantiam . . .*
19 *Registrum episcopatus Glasguensis*, ed. C. Innes (Maitland Club, Edinburgh, 1843), 3–7.

the Norman king of Sicily, who then added it to his style.[20] The First Crusade took the title 'prince' into the Latin East, where it was assumed by the ruler of Antioch in Syria. The inspiration is obvious, for the first prince of Antioch, Bohemond, was a Norman from southern Italy. French crusaders in turn brought the title into Spain, where in the early twelfth century it was taken up by the Norman, Robert Burdet, with papal sanction, when he became ruler of the Crusading state of Tarragona, lately conquered from the Moors. These new princes may have been part of the inspiration for the Welsh. Welshmen went to the Holy Land, and were visiting Rome with increasing frequency after 1100 (they were by no means strangers to Rome before 1100).

For a Welsh *tywysog*, the equivalent of 'prince' was a happy choice. It may have been a step down from king, but it retained the impression that its user ruled a realm of some sort, and – a sideswipe at the English earls, this – was a ruler over counts. So it became incorporated in the official styles of the rulers of independent Powys and Gwynedd (now called principalities) as they moved into the thirteenth century, and it was as princes that the English Chancery clerks came to address them. Llywelyn the Great, prince of Gwynedd, favoured the Anglo-Welsh style first known to be used by his uncle, Dafydd, *princeps Norwallie*. Late in his principate he altered this style to *princeps de Aberfrau et dominus Snowdini*.[21] Aberffraw was (with Marthrafal and Dynefwr) one of the three royal seats of the Welsh, according to Welsh lawbooks. The princes of Gwynedd still occupied theirs, and the allusion in this later style is to ancient royalty. The contemporary and rival princes of Powys imitated those of Gwynedd, and an instance survives of Llywelyn's enemy, Gwenwynwyn ab Owain, styling himself *Powisie princeps et dominus Arwistili*, either in rivalry or mockery.[22]

For the prince of Gwynedd the climax of this fitful search for status came in 1240. Llywelyn the Great of Gwynedd had recently died, and the heir to his principality was his son Dafydd. Dafydd was, through his mother, a nephew of King Henry III of England. King Henry was a man who could be more than liberal in his favours with his nearest relations, and at Gloucester in May 1240

20 *Rogerii II regis: Diplomata Latina*, ed C. Brühl (Codex diplomaticus regni Siciliae, ii, pt 1, 1987), 111–15.
21 D. Stephenson, *The Governance of Gwynedd* (Cardiff, 1984), 199–203.
22 National Library of Wales, Wynnstay Collection, Strata Marcella Deed no. 22.

he proved it by knighting his nephew, confirming his pre-eminent position in Wales, and allowing him a privilege no English magnate enjoyed either then or for long afterwards; the right to wear a coronet, the lesser crown called the 'garland' (for more on this see Chapter 6). The significance of this act becomes clear when we note that a circlet called 'the garland' had been used in the coronation of Dafydd's grandfather, John, as duke of Normandy in 1199. A direct correspondence was thus made between a Welsh prince and a Norman duke.[23] The events of 1240 can be interpreted as Dafydd being given formal precedence over the English earls, and the status of a ruler of a realm with its own distinct customs and law. Indeed Prince Dafydd's affectation of the style 'prince of Wales' may well be associated with the primacy in law Welsh jurists were constructing for the Venedotian dynasty. His realm was dependent on an outside king, but until Edward I lost patience with Prince Llywelyn in 1277 it was a dependence expressed solely through an act of homage, only later by military service and summons to English parliaments.

The native-ruled principality of Gwynedd, or Wales, came to an end in 1282 when the last Llywelyn fell in an ambush in mid-Wales. His principality was confiscated by the English king and became part of the royal estates. The other major principality in Wales, Powys, continued to be ruled by its Welsh dynasty, but it had never been conceded the same privileges as Gwynedd, and by the 1260s, under pressure from Gwynedd, its ruler, Gruffudd ap Gwenwynwyn, had dropped the title prince in favour of the ambiguous title 'lord' (Lat. *dominus*; Wel. *arglwydd*). In time he Frenchified his name to 'Griffin de la Pole' ('Pole' referring to his chief seat of Welshpool) and was absorbed into the English baronage. However, this was by no means the end of princely status in the British Isles. The principality of Wales remained intact as an administrative unit of the royal estates, and in 1301, casting around for a suitable endowment for his eldest son, Edward I gave the youthful Edward of Caernarvon the earldom of Chester he had himself once enjoyed, and added to it Wales. The title of prince may not have been formally given, but Edward

23 On the one fragmentary impression of a seal purporting to be Dafydd's, once amongst the muniments of the earl of Bridgewater, he is shown seated on a throne, holding a sword upright in his right hand. This could well be a wonderful example of a Welsh prince conforming on his seal to the standard ducal image, see H. Owen and J.B. Blakeway, *A History of Shrewsbury* (2 vols, London, 1825), i, 117–19; see below pp. 246–7.

was using it within a few months of receiving the lands of the principality.

This was the first time any member of the English royal family used the title of prince. We have long been used to the dignity of prince or princess being automatically bestowed on the children and grandchildren of English monarchs, but this was not the medieval practice. Before 1066 there was indeed something of an analogous situation where those male members of the royal family in a position to succeed the king were dignified by the title *atheling*, Latinised as *Clito*. Welsh kings adopted a similar practice and called their designated heir by the borrowed word, *edling*; something they were still doing early in the thirteenth century.[24] In the first years of the twelfth century Henry I's only legitimate son, William, was called 'atheling', but on his death by drowning in 1120 the title lapsed in England, never to revive. Until Edward, son of Edward I, was invested as prince of Wales, the eldest sons of English kings were known by a variety of titles. Stephen's eldest son, Eustace, was count of Boulogne; Henry II's eldest son, the Young Henry, was accorded the unique dignity in England of coronation as king in 1170 in his father's lifetime. He died in 1183 and the process was not repeated for his next eldest brother, Richard, whose title was count of Poitou until he succeeded his father. Henry III's eldest son Edward was given the estates of the earldom of Chester, but rarely used the title. In his charters he was most frequently known as *primogenitus* 'the king's (eldest) son'. His brother Edmund was almost invariably 'the king's son' even though he was in fact also earl of Lancaster, Derby and Leicester. Appanage was of less consequence than parentage. The relationship to the fount of majesty was all-important to the dignity of royal cadets and by-blows. 'The king's son', or less usually, 'the king's brother' and 'the king's uncle' were the formal titles most frequently employed by both legitimate and bastard sons of the English and French kings, whether on their seals or in their charter styles. When he became prince of Wales, Edward of Caernarvon did not wholly turn from this older style, and in his charters and letters he was 'Edward *the king's son*, prince of Wales'.

After Edward II became king in 1307 the title of Wales temporarily lapsed. The future Edward III was made in 1326, like his

24 T.M. Charles-Edwards, 'The Heir Apparent in Irish and Welsh Law', *Celtica*, ix (1971), 180–90.

predecessors, earl of Chester, but the title of duke of Aquitaine was his main style. However, in 1343, Edward III revived the principality of Wales for his eldest son Edward (the Black Prince). Edward had already been made earl of Chester and duke of Cornwall in 1337, but the title of prince was resurrected for the boy later for unknown reasons. It is interesting to find that when it was revived it became the boy's chief style, taking precedence even over the ducal title of Cornwall. This was a departure from the Continental practice. There the position of the princes was never clear cut in relation to the dukes, to many of whom they were inferior. There the prince was not thought of as royal at all. In what may have been a memory of the dignity of Gwynedd and Normandy before it, the new prince was invested before the English parliament with a coronet, a gold ring and a silver rod or sceptre.[25] Certainly the charter of creation says that everything was done 'according to custom' (*iuxta morem*), which must refer back to an accepted earlier practice, and, as we will see, the ring and coronet had already been long accepted as part of the proper princely regalia.

THE DUKE

The formal appearance of the duke in England was late, and in Scotland, even later. The first English duke was the young Edward, son of Edward III, who was 'girded' duke of Cornwall in 1337. The first two Scottish dukes, Albany and Rothesay, were created in 1398. In the cases of both countries, native dukedoms were bestowed first on the sons of reigning kings. This does not mean, however, that the English had not been long acquainted with dukes. Before 1066 native ealdormen and earls had been equated in dignity with the Continental dukes. After 1066 for the best part of three centuries their king had also been a French duke, whether of Normandy or Aquitaine. The arms of the Continental dukes appeared on the thirteenth-century rolls of arms in which noble English boys were instructed, for they might later meet their owners on Continental tournament and battlefields. Good and evil dukes populated the

---

25 *The Fifth Report from the Lords Committees touching the Dignity of a Peer of the Realm* (London, 1829), 43–4. Since the word used for 'coronet' was *sertum*, meaning a 'chaplet', this may actually betoken the original 'garland' of the princes of Gwynedd (and perhaps of Normandy before that), making yet another appearance. We know that the Black Prince left it in his will to his brother Lionel; after that we lose sight of it.

twelfth- and thirteenth-century romances that were written and read in England. Bracton, almost absently, included dukes in his secular scheme of things, even though when he wrote there were no dukes in England nor were there to be for nearly a century. The idea of the duke was part of the English appreciation of aristocracy and hierarchy, for why else would the word 'duke' have penetrated the English language by the thirteenth century?

It is a little strange in view of this why no dukes were created in England long before the fourteenth century. The only obvious reason would be that the king did not like the idea of a number of his subjects carrying the same title as he did, even though it was his secondary title. This would be one explanation of the Norman suppression of the Latin title *dux* for earl in the 1070s. As Powell and Wallis suggest, it is perhaps significant that when Edward III created his son a duke he was on the verge of claiming the crown of France, which would have submerged his secondary style of duke of Aquitaine in something far greater.

The basic etymological meaning of the word 'duke' was 'leader', and it became a formal military office in the reign of the Roman emperor Diocletian (AD 284–305). There was less confusion about the use of duke as a title than there was over prince, but the basic meaning allowed a certain leeway to the pretentious even in dukeless England. The twelfth-century writers, Geoffrey of Monmouth and William of Malmesbury, determined to flatter, called their patron, Robert (in fact earl of Gloucester) 'duke' in the 1130s. This would be less revealing if the same earl had not been so experimental in his own use of titles. He methodically avoided the Latin *comes* for the less usual and pretentious title *consul*, which was its occasional synonym (probably because – as Marc Bloch said – it resembled the Middle French word for count, *cuens*). As like as not, Geoffrey and William knew their man, and were pandering to Earl Robert by bestowing on him the title used by the 'ducal' earls before the Conquest. 'Duke' was used by one of the Latin chroniclers in Wales for the prince of Gwynedd around the year 1200, but it was a passing fad that never challenged the title 'prince'.

The creation of Edward of Woodstock, eldest son of Edward III (the future Black Prince), as duke of Cornwall was marked by no particular ceremony special to a duke, probably because there was no easy precedent for it in England. King Edward was in some way a little defensive about the business. He was pushed to the uneasy assertion that in raising his son to be duke of Cornwall – 'over which dukes had for much time presided in due order' – he was restoring Cornwall's ducal dignity.[26] He was alluding here to that rich mine of dynastic mythology which had long provided the materials to decorate his family's imperial ambitions: Geoffrey of Monmouth's *History of the Kings of Britain* (a work of the mid-1130s). It had already provided the Plantagenets with the propaganda gift of King Arthur; now Geoffrey's imaginary Celtic duchy of Cornwall was being used as a precedent to justify a small revolution in dignity in England.[27] We could not find a better example than this of the world of aristocracy being found principally in the baroque imaginings of the human mind.

Historical sources were not so forthcoming about how the little duke Edward might be invested. Neither Welsh precedents nor Norman ones were suitable, for the duke of Cornwall could not be compared to rulers of the semi-independent status of realms such as the duke of Normandy and prince of Gwynedd had ruled. Instead Edward appears to have been simply belted: 'as is the custom', so his father said – how, I wonder, might a six-year old boy have a sword belted to him; was it vice versa? The same ceremony was resorted to in 1351 when the first non-royal duke was created, Henry of Lancaster, the king's second cousin. But Edward III, the English Constantine, lover of panoply and parade as he was, was not baffled for too long. In 1362, when he created his sons Lionel and John dukes of Clarence and Lancaster, Edward staged a handsome ceremony for John in Parliament involving the girding with a sword, but followed by the conferring of a fur-trimmed, scarlet cap, and around it a jewelled circlet of gold. Lionel (then in Ireland) had his coronet conferred subsequently, as we learn from his will.

THE MARQUIS

The marquis was not an ancient title; it had no Roman origins, and this may be what lies behind the diffidence with which aristocratic society long treated it. It began in a vague way in Carolingian times. There was then a move to organise particularly exposed counties under a 'super-count'. The word for a border area had

---

26 ibid, 32.
27 Geoffrey in fact was not precise about the dukes of Cornwall; sometimes its rulers are dukes (Henwin, Tenvantius, Asclepiodotus, Gorlois, Cador and Blederic), but Dunvallo Molmutius is referred to as its king. The Tristan legend also has Cornwall ruled by a king, Mark.

long been a 'march', and rather than concede the superior office of 'duke' to these new creations, the tendency was to call them 'counts-marcher' (still the meaning behind the German word for marquis: *Margraf*). Alongside this a new word was coined for them in Latin, *marchio* (first appearing in the early years of the ninth century), which must have come into circulation at much the same time as the vernacular word *marchis*. The title did not catch on, and in general the counts-marcher tended to call themselves or be called 'counts' rather than 'marquises'. But the title remained current and when the greater counts of France were looking for titles to exalt themselves above the lesser counts who were their subordinates, they might well experiment with *marchio*. Hugh Capet, the over-mighty magnate who put his family on the throne of France in the tenth century is a case in point. In his search for status he was at one time 'count and marquis' and later 'duke and marquis'.[28] The rulers of Burgundy, Normandy, Aquitaine and Flanders played with the title 'marquis' in the tenth and eleventh centuries, although to no eventual purpose. The first three opted in the end to be dukes, and the ruler of Flanders stuck to the title of count. But elsewhere in the world, particularly in Italy, the title had settled into some sort of regular use: the rulers of Ivrea, Tuscany, Montferrat, Provence and Turin used it consistently for long periods of time.[29]

The title was not used in England until after the end of the period of this book. That does not mean that the words *marchio* or *marchis* were not known nor used here earlier. There was a double meaning: they might betoken the title 'marquis', but on the other hand, they might just mean 'marcher', a man who lived in the March.[30] A rather bizarre instance which fully exploited this ambiguity occured in the twelfth century. Brian fitz Count, a bastard of the ruling house of Brittany, was one of the most trusted intimates of King Henry I and was endowed by the king with the heiress of Wallingford, Berks, and the lordship of Abergavenny in the Welsh March. In Stephen's

---

28 *Cartulaire de Notre-Dame de Chartres*, ed. E. de Lépinois and L. Merlet (3 vols, Chartres, 1862–5), i, 74; *Recueil de chartes et documents de St-Martin-des-Champs monastère Parisien*, ed. J. Depoin (5 vols, Paris, 1912–21), i, 6-7.

29 *Rodulfi Glaber: Historiarum Libri Quinque*, ed. J. France (Oxford, 1989), 172, in the 1040s can refer generally to 'the marquises of Italy' being divided as to whether they would accept Conrad as emperor.

30 As for instance at the coronation of Queen Eleanor in 1236 when four prominent 'marchers from the March of Wales' (*marchiones de marchia Walliae*) upheld the canopy above the queen in the coronation procession, *Red Book of the Exchequer*, ed. H. Hall (3 vols, Rolls Series, 1896), ii, 756.

reign Brian was notably loyal to the cause of Mathilda, Henry I's daughter, and his castle of Wallingford was an island of support for her cause in the Thames valley from 1138 to the end of the civil war in 1154. Because of this (rather than because of the Marcher lordship he also held, which he had sold early in Stephen's reign) one writer called Brian 'the marquis of Wallingford' or perhaps more accurately 'the marcher of Wallingford', because his castle was an outpost of the West Country heartland of Mathilda's cause.[31] This might not be so bizarre if the word 'marquis' had not later become attached as a matter of course to the lord of Wallingford. In the famous early thirteenth-century English romance *Guy of Warwick* one of the heroes, Heralt of Arden, is called *le marchis* because he was supposed to have been the ancestor of the lords of Wallingford.[32]

Whether or not we can regard Brian fitz Count as the first English marquis (and to do so would be to miss the point of the early use of titles) the addition of the title to the repertoire of dignities in the gift of the king was a late fourteenth-century decision. We need not pursue the history of its introduction, therefore, except to note one revealing comment to which it gave rise. Richard II (1377–99) created a marquisate (his second) in 1397 under the title of Dorset for his illegitimate cousin, John Beaufort (a bastard of John of Gaunt), already earl of Somerset. Marquis John did not keep the title long, and it was suppressed by Henry IV in 1399 with a lot of other new titles Richard had created. A move to have the title restored to him in parliament three years later was frustrated by John himself. He explained that although he was grateful for the goodwill of the Lords and Commons 'as the name of marquis was a foreign name in this kingdom, with the king's consent he did not want it to be given him, or to bear or take it in any way'. Neither he nor his audience seems to have appreciated the irony of his remark: how little that was truly English lay in the English use of titles.

THE VISCOUNT

'Viscount' was a title that was not given to an Englishman by his king until the fifteenth century, so that aspect of it is outside our scope. But the Latin word for it, *vicecomes*, was used in England as an

31 William of Malmesbury, *Historia Novella*, ed. K.R. Potter (London, 1955), 51.
32 *Gui de Warewic: roman du xiiie siècle*, ed. A. Ewert (2 vols, Classiques français du moyen âge, 1932), i, p. 113.

equivalent to the English 'sheriff' soon after the Normans conquered England (the English before 1066 had used the Latin equivalents *prefecti* or *prepositi*). The pre-Conquest sheriffs were for the most part insignificant men, some may not even have been landholders. The post-Conquest sheriffs appointed by the king were, on the other hand, often baronial figures, filling a position closer to the pre-Conquest English earl than the sheriff. An equation was made after 1066 between the English sheriffs and the viscounts of the Norman *pays* (the Avranchin, Bessin, Cotentin, Hièmois, Lieuvin, Roumois and Talou) who were, except for the Roumois, magnates who had hereditary control over the office from at least 1000. They were nonetheless working officials, with responsibility for justice, and were genuinely 'in the count's place' – which is what the title meant – if we interpret 'count' as the 'count of Normandy'. Some of the greater men who obtained the English shrievalties were able to secure a hereditary interest in them which lasted on occasion well into the thirteenth century. Such were the Pitres family, sheriffs of Gloucester, the Beauchamps, sheriffs of Worcester, and the Salisbury family, sheriffs of Wiltshire, and others beside.

The Norman viscounties were titles of some dignity because of the people who held them. On at least one occasion a Norman viscount, Goscelin of Arques-Talou, claimed God's grace for his title.[33] Just as with counts, their wives shared their dignity. There are a couple of known examples before 1066 of Norman woman called 'viscount-ess': Emmelina, wife of Goscelin, viscount of Arques-Talou, and Mabel, wife of Roger de Montgomery, viscount of the Hièmois.[34] It is this last indication of dignity which tells us that the Norman view of viscounts was transferred to English sheriffs, for in the 1120s, Adeliza, the widow of Durand de Pitres, *vicomes* of Gloucester, was using the title *vicecomitissa*.[35] Her use of it was plainly intended to be a reflection of a dignity her husband enjoyed and which transcended his death. The practice is met with in the later twelfth century: we find a Joan 'viscountess of Gloucester' and a 'Viscountess Bertha' wife of Ranulf de Glanville, sheriff of Yorkshire for many years

33 *Chartularium Monasterii Sanctae Trinitatis de Monte Rothomagi*, ed. A. Deville, in *Cartulaire de St-Bertin*, ed. B. Guerard (Paris, 1841), 433–4, *Gozelinus dei gratia vicecomes*, his wife Emmelina is *vicecomitissa* in the same document.
34 *Recueil des actes des ducs de Normandie (911–1066)*, de. M. Fauroux (Caen, 1961), no. 84; *Cartulaire de St-Aubin d'Angers*, ed. A. Bertrand de Brousillon (Paris, 1903), 421.
35 *Historia et Cartularium monasterii sancti Petri de Gloucestria*, ed. W. Hart (3 vols, Rolls Series, 1896), i, 188.

in the reign of Henry II, but here the women were wives of non-hereditary officials, and it is by no means clear if they would have continued to use the title when their husbands had given up office.[36] The viscountess, as wife of a hereditary sheriff, is not met with in the thirteenth century, and there are other reasons for thinking it was an idea that had by then faded. Many of the early Norman hereditary sheriffs had disappeared; most of them were granted earldoms by Stephen or Mathilda. Their need for dignity was therefore softened in another way, and this mild and unlicensed intrusion of a Continental dignity dissipated before it could get any hold on the English aristocratic mentality.

KING AND PEERS

The story of English hereditary titles after 1000 is a full one, but not in fact very complicated. On one level, a political level, it is a warning that ideas about titles did not stay constant. A twelfth-century earl was not the same as a fourteenth-century one. Tempting though it is to look at lists of earls spanning the centuries and think that we have an unchanging succession of ideas, it would be an error. It is important to remember that in the twelfth century kings were not the only arbiters of dignity; people had their own views and royal licence was but one influence. There was something communal about the use of titles. Earls and counts should be *created* by kings; the people of England, Normandy and Scotland would have been agreed on that. But they would have been less sure of a king's right to control or terminate the title he had brought into being. Until the fourteenth century, kings of England found it more difficult to suppress a titled dignity than dispossess a family of its lands. The reason is clear enough: a title brought no revenue and hardly any privileges, but it did cast about its possessor that rich mantle of dignity which set him apart from the rest of the aristocracy. This sole attribute of the title may seem puny in our age, but it should not be underestimated. Land gave a man power, but only a title could give him an open and communal sanction for his power. The main point about the title for the present purpose is that this gift of deference and dignity lay partly at the disposal of society. If his fellows chose

36 *Historia et Cartularium Monasterii de Gloucestria*, ed. Hart, i, 188; *Cartularium abbathiae de Rievalle*, ed. J.C. Atkinson (Surtees Soc., lxxxiii, 1889 for 1887), 62. Bertha was wife of Ranulf.

to honour a man or his son as an earl there was little the king could do about it. Countesses seemed likewise to have suited themselves in their use of title.

Because of this the king devised rituals and sanctions to check the succession of earldoms. The use of investiture to attempt to monitor succession is a symptom of this royal insecurity; it was an attempt on the king's part to extend his control over society's attitudes. The king might express forcibly his own views on a man's style by saying how he was to be announced at the door of the royal hall. The productions of the royal writing offices, whether of the Chancery or the Exchequer, were another aid in moulding society's view of titles to the king's pattern. It is rare to find an earl who was not invested by the king credited as earl in a royal act, and it is frequent enough to find men who were properly invested lacking their due title in royal documents.

It remained the case well into the thirteenth century that the king might banish an earl and confiscate his estates, but still could not suppress the earldom as simply as he could squash an earl. Here we may see the resilience of this aspect of the image. Earldoms had lives of their own because people had ideas of their own, ideas the king could not wholly control, and on occasion he was forced to recognise this: re-erecting titles for claimants who could not be resisted, or whose support he needed. The examples of the English countesses and viscountesses of the twelfth century, and of that odd creature, the 'marquis of Wallingford' (let alone that of the Welsh kings and princes) opens up a door on a whole fairyland of contemporary attitudes where the king might not tread and where he had no control. The title was a creature of two lands. It lived in the royal reserve of patronage, to be let loose at his whim, but it lived also in men's minds and imagination, the source from which it drew its peculiar ability to dignify. Some titles (earls, counts and later, dukes and marquises) were more under royal influence, but others lived wholly outside royal control. The next chapters will explore this strange country (a land populated by barons, knights and squires) in greater detail, but it is important to realise that even with hereditary titles the king's licence in the earlier period was not always necessary to the aristocracy. It is not until the fourteenth century that we find an aristocracy hardening into the mould the king must have considered more to his liking. It is interesting that it was this century that saw kings becoming experimental and even profligate in the use of hereditary titles. Whatever causes the king

103

might still have to suspect and fear his aristocracy, its own wilfulness in the matter of dignities was no longer one of them.

PEERAGE

The concept of an English peerage is relevant both to the use of titles and to our other theme of social divisions and status groups. As we have already seen, the idea of a dominant group of magnates at the head of society had been long established at the beginning of our period. That this was transmuted through the evolution of the institution of Parliament into a 'parliamentary peerage' by the fifteenth century is well known. Certain families obtained the right to a hereditary personal summons by the king to attend parliament. Dukes, marquises, earls and viscounts, all those with lay titles of honour, were part of this group. Those men who did not possess such a dignity made do with the title of baron, revamped as a title of honour, rather than a social dignity.[37]

Before the fourteenth century, there were some developments which prefigured the development of an English 'peerage'. Not the least of these was the curious exchange between Earl Richard Marshal and Peter des Roches, bishop of Winchester, recorded by Matthew Paris. It was inspired by Magna Carta, which in its clause 39 (of 1215) and clause 29 (of the 1225 reissue) proclaimed that no man might be acted against 'except by the lawful judgement of his peers'.[38] Peers in this case meant 'equals', but it was a trifle ambiguous as to who the equals of an earl might be; could every free man claim to be Earl Richard's equal? When in 1233 Earl Richard Marshal made such an appeal, it was taken by his enemy, des Roches, as a special appeal to the other magnates, and hotly denied: there were no such things as peers in England 'as there were in the realm of France'.[39]

The bishop may have been deliberately obtuse to serve his own purposes. Since the end of the twelfth century, under the influence of the Charlemagne legend, it had been accepted that twelve *pairs* (six prelates and six magnates) headed the aristocracy of France under the king. It is unlikely that Earl Richard was claiming that

37 This is sketched by C. Given-Wilson, *The English Nobility in the Later Middle Ages* (London, 1987), 62–6.
38 J.C. Holt, *Magna Carta* (Cambridge, 1965), 226–9, 326–7, 355.
39 Matthew Paris, *Chronica Majora*, ed. H.R. Luard (7 vols, Rolls Series, 1872–83), iii, 252. I must thank Nicholas Vincent for discussing this passage with me.

England had its twelve peers too, but the bishop's waspish reaction to the suggestion is significant. He and his sympathisers wanted no such formal expression of the status of the magnates against royal authority. But he was willing to credit the magnates as seeking such a status. It may be that he was right to be suspicious. The reference to themselves as 'peers' became current amongst the English magnates throughout the thirteenth century. William de Beauchamp of Bedford referred in 1250 to 'the earls and other barons, his *pares*, in England' when asserting his rights to advocacy over a priory.[40] By the reign of Edward II (1307–27) writers had got into the habit of calling the magnates just that: 'peers of the realm'. It was under this soubriquet that they presumed to challenge the king; which might be seen as a fulfilment of the fears of Peter des Roches.[41]

The consolidation of the status level of the magnate was in part a slow consequence of the transformation of the status of knight. In the expanded aristocracy of the end of the thirteenth century, there was a necessary elaboration in levels of status within it. Summons to councils and parliaments were one convenient delineation of the highest level. As we will see, this was matched by the rapid evolution of a superior form of knight, the banneret, who might be (but was not invariably) summoned to councils in person. The patching together of the titled aristocracy and the barons and bannerets of the thirteenth century into the parliamentary peerage was a product of the fourteenth century. But we can see the mechanism at work rather earlier.

40 PRO, KB26/141, m. 25d.
41 S.L. Waugh, *England in the Reign of Edward III* (Cambridge, 1991), 119–20.

3

SOCIAL DIGNITIES: BARONS AND BANNERETS

In analysing such social groups as the medieval mind understood, it is useless expecting to have the exercise cut and tied. As soon as the whole unwieldy mess seems neatly parcelled a corner gives way and disgorges some part of its contents. The fact is that different medieval writers had different perceptions. Those amongst medieval men who were quirky enough to want to sit down and write about their society were often indeed quirky men with their own opinions. The key to the business is not to be too particular. The great hereditary dignities registered in the medieval consciousness as a clear social group, as is evident from the addresses of royal charters. A charter of Henry I (1100–35) would commence typically with an address to 'his earls, sheriffs, barons and men'; a charter of Richard II (1377–99) would be addressed to 'his dukes, marquises, earls, sheriffs, barons, knights and men'. It is the 'barons, knights and men' with whom the following chapters are concerned; the ill-defined 'others' within the medieval consciousness of its society. These 'others' were for the most part men who carried no hereditary title. But here a corner of our package rips. There were, for instance, families in England and Ireland whose chiefs carried the hereditary style of 'baron' long before it was a title recognised and awarded by the king. There were also other hereditary dignities which arose within society, titles which derived from household offices but with which a family's importance and dignity became inextricably entangled. All these come within the classification here of 'social dignities': titles in use in society which the king had no pretensions to control, and which were (in general) outside his gift.

THE BARON

The 'baron' (Lat. *baro*; Fr. *ber*), like the 'prince', was a shapeless creature, or rather, a many-headed one. The word had a series of meanings and might be tailored to meet a great number of circumstances. On the other hand, like the 'prince', some of the meanings were precise and had a narrow social focus. The word 'baron' was an old word by the end of the first millenium. It was known to Isidore of Seville, who thought that it had a Greek origin and signified a hired hand. He was wrong about the derivation, but he must be trusted on the subject of its sixth-century application.[1] Like 'vassal', or 'knight', the word 'baron' had and continued to have into the High Middle Ages its original, simple application of 'man'; as in the French *barun et femme*, that is 'man and wife'. A baron in this sense was a man, and a full-grown, mature man. It is in the vernacular that we see quite a range of applications of this sense of the word.[2] In the William of Orange cycle, written down in the mid-twelfth century, the hero is described as *molt gentix et ber*, that is, 'most noble and manly'.[3] Other examples are to be found in Jordan Fantosme's depiction of Roger de Stuteville addressing his men; *'baruns chevaliers'* he called them: 'seasoned knights'. Jordan also talks of Duncan of Fife offering his king 'baron-like' advice, meaning advice of mature wisdom, as opposed to the rash advice given by the king's young military household.[4] The French collective noun *barnage* did not necessarily mean a collection of barons, but the assembled strength of a king or lord's following, his 'manpower', in effect. In Latin, on the other hand, we are more likely to find 'baron' being used in a sense close to that by which modern English understands the word.

This more precise Latin application is the one that comprehends a distinct group, recognisable to medieval people. The word *baro* already had a long history before it came into what might be called a vogue amongst Latin scribes in England in the late eleventh century. In England and France *baro* was used to comprehend a king or

---

1 *Mercenarii sunt qui serviunt accepta mercede; iidem et barones Graeco nomine, quod sint fortes in laboribus; 'barus' enim dicitur gravis, quod sit 'fortis'.* Isidore of Seville, *Etymologiae* IX c.4.31.
2 This has been explored extensively for France in Guilhiermoz, *Essai sur la noblesse du moyen âge* (Paris, 1902), 156–9.
3 *Le Charroi de Nîmes*, ed. J-L. Perrier (Classiques français du moyen âge, 1982), l. 29.
4 *Jordan Fantosme's Chronicle*, ed. R.C. Johnston (Oxford, 1981), 38; Stenton, *The First Century of English Feudalism 1066–1166* (2nd edn, Oxford, 1961), 95n.

lord's followers, where the words *fideles, homines* or *vassali* might also have done. Richard I of Normandy (died 996) referred on one occasion to 'his barons' with him on the occasion of a grant to an abbey under his patronage. His descendants, Robert I and William the Conqueror, also used it of their immediate lay followers and magnates. For the Conqueror, this may have meant the Norman magnates who were his closest cronies, the small group which William de Poitiers said was worth more than the 200 senators of ancient Rome.[5] From the late eleventh century in England we find a larger group of men known as the '*barones regis*', the 'king's barons'. 'Baron' was in this sense one of over a dozen attractive Latin synonyms which a writer might use to convey the idea of magnates, words like *proceres, primates* and *principes*.

The phrase *barones regis* seems to have had a certain precision to it that made it very attractive, particularly for writers of charters and surveys, and particularly in England. The Normans may have found it especially useful in England, because they needed such a word to describe those men of influence who attended shire and hundred courts. In this sense of 'leading men of the province', the word *barones* is frequently found in northern France too in the eleventh and twelfth centuries.[6] Other words used in France in the eleventh and twelfth centuries for the group of leading men (who had no hereditary titles) around a prince were the *dominici* (Fr. *demaines*) or the variant, *casati*. Both words are associated with the prince's household in which these great men attend, his *domus* or *casa*. But the *dominicus* or *casatus* is rarely found in Normandy or in England, except when Walter Map in the 1180s noted the absence of the word *dominicus* in Anglo-Norman usage.[7]

5 *Recueil des actes des ducs de Normandie (911–1066)*, ed. M. Fauroux (Caen, 1961), 76, 195, 265.
6 Note the address by Waleran count of Meulan to his *barones* of the county of Meulan and his lands in the Ile de France, Bibliothèque Nationale, Collection du Vexin xii, fo. 145v; *Chartes de l'abbaye de Jumièges*, ed. J-J. Vernier (2 vols, Rouen, 1916), i, 150–1; *Recueil de chartes et documents de St-Martin-des-Champs, monastère Parisien*, ed. J. Depoin, (5 vols, Paris, 1912–21), ii, 158. For other French examples, see Guilhiermoz, *Essai*, 157nn.
7 For *dominicus*, see P. Guilhiermoz, *Essai sur la noblesse du moyen âge* (Paris, 1902), 156n.; for *casatus*, Guyotjeannin, *Episcopus et Comes* (Geneva, 1987), 96–100. See for England, Walter Map, *De Nugis Curialium*, 314. Henry I in 1109 does, however, refer to *dominicos barones meos*, meaning his magnates, in a general writ concerning the shire courts, W. Stubbs, *Select Charters and other Illustrations of English Constitutional History*, ed. H.W.C. Davis (9th edn, Oxford, 1913), 122. *Dominicus* here is an adjective, but the same sense of 'intimate follower' is intended.

Being the Norman term for 'leading man', it was natural that 'baron' would be the word applied to suitors at the English communal courts in early twelfth-century records, when the Anglo-Norman clerks found that they needed a word for such men. The phrase 'king's barons' might have been intended to have a similar sense. They were those men who were summoned to pay suit to the king. The 'king's barons' are a group we find again and again throughout our period, from Domesday Book onwards. When the phrase was used it invariably meant the greatest men in the aristocracy (whether they were earls, barons or not), men habitually at court, lords of great estates, those indeed whom the king consulted in the affairs of the realm. As the twelfth century progressed, the word *pairs* (Fr.) or *pares* (Lat.) – from which we get our 'peers' – would be employed for the leading men of the kingdom of France, but this was a sense which did not penetrate England until the next century.

The estates of a baron might be called a 'barony' (Lat: *baronia*). The term has a general meaning. Many words were used in the eleventh and twelfth centuries for a complex of estates, and one was indeed 'barony', although it was less popular in England than the word 'honor'.[8] 'Fee' (*feodum*) was yet another such word, employed both for a complex of estates and for a single estate. 'Land' (*terra*) is a word which has many applications, and it is no coincidence that in vernacular French writings of the twelfth century *terre* is a word

---

8 H.M. Chew, *The English Ecclesiastical Tenants-in-Chief* (Oxford, 1932), 160–1, treated *baronia* and *honor* as distinct terms. Although she did not give any reason, she seems to have been drawing the distinction both from the consistent use of the word in the relief '*per baroniam*', and from Magna Carta (c.43) which refers to the *baronie* of the leading tenants of the *honores* of Wallingford, Boulogne, etc. But this last distinction would seem to be no more than a change of term for the sake of clarity. In 1196 we hear of similar men who held *baronie* in the vacant *episcopatus* of Durham, see *Chancellor's Roll of 8 Richard I*, 260–1. To turn Chew's example on its head, we find in 1148 x 66 a tenant of the earl of Gloucester, Maurice de Londres, addressing a charter *omnibus hominibus* honoris *de Uggom[ora]*, see facsimile in J. Conway Davies 'Ewenny Priory: Some Recently Discovered Deeds', *Journal of the National Library of Wales*, iii (1943–4), 109. For Ogmore, a dependency of the lordship of Glamorgan, see R.R. Davies 'The Lordship of Ogmore' in *Glamorgan County History*, iii, *The Middle Ages*, ed. T.B. Pugh (Cardiff, 1971), 285–91. In 1137 x 38, Geoffrey de Clinton II could refer to the *honor* he held, not from the king, but from the earl of Warwick, Cartulary of Kenilworth, Brit. Libr., ms Harley 3650 fo. 69v. Stenton provides a further example of this 'sub-honor' in the tenancy of Osmund de Stuteville of the earldom of Warenne, Stenton, *First Century of English Feudalism*, 56n. We may conclude from this that the word 'honor' might be applied indifferently by an Anglo-Norman clerk to any substantial estate, whoever held it and whoever he held it from.

commonly employed for the estates of a baron. In the mid-twelfth century the word *potestas* came into fashion in England to describe the area of authority of a baron. But here the emphasis is as much on jurisdiction as on land.[9] Nevertheless, some historians have sought to find a technical meaning in the word 'barony' and apply it by transference to the 'baron'. If a man held a barony that raised him to the status of a 'baron', it is said, because a 'barony' was held '*per baroniam*', that is 'by the service of a baron'. This is at first sight a circular argument with nothing to support it. Indeed, this application of the word 'baron' would have made no sense in the twelfth century. But by the mid-thirteenth century the paying of a baron's relief – however small the barony – had acquired some touch of status. We can see this from the middle-aged King Henry III's engaging boast that he could still remember the names of 250 baronies and their holders. The king was set to learn them because these people owed him more money than others, yet even so there was a status of sorts in being in the king's mind.

One contemporary alone offers us what might be a definition of the position of a baron. Archbishop Theobald of Canterbury around the year 1145 advised the Norfolk magnate Roger de Valognes that the control of the service of six knights made a man *nobilis et liberalis*.[10] This remark is useful but it seems clearer than it is. Theobald was a Norman, and had only been in England for about six years when he made that remark. If he meant six *English* knights' fees, then it took very little in the way of resources to be considered a man who was 'noble and wealthy'. Six *Norman* fees, on the other hand, was a wholly different measure of status. It is now well known that a Norman fee was the equivalent of a number of English fees, perhaps as many as three.[11] For myself, I think that Archbishop Theobald was talking in the terms with which he was familiar, and that he was in fact offering us a definition of wealth and status that was rather more substantial than appears at first sight: fifteen to eighteen English knights' fees to support the status of a magnate.

9 E. King, 'The Anarchy of King Stephen's Reign', *Transactions of the Royal Historical Society*, 5th ser., xxxv (1984), 133–5. However, the occasional association of *terra* and *potestas* is demonstrated in 1212 by a letter of King John, referring to the '*terra vel potestate Willelmi comitis Marescalli*', *Rotuli Litterarum Clausarum* ed. T.D. Hardy (2 vols, Record Commission, 1833–44), i, 122.
10 Stenton, *First Century of English Feudalism*, 260.
11 T.K. Keefe, *Feudal Assessments and the Political Community under Henry II and his sons* (Berkeley, Calif., 1983), 95–6, works out a differential of 1:3 between Norman and English fees.

The twelfth and thirteenth centuries read little that was precise in the way of status into the word 'baron'. It was sufficient, as the good archbishop said, to be known to have reasonable resources to be considered *nobilis et liberalis*. The title 'baron' had a general application to obviously great men; an idiosyncratic application to the heads of certain families, but nothing more beyond that other than an application in the plural to any group of leading men.[12] 'The barons of the county of Shropshire' were those active men in the county court who were consulted as to its past doings by the king's agent, Richard de Beaumeis, in the 1120s.[13] Another well-known application of the phrase in this context is its use to describe the leaders and magistrates of English cities and towns, such as London, Bristol and the Cinque Ports. A record of a plea held at Sandwich as early as 1127 referred to the *barones* of St Margaret as being amongst the leading men of the neighbourhood, and then provides a list of men with impeccably English names.[14]

The sense of 'leading men' makes another, although transitory appearance in England in the late eleventh and twelfth centuries. In the early twelfth-century legal treatise known as the 'Laws of Henry I' there is a reference to 'the barons of the king, *or of other men*'.[15] Earls, or even lesser lords, might be said to have their own barons. When an earl's charters addressed 'all his barons and men', he was talking of his leading and lesser followers. It is also more than likely that in talking of his own barons an earl was attempting to parade his dignity in regal style. If so, it was another example of downward diffusion of social habits. Men less than earls in the twelfth century would talk of their 'barons', but such men were almost always great men little less than earls in status, such as the

12 On definitions of the word 'baron', C. Given-Wilson, *The English Nobility in the Later Middle Ages* (London, 1987), 60–1, taking issue with K.B. McFarlane, *The Nobility of Late Medieval England* (Oxford, 1973), 269.

13 *The Cartulary of Shrewsbury Abbey*, ed. U. Rees (2 vols, Aberystwyth, 1975), ii, 318–19. The *Leges Henrici Primi*, ed. L.J. Downer (Cambridge, 1972), c. 29.1 in the previous decade also refers to *barones comitatus*, and implies that the men described under those words stood above other freeholders in the county, H.G. Richardson and G.O. Sayles, *The Governance of Medieval England* (Edinburgh, 1963), 183.

14 The estates of the leading landowners in the town of Bristol were being called *'baroniae'* in the mid-twelfth century, Cartulary of Bristol abbey, Berkeley Castle muniments, fo. 34r. For the Sandwich plea, D.M. Stenton, *English Justice between the Norman Conquest and the Great Charter, 1066–1215* (London, 1965), 116–22.

15 *Leges Henrici Primi*, ed. Downer, c. 7.7.

lords of Clare and Stafford, or the Briouze lords of Brecon and Bramber.[16]

More may have been read into the appearance of 'barons' barons' than the twelfth century intended. Looking for a label for the leading men of an honor, Sir Frank Stenton coined the phrase 'honorial baronage'. The temptation thereafter was to invest the 'honorial barons' with the same significance as 'the king's barons', a recognised group at the head of affairs. It was one of the reasons why Stenton crafted the famous simile was that an honor was like a kingdom in miniature. It led him to postulate an unlikely social division between the barons and the 'mere' knights of an honor; he suggested that a baron was a principal tenant and selected counsellor. *Barones*, he says – echoing the addresses of charters – were distinguished from *homines* in post-Conquest English documents because they were greater men. But in fact the use of *baro* is inconsistent. This can be seen when we get a rare list which names specific 'honorial barons'. Stenton found a list of the barons of the abbot of Westminster present at a grant. Instead of men answering for over five knights' service, which was one way he defined baronial status, he found they all possessed less than that, some much less. He felt obliged to dismiss the list as having been made 'without any regard for the niceties of terminology'. But this has since been exposed as no more than special pleading. There was no strict terminology to be nice about at the time.[17]

Eventually during the twelfth century there came a point when great men would address only 'their men and friends', and refer no longer to their 'barons'. The social conceit (for such I think it largely was) of 'barons' barons' began to go out of fashion towards the end of the twelfth century. I hasten to say that the habit did not entirely lapse, for there were exceptions. When Ranulf III, earl of Chester, granted his own 'Magna Carta' to Cheshire, he granted it to his 'barons'.[18] The bishops of Durham too continued to talk of their

16 Stenton, *First Century of English Feudalism*, 84–94.

17 Stenton, *First Century of English Feudalism*, 96–7. Dr English finds that Count William of Aumale made no real distinction between his *barones* and *homines*, and finds two *barones* of Holderness holding less than a knight's fee, *The Lords of Holderness, 1086–1260* (Oxford, 1979), 138–9.

18 In *Charters of the Anglo-Norman Earls of Chester, c. 1071–1237*, ed. G. Barraclough (Record Soc. of Lancashire and Cheshire, cxxvi, 1988), 388, the Magna Carta of Cheshire was said to have been granted . . . *pro amore dei et ad petitionem baronum meorum Cestresirie*. In fact Ranulf III and John le Scot of Chester, like the king, continued to make occasional use of the address to his officers, barons and men, long after 1200. In this they were exceptional.

barons, but in general such a use is rare after 1200. However, the fact that the exceptions were men of unusual power is significant. Only a few men would stake a claim to the prestige of having subordinate barons any more, and this was probably because the word 'baron' was at last attaining in England an aura of exclusivity and status. At this point the use of the word 'baron' becomes more and more limited to only one of its functions: a great man within the kingdom close to the king. We see this elsewhere. After the mid-twelfth century we hear little of the 'barons' of a shire court, but its 'knights' or its *buzones*.

There are several other signs along the way by which the use of the word 'baron' within English (and Irish) society became limited. William fitz Stephen, in his panegyric on his native city of London in the 1170s makes the curious observation that though other towns had citizens (*civites*) London in its greatness had barons (*barones*). Although this was demonstrably untrue, nonetheless it tells us that William regarded *baro* as a word of high prestige fitted for a city of such nobility as London (see above p. 25). Another milestone is when certain lords began to use 'baron' as an individual style. The earliest such example comes from around 1200 when William, the fitz Gerald lord of Naas (co. Kildare), one of the leading lords of the Anglo-Irish community, took for himself the title *Baro de Naas*, that is, 'the baron of Naas'. He was succeeded in it by his sons. In later thirteenth-century England a few great men who were not earls also appropriated the word as an unauthorised title, such as 'the baron of Stafford', the 'baron of Helton' or 'the baron of Greystoke'.[19] Though few men took up such a style, the fact that a few did has a certain significance. As we will see, it was one of a range of options by which great men who lacked formal titles bolstered their dignity, with the collusion of general society. 'Baron' in this case carried implications of both social superiority and patriarchy, without being a style subject to regulation. It may be that such thirteenth-century informal, hereditary styles had something in common with nicknames, but the fact of the wealth and power of these men raised their titles above the level of a Robert 'bentnose' or Geoffrey 'abbot'.

In the thirteenth and fourteenth centuries, however, these hereditary

---

19 G.E. Cockayne, *The Complete Peerage*, ed. V. Gibbs *et al.* (13 vols in 14, London, 1910–59), xii pt 1, 172–3; McFarlane, *The Nobility of Later Medieval England*, 269n., makes the useful point that the 'baron of Helton' did not in fact possess an honor which paid a baronial relief.

'baronial' families were few. The reason can be found in the competition of the title 'baron' with a new title that had more general cachet: the 'banneret'. Coming into common usage in the early thirteenth century, the title *banneretus* remained popular amongst the non-comital aristocracy to the end of the fourteenth century, when it abruptly went out of fashion (see below for a lengthier consideration of this). The disappearance of the *banneretti* made way for the adoption of 'baron' as a dignity conferred by the Crown in the fifteenth century: a grade within the peerage, rather than a more vague social dignity. The first such royal creation was when Richard II (that great experimenter in dignities) elevated John de Beauchamp of Holt to the rank of 'baron' by letters patent in 1387. He survived to enjoy the dignity for less than a year; sadly, often the case with Richard's experiments.

THE BANNERET

One of the more curious episodes in the history of the self-image of the medieval Anglo-French aristocracy is the rise and decline of the use of the title of 'banneret'. For a time, and a considerable time at that, it was almost a recognisable and recognised grade of peerage, although it was never strictly hereditable. Tout compared it to the 'life peer'.[20] The title's disappearance towards the end of the fourteenth century has much that is curious and unaccountable. Its origins however are clear enough.

We will see in a later chapter how the banner (or gonfanon: the words are synonyms at this time) became an early item of aristocratic insignia in Western Europe; its use limited around 1100 to kings, dukes and counts, and perhaps a few other great men. Men who had banners were great men, for the practical reason that only a man with the resources to lead a company of troops would need such an item to distinguish himself from others. Banners were the first aristocratic accessory on which individual lords advertised their presence by distinctive and recognisable symbols. Some great lords, kings or counts, included in their baggage sacred banners, conferred on them by particular abbeys as a symbol of divine approval as well as social and political consequence. Banners were not to flutter above the head of just any man. Wace puts it neatly for us when describing a

20 Although modern life peers were not created till 1958 (long after Tout's death), the term had been current in political debate since the 1860s, and in effect life peers existed after the promotion of senior judges to baronies for life in the 1870s.

mid-twelfth century army being marshalled for battle: 'All had their swords girded on, and rode on to the plain with lances raised. *The barons carried gonfanons, the knights had pennants.*'[21]

An awareness that a banner could be a social as well as a military accessory grew through the twelfth century. It was in the second half of the century that clumsy attempts began to endow banner-carrying into a formal expression of status. An odd French circumlocution that certain magnates were *banières portants* (carrying banners) is to be found in the tourney roll of Lagny of 1180 (a lost document partly preserved in the biographical poem on William Marshal).[22] Since the poem was composed in the late 1220s this might be thought an anachronism projected back into the twelfth century, but a similar Latin phrase appears in the life of Abbot Samson of Bury St Edmunds. In 1193 the good abbot rallied to the justiciars against Count John. He himself led his contingent to the siege of Windsor 'wearing armour (*armatus*), with certain other English abbots, having his own banner (*vexillum proprium habens*) and many knights'.[23]

By 1207 the social meaning of the capability of carrying a banner was clear, particularly in northern France. The new Capetian administration of Normandy produced a list for Philip Augustus of sixty Norman magnates 'who carry banners'. The use of the phrase is here a comprehensive one, because it included the one surviving Norman count, the count of Alençon. For these clerks, the status of carrying the banner was a way of defining the magnate, and they listed 566 of them in the various regions of France subject to Philip Augustus, north of the River Loire.[24] Rigord's biography of Philip Augustus is more nice in its use of the phrase. In describing the events of 1214 he refers to the capture of five counts *and* twenty 'knights of such nobility that they rejoiced in the insignia of a banner'.[25]

So there already seem to have been two strains of thought about

21 M. Bennett, 'Wace and Warfare', in *Anglo-Norman Studies*, ed. R.A. Brown, xi (1988), 46. Wace was in fact describing the disembarkation of the army of the Conqueror in England in 1066, but drew the details from his own day and age nearly a century later.

22 *Histoire de Guillaume le Maréchal*, ed. P. Meyer (3 vols, Paris, 1899–1909), ll. 4496–4654.

23 *The Chronicle of Jocelin of Brakelond*, ed. H.E. Butler (London, 1949), 55.

24 J. Baldwin, *The Government of Philip Augustus* (Berkeley, Calif., 1986), 262.

25 *Recueil des Historiens des Gaules et de la France*, ed. M. Bouquet et al. (24 vols, Paris, 1869–1904), xvii, 99.

what this 'proto-banneret' was. We see it again in the English royal accounts of the later thirteenth century which treat a banneret as a superior knight, qualifying for a higher daily wage (usually four shillings a day). The same source classes an earl, if he received wages, as a banneret; it deals in this way with Henry de Lacy, earl of Lincoln, in 1277.[26] This can only be because the word was being used in a specialised fiscal sense. But on other occasions the word has clear overtones of a specific social rank, above the dubbed knight, but below the greater baron or hereditary dignitary. William of Rishanger can thus talk of 'barons and bannerets' captured at Kenilworth priory in 1265, seemingly distinguishing the one from the other.[27] This may account for the occasional practice amongst writers of the fourteenth century in using the word *baronetti* 'little barons' of men between the ranks of baron and knight, in the place where otherwise the word 'banneret' might be used.[28]

The move to the term 'banneret' may have been made in at least the vernacular by the mid-thirteenth century. Certainly the Latin word *vexillifer* (sometimes employed as *miles vexillifer*), trawled from accounts of the Roman army, was current in the mid-thirteenth century for a leading knight, and this may well be the Latinisation of a contemporary vernacular term. Matthew Paris uses the word in the 1250s, as do the chroniclers of Evesham when dealing with the events of the 1260s. In the royal household accounts of the reign of Henry III, beginning in 1260, *milites regis bannericiis* occur as the senior knights of the royal household. The term was in that year used of the minor magnate, Marmaduke of Thweng.[29] As we have seen, 'banneret' in these and other thirteenth-century references is not always used with any great clarity. But at some time on either side of 1300 it becomes clear that the 'banneret' took on a more distinct meaning: a senior knight, or a lesser magnate, and was no longer used to embrace the whole class of banner-bearing magnates, as it had been a century earlier.

To reinforce this idea, or as a consequence of it, it became customary to institute a banneret by a separate investiture (*ad modum bannereti*). Reference was already being made in 1338 to 'the

---

26 J.E. Powell and K. Wallis, *The House of Lords in the Middle Ages* (London, 1968), 288.
27 *The Chronicle of William de Rishanger of the Barons' War*, ed. J.O. Haliwell (Camden Soc., xv, 1840), 44.
28 *Dictionary of Medieval Latin from British Sources*, fasc. I, s.v. *baronettus*.
29 *Close Rolls of the Reign of Henry III preserved in the Public Record Office* (14 vols, PRO, 1902–38), *1259–61*, 315.

estate of banneret' into which Sir Reginald Cobham of Sterborough was raised by Edward III from that of simple knight, and given sufficient income to support his new status.[30] This indirectly implies some sort of rite of passage, or at least formula of admission into a superior order. There are hints of such a ceremony in the late thirteenth century. John de Beauchamp was killed in 1265 at the battle of Evesham. William of Rishanger notes with what appears to be irony that Beauchamp had 'raised that day his banner for the first time'.[31] Was this a reference to a public ceremony admitting John into a higher order, or a routine comment on a young magnate entering the field?

A description of what must be such an investiture comes in 1367 when, just before the battle of Najera, the Black Prince, assisted by the duke of Lancaster and pretender to the throne of Castile, formally raised Sir John Chandos to the rank of banneret. Sir John brought the prince his banner, stated his ability to support his rank in land, and requested his investiture (*que je puisse à baniere estre*). The prince and the others then displayed the banner and lowered it for Chandos to take, invoking God's blessing on him. Chandos then, significantly, passed its keeping on to his company of knights with the words 'Good sirs, here is my banner, defend it as your own, for it is as well yours as mine.'[32] In both 1335 and 1367 care was taken that the new banneret have the revenue to support his rank. In 1367 the stress is on the banner itself, in a way that recalls French ducal investitures of the twelfth century. What is more, the ceremony has much in it that recalls the twelfth-century antecedents of the 'banneret': its owner's need to ensign his company of knights. Another point here is that it was not the king who created Chandos a banneret, but the king's son. True, the Black Prince was prince of Aquitaine and lieutenant of the king in France, but the appearance

---

30 *Calendar of Patent Rolls preserved in the Public Record Office, 1216–1509* (PRO, 1906–16), *1338–40*, 105–6.

31 *Chronicle of William de Rishanger*, ed. Halliwell, 47. Sir John de Beauchamp was a Bedfordshire knight and last holder of the barony of Beauchamp of Bedford; he had succeeded his brother only a year or two before Evesham.

32 Chandos Herald, *Life of the Black Prince*, ed. M.K. Pope and E.C. Lodge (Oxford, 1910), 95–6. There are some invaluable comments on this incident and bannerets generally in N. Saul, *Knights and Esquires: The Gloucestershire Gentry in the Fourteenth Century* (Oxford, 1981), 7–10. A related but later account by Froissart has Chandos handing over to the prince not a banner, but a large pennon, from which the prince cut off the tail. This detail points up the contrast between simple knight and banneret quite neatly, but it may well be Froissart's addition; see the translation of this passage in M. Keen, *Chivalry* (London, 1984), 168.

of bannerets in the retinues of the earls and dukes of Lancaster, the earls of March and others in the fourteenth century, suggests that (like knights) bannerets might be created by others than the king.

The most curious aspect of the story of the banneret is its use in relation to Parliament. This is a little beyond the scope of this book, but having started the story of the banneret, I cannot quite put it down. A summons to Parliament in 1344 brought to Westminster not just prelates, earls and certain established non-comital magnates but 'other barons and bannerets', to make up the number of peers in Parliament.[33] The distinction here is unequivocal and is repeated on many later occasions. Bannerets (or at least the king's bannerets), being, as we have seen, men of a certain level of wealth and often intimate with the king, might well be summoned to Parliament individually (that is as peers of the realm). Furthermore, in 1383, Richard II discharged Thomas Camoys 'who is a banneret, as were many of his ancestors' from service as a knight of the shire for Surrey, because bannerets were said by the king to have long been ineligible for election.[34] Taking these two references together, it might be thought that bannerets were a lower degree of peerage which customarily sat in Parliament by right of its rank. But, as Given-Wilson points out, there are numerous instances of bannerets never summoned to Parliament, even though in some cases their fathers had been.[35] The answer seems to be that the bannerets in Parliament were simply those of that rank whom the king wished to honour with a summons to his council, as opposed to the 'barons'. The barons were those great men whose wealth, lineage and influence guaranteed them a summons, and who, for the same reasons did not need the social cachet of a personal creation as banneret.

The fact that bannerets were said to be ineligible for election to Parliament as county knights has some retrospective value for the status of the 'banneret' in the thirteenth century. Here, in local society before the rank of banneret evolved fully, the wealthiest knights in county society (those whose manors were numerous and spread over a number of shires) were never subjected to the same demands made on other men of knightly rank, to serve in local office, or on juries, assizes or views. To take the example of

---

33 Powell and Wallis, *House of Lords in the Middle Ages*, 352.
34 *Reports of the Lords Committees touching the Dignity of a Peer of the Realm* (5 vols, London, 1829), iv, 707.
35 Given-Wilson, *The English Nobility in the Late Middle Ages*, 61–2.

Warwickshire and Leicestershire in the thirteenth century, there the dominant knightly families of Harcourt of Bosworth, Du Bois of Thorpe Arnold, Cantilupe of Aston Cantlow, and Montfort of Beaudesert, did not contribute a juror or justice to the county. Yet they were knights domiciled in the counties and not tenants-in-chief in any significant degree. The fact that they had castles or great houses in the area, a multitude of manors, and close connections with the court and great magnates must simply have raised them above the level where routine administrative demands might safely be made of them. Nowhere is this exemption stated formally (as it is in the case of those holding baronies)[36] but it must just have been regarded as undignified that certain greater knights should be called on in this way, even though they were not magnates and not summoned to the king's council.

The end of the useful life of the term 'banneret' had come by the early fifteenth century. The class literally fell apart. It is easy to say why this happened. Those bannerets who had received summonses to Parliament, to be followed by their sons in the same privilege, simply disappeared amongst the established baronial families. Those sons who failed to follow their fathers into Parliament disappeared amongst the knights. The beginning of the practice of creating 'barons' by letters patent in the reign of Richard II devalued the rank of banneret. After 1400 it became an increasingly rare survival.[37]

36 As in 1293 in the case of Thomas Jardin, who held the barony of Cogges, PRO, CP40/144 m. 184d., quoted in J. Quick, 'The Number and Distribution of Knights in Thirteenth-Century England: the Evidence of the Grand Assize Lists', in *Thirteenth-Century England*, i, ed. P.R. Coss and S.D. Lloyd (Woodbridge, 1986), 116 and n.
37 N. Saul, *Knights and Esquires, The Gloucestershire Gentry in the Fourteenth Century* (Oxford, 1981), 10; Given-Wilson, *The English Nobility in the Late Middle Ages*, 62.

4

THE KNIGHT

THE FRENCH ROOTS OF KNIGHTHOOD

The beginnings of knighthood do not indeed lie in England, but in the lands of the Western Franks. All that pre-Norman England has given later knighthood is the modern vernacular name for it, from the Old English *cniht*. So it is only appropriate that we should go to French historians for an explanation of the appearance of knighthood. Over the past century, the French have been industrious in framing, rejecting and re-erecting theories to explain the knight, to a degree that shames the English historical establishment. Since the Second World War a distinguished generation of French historians (Génicot, Fossier and Duby), and their pupils have exhaustively considered the question of the development of the knight. The knight and his status in society has long been for the French – and continues to be – the key development in the 'enlargement' or the 'transformation' of the twelfth-century aristocracy.

English concerns over the past century have not been those of French historians. The English have long been obsessed with nineteenth-century questions about the size of the knight's fee, the precise numbers and timing of enfeoffment of knights, and the mechanics of the customary obligations that went with tenure of land by knight service. The English have been searching for the origins of the 'gentry'; the class which the Whigs credited with the creation of an assertive Commons, and hence the British constitution. The quality of the evidence means that the English have at least had more to chew on than the French when considering these sorts of questions. But the nature of that evidence makes any authoritative answer to them unlikely. Perhaps it might have been kinder if Fate, the Chancery and the Exchequer had been less generous in preserving early surveys and lists of fees and forced us to concentrate on more basic questions.

There is now a wide context in which to set the story of knighthood in Britain, and it is high time that such a task was attempted. England in the twelfth century was firmly part of the French cultural world, and is now the most systematically documented part of it. It will be the business of this part of the chapter both to put the English and Scottish evidence in context, and to demonstrate what it has to offer. It is also the business of this chapter to look at an area strange to but a few: the story of knighthood in Wales. Perhaps Welsh 'knighthood' is putting it crassly, when what I will be looking at is the ways that the Anglo-French military aristocracy influenced the equally militant Welsh aristocracy. Even so, 'knighthood' was an idea not entirely alien to twelfth- and thirteenth-century Wales.

We must first begin in France, however. For the French the current belief is that the story of the knight begins, if anywhere, in the 970s. French historians see the assumption of the Latin word *miles* by individual landholders as a title as the significant development. It first appeared in a social context in documents of the region of the Mâconnais (in French Burgundy) in the 970s, gradually superseding the word *nobilis* in charters by the second quarter of the eleventh century.[1] In Picardy on the borders of Flanders, the same shift to *miles* happened at much the same time, and as in the Mâconnais the word was general in charters by 1030.[2] In Berry, south of the Parisian region, *miles* appears in the 990s, and again, is general by the 1030s.[3] In Normandy, where early documentation is much thinner than in other parts of northern France, the use of the word *miles* nonetheless follows a similar chronology.[4] The word is also found in Languedoc, Catalonia and Lombardy by the mid-eleventh

---

1 G. Duby, *La Société aux xie et xiie siècles dans la région mâconnaise*, (repr. Ecole des Hautes Etudes, 1982), 191-6; idem, 'Lineage, Nobility and Knighthood: the Mâconnais in the Twelfth Century – a Revision', in *The Chivalrous Society*, trans. C. Postan (London, 1977), 75–9. Brief and useful summaries of French historiography on the subject of the knight are to be found in J-P. Poly and E. Bournazel, *La Mutation féodale, xe–xiie siècle* (Nouvelle Clio, xvi, 1980), 171–83, and in more detail in J. Flori, *L'Essor de chevalerie, xie–xiie siècles* (Geneva, 1986), 9–42. For French and English historiography, see also T. Hunt, 'The Emergence of the Knight in France and England, 1000–1200', in *Knighthood in Medieval Literature*, ed. W.H. Jackson (Woodbridge, 1981), 1–22.
2 R. Fossier, *La Terre et les hommes en Picardie jusqu'à la fin du xiiie siècle* (2 vols, Paris, 1968), 538–9.
3 G. Devailly, *Le Berry du xe siècle au milieu du xiiie siècle* (Paris, 1973), 187–8.
4 D. R. Bates, *Normandy before 1066* (London, 1982), 109–10.

century; indeed it seems to be general to France by that time. It is, however, singularly absent in the Empire. There, the social grouping of men as *milites* is lacking until the twelfth century.[5]

It is argued that the shift in vocabulary is significant. The fact that *milites* are contrasted in the writings of Richer of Reims in the 990s with *pedites* (footsoldiers) certainly indicates that contemporaries used the Latin word to signify a horse-soldier rather than any sort of soldier (its original Classical and Late Latin meaning).[6] The earlier word for horse-soldier was *caballarius*. It was a word derived from the Frankish word for horseman, the word that produced the vernacular French word, *chivaler* (the word that gave the English language 'cavalier' and 'chivalry'). The Latin word *caballarius* went slowly out of fashion during the eleventh century in the north of France, probably for no other reason than that for the scholar of the High Middle Ages it was contaminated by too close a relation to the vernacular, and Classical Latin alternatives had more intellectual chic. Doubtless for the same reason, the Classical Latin *eques* was frequently used as a synonym of *miles*.[7] The *equites* in the Rome of Cicero were a distinct group within the aristocracy, above the plebs but below the patrician order. Since the *equites* had originally been the more substantial citizens of Rome, charged with providing its army with horsemen, there was some significance in the choice. It more than hints that the new knights were seen as a social group, not just a military trade.

THE SOCIAL CONTEXT OF KNIGHTHOOD

The amount of serious academic literature written on various aspects of the knight makes any attempt to form a coherent story out of the idea of the knight very difficult. For our purposes here I will be concentrating on but one aspect: the place of the knight and knighthood in society. Even so, just this one aspect of the knight is burdened with a great weight of scholarship; nevertheless, it is essential to struggle uphill with it. The understanding of what was meant by a 'knight' and the behaviour of knights in the High Middle Ages, and the inferences we can draw from these, lie at the centre of this book. It will be seen that slow internal movements in

5 G. Duby 'The Origins of Knighthood' in *The Chivalrous Society*, 160–1.
6 P. Contamine, *War in the Middle Ages*, trans. M. Jones (Oxford, 1984), 31.
7 Orderic Vitalis, for instance, will talk sometimes of an *eques pagensis*, sometimes of a *miles pagensis*.

society caused the knight to move within the confines of aristocracy. Knights are for us the mercury in the barometer of social pressure.

The argument about the origins of the ministerial knight, the German serf-knight, will not be considered here. Nonetheless, it cautions us that at its very roots and in some areas, the group we call knights, the élite horse-warriors, may not even have been made up of free warriors. However, in French society in 1000, when our particular story begins, knights were a recognisable group, and they were free. In the tenth century, the resemblance to a social group was already clear; for the knight was believed to have innate characteristics. Richer of Reims explains the failure of the Carolingian, Charles of Lorraine to prevent the takeover of the West Frankish throne by the Capetians by saying that – apart from his laziness and faithlessness – Charles had put himself out of the running by taking to wife 'a woman who was not of his degree (*ordo*), a woman from people of the rank of knight (*de militari ordine*)'. How could anyone have taken such a woman seriously as queen?[8] Knights, he is saying, are all very well, but would you like your daughter to marry one?

Richer's distaste was the distaste of a churchman for a group seen as disruptive in society. Yet the likely grounds for his suspicions of knights are significant. However you translate *ordo*, his use of it is intended to conjure up a recognised group within society. More than function is at issue here, for the profession of the knight tainted for Richer the female children of knights. What was so objectionable about knights was their profession of arms. They were the men from amongst whom kings and princes recruited their horse-soldiers; they were the hired military help (the suspicion with which contemporary society views private security guards leaps irresistibly to mind). The Church at the time particularly loathed the knights for that reason. Their swords were for hire; they were unheeding agents of the breakdown of public order in the West Frankish lands. Knights were the means by which the magnates of France could defy the natural protector of order and justice, the king. It was against the knights and their masters that the movement known as the Truce (or Peace) of God was formulated by French bishops in the eleventh century.[9]

8 *Richeri Historiarum Libri Quatuor*, ed. J. Guadet (2 vols, Paris, 1845), ii, 156; J.M. van Winter, 'Uxorem de militari ordine sibi imponens', in *Miscellanea in memoriam J.F. Niermeyer* (Gröningen, 1961), 119–20.
9 H.E.J. Cowdrey, 'The Peace and the Truce of God in the Eleventh Century', *Past and Present*, xlvi (1970), 42–67; G. Duby, *The Three Orders: Feudal Society Imagined*, trans. A. Goldhammer (Chicago, 1980), 134–8.

Other eleventh-century sources are admittedly less hostile to the *milites*. Their knightly qualities (*militia*) projected manly glamour. *Militia* was a quality desirable in kings and princes. To be called a *miles* was not in that sense an insult, quite the opposite. As early as the time of Nithard, in the mid-ninth century, as Janet Nelson has demonstrated, Carolingian rulers had been associating themselves with the army, its skills and rituals. This remained a constant theme. One mid-eleventh century writer complimented King Henry I of France (1031–60) for being 'a spirited knight' (*miles accerimus*).[10] It was quite usual at that date for men of high rank in society, counts and castellans, to have attributed to them the status of knight, as for instance Ralph, the Norman progenitor of the great house of Warenne and lord of Bellencombre, called 'Ralph a certain knight of Warenne' in a deed of 1050 x 51.[11] This can only be because people in general saw knightliness as an asset, however humble in means the generality of knights may have been. What the knight *was* did not give him much status, but what the knight *did* gave a man a sort of glamour. This seems to be the only way to account for the rich men who are credited with knightliness.

Over and above this was the fact that the knight was a man on horseback. Horse-riding had high status. The horse had long been a necessary accessory of the great man, lay magnate or bishop: Bede reports that the demands of status forced Bishop Chad (who preferred to go on foot in apostolic humility like his master, Aidan) to take to horseback. Humble English bishops were seen as letting down the side of the Church in comparison with the grandeur of their contemporary Gaulish colleagues.[12] What was true for an Anglo-Saxon bishop was as true, and more urgent, for a Carolingian aristocrat and king, product of a culture whose basic values were military. As a result the horseback posings of kings and

---

10 M. Bur, *La Formation du comté de Champagne, v.950–1150* (Mémoires des annales de l'Est, liv, Nancy, 1977), 417.

11 *Quidam miles de Warenna Radulfus nomine . . .* Cartulary of St Peter of Préaux, archives départementales de l'Eure H 711, fo. 137r. For further Norman examples see L. Musset, 'L'Aristocratie Normande au xie siècle', in *La Noblesse au moyen âge, xie–xve siècles: essais à la mémoire de Robert Boutruche*, ed. P. Contamine (Paris, 1976), 89; Bates, *Normandy before 1066*, 110. For French examples see, P. van Luyn, 'Les Milites dans la France du xie siècle: examen des sources narratives' *Le Moyen Age*, lxxvii (1971), 215–16.

12 Aidan's eccentricity and the significance of the horse in the matter of dignity is discussed in H. Mayr-Harting, *The Coming of Christianity to Anglo-Saxon England* (London, 1972), 95–7.

dukes enhanced the common cavalryman's standing. The *nobilitas* of the horseman was attested by Nithard in a context which implies at the least 'worthiness' or 'respectability', and maybe more.[13]

Status by association did really occur, I am sure, by the early eleventh century. We get what must be inklings of it in standards of behaviour which are attributed to *milites* by the odd writer. Knights were expected to live up to a standard of bravery and loyalty, as for instance the Italian commander who refused to succumb to the bribery of the Emperor Otto 'as a sworn knight'.[14] Already by the early eleventh century knights could expect special treatment in battle. This can only reflect on their status. One revealing source is the treaty between Hugh, lord of Lusignan, and his sometime lord, sometime opponent, Count William V of Aquitaine, reached in the first quarter of the eleventh century. Relations had not always been good between Hugh and his nominal lord, the count, nor between Hugh and his other neighbours. During a quarrel between Hugh and Geoffrey of Thouars, Geoffrey took Hugh's fortress of Mouzeil. Geoffrey chose to be vindictive and had the hands of those of Hugh's horsemen (*caballarios*) he captured cut off.

It is true that – at first sight – there is not much sign here of any fellow-feeling amongst warriors. Yet at least we know that things might have been different if the parties were agreed. The norm of behaviour was that knights should be treated better; how otherwise account for Hugh's outrage? When Hugh later took prisoner forty-three of Geoffrey's best horsemen, we are told that he had the option of returning them for a substantial ransom. But instead Hugh chose to take revenge and held them captive (until Count William ordered their surrender to him instead). Again, Hugh was departing from a norm of behaviour. As a result, the count, his lord, had the captured knights delivered to him and disposed of them by ransom. Count William himself, of course, as a great magnate was above such indignity; his 'city and person' were expressly exempted

---

13 J. Nelson, 'Ninth-century Knighthood: the evidence of Nithard', in *Studies in Medieval History presented to R. Allen Brown*, ed. C. Harper-Bill *et al.* (Woodbridge, 1989), 255–66, particularly, 261–2, 263–4.
14 . . . *utpote miles adiuratus*, Glaber, *Vita Domni Willelmi Abbatis* in *Historia Quinque Lion*, 256. The reference is ultimately to the military oath taken by Roman soldiers, but the circumstances admirably fitted the eleventh century too. It is known – interestingly, in this context – that the military inner retinue of King John of England were bound by an oath to respect their master's interests, *Curia Regis Rolls of the Reigns of Richard I, John and Henry III* (16 vols, HMSO, 1922–79), vii, 170.

when Hugh de Lusignan had put up with so much of his deceit that he threw over his allegiance to him.[15]

Here there are, as in Nithard's day, indications of a military code. Ransom of a captured knight was possible, and Hugh of Lusignan was plainly affronted by the mutilation of his horsemen (although we do not know if it was the act or the insult intended to him that rankled most). A century after Hugh and his troubles, the safety of the captured knight seems to have been more assured. Guibert de Nogent was as outraged as Hugh could have been at the maltreatment of knights by a particularly brutal ruler of the generation before. The brute in question was William the Conqueror; the knight on whose behalf he was outraged was Guibert's father. Writing of the 1050s Guibert talks of the terrible Duke William of Normandy 'whose habit it was never to take prisoners for ransom, but to condemn them to imprisonment for life'.[16] But Guibert was condemning the poor standards of earlier times. His days may well have had a more established custom of clemency, and if practice did not always quite match it, the feeling was nevertheless that one should hold one's hand against stricken knights. This may not necessarily have been because knights were perceived to be aristocratic, set apart from lesser men. The solidarity of the camp and the field would account for it too (as also would the incentive of ransom). Orderic Vitalis's near-contemporary account of the aftermath of the Norman victory over the French at Brémule (1119) implies as much:

> I have been told that in the battle of the two kings, in which about nine hundred knights were engaged, only three were killed. They were clad in mail and spared each other on both sides, out of fear of God and fellowship in arms (*notitiaque contubernii*); they were more concerned to capture than to kill the fugitives.[17]

Knights spared knights because (apart from their common Christianity) they were *contubernii*: tent-fellows, the name the Roman army applied to the basic unit of the legion, the *contubernium*, a small

15 Martindale, '*Conventum inter Guillelmum Aquitanorum comes et Hugonem Chiliarchum*', *English Historical Review*, lxxxiv (1969), 542–3, 547. I must acknowledge my debt here to a translation of this strange document, prepared by a seminar chaired by Dr Susan Reynolds.
16 Guibert de Nogent, *De Vita Sua*, ed. E.R. Labande (Paris, 1981), 88.
17 Orderic Vitalis, *The Ecclesiastical History*, ed. M. Chibnall (6 vols, Oxford, 1969–80), vi, 240.

detachment which shared the large military tent. I would imagine that the fear of God played a less important part in the good feeling of knight for knight than did the comfort of fellowship.

I hesitate to call the knight aristocratic in the eleventh century. The generality of knights clearly did not belong to the recognisable magnate class. Knights are, for instance, distinguished from *nobiles* in some eleventh-century Norman sources, which echo contemporary sources from the Ile de France which distinguish knights from the *casati* (chief followers) of princes. Elsewhere, the horse-soldiers of Hugh of Lusignan were to be commanded and disposed of by Hugh (the 'chiliarch' as his clerk called him). Hugh was a magnate, so was the count his adversary. His knights, on the other hand, were subordinates. We see this subordination clearly elsewhere, where the possessive pronoun is attached to the knight in documents: here a lord will talk of 'my' knight(s). French historians often describe such common knights as *milites castri*, the knights who are attached to garrisons of particular fortresses.

Yet, subordinates or not, some other pointers to a group identity surround the knights of that century, other than battlefield solidarity and horse-riding. One such pointer is the wearing of the golden spur. It is found established as a knightly accessory by the time the 'Song of Roland' was committed to parchment around 1100; it must be an older practice than that. The *golden* spur cannot be other than a measure of status accorded to the knight, however limited that status was. It is remarkable how little attention has been paid to this particular badge of knighthood; the act of dubbing seems to have monopolised academic thinking. A pair of heavy gold spurs appear in the coronation regalia of Richard I of England in 1189 carried by the hereditary marshal. The significance appears to be the proclamation of the king's military prowess (for the marshal was a military officer). In this way we find echoes of the description of Henry I of France over a century before as a 'spirited knight' (see p. 124). By 1189 even the king was bearing, indeed flaunting, the badge of the fellowship of knighthood.

Yet another indicator of the fellowship and solidarity of knighthood is the consistent use of the word *miles* as a description appropriate to a man of moderate landed resources. We find it throughout the eleventh century. Early narrative cartularies of northern France and England (like Les Préaux, St-Martin-des-Champs, Jumièges and Abingdon) will talk of this or that 'certain knight' who made such and such a benefaction. *Milites* feature in the long lists of significant people present when the great diplomats of the eleventh century were drawn up. They are not amongst the magnates present, but are clearly important. The early twelfth-century Life of St Hildeburgh of Ivry can talk of a suitor of its subject as 'a certain noble knight, rejoicing in wealth and honours'. It might have done so to underline Hildeburgh's virtue in rejecting such a man, despite the urgings of her kinsfolk, but plainly the writer thought that there were such knights.[18]

People called *milites* in the late eleventh century could be people of some account, rich and noble, so much is clear. Yet they might be poor and non-noble too. Eleventh-century writers often noted this by implication. Glaber, for instance, notes a knight of low birth (*generis infimi*) which implies as a matter of course that there were as well knights of good or distinguished birth, and proclaims knighthood to be a social continuum.[19] There was an economic continuum of knighthood too, and the wide range of English sources, if any, should give us material to detect the poor knight. Sally Harvey (in particular) has pointed to the existence of nearly five hundred 'knights' in Domesday Book; men called *milites* whose recorded holdings were little more than that of a well-off peasant. There have to be some reservations about the Domesday evidence. It may well be that many of the poor knights had more resources than Domesday Book recorded. It may well be also that what Domesday Book meant by *milites* could be debated, especially because a number of them were deliberately called 'English knights' (see below). Nonetheless, the weight of numbers of such examples means that it would be unreasonable to quarrel with Dr Harvey's broad conclusions, and that many (perhaps very many) knights were indeed poor knights.[20]

18 *Cartulaire de l'abbaye de St-Martin de Pontoise*, ed. J. Depoin (Pontoise, 1895), 51 . . . *quidam miles nobilis, divitiis honoribusque fulgens.*
19 Ralph Glaber, *Historiarum Libri Quinque*, ed. J. France (Oxford, 1989), 212.
20 Harvey 'The Knight and Knight's Fee in England', *Past and Present*, xlix (1970), 15, 21. The attempt to undermine this viewpoint by R. Allen Brown, who saw knights *per se* as an élite, fails because he could not see knights as being a group whose incomes fell within an economic continuum. Rich magnates could afford to pose as knights and enjoy the aristocratic life, poorer *milites* depended for their standing on their arms, 'The Status of the Norman Knight', in *War and Government in the Middle Ages*, 18–32. More serious reservations about the Domesday evidence are raised by D.F. Fleming, 'Landholding by Milites in Domesday Book', in *Anglo-Norman Studies*, xiii (1990), ed. M. Chibnall, 83–98, who suggests, as I do, that we should look more to a continuum of levels of wealth amongst men called *milites*.

As many knights again, perhaps, survived on their upkeep or wages from a greater magnate and had no land at all. Such had been a large number of the knights who came with the Conqueror: attracted to him as much by generous pay (as William of Poitiers says) as by the justice of his cause.[21] The abbot of Abingdon kept a group of such soldiers in his household after the Conquest, to meet the military impositions of the king, before later setting aside abbey lands to maintain them on a more permanent basis.[22] In the great French epic, the 'Song of Roland', we find mention of the paid knights (*soldeiers*) who served Charlemagne.[23] Anselm, archbishop of Canterbury, around 1097 used the shiftlessness of such knights (*stipendarii*) to offset what he saw as the virtues of the tenured knight.[24] The 'Laws of Henry I' refer as a commonplace to the detachments of such men (*conducticii, solidarii* or *stipendarii*) to be found in the great man's household.[25]

In the light of the work of French historians we can see the affinity of such a society with that of the French homeland. Many knights in both England and France in the late eleventh and early twelfth centuries seem to have lived on a shoestring. A large number did without land altogether, and made precarious careers in the households of greater men. There they had their keep and a roof over their heads and, if they were lucky, some sort of salary. There is nothing like the Domesday Survey for France, but we have scattered testimony to a similar situation. For example, writing early in the twelfth century, the aged Guibert de Nogent recalled the situation of his younger brother, a knight in the 1070s in the garrison of Clermont and in the pay of its count. The brother's wages were in arrears, and Guibert's relatives suggested that Guibert be provided with a benefice by the count in lieu.[26] An exactly contemporary

21 William of Poitiers, *Gesta Guillelmi ducis Normannorum et regis Anglorum*, ed. R. Foreville (Paris, 1952), 150.
22 *Chronicon monasterii de Abingdon*, ed. J. Stevenson (2 vols, Rolls Series, 1859), ii, 3–4.
23 The Latin *stipendarius* is translated by the French *soldeier* in an early French translation of Magna Carta, see J.C. Holt, 'A Vernacular-French Text of Magna Carta', *English Historical Review*, lxxxix (1974), at clause 51.
24 Eadmer, *Life of St Anselm*, ed. R.W. Southern (repr. Oxford, 1972), 94–5. Rather later we find another comparison between enfeoffed knights and mercenaries in the household of Robert de Belleme in 1102, written by Orderic Vitalis in the 1130s, *Ecclesiastical History*, ed. Chibnall, vi, 26–8.
25 *Leges Henrici Primi*, ed. L.J. Downer (Cambridge, 1972), c.8, 2a.
26 *De Vita Sua*, ed. Labande, 42; Guibert says he is unsure whether the wages were a *donativum*, or *feodale debitum*, meaning either paid at the count's will, or regularly out of his revenues, as a cash fee.

reference from a Norman cartulary shows us a poor, landed knight: a Ralph 'from the Pays de Caux' who on entering the abbey of Préaux made a grant of the vavassor whose rents had supported him, with the consent of the magnate William Malet 'for whom he exercised his knightly skills'.[27]

For this reason, the conquered English had by the 1090s begun to fix on the word *cniht* as their vernacular equivalent to the French *chivaler*: *cniht* signified a household retainer of a great man, not even necessarily a soldier. This duality of meaning was not always thought appropriate. In the immediate aftermath of the Conquest, *cniht* would not always do to mean *miles/chivaler* if the *chivaler* in question was a great man. In 1086 the Anglo-Saxon chronicle recorded the dubbing of Henry, the youngest son of the Conqueror. It did not then call him a *cniht*, it called him a *ridere*, a more direct approximation of the knight and a word with no servile associations.[28] The grubby associations of the word *cniht* did, however, make it a close synonym of another French word for a knight (particularly a young, retained knight) *bacheler* (Lat: *baccelarius*), which had much the same sense; warrior and servant.[29] Being confronted by these armed and mounted retinues of *bachelers* or *chivalers* in the aftermath of the Conquest, it is easy to understand why the English made the equation with *cniht*. It was therefore quite as natural that some Englishmen were being characterised in the guise of *milites* by the Conqueror's clerks. Abingdon abbey had a hide of land in Chesterton, Warwickshire, 'and there are there five English *milites*, having four-and-a-half ploughlands'.[30] Were

---

27 Cartulary of St Peter of Préaux, Archives départementales de l'Eure, H 711, fo. 145r: *iussu ... Willelmi Maleth cui idem miles militabat.*

28 F.M. Stenton, *The First Century of English Feudalism, 1066–1166* (2nd edn, Oxford, 1961), 132–4. This was a word which compared with German *Ritter* in use in the late eleventh century. In 1086 the Anglo-Saxon chronicle says that King William *dubbade his sunu Henric to ridere* at Westminster.

29 The special application of the word *bacheler* to a particular variety of knight is evident at its first appearance around 1100 in the Song of Roland (l. 113) where Charlemagne's elder followers sit around playing board games while the *bacheler leger* indulge in exercises of arms. But, just like the word *cniht*, the *bacheler* might in the twelfth century signify a household servant, such as the Irishman, Maurice Regan, the interpreter of King Diarmait of Leinster, *Song of Dermot and the Earl*, ed. G. Orpen (Oxford, 1892), 2. On the subject of the *bacheler*, see J.M.W. Bean, '"Bachelor" and Retainer', *Medievalia et Humanistica*, new ser., iii (1972), 117–31; J. Flori, 'Qu'est-ce qu'un bacheler?', *Romania*, xcvi (1975), 289–314.

30 *Domesday Book seu Liber Censualis Willelmi primi regis Angliae*, ed. A. Farley *et al.* (4 vols, London, 1783–1816), i, fo 241d: ... *ibi sunt .v. milites Angli habentes .iiii. carrucatas et dimidiam.*

they attendants, paid guards, or what? There is some evidence that Englishmen in the Norman period might have lived up fully to the description of *milites*, for English soldiers of good birth participated in Henry I's victory over the Normans at Tinchebray in 1106.

The continuing precariousness of the existence of the household knight in England is best demonstrated by digressing into the later twelfth century. At this time it was still common for knights, young and old, to live for decades of their lives in the households of the great, dependent on them for horse, arms and daily bread. One of the most famous of knights at that time was William Marshal. He was born around 1147, the younger son of a baronial, rather than knightly family. His mother's family, that of the earls of Salisbury, placed him early in the 1160s in the household of a kinsman, William de Tancarville, a great Norman magnate. In Normandy he was brought up and came to manhood as a squire of the Tancarville household. In 1167 he was knighted (by belting) by his master and fought well for him in a skirmish on the Norman frontier. Nevertheless, William de Tancarville decided to slim down his over-large household after the campaign, and by withdrawing his maintenance gave William a broad hint that he must look elsewhere for support. William was at a loss at this point. His father had died a year before and left him, as third surviving son, penniless and landless. He was saved from embarrassing poverty by Tancarville's decision to reprieve him for the purpose of taking him on a tournament tour of northern France. But once that was over, William was once again at a loose end. He invested his tournament winnings in a return trip to England, where he was lucky enough to find his uncle, the earl of Salisbury, fitting out for an expedition to Poitou, and was taken on by him. Unfortunately, the earl met his end by an assassin's sword only months later, leaving William Marshal a captive in a foreign land.

Although Marshal retrieved his fortunes by an unlikely stroke of luck – Queen Eleanor of England was rather taken by his youthful charm – his early career demonstrates the appalling uncertainty that dogged the stipendiary knight's feet, as he hopped from berth to berth. At one critical point in his career when he was between patrons, William had to trust for his support to a whip-round amongst friendly barons and courtiers. William Marshal continued to live in such a state of uncertainty until he was in his early forties, yet he was a man of good family with several rather grand connections, nephew to both an English earl (Salisbury) and a leading French count (Perche).[31] This is a point worth repeating. There was no dishonour in serving a lord as a knight for money, which is why a young man of such high connections as William Marshal took to the life. Stipendiary knights were not debarred from such status as attached to their profession for that reason.[32] Nonetheless, the rootlessness of the life meant that paid knights like William Marshal had at some time to try to secure a more settled source of income.

THE TRANSFORMATION OF KNIGHTHOOD

Some years before William Marshal was born a slow change in the perceptions of a knight had become noticeable. Perhaps 'slow change' is insufficient to describe what was happening; for it might be better to call it a closer definition of the level of status which the knight enjoyed. We can pinpoint a number of contributory developments. The attitude of the Church is important here. In the mid-eleventh century, as we have seen, the Church abhorred the violence of the knight and his employer. But even so, there are indications that the Church was increasingly willing to acknowledge that the knight might fight for peace and for God.[33] The First Crusade reinforced that attitude, for in 1097 Pope Urban made a direct plea to the knights of Christendom to direct their warlike skills towards the recovery of Jerusalem. With the success of the First Crusade, knighthood gained a new respectability. Writers turned their pens to praise the good knight, even to call him 'the knight of Christ'; a phrase formerly reserved for monks, long the front line against Satan. Guibert de Nogent, in his history of the First Crusade, composed not long after the event, marks the change. 'In our time God has instituted holy warfare so that the knightly order (*ordo equestris*) and the unsettled populace . . . should find a new way of deserving salvation.'[34]

After 1100 it was often said to be the knight who was to protect the

---

31 D. Crouch, *William Marshal: Court, Career and Chivalry in the Angevin Empire* (London, 1990), 21–59.
32 S.D.B. Brown, 'Military Service and Monetary Reward in the Eleventh and Twelfth Centuries', *History*, lxxiv (1989), 20–38, pursues this point to good effect.
33 See the review of the historiography of this question by Hunt, 'The Emergence of the Knight', 4–5.
34 Quoted, with comments, by C. Morris, '*Equestris Ordo*: Chivalry as a Vocation in the twelfth century', in *Studies in Church History*, xv (1978), ed. D. Baker, 87–8.

poor and churches by the arms committed to him; a duty previously seen to belong to the king. Writers all over the French world were at pains to point out to the knight the virtues he was to cultivate, the vices he was to avoid. The Church had discovered an ideal knight with which to preach against the all-too-fallible real one. In the early twelfth century Eadmer holds up for our approval the godly firmness of a certain knight called Cadulus, who was beset by devils in a wayside church, but who virtuously kept to his vigil in the church despite their tricks.[35] Writers of tracts such as that called the *Similitudo militis* chose the knight at this time as a suitable allegory of proper Christian conduct. The *Similitudo* (at one time attributed to St Anselm of Canterbury, and deriving from the earlier part of the reign of Henry I) details the equipment of a knight: the horse 'his most faithful friend', his saddle, his spurs, his hauberk, helmet, shield, lance and sword. Taking each in turn, the author draws from them a spiritual significance. The horse, for instance, is the body, which a Christian must control and bit, and use to pursue and conquer the devil. His hauberk of mail represents right conduct – which if any sin is able to tear (like an arrow) can be rendered useless at once.[36] The choice of such a subject for allegory says a lot about early twelfth-century knighthood, particularly about the tensions and flaws visible to all in the contemporary knight.

The creation of the order of Knights Templar in 1119 added to the debate; here indeed were monks and knights both. In a tract of 1130 addressed to the first master of the Temple, St Bernard of Clairvaux rejoiced in what he called the 'new knighthood'. As a matter of course Bernard was quite keen to deplore the old knighthood: the 'worldly knights'. All their efforts will bring them nothing but death, such are the wages of sin. Then he moves on to ridicule the luxury in which they revel – the luxury he himself denied to the order of the Temple when he helped draft its constitution some years earlier. Worldly knights delighted in silken caparisons for their horses; voluminous robes over their hauberks; painted spears, shields and saddles; bits and spurs of silver and gold, all flashing with gems. They grow their hair long and wrap their limbs in rich shirts. St Bernard's message is rather crude, taunting contemporary knighthood with its effeminacy when contrasted with the ascetic excellence of the Templars.

35 *Life of St Anselm*, ed. Southern 42.
36 *Memorials of St Anselm*, ed. R.W. Southern and F.S. Schmitt (Auctores Brittanici medii aevi, i, British Academy, 1969), 97–102.

To the historian, however, Bernard gives a more subtle and unintended message. He registers – as no man of a previous generation had done – that knights were a group of material consequence in society, given to posturing in luxury clothes. When writers like Glaber and Guibert de Nogent had earlier deplored 'effeminate' display of silks and gold, long hair and outlandish fashion, they had done so with reference to magnates and to the courts of princes.[37] But here the rebuke is directed at a much lowlier social group. St Bernard was not alone in noticing that knights had entered the world of Paris fashion. The movement had embraced England. In 1130 William of Malmesbury describes 'a certain county knight' (*quidam provincialium militum*) who had taken up the court fashion of the *criniti* (the long-haired layabouts).[38] There were indeed men called *milites* with a recognised station at court, who could perhaps set a standard for such country knights. In the reign of Henry I of England (1100–35) officers at court noticed as *milites*, such as the knights-marshal, the knights-usher and knights-huntsman, drew higher wages than the same officers who were not knights. Their title carried with it a few pence-worth of prestige.[39]

Such posturings, however much they opened knights to ridicule, certainly point to a new self-awareness amongst them. Even county knights might become as dedicated followers of fashion as the knights of the royal household. In part it was due to centuries of knightly posturing by princes and magnates and the closeness of the household knight to his master. In part also the change was, as I have said, attributable to the Church, which had now recognised knights as a group within Christian society which had superior skills and standing; indeed, a group which ought to act the part of Christian gentlemen.[40] And another new contribution to this feeling of knightly solidarity was the tournament. In 1130 the pope was provoked to condemn unauthorised and international gatherings of knights in France for the purpose of sporting exercise

37 Glaber, *Historiarum Libri Quinque*, 164–6, accuses the Aquitanian followers of Queen Constance, wife of Robert II of France, of importing vain and curious fashions into the French court. Guibert, *De Vita Sua*, 54, describes a commoner posing as the count of Breteuil wearing such a get-up in the late eleventh century. Orderic Vitalis, *Ecclesiastical History*, ed. Chibnall, vi, 64–6, describes the courtiers of Henry I in 1105 in extravagant gear and long hair.
38 William of Malmesbury, *Historia Novella*, ed. K.R. Potter (London, 1955), 6.
39 *Constitutio Domus Regis*, in *Dialogus de Scaccario*, ed. C. Johnson *et al.* (2nd edn, Oxford, 1983), 134 (*bis*), 135.
40 Morris, '*Equestris Ordo*', 91–3.

– mock combat. Innocent II, speaking at Clermont in the north of France, denied Christian burial to those who fell in them. The Church deplored the dissipation of military energy in tournaments which might have been directed towards a more godly purpose – killing Saracens. This was the 'tournament between Heaven and Hell' as one Crusading propagandist put it in 1147 on the eve of the Second Crusade, tailoring his message to his audience.[41] But condemnation by the pope, just as much as the strictures of St Bernard, was futile. Fashion and fun were stronger than censure. The excitement of a pseudo-battle, with the added interest of possible profit, drew common knights to these gatherings from all over the Anglo-French world. It seems that at first magnates stood aloof from the fun and games. Magnates did not participate in, and sponsor, these occasions till later in the twelfth century. Nonetheless their popularity amongst free warriors was remarkable, and irrepressible.

The tournament is well attested in England by the 1140s, and seems to have thrived in the reign of the knightly king, Stephen (1135-54). Tournaments or military games at that time are mentioned by William of Malmesbury, by the chronicle of Wigmore abbey, and in the reminiscences of William Marshal about his father. Even men of English blood were sucked into the pursuit. At some time in the 1130s or 1140s, perhaps even as early as the last years of Henry I, the possessor of the large estate of Kingsbury in north Warwickshire was Osbert of Arden. Osbert had a Norman name, but his descent was impeccably English. His great-grandfather was Aethelwine, one of Edward the Confessor's sheriffs. His grandfather had been called Thurkil, and his father was called Siward. At some time in the 1130s or 1140s Osbert retained a servant, one Thurkil Fundu (fairly evidently also not a Frenchman) and gave him land near Kingsbury. Thurkil's duties were committed to writing since land was involved. He was to ride at his own expense with Osbert whenever Osbert went to tournaments as far as Northampton or London. If Osbert crossed the sea for a tournament, Osbert himself would pay Thurkil's expenses. Apart from being a riding attendant, Thurkil's duties were to keep Osbert's painted lances. Osbert of Arden was an active knight in his day – his career took him as far as Scotland, where he was for many years in the household of

41 J. Bédier, *Les Chansons de croisade* (Paris, 1909), no. 1, quoted by Morris, 'Equestris Ordo', 93.

King David, but he was never more, materially, than the owner of one manor, albeit a large one.

By the middle of the twelfth century the solidarity of those who called themselves knights was being heavily reinforced both from within and without. Knights were recognised by the Church as an important, if wayward group in society. Knights themselves were copying aristocratic modes of dress and display, affecting to be good Christian gentlemen, and in peacetime were gathering for military games in which they were the chief performers. The aristocracy for its part was still affecting the manly pursuit of *chevalerie*. It remained a routine compliment to associate the status of knight with greater aristocrats. Abbot Suger in the 1130s flattered great men in this way: Guy, count of Rochefort (*miles emeritus*); the castellan of Gournay-sur-Marne (*miles strenuus*); Aumary de Montfort, count of Evreux (*egregius miles*).[42] In England in the latter part of the same decade a charter of Reginald, son of Roger de Breteuil sometime earl of Hereford, is attested by a party of men noted as 'knights of the king' (viz. Stephen); the group included such a major figure-about-court as Richard de Canville, the king's favourite.[43] It is hardly surprising in the circumstances that the customs and behaviour of either end of the economic continuum comprehended by the title *miles* should draw together.

Such a development in the first half of the twelfth century may have been the adoption of the rite of the delivery of arms to mark the passage of a postulant into the 'order' of knighthood.[44] One cannot be certain of this, because it is always possible (and to me seems likely) that there had long been some informal way in which common knights had marked their coming to manhood: perhaps it was the ritual blow (*colée*) or dubbing that is linked to the delivery of arms later in the twelfth century. The insistence by chroniclers and cartulary writers, long before records of dubbing of knights, that some men were emphatically of that status indicates to me that some public, camp ceremony had been performed on the humbler

42 *Oeuvres complètes de Suger*, ed. A. Lecoy de la Marche (Paris, 1867), 25, 41, 67.

43 Cartulary of Godstow, PRO, E164/22 fo. 29r.

44 Keen, *Chivalry*, 66–8, also considers the dual nature of such ceremonies, in his case the entry to the warband, and the entry into majority or inheritance. J. Flori, 'Chevalerie et liturgie', *Le Moyen Age*, lxxxiv (1978), 245–78, 410–42; idem, 'Les Origines de l'adoubement chevaleresque: étude des remises d'armes et du vocabulaire qui les exprime dans les sources historiques latines jusqu'au début du xiiie siècle', *Traditio*, xxxv (1979), 209–72; idem, *L'Essor de Chevalerie*, 51–3.

warrior.[45] But on the other hand, the girding of humble men with the sword begins to register in the sources only at the very end of the eleventh century. What is more, the phrase 'girded knight' (*miles accinctus*) appears newly-coined in English sources in the reign of Stephen. In its more complicated ceremonial, knighting by girding must have been something new in the first quarter of the twelfth century.

Before 1100 the delivery of arms to young warriors is only noted in the case of children of the royal families and those of high aristocracy. So in his autobiography Count Fulk le Réchin of Anjou recalled how his uncle, Count Geoffrey, 'girded to me the sword in the city of Angers' at Pentecost 1060 when he came of age.[46] The ceremony, or something like it, was not unknown to the English. The Norman aristocrat, Robert of Rhuddlan, had been at the court of King Edward the Confessor as a young man. According to Orderic Vitalis, King Edward bestowed investiture with a sword on him. The same writer tells us that in 1086 the future King Henry I of England received investiture with hauberk, helmet and swordbelt on coming of age from Lanfranc, archbishop of Canterbury. Such families continued to use the delivery of arms to mark their sons' passage into manhood.[47] In the Marches of Wales in 1128, Simon son and heir of Richard fitz Pons, the lord of Clifford and Cantref Bychan, received investiture as a knight, perhaps from his father himself.[48] Two years later, the Pipe Roll of the Exchequer is already deploying the undertaking of knighthood as a synonym for coming of age amongst landed families.[49]

45 There are known cases of impostors. Roger 'le Chaplain' of Bishops Stortford, Herts, was arrested in 1211 'for pretending sometimes he was a knight, and sometimes a priest', *Curia Regis Rolls*, vi, 146. The fact that he was arrested indicates that it was not easy to get away with such impostures in an intensely localised medieval society, presided over by a small and interbred national aristocracy.
46 *Chroniques des comtes d'Anjou et des seigneurs d'Amboise*, ed. L. Halphen and R. Poupardin (Paris, 1913), 236.
47 *The Ecclesiastical History*, ed. Chibnall, iv, 120, 136.
48 Llanthony Cartulary, PRO C115/K1/6681, fo. 182r.
49 *Pipe Roll of 31 Henry I*, ed. J. Hunter (Record Commission, 1833), 24 (son of Nigel d'Aubigny), 94 (son of Geoffrey de Faverches), 117 (Robert Marmion) 119 (Ralph fitz Simon of Driby). *Regesta regum Anglo-Normannorum*, iii, no. 482, gives a later instance of this, referring to the end of the wardship of the son of Alice de Condet to come when the boy 'could hold land and become a knight'. The West Country baron, Henry de Tracy, recalled in 1220 that King John had delivered his inheritance to him (in 1213) 'when he made him a knight' (*quando eum fecit militem*) *Curia Regis Rolls*, viii, 365. *Curia Regis Rolls*, iii, 143, gives a case around 1204 where an under-age tenant of the bishop of Lincoln had himself knighted in order to escape wardship.

Around 1100, however, the belting ritual begins to be associated with lesser men. In 1101 King Baldwin I of Jerusalem promised a squire sent on a daring mission that he would make him a knight if he succeeded, and when he did the king recognised his bravery by endowing him with the arms of a knight.[50] In the family of Gerald of Wales, it was long remembered how in the 1100s his ancestor, the constable of Pembroke, had made good the desertion of a party of knights from the defence of the castle by girding their squires with the knightly belt.[51] John of Marmoutier, writing in the 1160s, talks of many poorer men being made knights alongside the young Count Geoffrey Plantagenet of Anjou in a lavish ceremony at Rouen in 1128.[52] Such men might well have been the 'girded knights' of the mid-twelfth century. Not all knights were then so qualified. There were 'common knights' (*milites gregarii*) or the less easily translated *milites pagenses*, who might be intended to be 'country knights' or a less complimentary version of William of Malmesbury's *milites provinciales*, 'county knights' (*pagus* was a word often applied to the English shire). Were these an older style of knight? Were they men who had come to the rank by a military apprenticeship and general recognition by their fellows in the camp? Or were they simply poor knights? Whatever the case, the terminology indicates a fissure already opening up in the knightly class: the poorer ones, or the unconcerned ones, dropping out of the new game of pretension and fashion.

Seals tell us the same story. This is a subject I will be dealing with in greater detail in a subsequent chapter, but it is worth considering now. Although the use of seals was widespread throughout medieval society, the great round seal, six centimetres or so across, was a preserve of kings and magnates until the mid-twelfth century. But around the 1140s lesser men take them up. In doing so they are trying to make a point. They copy the design which first featured on the great seal of William the Conqueror: a mounted knight. In doing so they are declaring their status and at the same time trespassing on the dignity of their betters. To do so was an act ot temerity, and at least one knight suffered for it. Richard de Lucy, justiciar of England, publicly rebuked Gilbert de Bailleul, a county knight

50 *The Ecclesiastical History*, ed, Chibnall, v, 346.
51 *Itinerarium Kambriae*, in *Opera*, vi, ed. J.F. Dimock (8 vols, Rolls Series, 1861–91), 90.
52 John of Mamoutier, *Chroniques des comtes d'Anjou*, ed. L. Halphen and R. Poupardin (Paris, 1913), 179–80.

who appeared before him and who had talked out of turn about his seal. He called him contemptuously a 'petty knight' or 'knightlet' (*militulus*): seals 'are appropriate for kings and great men (*precipuis . . . personis*) only'. Yet Gilbert's lands answered for the respectable total of three knights' service.[53] Such ridicule was, however, already ineffective. Every surviving archive of charters from the later twelfth century is full of impressions of such seals. It can only be that any substantial freeholder of the time felt justified in taking up that particular trapping.

By the 1170s the knight had come to a new height of status. Whereas in the past the bulk of French and English knights may have been free, but had hardly been aristocratic, their situation had moved to one where anyone who was a knight might claim some of the trappings of the magnate. For this reason, the writer and eminent churchman, Stephen de Fougères, wrote soon after the middle of the century of the 'high order' of knighthood. His *Livre des manières* was composed in the Continental realms of the Plantagenet king of England. It is a good indicator of how the educated in society regarded knights in the third quarter of the twelfth century. Stephen elevated knighthood for the same reason as did St Bernard, to hold up the ideal knight so as to shame the all too imperfect real one. Stephen saw knights as prey to many forms of worldly weakness: dancing, luxury, posturing, tourneying and needless violence. This in itself tells us something of the aspirations of the knight of the time: the knight was seen as heedless playboy, not merely as the bloodthirsty brute of earlier days. Stephen expected his knights to be born of free parents, to respect the Church and all Christian folk, to maintain justice and condemn the vicious. In stating such an ideal Stephen was echoing eleventh-century writers, and indeed those of only the generation before himself, such as Suger. But Suger had expected such qualities of kings and princes, not of simple knights. For Stephen, then, knighthood was indeed a high order. For him, it must be undertaken in a church, where princes also were hallowed.[54] John of Salisbury (who lived in the same circles as Stephen de Fougères and like him became a French bishop) had much the same ideal view of the status of the knight. The passages about knights in the sixth book of his *Policraticus* (written around

53 *The Chronicle of Battle Abbey*, ed. E. Searle (Oxford, 1980), 214, 215n.
54 Stephen de Fougères, *Le Livre des manières*, ed. R.A. Lodge (Geneva, 1979), l. 585 (*haut ordre fut chevalerie*) note the past tense which gives the tone of the piece, ll. 585–672.

1159) give examples of knightly behaviour which clearly transfer what had been the ancient royal ethos to the knight, who was to John honourable for being, like the Roman legionary, in the service of Caesar.[55] From both of these courtier-bishops we receive the drift of the argument about the ideal and reality of knights and knighthood as it was being discussed in some circles at least of the court of Henry II their master, the greatest prince in Christendom.

Stephen's and John's younger contemporary, a more raffish sort of French clergyman, Andrew the Chaplain, was even more explicit on the high status of knighthood. In the 1180s Andrew wrote a textbook on love. In the first book, Andrew imagines dialogues (with amorous intent) between assorted couples of three ranks of society: plebeians, nobles (*nobiles*) and great nobles (*nobiliores*). From the use of synonyms in the text, it is clear that he intended the plebeians to be taken as rich merchants, the nobles to be taken as knights and ladies, and the great nobles to be counts and countesses. In the dialogue between a commoner ambitious to seduce a countess we hear a lot about nobility and status. The countess (a remarkably patient woman) explains to the burgher that although it is true that a man's integrity can make him truly noble, it cannot of itself alter his rank, excepting only that a prince, if he were so minded, might confer nobility (*nobilitatem adiungere*) on any person of good character. Andrew conflates 'nobility' with 'knighthood'. Here then is what appears to be an unequivocal statement from a man of the world of central France that knighthood is a superior level of status, set above common men, however wealthy. Indeed, his language suggests that the 'noble' knight has more in common with the 'more-noble' count than he has with other free men. Andrew's dialogues even explore the idea that the noble should be handsome, with shapely calves and feet, unlike the bandy, big-footed burgher the countess has to tolerate.[56]

The late twelfth-century romances of Chrétien de Troyes and Marie de France (herself a lady with English and Norman connections) complement Andrew's observations. Here, if the heroes are not kings or the sons of kings, they are called indifferently *baruns* or *chivalers*; they are always wealthy men with retinues of *chivalers* of their own. The knight of the romance is idealised. When we find the rare knight who makes his living by his military

55 John of Salisbury, *Policraticus*, ed. C.C.I. Webb (2 vols, Oxford, 1919), ii, 2–37; Flori, *L'Essor de la chevalerie*, 280–9.
56 Andrew the Chaplain *Tractatum Amoris*, ed. P.G. Walsh (London, 1982), 78.

skills for a lord, like Marie's Eliduc, he still somehow never seems distressed for funds to keep up a substantial household. The degree of idealisation is significant, however. The poorer knight is rarely to be found, although such men are implied in the retinues which attend the heroes, and the vagabond knights they dispatch in great numbers must be others such. The knight-hero of the romance is in fact a banneret, and that assumption speaks of a conscious conflation of the knight and the magnate in the heads of the romancers.

It is as well that we know at least some of the ideas about the status of the knight that were current in Henry II's and Philip II's courts. It was the decisions of Henry II and his advisers that did more than anything else to establish the English knight as an aristocrat. I will go on to consider this in a moment, but for now we need to digress a little. In talking of the aristocratic knight we are confronted with the problem of definition once again: what is aristocracy? But I think that the status of the knight by the later twelfth century had come to fulfil a number of the possible definitions of aristocracy. I have been arguing over the past few pages that the knight's status was rising in the twelfth century because knights (and not solely the wealthier knights) were affecting the behaviour of the magnate class. Service to the monarch is another characteristic of aristocracy.[57] Service, paradoxically, brought power; power through exercising office, and power through closeness to the centre of affairs. The magnates had long had this power, but knights had not. They were the servants of the king's servants, and at one remove from the Crown, holding no public office. When this changed, and knights became royal agents, then arguably they had become aristocratic.

In the Assize of Clarendon of 1166 the king, for the first time in any royal act, noticed the existence of knights as a distinct group within society between the barons and the other freemen. Ten years later, in the Assize of Northampton, the king went further, and charged the knights of each hundred to report to the royal justices those suspected of crimes against the king's peace.[58] This one clause recognised the local knights as a group with enough authority to speak for the other freeholders; being to their neighbourhoods what the barons were to the kingdom. As such the king was prepared to let

---

57 M. Bush, *The English Aristocracy: a Comparative Synthesis* (Manchester, 1984), 48–9.
58 W. Stubbs, *Select Charters and other Illustrations of English Constitutional History*, ed. H.W.C. Davis (9th edn, Oxford, 1913), 173, 179.

them speak to him as representatives of their neighbourhoods.[59] By the end of Henry II's reign, as the legal treatise known as 'Glanvill' makes clear, knights were already the mainstay of local justice, chief actors in the proceedings of the county courts.[60] Like the barons, knights had now a recognised stake in their land (their *patria*, as the writs have it, meaning 'neighbourhood') and a responsibility for its tranquillity. They were more clearly set apart from others. As early as 1178 a Yorkshire deed is already reflecting this local superiority. The long witness list of a charter of John, constable of Chester issued at his manor of Scroby, is begun by five men noted as *milites*, taking precedence over other freemen present.[61] The exclusivity attaching itself to the landed knights in the later twelfth century does mark them as aristocratic. They had attained a new level of status, crossing from one side of the picket fence of the social divide to the other.

At this point we begin to see more and clearer symptoms of the instability of the knightly 'class'. It had long comprehended a whole range of sorts of men, from lords of several manors down to the freeholders of small patches of land. Knighthood also included men who had no land at all, but lived off the pay and maintenance offered by magnates, men like William Marshal, whom I have already mentioned. Such men might easily fit into the group in the early twelfth century, but two generations later, when knights aspired to an aristocratic style of life, and *landed* knights were recognised as a superior group by the Crown, the economic continuum of the group could not hold. There had to be a schism somewhere within it, as the poorer knights were squeezed out. In the Herefordshire of 1220 we have just such an example. A knight, Robert de Vernay, was removed from a panel of knights of the county court sent to examine a man who had pleaded illness as a

59 J.C. Holt, 'The Prehistory of Parliament', in *The English Parliament in the Middle Ages*, ed. R.G. Davies and J.H. Denton (Manchester, 1981), 5-9.
60 *The Treatise on the Laws and Customs of England commonly called Glanvill*, ed. G.D.G. Hall (London, 1965), 11–12, 30–7, 99, 102. As Peter Coss points out, the 1166 *carta* of the earl of Arundel shows *milites* as the leading members of the honor court of Arundel, *Red Book of the Exchequer*, ed. Hall, i, 200–1, quoted in Coss, *Lordship, Knighthood and Locality: a Study in English Society, c.1180–c.1280* (Cambridge, 1991), 211–12. Such *milites* might have been called 'barons' in other earlier or contemporary documents emanating from honor courts; perhaps, therefore, the main significance of the Arundel *carta* is to provide further examples of how the terminology of social groups was changing in private charters.
61 Cartulary of York, Brit. Libr., ms Landsdowne 402, fo. 107v.

reason for non-attendance at a plea, because 'he is in a household (*familia*) and has no land'.[62] Was this because he was regarded as a cut below the landed knights and having no stake in county affairs? Was it because his dependency on his master opened him to undue influence? In either case, he was denied a place in a public assembly because he did not have the land that gave its holder status in the assembly's doings.

At the wealthier end of the knightly class, magnates who had no formal title but who were lords of wide lands began to feel uncomfortable about the association with a group which had a recognised but subordinate place in the Plantagenet scheme of things. There is abundant evidence that great families in the twelfth century had their sons knighted and rejoiced in the glamour of knighthood, so much so that 'becoming a knight' was a synonym for 'coming of age'. As early as the Pipe Roll of 1130 in England the act of knighting was understood to end the minority of an heir and launch him into adulthood (see p. 138). All untitled magnates were therefore knights, and we can see the confusing association of knighthood with magnates clearly and at an early date. A charter of around 1081 concerning the English lands of St-Florent of Saumur describes a baron and benefactor of the abbey, Wihenoc of Monmouth, as a *miles*, but also talks of the *milites* 'who hold lands from him'.[63] In the mind of that one clerk who drew up the charter at Salisbury the upper levels of society formed a knightly continuum.

In the earlier part of the twelfth century it would have been customary for the description *miles* to be applied to both magnates and their followers. Not much social significance could be attached to it, for knighthood was then not a definition of aristocracy, but a badge of adult virtue. Even so, the increasing use in the twelfth century of the status word 'baron' for royal followers and major sub-tenants might be seen as a consciousness of the need for some social distinction in the eleventh century. But by the end of the century, the title of knight could become a real danger to the dignity of the magnate since it lumped him in with the county knight as one class. Richard de Lucy's tirade at the hapless Sussex *militulus* before the Exchequer is only one example of this. He and many of his class can only have felt crowded by the posturing of

---

62 *Curia Regis Rolls*, ix, 157.
63 Archives départementales de Maine-et-Loire H 3710, no. 1. I owe this reference to Dr David Bates.

their economic inferiors. So it was that by the 1180s the magnates, not just of England, but also of France, embraced a modified title. No longer were they simple knights, but knights 'carrying banners' (*portant bannière*). This was a new way of categorising men, and demonstrated the difference between the untitled magnates and the cuckoo aristocrats who had been placed in their nest. The knights *portant bannière* were knights rich enough to lead other knights; they had banners because they needed an ensign to mark off their companies in the field, and to act as a rallying point. What was more, they had individual heraldic designs to display on these banners: family devices, some going back as far as the eleventh century, symbols of pride and high lineage. By the thirteenth century these magnate-knights were being called on occasion 'bannerets', and eventually secured a recognised higher status and superior investiture (see Chapter 3).

At the lower end of the continuum there had long been symptoms of division. If knights were *nobiles*, there were always some knights who were *nobiliores*. If there were knights who were 'girded' or 'active', there were also knights who were 'common' or 'country' knights. In the later twelfth century there is an abundance of evidence that people perceived knighthood to include both noble, active knights, and lesser, rustic knights.[64] Walter Map in the early 1180s distinguished in one of his stories a worthy and famous knight from the 'ignoble and worthless knight' (a*b ignobili nulliusque precii milite*) who had the luck to strike down his superior. By the end of the twelfth century it is clear that knights were being weeded out. This may have been going on for some time, but large-scale systematic royal record-keeping only begins in 1189, and it is not until after 1189 that we know who it was who were the county knights of England. For it was in royal records that such men were first credited with the title of knight with any regularity. By 1220 it is clear that in England – where sources are prolific enough to tell us – knightly status was only being kept up in the wealthier families, and poorer families were no longer seeking the dignity.[65]

My own observations, and those of others, lead to the conclusion that by the second half of the thirteenth century in England only

---

64 Coss, *Lordship, Knighthood and Locality*, 212–14, cites a number of references of perceived divisions between noble and ignoble, or active and bucolic, knights.
65 P.R. Coss 'Knighthood and the Early Thirteenth-century County Court', in *Thirteenth Century England*, ii ed. P.R. Coss and S.D. Lloyd (Woodbridge, 1988), 53–4.

men (or the sons of men) holding a substantial property would take up knighthood. Indeed, such had become the status and obligations of knighthood that many men of substance preferred not to take it up at all. English historians have long noticed this tendency. Indeed, calculating numbers of all sorts of things in the Middle Ages has long been an English obsession. The existence of Domesday Book and the 1166 returns of knight service have enticed them that way. J.H. Round arrived at a figure of around 5,000 knights in mid twelfth-century England calculating from the 1166 returns (themselves incomplete).[66] But even that apparently reasonable figure cannot be wholly justified; it depends on the assumption that there were enough knights in England to answer for all the knights' fees which had been created since 1066. It also depends on the assumption that the king could not negotiate the totals up for fiscal reasons. Professor Keefe's computer-generated figures reveal just over 6,500 fees assessed for scutage in the period 1190–1210, a rise of 1,500 on the figure suggested for 1166.[67] All this has nothing to do with the question of how many knights actually answered a royal summons in the twelfth century. We cannot say how many. Even if we knew, we could not say how proportional a figure those who came were to the total who *might have* come.

The thirteenth century can bring us nearer actual campaign totals for active knights in the royal armies. A total of 300–400 was all that John or Henry III might expect for a foreign campaign. Edward I did not have many more at his disposal, although other horsemen (serjeants or squires) might increase the total of cavalry in his army to above 1,000. But how many actual knights were there at large in the countryside in this century? Denholm-Young made a reasoned guess at 1,250 at any one time. Jeremy Quick has made a more soundly based estimate of a little above 1,500, working from lists of knights serving on grand assizes.[68] Had the total dropped from the beginning of the century? Can we make any sensible conclusion

---

66 J.H. Round, 'The Introduction of Knight Service into England', in *Feudal England* (repr. Westport, Conn., 1979), 228–30.

67 Keefe, *Feudal Assessments and the Political Community under Henry II and his Sons* (Berkeley, Calif., 1983), 57–9.

68 N. Denholm-Young, 'Feudal Society in the Thirteenth Century: the Knights', in *Collected Papers* (Cardiff, 1969), 83–5; J. Quick, 'The Number and Distribution of Knights in Thirteenth-Century England: the Evidence of the Grand Assize Lists', in *Thirteenth-Century England*, i, ed. P.R. Coss and S.D. Lloyd (Woodbridge, 1986), 119.

on this question if we do not know how many knights there were in the twelfth century? Certainly, Peter Coss is convincing in his assertion that lesser men were no longer seeking out knighthood by the mid-thirteenth century, as they had been in John's reign. This argument implies that there should have been fewer knights by the end of Henry III's reign. Complaints that there were insufficient knights to form juries in the county courts of England were not unusual in the reign of Henry III, and give the impression of shrinking numbers.

The decline in number of knights is best demonstrated, as Denholm-Young concluded, from the measures taken by the government of Henry III to increase them. In 1224 the young king's advisers attempted to fine (or 'distrain') men who had sufficient income to become knights, but had not done so. Such genteel witch-hunts occurred periodically throughout the thirteenth century, and are often associated with impending military campaigns. Peter Coss suggests that royal anxiety about the numbers of knights increased after 1241, when for the first time distraint was extended to men who did not hold their fees directly from the king.[69] It is impossible to assess the effect of these measures at all closely. Interest could be made by potential victims to secure or to buy pardons from distraint. The complaints about lack of knights did not dry up, either. It may well be that the administrative and not the military problems posed by lack of knights was what eventually concerned the king more than anything else. The military problem was not insuperable. If there were not enough knights, then by the end of the century there were plenty of squires who would go to war equipped quite as adequately as knights. The shortage of dubbed knights on the battlefield was not necessarily a great worry.

Reasons for not taking up knighthood often appear to have been civil. Take the particular example of Anschetil de Martinwast, lord of Noseley, Leicestershire, in the latter part of the reign of Henry III. He successfully evaded knighthood for many years after inheriting the family estate in 1246; he had respites from Henry III from distraint in 1251 and 1252.[70] Yet he was the son of a knight, William de Martinwast, a former sheriff, and he was a man of no small income. By 1256 he must have changed his mind about being a knight, for he had an exemption from assizes, juries and

---

69 Coss, *Lordship, Knighthood and Locality*, 241–4 (and references cited there).
70 *Close Rolls of the Reign of Henry III preserved in the Public Record Office* (14 vols, PRO, 1902–38), *1247–51*, 564; *Close Rolls, 1251–53*, 425.

recognitions, and from being made sheriff.[71] He was willing to become a knight, providing he was not inconvenienced by civil demands. How was he able to get away with such preferential terms? The reason for his rejection of knighthood, his preferential treatment, and then public activity must lie in his connection with Simon de Montfort, earl of Leicester. In August 1258 Anschetil suddenly appears in the public arena, as one of four knights to inquire according to the Provisions of Oxford into late excesses in the county of Leicestershire, and in October 1258 he was appointed joint keeper of the counties of Warwickshire and Leicestershire.[72] Although he makes no known appearance in the earl's charters, he appears in the neighbourhood of the great Montfort castle of Kenilworth in 1253, and he is recorded as the earl's seneschal both in a suit of 1263, and in an undated charter subsequent to 1256.[73]

I am inclined to discount Denholm-Young's assumption that the rising cost of military equipment shook out the less well-off knights. It is the argument of this book that the rise in knightly status involved more than this. In fact, military equipment did not change much in essentials between 1150 and 1250. Heraldry and livery, mail and plate armour, and high-status clothing were all in evidence in knightly equipment by the second half of the twelfth century, and could be inherited as much as purchased. Inflation would seem to have been rather more dangerous to the knight of modest resources than rising expectations. It made inroads into seigneurial incomes at the end of the twelfth century (prices doubling between 1180 and 1220) and the means to increase income to meet increased demand were not there.[74]

The tendency towards a shakeout in the 'knightly class' can be distinguished long before 1180. It rests in the aspirations of the landed knight earlier in the century. If county knights wished to adopt court fashion, and what they could afford of the life-style of the magnate class, then they had to pay for it. The great numbers of the debtors of William Cade and Aaron of Lincoln (already out of

71 *Calendar of Patent Rolls preserved in the Public Record Office, 1216–1509* (PRO, 1906–16), *1247–58*, 536.
72 ibid., 646, 655.
73 '*Anketillum de Martiuaus seneschallum S. de Monteforti comitis Leyc*', PRO, KB26/173 m 19d; *Report on the MSS. of the late Reginald Rawdon Hastings, Esq., of the Manor House, Ashby de la Zouche* (4 vols, Historical Manuscripts Commission, 1928–47), i, 42.
74 P.D.A. Harvey, 'The English Inflation of 1180–1220', *Past and Present*, no. 61 (1973), 3–4.

business by 1180) tell us of an insatiable demand for credit amongst the landed. The 'great necessity' which impelled landowners to mortgage away their lands must have been in part the need to answer social imperatives.[75] Walter Map, writing around 1180, was well aware of the problems of 'knights . . . who either eat up their patrimony or are shackled by debts', and the particular problems of indebted knights are carefully considered even earlier, in the 'Dialogue of the Exchequer'.[76] To build appropriate residences, to dress and dine up to the magnates, to endow the religious, to enclose a park; these were the imperatives which brought knights into the magnate class, or resigned their heirs to more realistic social expectations.

THE LANGUAGE OF DEFERENCE

To live the aristocratic life took money, and when, by the 1180s, it was a necessity for a knight to live up to the standard of his betters in order to be seen to be a knight, then poorer men had no business being knights. It was not just that knightly equipment was becoming more complex and expensive (in fact, that was something that had happened earlier in the century). The problem lay deeper. An aristocratic knight had to have more numerous servants, an appropriate residence, jewels, relics, plate, chaplains: all the symbols of higher status. Chrétien de Troyes writing in the 1170s is full of asides as to the dignity of the knight. When the young and unsophisticated Perceval was knighted by Count Gornemont of Gohort, he was dressed in fine linen and Indian silk, given spurs of gold, and charged to be free of baseness, for he was entering the highest order ordained by God.[77] Only a man dressed in such a way in 1200 could claim – without inviting ridicule – the all-important title of *messire*: 'my lord'. This deferential word marked the knight off as an object of public reverence and respect.

The language of deference ought to be a very important indicator of the whereabouts of the borders of aristocracy. Georges Duby devised a neat model in his study of the Mâconnais where the

75 The earliest I have seen this characteristic phrase in mortgages is in the mid-twelfth century: see a deed of Roger de Bercherolles in Register of Glastonbury, Cambridge, Trinity Collge ms R.5.33, fo. 106v. For indebtedness amongst knightly families, see generally, Coss, *Lordship, Knighthood and Locality*, 264–304.
76 Walter Map, *De Nugis Curialium*, trans. M.R. James (revised edn, Oxford, 1983), 8; *Dialogus de Scaccario*, ed. Johnson *et al*. 111.
77 *Le Conte de Graal*, ll. 1593–1660.

title of *dominus* is first borne by the castellan and possessor of the *ban*, and then, early in the thirteenth century, filters down to the socially ambitious knight; a model of cultural diffusion.[78] However, for me and for others the uses of deferential language are more complicated than might first appear from this persuasively coherent model. To begin with, there is an unacknowledged problem in the sources. Duby used charters for his evidence, but they do not tell the whole story, by any means. We only learn about modes of deferential language in general society from the reported speech of chroniclers and romancers, or from the sycophantic language of authors dedicating their work to potential patrons. From these we will usually hear only how knights or clerics addressed great men or kings, and how they replied. How knights talked to other knights, is occasionally featured, and it seems that they were calling each other *sire* by the later twelfth century. But how did burgesses talk to other burgesses, ordinary free tenants to knights, or squires to squires? Then there is the problem of date. Romances are a twelfth-century cultural phenomenon; reported speech from the eleventh century will be in Latin alone, and relatively rare.

I would say that deference was not simply paid by inferiors to their betters in the eleventh and twelfth centuries. Deference must indeed be paid to a superior, but in a society where men habitually carried edged weapons it had to be paid to equals and near-equals too. A good example can be found in early twelfth-century Wales, not much touched as yet by Anglo-French customs. Yet in the poetry of the *Mabinogion* is a marked consciousness of politeness by its heroes to all and sundry, especially on the dangerous first meeting. Deference was apparently spread liberally around Welsh society, from the greatest kings to the common freeholders. There were, however, marked *gradations* of deference, sensitively applied.[79] We must match contemporary society with a similar sensitivity if we are to be able to use such clues as deference applies to status.

---

78 Restated in 'The Nobility in Medieval France', in *The Chivalrous Society*, 108.

79 See Charles-Edwards, 'Honour and Status in some Irish and Welsh Prose Tales', *Ériu*, xxix (1978), 123–41, notably, 124–7 for the conversation between Pwyll, king of Dyfed, and Arawn, king of the Underworld, and the interplay between the use of respectful addresses such as *unben* and *arglwydd*. In the Vexin on the Norman border in the 1160s the baron *dominus* Theobald de Gisors appears accompanied by *dominus* Dreux de St-Cyr 'his knight' (*miles eius*). Here the same title applies both to a magnate and a knight of his *mesnie*, *Cartulaire de l'abbaye de Pontoise*, ed. Depoin, 123.

I have already discussed the rarefied styles applied to the earl and count after 1000. At this level there was no doubt that 'your serenity', as William of Malmesbury addressed Earl Robert of Gloucester, was intended to convey the humility of a lesser man in the presence of a greater. But deferential styles might have been applied to William of Malmesbury himself. His pupils in the cloister would have called him in Latin *domine*, signifying 'master'. Outsiders talking to William in the vernacular would have referred to the learned and senior monk in the vernacular equivalents, *dan* or *sire* (from Lat. *senior*). These words and their female equivalent *dame* (from Lat. *domina*) were liberally spread about in conversation in the early and mid-twelfth century, when vernacular sources become plentiful enough for us to see it. This is quite the opposite of the restricted use seen by Duby.

It is very likely that *dan*, *dame* and *sire* as terms of deference had been found in earlier times too. The way that Latin *dominus* had been worn down into the vernacular form *dame* (as still seen in the rare vernacular title *vidame* (from Lat. *vicedominus*), and then down into *dan*, bespeaks centuries of popular use.[80] As other evidence for this we find well established in the mid-twelfth century (in the writings of Wace, for instance) the diminutives *demoisel* (Lat. *domicellus*) and *demoiselle* (Lat. *domicella*; from which English draws the word 'damsel') for young men and women. From this we can conclude that *dan* and *dame* had been in general use in society for time enough before the twelfth century for them to have spawned vernacular diminutives.

The titles *dan* and *sire* had already, it seems, a wide application in mid twelfth-century France and its cultural colonies. Both are established as near-synonyms by the time of the writing down of the 'Song of Roland' around 1100. They are applied liberally to the characters of the epic (although *sire* is the more frequent). By the mid-twelfth century the evidence of the growing number of epics and romances gives ample testimony that merchants too might be addressed in the vernacular as *dan* or *sire*, and they continue to be so addressed until late in the thirteenth century.[81] This is a courtesy found in English historical sources too. Jordan Fantosme referred to a large number of his contemporaries as *dan*. Although most of them were clearly magnates of some distinction, at least one

---

80 L. Foulet, 'Sire, messire', *Romania*, lxxi (1950), 1–48, 180–221, particularly 2–3.
81 ibid., 7–8, 14, 181–2.

was not. Jordan referred to one lesser man, Henry Blunt, as *dan*; Henry was a leading citizen of London, a rich man undoubtedly, but a man Andrew the Chaplain, at least, would not have considered as remotely knightly.[82] We need not be surprised at this blanket use of respectful titles, for one application of *dominus*, after all, was to a husband. The female title *domina* or *dame* was used liberally in the twelfth century of respectable, propertied women who were not at all aristocratic, as for instance the Englishwoman, Ingrid of Hurley, a minor landowner in north Warwickshire. Widows in the early thirteenth century also receive the title, as being propertied and independent.[83]

In the mid-1170s this general application of the deferential *dan* and *sire* was still the case. This situation did not continue, however, and indeed was already changing. Just before the end of the twelfth century the witness lists of Latin deeds in England and France begin to refer to knights (and no one of lesser rank) as *dominus*. Although the vernacular *dan* and *sire* remain applied widely in society, a new vernacular usage reflects the limitation of *dominus* to aristocrats. In the 1170s, notably in the works of Chrétien de Troyes, the new title *messire* 'my lord' is applied to lay magnates and knights. The people who were being so addressed were not always the lords of those people addressing them; but it was a new measure of deference nonetheless, because it implied a social genuflection, even between equals, which neither *sire* or *dan* had done. *Sire* becomes less often used as the thirteenth century progresses, and *dan* becomes limited to addressing clergy (with the modified Latin equivalent of *domnus*, instead of *dominus*).[84]

By the 1220s the process of limitation had gone further, because the lesser style of *domicellus* began to be reserved in France for young men of good family who were squires, but were presumably intending to be knights. Though not a development that was transmitted to England, it bespeaks a remarkable and rapid hardening of

---

82 *Jordan Fantosme's Chronicle*, ed. R.C. Johnston (Oxford, 1981), 72, 142.
83 For Ingrid of Hurley, *Report on the MSS. of Lord Middleton preserved at Wollaton Hall, Nottinghamshire* (Historical Manuscripts Commission, 1911), 21; for widows known as 'dame', *Lay Subsidy Rolls, 1225, 1232*, ed. F.A. and A.P. Cazel (Pipe Roll Soc., 1983), 18, 20. *Domina* was applied fairly consistently to women who were aristocratic, such as Bertha, wife of the magnate Gilbert of Monmouth. She is *domina* in two of her husband's nine extant charters, Brit. Libr. ms Harley 2044 fo. 182v.; National Library of Wales, Penrice & Margam charter 53.
84 Foulet, 'Sire, messire', 17–30, 180–1, 211–17.

deferential language, with certain ranks being able to appropriate certain words to themselves and deny it to others. To explain these shifts is not easy, but their relation to other developments in society concerning the status of the knight and cleric is obvious, as indeed is the fact that the power-house of these changes was vernacular usage, and Latin scurried along behind.

THE HARDENING OF SOCIAL LEVELS

It did not take much more than a generation after the death of Henry II for knights to make their final claim on the trappings of aristocracy. As we will see in Chapter 6, the display of family devices which later grew into the European system of heraldry began as the prerogative of kings, princes and counts, spreading from northern France throughout Christendom by the 1160s. By the 1180s magnates in England were generally deploying such devices too. Knights, on the other hand, do not seems to have aspired to individual devices until much later. The evidence of seals, however, shows that by the 1230s they too (and their wives) were parading armorial shields. They went about it cautiously, as will be explained later, but nonetheless the process of social aggrandisement brought them their desire, and consolidated their position as aristocrats.

By the 1230s at the latest English knights clearly formed a level of status within the aristocracy. This had been achieved by several generations of persistent social aspiration amongst substantial free landowners. But if the status and numbers of knights were transformed in the process, then so was aristocracy itself. From a group of around a hundred influential magnates, the aristocracy in England had widened out, but in the push and shove of upward knightly mobility it had found definition. The titled élite remained at the head of the magnate group, with a class of barons filling out a second level of status. But now barons were marked as superior in England by their rank of banneret, an invention to differentiate deliberately magnate knighthood from that of magnates' retainers. County knights themselves were the third level of status; by their acknowledged pretensions, aristocrats. But a fourth level of status had already formed by the 1230s, that of the squire. Its position within the aristocracy was ambiguous; its members aspired to some aristocratic trappings, but, as we will see at the end of this chapter, it included men who had no desire to be knights as well as those who had not the resources. This was the product of a century of social definition after the death of Henry I, in whose reign we discern the first movements towards it. The process was still working itself out in he fourteenth century, when 'gentlemen' and 'yeomen' became new levels of status within what we should by then call the gentry.

In that it was knights who began this long process, we can say with Duby that they transformed the aristocracy. But I do not agree with Duby that the knightliness of the magnate affected the process much, producing a homogeneous ethos within the aristocracy: this had been going on for centuries. In England, magnates took care to create a superior knighthood for themselves; magnates and simple knights did not fuse into one group, as Duby suggests for France. In England the shove of aspiring, wealthy knights from below forced people to think more clearly about their position within society, and to define their aspirations, and thus their position in society, hence the more obvious definition of grades. I would suggest that it is the use of prestigious, aristocratic trappings (another trend identified by Duby) rather than the spread of the custom of *adoubement* which gives us the true measure of this movement.

THE KNIGHT IN SCOTLAND

Knighthood, however you define it, was unknown in Scotland until after the reign of Malcolm III. That Malcolm III, and perhaps even his predecessors, knew of Continental knighthood by repute is probable. Malcolm III and his kingdom certainly suffered from the military prowess of William the Conqueror's knights. Duncan, Malcolm's son, had delivery of arms, either from Duke Robert or William Rufus (depending on your source), in 1087. But Scotland would not have had any direct experience of the social aspects of knighthood until the early twelfth century. Malcolm's younger son, David, was probably the first native Scot (or Anglo-Scot) to study and embrace the rituals and ethos of knighthood.[85] He followed his sister Edith (Mathilda) to England around 1103 and was received by her husband, King Henry I. There he was made earl of Huntingdon and became a leading courtier. Orderic Vitalis records that David had 'magnificent arms' conferred on him by Henry I.[86] King David was regarded as a distinguished enough warrior to knight in turn the

85 R.R. Davies, *Domination and Conquest: the experience of Ireland, Scotland and Wales, 1100–1300* (Cambridge, 1990), 51.
86 For David's knighting see *The Ecclesiastical History*, ed. Chibnall, iv, 274.

teenage Henry Plantagenet at Carlisle in 1149, to mark his coming of age in the great world of power politics.

All the subsequent leading members of the Scottish royal house were knighted. Henry, earl of Northumbria, David's only son and heir, received arms when he came of age, and Henry's contemporary, St Bernard, called him 'a brave and prudent knight'.[87] In due course, Earl Henry's son, King Malcolm IV, received arms from Henry II of England, at the siege of Toulouse in 1159. In the meantime the profession and social grouping represented by the knight had established itself in Scotland. Even before David became king in 1124, his agreement with the bishop of Glasgow reveals him attended by his 'barons and knights' (*proceres et milites*) who were called upon to witness it.[88] David I, once he was king, was the agent of wider change. Firstly, he established in his new realm numerous Anglo-Norman aristocratic colonists, who brought the ideas and practices of knighthood with them. King David made a grant of land in Berwickshire to 'his knight' Ernulf before 1153. In the reign of Malcolm IV the witness list of a charter of a royal butler has as first lay witnesses three men categorised as his 'knights'. In the time of King William the Lion, Scottish knights and earls were tourneying in France. As in England, Scottish knights were generally using seals and leading witness lists by 1240.

However, when knights appear in Scotland they bear names that indicate an English or even Continental origin. What therefore of the native Scot? The general opinion in the mid-twelfth century was that the Scots were barbarians. However, when they did associate with other European peoples – on Crusade for instance – there was occasionally surprise at their courtesy.[89] Maybe they had by then absorbed sufficient Anglo-French culture to fit in when abroad. There is certainly evidence that native Scottish magnates other than the king were not unaffected by the new fashion. By the early thirteenth century the entourages of the indigenous earls of Strathern, Fife, Athol and Lennox were featuring men described as 'knights'. Again, these knights do not bear Scottish names. But their

87 *Vita Sancti Waldevi* in *Vitae Sanctorum Britanniae et Genealogiae*, ed. A.W. Wade-Evans (Cardiff, 1944), 126; *Patrologia Latina*, clxxxii cols 1095–6.
88 *Early Scottish Charters prior to AD 1153*, ed. A.C. Lawrie (Glasgow, 1905), 41–2.
89 *De Expugnatione Lyxbonensi*, ed. C.W. David (New York, 1936), 106, gives the opinion of the Norfolk knight, Hervey de Glanville, 'Who indeed would deny that the Scots are barbarians? Yet among us in this enterprise they have never overstepped the bounds of due friendship.'

appearance attests that the Scottish magnates were absorbing the alien fashion. The first consideration would have been the military value of the knight, but the social implications came along in the knight's baggage. Scottish earls' seals conform by 1200 to the Anglo-French norm, and show their users cantering across the obverse armed and habited as knights. As I have said, this is not conclusive proof that the Scottish earls had been knighted, but it was a big step towards absorbing a foreign fashion. The establishment of quotas of knights for the great Scottish honors would have hastened the process: if a Scottish magnate granted a military tenure to a dependant by knight service, it could be argued that the dependant was *ipso facto* a knight. The fact that David II of Huntingdon, younger son of King William, granted a knight's fee in the lordship of Garioch (co. Aberdeen) in the early thirteenth century to an Anglo-Scot, Malcolm son of Bertolf, brought Malcolm bodily into the world of French knighthood. There must have been many other men of indigenous families who experienced the same cultural shift as this Malcolm.[90]

THE KNIGHT IN WALES

The ethos and status of knighthood did not have as much of a social impact on Wales as it had on Scotland. In many ways this is a surprising fact when the evidence of Welsh aristocratic life is fully marshalled. English colonists who embraced the ethos of knighthood populated the March. In places like Upper Gwent, Brecon and West Glamorgan Welsh and English landed families lived cheek-by-jowl. The Welsh royal houses were exposed early on to knighthood. Indeed, after 1100, numerous Welsh nobles and children were resident at the court of Henry I as hostages, and at least one scion of Welsh royalty may have gone through the ceremony of delivery of arms at the hands of Henry I – Owain ap Cadwgan of the house of Powys. In 1114 King Henry promised to make him what the editor of the *Brut y Tywysogyon* translates as an 'ordained knight' (*varchawc urdawl*) as a sign of favour. What the Latin original of the *Brut* might have said was that Henry was to admit Owain to the order of knighthood (the original Latin phrase of which the Welsh is a translation is not recoverable, and that it might have been *miles ordinatus* does not sound right, but if it had

90 For this section see in general, G.W.S. Barrow, *The Anglo-Norman Era in Scottish History* (Oxford, 1980), 118ff.

said that Owain was to be admitted into the *ordo militaris*, then this would justify the Welsh phrase). Two years later the Normans introduced the custom of castle guard to the Welsh magnates of Glamorgan and Gwent, several of whom were obliged to do a stint of a fortnight at the royal stronghold of Carmarthen.[91] It can only be significant that the earliest extant seal of a Welsh king, that of Cadell ap Gruffudd of Deheubarth, is modelled on the contemporary seal of an English earl. It dates between 1147 and 1154 and shows King Cadell cantering across its face in helmet and chain mail, habited as the complete Norman knight.[92] Needless to say, the seal effigy of Cadell is not to be taken as an exact portrait of him riding to war; what is significant is that this was the image of power by which a Welsh king chose to be glorified to his men and neighbours in the mid-twelfth century.

The warrior society of the Welsh kingdoms found Anglo-French military technology exhilarating, and English and French armies congenial. As is well known, the Welsh had an abundance of opportunities to observe the military society of both England and France of their day. Welsh mercenaries served under their own kings in the armies of Robert of Gloucester and Ranulf of Chester in Stephen's reign. They contracted to serve both on foot and horse in the armies of Henry II and Richard in France. They joyfully embraced the new technology on display in England and France. As early as 1110 the Welsh were assiduously copying the Normans in building castles of their own. The paramount Welsh magnate of Glamorgan, the lord of Afan, a prince who had dangerous and intimate dealings with the Norman lord of Cardiff, had fortified his *llys* (that is, hall) of Plas Baglan with a stone wall and formidable square keep by the middle of the twelfth century.[93] Armour (much, no doubt, looted) and siege catapults are to be found in Welsh armies by the second half of the same century.[94]

Little stood in the way of adoption of the code and status of

91 *Brut y Tywysogyon: Red Book of Hergest Version*, ed. T. Jones (Cardiff, 1955), 82, 88.

92 Devon Record Office, 312M/TY18 (Hole of Park deeds), facsimile in Crouch, 'The Earliest Original Charter of a Welsh King', *Bulletin of the Board of Celtic Studies*, xxvi (1989), 131. Welsh aristocratic seals after 1176 (again mostly equestrian) are catalogued by M.P. Siddons, 'Welsh Equestrian Seals' *National Library of Wales Journal*, xxiii (1983–4), 292–317.

93 Communication by Mr Jack Spurgeon of the Royal Commission on Ancient and Historical Monuments, Wales: Plas Baglan will be described fully in the forthcoming RCAHM Glamorgan inventory, *Early Masonry Castles*.

94 *Brut*, ed. Jones, 114, 174, 176.

knighthood by the Welsh. Apart from the dangers of ambush, the land itself was no obstacle to horseback warfare; if knights could fight in the steep and narrow streets of Lincoln, as they did in 1217, the empty, grassy hills of Wales would be no problem. Mountains or not, the Welsh shared the common European belief that horseback travel was to be equated with status, and they may well have learned to fight on horseback before the Normans appeared. A clerk writing in Glamorgan in the time of Henry I wrote of a Welsh army which devastated Glamorgan in the previous reign as being of 3000 men, horse and foot.[95] Clearly the idea of mounted Welsh forces provoked no sense of immediate absurdity in the man. In 1115 we have an explicit reference to the military household of Gruffudd ap Cynan, king of Gwynedd (died 1137), as being mounted, in pursuit of his enemy. Gruffudd himself learned to ride in his youth in Ireland in the 1070s.[96]

The example of King Gruffudd tells us much more about the Welsh aristocracy and horses. From the lament composed for him by the court-poet of his day, Meilyr Brydydd, we learn that home-bred cavalry formed the backbone of the army of Gwynedd at this time and that the breeding and granting of horses was one of the principal mechanisms of lordship in Wales in the early twelfth century.[97] In fact studs are mentioned as a royal asset in Ceredigion as early as 1109.[98] Such a structure of Welsh lordship was resilient, for what was true in Gwynedd early in the twelfth century was as true in the days of Gruffudd's great-great-great-grandson, Llywelyn ap Gruffudd, prince of Wales (killed 1282). The good customs of his day were said by a jury of Welsh gentry to have included his openhandedness to his nobles with the colts of his own studs, as well as the colts he had in tribute from the Cistercian abbots of his principality.[99] Most of the evidence has been drawn so far from Gwynedd, but there

95 *Vitae Sanctorum Brittaniae et Genealogiae*, ed. A.W. Wade-Evans (Cardiff, 1944), 232, . . . *commotus est exercitus a Walensibus circiter tria milia armatorum equitum et peditum*.
96 *Brut*, ed. Jones, 84; *The History of Gruffydd son of Cynan*, ed. A. Jones (Manchester, 1910), 109; *The Life of Gruffudd ap Cynan*, ed. D. Simon Evans (Lampeter, 1990), 26–7.
97 A. French, 'Meilyr's Elegy for Gruffudd ap Cynan' *Etudes Celtiques*, xvi (1979), 268 'We in Snowdonia were rich in horses' (l.59); 'he defended his right with one thousand horsemen' (l.63); 'the leader of Wales, a bold horseman' (l.68); 'he hoarded neither trappings nor superfluous horses' (l.94).
98 *Brut*, ed. Jones, 60.
99 Ll. Beverley Smith 'The *Gravamina* of the Community of Gwynedd against Llywelyn ap Gruffudd', *Bulletin of the Board of Celtic Studies*, xxxi (1984), 176.

is corresponding evidence from the other principalities. Powys, according to Gerald of Wales, was famous for its exceedingly valuable horses, a breed he believed had been introduced there by Robert de Belleme, earl of Shrewsbury (exiled 1105).[100] Rhys ap Gruffudd, prince of Deheubarth, chose to honour Henry II in the native way in 1172 by a gift of eighty-six fine horses (we have already noted the presence of studs in his province of Ceredigion in 1109).[101]

There is therefore overwhelming evidence of the Welsh not just adopting Anglo-French military technology and dress but having been thoroughly exposed to the knightly ethos at an early date. Moreover, in 1100 the Welsh aristocracy was as much a horseback one as the intruding Norman marchers. This accounts for much of the success of a politically fragmented, poverty-stricken and sparsely inhabited region in holding off the power of an intruding and alien society for two centuries after Hastings. The English themselves recognised this common military culture. It is difficult otherwise to account for the demand made early in the 1170s by Earl Richard Strongbow on his follower, Walter Bloet, 'for the service of a Welsh knight (*per servitium unius militis Gual[ensis]*)' in return for the estate of Raglan in Gwent.[102] Walter Bloet was not Welsh, in fact he was the younger son of a distinguished Norman family. But he was being given a large estate in an area the earl his master had only recently conquered, or reconquered, from the Welsh of Gwent. The earl was asking for Walter to maintain for his service one of those mounted retainers who might otherwise have served in a Welsh magnate's *teulu*, or household. Earl Richard had taken many Welsh colonisers with him from West Wales into Ireland; he had fought such men to reconquer Usk from the dynasty of Caerleon. He knew what it was that he was getting in return for Raglan, and saw no reason not to dignify such a warrior as a knight. South Wales was rich in such human resources, and in later centuries 'Welsh knight service' was a recognised variant of military tenure in a number of lowland lordships of South Wales.[103] However, the use of the term 'knight' for mounted Welsh troops was not invariable. When in 1188 Henry II raised troops from amongst

100 *Itinerarium Kambriae*, in *Opera*, vi, ed. Dimock, 143.
101 *Brut*, ed. Jones, 154–6.
102 National Library of Wales, Badminton deeds, 1989 deposit, Box 3.
103 R.R. Davies, *Lordship and Society in the March of Wales, 1282–1400* (Oxford, 1978), 76.

the Welsh of Meisgyn in Glamorgan they included both mounted and foot contingents; but here, the horseback Welsh (despite twelve of them having sufficient resources to afford two horses) were called *servientes*, not 'knights'.[104] The reason can only be that the English Exchequer, unlike a Marcher earl, could not conceive of Welshmen as possessing more than the outward trappings of knighthood; the ethos of knighthood was quite a different matter.

The impact of the Norman knight on the Welsh remained a *military* one, and not a *social* one. How do we account for this? Welsh kings did not do as David of Scotland did: take Normans into their intimate counsels and give them land. Eleventh-century Welsh kings did employ Normans as mercenaries, such as those that served Caradog ap Gruffudd of Glamorgan at his victory on the river Rhymney in 1072 and later at his defeat by Rhys ap Tewdwr of Deheubarth at Mynydd Carn in 1081. One assumes that these mercenaries must have been knights, at least in part, although at Mynydd Carn a late source says they were crossbowmen (*albryswyr nordmannyeit*).[105] But thereafter Normans are absent from Welsh households. They became aggressors and colonisers, not employees, after the great incursions of 1093. A Powisian princeling was (perhaps) knighted by Henry I in 1114, but it is not till 1240 that we next hear of a Welshman being knighted, when Dafydd ap Llywelyn, prince of Gwynedd, received arms from his uncle, Henry III, at his investiture as prince at Gloucester. There is no clue as to whether either of the Llywelyns was knighted, great and well-documented men though they were. The only indirect evidence is that both princes bore coats of arms; but being such great noblemen was warrant enough for them to assume the privilege. By the fourteenth century there was an idea that it was just not Welsh to get knighted. When a later historian reported that Dafydd ap Gruffudd, brother of the last Llywelyn, was knighted, it was said to have been done 'contrary to the custom of his people'.[106]

Perhaps the main barrier to the ready adoption of knighthood by Welsh noblemen in the twelfth century was Welsh culture itself. Like Irish aristocratic culture, it remained for some time impervious to much more than the material attributes of Anglo-French aristocracy, only slowly shifting its perceptions of power in the thirteenth

---

104 *Pipe Roll of 34 Henry II*, 106.
105 *Brut*, ed. Jones, 26; *History of Gruffydd son of Cynan*, ed. Jones, 126.
106 *Eulogium Historiarum sive Temporis*, ed. F.S. Haydon (3 vols, Rolls Series, 1858–63), iii, 144.

century.[107] In the eleventh century, Welsh military life revolved around the *teulu*, the mercenary bodyguard of the Welsh king, prince and magnate. By the later twelfth century, the *teulu* may have been equipped for war and mounted like an Anglo-French baronial *mesnie*; it may have shared the same Latin name (*familia*), but there the resemblances stopped.[108] The *teulu* had little aristocratic cachet, it was very much a mixed bag; that of Gruffudd ap Cynan of Gwynedd had a large Irish contingent, the *teulu* of Glamorgan in the eleventh century contained Normans. The *teulu* had more of a direct relationship to the enforcing of lordship in Wales than the *mesnie* had in England. In England the *mesnie* rode about with its employer in an ostentatious parade of lordship. The robes and fees it offered were generally more important than the sharpness of its swords. In Wales, landed freemen were notoriously treacherous and fickle, and recognised no other bond between prince and subject than *force majeure*.

The *teulu* was a permanent military force billeted on his land which was all that stood between a Welsh prince and death and defiance, and all too frequently failed to prevent both. The Welsh Laws treat the *teulu* as an independent force within the king's household, of which it was the chief part, complete with its own bard and priest; the *penteulu* (captain of the *teulu*) was one of the king's chief ministers, preferably a kinsman, never one of his suspect gentry.[109] This impression of a body of men standing outside society – a cultural island – is reinforced by the Welsh court-poets. The famous poet Cynddelw was commissioned to praise the *teulu* of Madog ap Maredudd, king of Powys (died 1160). He praises them lavishly, in terms drawn from heroic verse. They are compared with the three faithful *teuloedd* of the Welsh triads, with that of the giant Benlli, with that of Arthur himself. They are the 'rampart of Britain', the terror of Lloegr (England).[110] They looked to a very

107 K. Simms, *From Kings to Warlords* (Woodbridge, 1987), 21–40.
108 *Annales Cambriae*, ed J. Williams 'Ab Ithel' (Rolls Series, 1860), 41, 42: the *familia* of Madog ap Maredudd of Powys (1138), the *familia* of Rhys ap Gruffudd (1159).
109 The 'Dream of Rhonabwy' has Madog ap Maredudd of Powys (died 1160) offer his brother Iorwerth the post of *penteulu*; thirteenth-century notes on the dynasty of Deheubarth have Morgan ap Rhys as *penteulu* of his brother Gruffudd (died 1201), and Cynwrig ap Rhys *penteulu* of his brother, Maelgwyn (died 1231), T. Jones. 'Cronica de Wallia', *Bulletin of the Board of Celtic Studies*, xii (1946), 41.
110 *The Law of Hywel Dda*, trans. D. Jenkins (Llandysul, 1986), 8–12, 20; J. Vendryes, 'Trois poèmes de Cynddelw', *Etudes Celtiques*, iv (1948), 22–3; W.F. Skene, *The Four Ancient Books of Wales* (2 vols, Edinburgh, 1868), ii, 461.

different Arthur from the contemporary knights of the Marcher lords, they had different heroes, different exemplars of behaviour. In that respect the minds of the Welsh military remained impervious to outside culture. They remained package tourists in France and England, travel did not broaden their minds, and the richness of their own ancient culture and tradition monopolised their attention.

The native gentry families (*uchelwyr*) of Wales began to adjust to Anglo-French social mores – as well as material culture – from the middle of the thirteenth century. There is evidence of a new direction in cultural curiosity about this time. If Welsh heroic poetry had provided the ultimate inspiration for the Anglo-French Arthurian romance, it seems but fair that eventually the Welsh gentry should return the interest by a curiosity about the 'matter of France'. The Song of Roland was translated from French for a Welsh audience early in the thirteenth century.[111] This would not have happened unless men of the Welsh upper class had begun to find it useful to know more about the basis of French culture. It did not necessarily imply that their own culture was suddenly of less weight; but it does demonstrate a move towards a cultural 'bilingualism' which was the precondition for Anglicisation. The Arthurian legend itself played a part. The royal house of Glamorgan was happy to take the Arthurian cult-centre of Caerleon as a toponym around 1200, and the royal house of Gwynedd had in its treasury 'Arthur's jewel'. By such affectations the highest level of Welsh society was putting itself well over the threshold of European culture. How much was this part of the growing political pressures on the Welsh by the English royal government? It is difficult to say whether the cultural and political processes were directly connected, for the house of Gwynedd was keen to adopt other Anglo-French customs, such as heraldry and castle-building. But the very fact that the English government put forward the serious proposal that Llywelyn ap Gruffudd should surrender his principality of Wales in exchange for an English earldom tells us that the English, at least, were having no difficulty comprehending the great Welsh magnates as part and parcel of their Anglo-French aristocratic world.

Anglicisation affected all levels of the Welsh aristocracy, from the princely houses to some modest *uchelwyr*. Glamorgan and Gwent, the areas open longest to colonisation, provide some notable

111 *Cân Rolant: The Medieval Welsh Version of the Song of Roland*, ed. A.C. Rejhon (Berkeley, Calif., 1983), 88–9.

examples, but by no means the only ones. The family of Afan, already referred to as early stone castle builders, was descended from Iestyn ap Gwrgant, a cadet of Glamorgan's ancient royal house and dominant Welsh magnate in western Glamorgan in the late eleventh and early twelfth centuries.[112] The direct line of the family survived in the area well into the fourteenth century, its possessions intact, if hardly untroubled. In the thirteenth century, however, its attitude to lordship began to change. After the mid-thirteenth century the then lord, Lleision ap Morgan, surrendered the quasi-princely status his father had enjoyed over the other Welsh of the region and began appearing regularly at the county court of the Marcher lordship of Cardiff, amongst the knights. Lleision's son, Sir Morgan, took knighthood and an English heiress to wife. He changed his name from the traditional patronym to Morgan 'de Avene', adopted a coat of arms (modelled on that of the Clare family, lords of Glamorgan), and became a member of the Glamorgan and Somerset gentry.[113] From Gwent comes the example of the family of Abadam. Its origin was not so high as that as Afan. The Abadams began as one of the dependent families of the princely house of Caerleon. The earliest known member of the family was Caradog, *distain* (steward) of the lords of Caerleon in the twelfth century. Caradog's son was Iorwerth and Iorwerth's son was the Adam who gave the family its later surname. Both succeeded Caradog as *distain* to the lord of Caerleon. Reginald ab Adam, Adam's youngest son, found a niche in the gentry, appearing amongst the suitors of the honor court of Lower Gwent in the later thirteenth century, and he married into the local knightly family of Knoville. A further good marriage raised Sir John Abadam, Reginald's son, to the rank of banneret and lord of Beverstone Castle, Glos; he received a summons to Parliament in 1297.[114] In his case the Welsh patronym was not abandoned, it simply lost its meaning (he did not become John ap Reginald), the 'ap' was treated in the same light as a Norman 'fitz' patronym.

112 Crouch, 'The Slow Death of Kingship in Glamorgan, 1067–1158', *Morgannwg*, xxix (1985), 30–1.
113 *Glamorgan County History* iii, *The Middle Ages*, ed. T.B. Pugh (Cardiff, 1971), 51–2; Rice Merrick (Rhys Meurig), *Morganniae Archaiographia*, ed. B. Ll. James (South Wales Record Soc., i, 1983), 57, 107–8, 160.
114 G.E. Cockayne, *The Complete Peerage*, ed. V. Gibbs *et al.* (13 vols in 14, London, 1910–59), i, 179–81; J. Bradney, *History of Monmouthshire* (4 vols, London, 1904–33), iii, 218, 220; *Calendar of Charter Rolls preserved in the Public Record Office* (6 vols, PRO, 1903–27), i, 294; Cartulary of Llanthony, fo. 288v.

The curious translation of the line of the steward of the kings of Glamorgan to the Parliament of Edward I was of course exceptional, although not unprecedented (compare the two lines of the 'de la Pole' family – sometime kings and princes – then lords of Powys and Mawddwy[115]). Such families represent the extreme of conscious Anglicisation, or all but the extreme. At least one Welsh gentleman, Rhys ap Gruffudd, migrated deep into England in the fourteenth century and settled into a comfortable gentry life, first in Shropshire and then Yorkshire. His descendants took the name of Griffiths.[116] The famous Lollard knight, Sir John Clanvow, came from a similar background: a Welsh family which had migrated into Herefordshire under Marcher patronage.[117] Other substantial Welsh aristocratic houses (like Glyndyfrydwy and Tudor) survived without making quite such apparently radical concessions to Anglo-French culture. But in fact all of them did no more than the Venedotian royal house had done. It too had Anglicised as far as it dared: took arms, remodelled its administration on Marcher lines, and tried (but ultimately failed) to jettison the deadly Welsh custom of partible succession. Abadam, Afan, Powys, and Tudor too, were able to dispense with that particular legacy, which is why their estates remained intact or grew.

Knighthood was taken up by a small number of Welshmen in the late thirteenth and fourteenth centuries, but it was exceptional amongst the less Anglicised part of the aristocracy.[118] This may have had more to do with the relative poverty of the Welsh baron or *uchelwr* compared with his English counterpart, rather than any royal policy of exclusion. There was also perhaps personal preference. The most famous Welsh warrior of the Hundred Years War, Owain ap Thomas ap Rhoddri (Yvain de Galles), the mercenary captain of the French kings and heir to Gwynedd, remained a squire until the end of his spectacular career. This cannot have been a prejudice stemming from his Welsh cultural background: he was brought up in the French royal court.

---

115 *Complete Peerage*, x, 641–2.
116 *Victoria History of East Yorkshire* ii, 108.
117 K.B. McFarlane, *Lancastrian Kings and Lollard Knights* (Oxford, 1972), 230–2
118 A.D. Carr, 'An Aristocracy in Decline: the Native Welsh Lords after the Edwardian Conquest', *Welsh History Review*, v (1970–1), 126–7.

5

THE SQUIRE AND
LESSER RANKS

THE SQUIRE

The word 'knight' had come to signify a member of a superior status group by the end of the eleventh century, indeed, probably some time before that. By the later twelfth century its use was closely restricted and well understood. But another, lesser, social rank shared with it the slow process of definition. We see during the twelfth century the dawning of an idea that there was a social rank lower than that of knight. Indeed, the very process of the social definition of knighthood must needs produce such a rank, by excluding respectable and substantial people from its number. Not every free man in the twelfth century would have wanted to become a knight and commit himself to the growing expense and public responsibility that being a knight entailed. Yet such a man might be as well or better endowed in worldly goods than many of his knightly neighbours. Society in general colluded in awarding a consolation prize that allowed him some of the comfort of rank.

Several words in the twelfth century hedge the seed-bed of the idea of a subordinate rank. The most common were *serviens* (MFr.: *serjanz*), *armiger*, *scutiger* or *scutifer* (equated with MFr.: *escuier*, which gave us the English 'esquire' or 'squire') and *valletus* i.e. 'little vassal' (MFr.: *vadlez* or *vaslet*, which gave us the English, or rather Franco-English, 'valet', and less flattering 'varlet'). Usage was not consistent and all of these words were employed in a context which might be called 'servile'. *Serviens* could mean a common servant (to use one of its less prestigious modern English derivatives) or bailiff.[1] *Valletus* also gave us the name of a modern household servant. But service to a social superior was not held to be demeaning in the Middle Ages, and all three words could on occasion be used in a more prestigious sense, taking no stain from their association with waiting and serving. Such a mixture of words with indeterminate status was not confined in Britain to Anglo-French society. The contemporary Welsh too had a selection of words for such a class of attendant-apprentices. Common was *gwas* (a Celtic cognate of the Late Latin *vassus*) a word directly comparable in root and meaning to *valet*: the *gwas ystafell* was the body-servant of a prince, his chamberlain. Then there were the more military attendants, equivalent to *escuier*, the *daryanogyon* (shield-bearers), who attend on the *uchelwyr*, the Welsh gentry. These words were not borrowings from French society, they are native descriptions of the components of a comparable social structure.

The appearance of the squire as a rank in society is not an easy one to chart. The multitude of words applied to what we call the squire is proof enough of a diversity of opinions about the reaches of society below the knight. In the twelfth century figures we call squires appear as humble attendants, as young men of good birth in training in a noble household, as second-rank horsemen or even as bailiffs. To add to the confusion the contemporary words were used interchangeably by some writers, but distinguished by others. But there was some consistency too. Wace's usage in the mid-twelfth century is significant. For him the *serjanz* was a mounted warrior inferior to the knight, whether because he had less armour, or less prestige, or was simply a trainee knight is not made clear. It was indeed customary in parts of France to contrast knights with sergeants.[2] We find traces of this practice in parts of France (Champagne being a case in point) as early as *c.*1100.[3] Later on in the twelfth century 'foot sergeants' are contrasted with 'mounted

---

1 See for instance a list of the tenured *servientes* of the earldom of Leicester in the early thirteenth century: the earl's falconer, fowler, cook and larderer, *Report on the MSS. of the late Reginald Rawdon Hastings Esq., of the Manor House Ashby de la Zouche* (4 vols, Historical Manuscripts Commission, 1928–47), i, 340. The ordinance of the Saladin Tithe of 1188 c.1 refers to the local representatives of the king or baron as *servientes*, W. Stubbs, *Select Charters and other Illustrations of English Constitutional History*, ed. H.W.C. Davis (9th edn, Oxford, 1913), 189. The so-called 'Laws of Edward the Confessor' dating from Stephen's reign list the *servientes* proper to a baron other than knights: stewards, butlers, chamberlains, cooks and bakers.

2 A good instance is when in 1170 Milo of Cogan commanded thirty knights to defend the West Gate of Dublin '. . . the serjeants (*serianz*) he caused to go in front to hurl their lances and shoot their arrows', *The Song of Dermot and the Earl*, ed. G.H. Orpen, (Oxford, 1892), 170–2.

3 Bur, *La formation du comté de Champagne*, 418.

sergeants', showing how the military usage was being widened. Before 1173, the Marcher lord, Osbert fitz Hugh of Richard's Castle, refers to the *servientes pedites* owed him from his lands in England for service in Wales.[4] It may well be the devaluation that this widening implies in the term *serviens/serjanz* that brought the 'squire' or 'valet' forward as an acceptable name for the rank of men below the knight. In the end, the word *serviens* had too many distracting implications for it to be used with any degree of social meaning. As early as the 1140s the contamination of the word is illustrated by Geoffrey Gaimar. He indulged in a little social comedy when he portrayed Earl Hugh the Fat of Chester indignantly rejecting William Rufus's offer that he carry a processional sword before him, like other earls. He would be no *sergant*, said the earl, at which the king laughed and gave him his golden sceptre, the ensign of his royalty, to carry.[5]

The terms *escuier* or *vaslet* were used by Wace in a civilian context, to describe servants and assistants to knights or their betters. Logically therefore, Wace might have described the same men by different titles: 'serjeants' when they were on campaign, 'squires' or 'valets' when they were in the hall. However, the common Latin equivalent *armiger*, and the less common *scutifer*, imply military service too: 'bearer of arms' or 'bearer of the shield'. We must simply face up to the confusing reality that although there was a perception that there was a social level below the knight, it attached to no particular word. There were a multitude of perceptions about *armigeri*, *valletti* or *servientes* in the twelfth century. But however precise some writers may have been in their ideas, the idea of the 'squire' has many facets, as has been well demonstrated by Matthew Bennett from the literary evidence.[6]

The servile aspects of the word are early demonstrated and long evident. St Anselm around 1100 mentioned in passing in an instructive story, the *scutarius* of a knight attending his master's horses and saddlebags outside a church.[7] Was this an *escuier* or something less? Matthew Bennett goes so far as to say that the twelfth-century squire's title signified a 'job' in the vast majority

4 Bodl. Libr. ms Dugdale 13 p. 445.
5 *L'Estoire des Engles*, ed. Bell, ll. 5975–6020.
6 M. Bennett 'The Status of the Squire: the Northern Evidence', in *The Ideals and Practice of Medieval Knighthood*, i, ed. C. Harper-Bill and R. Harvey (Woodbridge, 1986), 1–11.
7 Eadmer, *The Life of St Anselm*, ed. R.W. Southern (repr. Oxford, 1972), 42.

of cases. Certainly the functions of David and Roger *armigeri* of the prominent royal cleric, Bernard the scribe, seem unlikely to have been that of apprentice knight.[8] If we turn to other sources, we find that in the first half of the thirteenth century the squire still seems to have been seen by many as a domestic servant: there are, for example, the stories of 'Mamundus' (the Schwejk of his day) a stereotypical squire who was lazy and shiftless, calling in a dog from outside to check if its feet were wet when asked by his lord if it was raining.[9]

Kings and great noblemen were attended by a tail of attendants called *armigeri*, *scutiferi* or *scutigeri*; such men are often loosely called 'body-squires'. It is a term which covered a whole range of servants, greater and lesser. Examples are numerous and early. The households of earls in particular seem to have maintained a cloud of supernumerary squires as a token of their grandeur. Indeed the 'Laws of Edward the Confessor', which actually date to the middle of the twelfth century, assume that the households of magnates should contain, amongst the knights and titled officers, 'their squires (*armigeri*) and other servants (*servientes*)'.[10] Ranulf II of Chester (1129–53) had a squire called Nicholas (according to a later reference in a charter of his grandson) who held lands from him in Melton, Derbyshire.[11] William, earl of Warwick (1153–84), refers to his attendant squires in his privileges to his borough of Swansea.[12] A thirteenth-century source tells us more about an earl of Warwick's squire, and mentions in passing the robes and horses he claimed to receive from the earl his master, 'just as the earl's other squires of his household'. Significantly, the man claiming these squires' fees was the earl's master-cook and chamberlain, who held besides his fee a substantial holding in land in the suburbs of Warwick and a residence at Woodloes just outside the town.[13]

The 'body-squire', however, was already by this time to be found in much lesser households than those of kings and barons.

8 Bennett, 'Status of the Squire', 4; *Regesta Regum Anglo-Normannorum*, ed. H.W.C. Davis *et al.* (4 vols, Oxford, 1913–69), ii, no. 1364.
9 *A Selection of Latin Stories*, ed. T. Wright (Percy Soc., viii, 1842), 26.
10 Stubbs, *Select Charters*, 128.
11 *Charters of the Anglo-Norman Earls of Chester, c. 1071–1237*, ed. G. Barraclough (Record Soc. of Lancashire and Cheshire, cxxvi, 1988), no. 147.
12 PRO, E164/1 p. 478.
13 Bodl. Libr. ms Dugdale 13 pp. 521–2 (an interpolated charter of Alan the chamberlain of Woodloes).

The substantial Warwickshire county knight, Henry of Arden, had in the mid-twelfth century an *armiger* called Herbert, who ranked in his following below a reeve and a baker.[14] These were doubtless the lower end of the squirely continuum: humble men retained for cash payment, or even just bed and board. Greater men occasionally rewarded their squires with land and rents. At a humble level in the mid-twelfth century the English magnate, Robert fitz Harding, retained one squire with half a virgate of land and a shilling rent, no more than the holding of a peasant.[15] Other such men were more prosperous, like Thomas Noel who was granted a half knight's fee by Robert of Stafford 'so that he will keep my shield'.[16]

It is impossible to believe that most men who were called 'squires' in the twelfth century were of any account whatsoever. But it is equally plain that some men referred to by that rank were men of some substance, or at least lineage. In 1167, the newly-knighted William Marshal, who had not a penny of his own, is said to have retained a squire: what sort of Sancho Panza could he have been? Yet the same source talks of William Marshal himself as having been a squire 'for twenty years' before his knighting.[17] Later on, as his star rose, the Marshal was attended in 1180s by two known men called 'squires': Eustace de Bertremont and John of Earley. Eustace was a nobody, as far as anyone can tell, although he later took knighthood and served until at least 1214 as a retained *bacheler* of the Marshal. John of Earley on the other hand came from a line of royal chamberlains, his father a minor baron, founder of a priory, and lord of a hundred in Somerset.[18] Here, in a few lines of an early thirteenth-century poem is the nub of the problem of squires and their rank. A young man of noble blood who was an apprentice of arms filled the same job as an acknowledged social inferior. There has to have been some tension as a result, and the *Histoire* of Marshal's life notices as much. From its viewpoint in the thirteenth century it comments on the rising expectations of squires, who expect not just a roncin

---

14 Cartulary of Kenilworth, Brit. Libr. ms Harley 3650 fo. 19r.

15 A grant to *Ade Stut armigero meo in feodo et hereditate sibi et heredibus suis post eum* ... PRO, DL25/218. Of course, Adam might well have had other land elsewhere.

16 ... *ad seruitium proprii clipei mei*, Bodl. Libr. ms Ashmole 833 fo. 248v.

17 Both *escuier* and *vadlet* were words used to describe young men, notably young men before knighting, Guilhiermoz, *Essai*, 483–4n.

18 D. Crouch, *William Marshal: Court, Career and Chivalry in the Angevin Empire* (London, 1990), 195–6.

(an inexpensive horse) to ride, but a pack-horse as well for their own possessions.[19]

The significant development in squirehood happened in France in the thirteenth century. Before the middle of the century, all over northern France, a new usage appears in charters. Whereas knights had begun to be dignified in charters as '*Dominus* N. de P. *miles*' in the first quarter of the century, the next generation allowed the dignity 'N. de P. *armiger* [or *scutifer*]' to squires.[20] Sometimes also by the middle of the century, a squire was called *domicellus*, as a diminutive of the knightly *dominus*. The wife of a squire was *domicella*.[21] We have already seen that *domicellus* or *damoiseau* were words applied to young men in the mid-twelfth century. Now, just as knights were 'lords', in France squires were 'lordlets'. The same pursuits were attributed to both knights and their underlings in the middle of the thirteenth century: 'The young magnate, knight, *or other man-at-arms*, ought to strive after honour, and to triumph so as to earn a name for valour and attain worldly goods, riches and an inheritance', writes Philip de Novara.[22]

Of course the practice of social definition of the squire must have predated its appearance in charters by some years. Indeed, there is evidence from Normandy that it did. In the 1180s Norman charters, just as English ones, occasionally corral knights together at the head of lay witness lists, an acknowledgement of social pre-eminence; but what they also do is to go on to a second group labelled *servientes*

---

19 *Histoire de Guillaume le Maréchal*, ed. P. Meyer (3 vols, Paris, 1899–1909), ll. 767ff. The twenty years the Marshal had been a squire can only refer to his years before his knighting, for he was born *c*.1147; for this and for Eustace and John see Crouch, *William Marshal*, 25n, 136–7.

20 In Perche in 1205, Philip de Clévilliers *armiger*, *Cartulaire de Notre Dame de Josaphat*, ed. Ch. Métais (2 vols, Chartres, 1904–8), i, 362; in the Parisis in 1228, Peter de Ceverent *armiger*, *Recueil de Chartes et documents de St-Martin-des-Champs, monastère Parisien* ed. J. Depoin, (5 vols, Paris, 1912–21), iv, 58–9; in the Méresais in 1231, Simon de Alneto *armiger*, *Cartulaire de l'abbaye de Notre Dame des Vaux de Cernay, de l'ordre de Cîteaux au diocèse de Paris*, ed. L. Merlet and A. Moutié, (2 vols, Paris, 1857), i, 294; in the Vexin in 1245, Peter de Blameicort *scutifer*, *Recueil des chartes de St-Nicaise de Meulan*, ed. E. Houth (Paris, 1924), 126. These are all earlier than the examples given by P. Guilhiermoz, *Essai sur la noblesse du moyen âge* (Paris, 1902), 485n.

21 See the example of Baldwin de Pleineval, *domicellus* or *armiger* in his deeds and 'Bauduin le Damoisel' on his seal, 1250–54, *Cartulaire de la Maladerie de St-Lazare de Beauvais*, ed. V. Leblond (Paris, 1922), 274, 285, 286. For an *armiger* and a *domicella* his wife (1256), see ibid., 300, and another (1267), *Cartulaire des Vaux de Cernay*, ii, 632.

22 *Les Quatres âges de l'homme*, ed. M. de Fréville (Paris, 1888), pp. 38–9, c.66.

(one of the synonyms for squire), 'and many others'.[23] This being the case, there is good reason to think that the idea of the squire rose in society in the wake of the knight his master, for the chronology of the social definition of the squire does not lag far behind the higher rank. As we will see in the next chapter, the use of heraldry spread to the class of squire in the second half of the thirteenth century. Again, only a generation behind the knight.

The development of squiredom in England shows some differences from the way it developed in France. The social ranking represented by the conjunction of *domicellus–domicella* for a squire and his lady is not readily to be found in England. Although English squires began to call themselves 'N. of P. *armiger* [or *scutifer*]', they did not do so generally until the fourteenth century. Another provincial oddity is that the word *valletus* is much preferred to *armiger* for 'squire' in England throughout the thirteenth century and into the fourteenth. It was not until the mid-fourteenth century that *armiger* became the appropriate word and *valletus* was devalued to be the equivalent for the emerging inferior rank of 'yeoman'.[24] There cannot be any denial that English society ceased to be international at the level below the knight. The political divorce between England and the northern French Plantagenet dominions and the infrequency of military forays against the French in the reign of Henry III doubtless accounts for much of this insularity in at least Latin practice. In the vernacular, French and English squires would probably not have noticed any difference in status; both spoke and understood the language of chivalry and heraldry.

Was the squire aristocratic by the end of the thirteenth century in England? I have expressed doubts that he was, earlier in this chapter. The squires may not properly have formed a status level within the pale of aristocracy as did the knights, because knights and squires were often of the same families. Yet on the other hand, since many squires (like Anschetil de Martinwast) went on to be knights, it is tempting to say that squires were yet another status level appended to the magnate class on the argument that they formed a *cursus honorum*.

There is some support for appending the squires to the lower end of the aristocracy in observations like that attributed to

23 *Chartes de l'abbaye de Jumièges*, ed. J-J. Vernier (2 vols, Rouen, 1916), ii, 34–6, 80–2, 94–5, 207–9.
24 Saul, *Knights and Esquires: The Gloucestershire Gentry in the Fourteenth Century* (Oxford, 1981), 11–20.

Bishop Robert Grosseteste. He describes attendants in the ideal noble mesnie as knights, and others besides whom he calls *gentis hommes* who received robes from their lord with the knights.[25] Since these *gentis hommes* could only be what we call squires, then knights were clearly not the only men who could be considered *gentil* (noble) in the 1240s. Yet I think it would be a mistake to make too much of this. Many squires may have adopted or been brought up in aristocratic mores, but they lacked that essential voice in local and national affairs which the knights did possess. They did not have the right to the golden spur, and in England in 1297 the right of the squire to heraldic bearings was still in dispute. To talk of squires as *potential*, rather than actual, aristocrats would be safest before 1300.

VAVASSORS AND FRANKLINS

The 'squire' and all its signifiers does not exhaust the repertoire of words applied to individuals with the intention of giving them some social distinction. There are several others, but unlike the squire they none of them became attached to a recognisable and self-conscious social level. Nonetheless, some are worth considering, if only because a degree of meaning did attach to them.

The most widely used of such words was the *vavassor* (from Lat. *vassus vassorum*, a 'vassal of vassals'). Vavassor was a word with a long and widespread history behind it in 1000. It was made use of in all the Latin-derived languages in Europe. Its use, however, was never in any way regular. Vavassors might at various times and places be very great men, holders of castles, or they might be petty landowners. In Normandy in the eleventh century the word had the meaning of a lesser free landowner, and this is its most frequent manifestation there. A *vavassoria* was a holding owing services different to the customary exactions on a knight's fee.[26] Some examples show how the word was used in both Normandy and England. Grants by greater landowners of vavassors to Norman abbeys are not uncommon. A particularly good example is that where a *miles*, Ralph de Caux, gave to the abbey of Préaux 'his

---

25 *Walter of Henley and other Treatises on Estate Management and Accounting*, ed. D.M. Oschinsky (Oxford, 1971), 402.
26 The ample bibliography on the subject is surveyed by P.R. Coss, 'Literature and Social Terminology: the Vavasour in England', in *Social Relations and Ideas: Essays in Honour of R.H. Hilton*, ed. T.H. Aston (Cambridge, 1983), 112–17.

land, that is, the land of a vavassor in Buletoth'; the vavassor is seen here as the subordinate of a landholding knight.[27] The abbey of Le Tréport had two tenants with the unusual name of Alfred in the late eleventh century and early twelfth century. One was distinguished as 'Alfred the knight', the other as 'Alfred the vavassor', and the Alfred who was knight always preceded the Alfred who was a vavassor on their numerous joint appearances in the abbey's documents.[28] These examples (which could easily be multiplied) give a clear social context for the early Norman vavassor.

This Norman position was reproduced in England, as can be seen from the appearance of vavassors as small landowners in Domesday Book, but only temporarily. Texts and writs of the reign of Henry I portray the vavassor not as a small landowner but as any freeholder who is less than a baron, or a tenant of one.[29] What we probably see surfacing here is the common French vernacular usage where a 'vavassor' is seemingly any sort of landowner. A vavassor might be in modest circumstances, he might be a retired knight, or he might be a rich man (Peter Coss has collected examples of all these), or again, as in the writs of Henry I, he might be any landowner who is not a magnate, including powerful castellans.[30]

It is for this reason that the word 'vavassor' never came to be taken to signify the rank of free man below the knight. Vernacular use and Latin usage never agreed on what it was. To the poor vavassor might always be opposed the view of the vavassor as any landowner holding of another, and therefore a rich man. The 'franklin' (Lat. *francolanus*) is another word that acquired something approaching social meaning. It resembled one of the meanings of vavassor – that of a modest, free landowner – and therefore might be seen as a synonym of vavassor. A document of 1150 records a perambulation of the bounds of the Warwickshire parishes of Shrewley and Rowington by the substantial county knight, Hugh fitz Richard. Hugh was accompanied by a party of free men,

27 Cartulary of Préaux, Archives départementales de l'Eure, H 711, fo. 145r.
28 *Cartulaire de l'abbaye de St-Michel du Tréport*, ed. P. Laffleur de Kermaingant (Paris, 1880), 18–28.
29 In the *Leges Henrici Primi*, ed. L.J. Downer (Cambridge 1972), cc.7.2., 27.1., *vavasores* follow *barones* as suitors in the shire courts, and are credited with the right to hold their own courts. The 1109 writ relating to shire courts rate *vavasores* simply as the tenants of barons, W. Stubbs, *Select Charters and Other Illustrations of English Constitutional History*, ed. H.W.C. Davis (9th edn, Oxford, 1913), 122. See F.M. Stenton, *The First Century of English Feudalism, 1066–1166* (2nd edn, Oxford, 1961), 19–20; Coss, 'Literature and Social Terminology', 117–21.
30 Coss, 'Literature and Social Terminology', 121–7.

'namely' as the document says, 'knights, clerks and *frankel[anos]*'.[31]
If the document had been a Norman document the word vavassor
might well have been substituted for franklin. Franklin remains a
rare word in Latin documents. Another Warwickshire reference of
the late twelfth century refers to the *francolani* of the parish of
Pillerton Priors who owe tithes to the abbey of St-Evroult.[32] The
rarity might be accounted for by the much more common reference
in documents to knights 'and other free men' (*liberi homines*) of an
area. *Francolanus* meant 'free man' if it meant anything. The French
vernacular *francs* or *francs hommes* comprehended the same idea.
The *francolanus* might be made to have a less wide application to
a substantial free farmer, but it happened later than the period of
this book, when the word had made its transition into the English
language.

31 Cartulary of Reading, Brit. Libr., ms. Harley 1708, fo. 123v.
32 Cartulary of St-Evroult, Bibliothèque Nationale ms. latin 11055, fo. 33r.

Part II

TRAPPINGS AND INSIGNIA

6

THE GREATER INSIGNIA

We have now considered the use and meaning of titles in England and Scotland in the High Middle Ages. The titles of knight banneret, knight and squire, and their development and use give us a picture of slow change in the aristocracy throughout the twelfth century, intensifying rather in the years between 1180 and 1230. In those two generations – the time of Richard the Lionheart, John and Philip Augustus – the aristocracy became both larger, and better defined. Status levels multiplied and social dignities evolved to meet the change. These were times of change too in Wales; a time when the native aristocracy was forced under outside pressure to change its own use of the ancient royal title, and find and define a new title which had a relevance to wider European developments. The society of Wales had to adapt to the military trappings, at least, of Anglo-French knightly society. Welsh aristocratic society was considerably less insular by 1230 than it had been in 1150.

In this second part we will be comparing chronology with other developments in aristocratic society. The use of material trappings was another way of recognising and defining aristocracy. We will be examining the use and development of such things as coronets and rods, banners and heraldry; the elaboration of homes, dress and households, and the evolution of aristocratic piety and religious patronage. A similar chronology and trend of enlargement of the aristocracy is clear to see. What is also clear is that the process of defining status levels is also at work. By the mid-thirteenth century we find in this field too a better defined and more self-conscious aristocracy in England and its satellite societies.

Already, by 1000, a great deal of money was in circulation in Europe, not least in England. Its aristocracy had the capacity to spend: what did it buy? Literary sources leave us in no doubt.

Kings and princes acquired stores of treasure: jewels, silks, furs, precious vessels and rings, horses, hawks and dogs, brocaded and embroidered mantles, fine weapons and armour. Many great men and women in England and Normandy from the eleventh to the thirteenth centuries invested some of their surplus wealth in ecclesiastical finery. Countess Adelaide, the sister of William the Conqueror, was able to give the canons of her church of St Martin of Auchy six rich copes, a dalmatic of silk, an alb, two fine bells and seventeen reliquaries; her daughter, Countess Judith, added a cope, a silver cross and a wall-hanging. Even more impressive is what the countess's tenants gave: more silken vestments, bells, a silver chalice, gold and silver crosses. The countesses might have been expected to have such treasures to give (female households in fact were vestment workshops), but hardly their dependants. There was a considerable amount of treasure available for patronage in a small corner of Normandy in the late eleventh century; in part the spoils of England, perhaps.[1]

We find much the same in the twelfth and thirteenth centuries. Magnates like Roger, earl of Hereford, William de Mandeville, earl of Essex, Isabel, countess of Gloucester and William Longespée, earl of Salisbury stored up copes of brocade, albs, dalmatics; precious chalices, crosses, relics, even books; stocking up private chapels as lavish as any bishop's.[2] From one of the chronicles of Walden abbey, we find that the chief monastery of a great magnate expected to receive the precious vessels, books, relics and ornaments of his chapel when he died. Should the monks not get it, it represented a grievous loss to their sacristy.[3] In part this accumulation of goods was for display, and in part for patronage. The openhanded giving of gifts was praised in a lord, as much by

---

1 Archives départementales de la Seine Maritime, printed in L. Musset, 'Recherches sur les Communautés de Clercs Séculiers en Normandie au xie. siècle', *Bulletin de la Société des Antiquaires de Normandie*, lv (1959–60), 32–5.

2 For Earl Roger's relics, D. Walker, 'Ralph son of Pichard', *Bulletin of the Institute of Historical Research*, xxxiii (1966), 201; for the contents of Countess Isabel's considerable chapel, which she left to Tewkesbury abbey, *Annales de Theokesburia*, in *Annales Monastici*, ed. H.R. Luard (5 vols, Rolls Series, 1864–9), ii, 113–14; for William Longespée, *Rotuli Litterarum Clausarum*, ed. T.D. Hardy (2 vols, Record Commission 1833–44), ii, 71. Substantial county knights might also have vestments, books or chalices in their possession, such as the Warwickshire knight, William of Bishopton, who stocked his own chantry with such things in John's reign, Bodl. Libr. ms Dugdale 13 p. 79.

3 *Liber de fundatione abbathiae de Walden*, in *Monasticon Anglicanum* ed. J. Caley *et al.* (8 vols, London, 1817–30), iv, 142, 144.

monasteries as among the writers and songsters who competed for patronage.

But by 1000, and doubtless for some time before, the crude measure of wealth in society was not subtle enough for the satisfaction of the greater aristocracy. After all, the common merchant also might acquire wealth and valuable goods. In England, at least, the simple acquisition of wealth allowed the most successful of the town-dwelling entrepreneurs to merge into the lower reaches of the aristocracy with no apparent difficulty. There was nothing incongruous in England, or, I suspect, in France, in a rich merchant who took up the lesser symbols of social eminence in the twelfth century: the *chlamys*, the mantle of a knight or gentleman, or even the golden spurs of knighthood: men like Robert fitz Harding, Gervase of Cornhill or Osbert Huitdeniers, to name but the greatest amongst them. But very visible, material barriers were lowered against further mingling. The really great – those men who were titled or untitled, but who could talk of their *potestas*, *honor*, and their *terrae*, and mean their jurisdiction over wide lands and numbers of men – such men associated with themselves trappings invested with a more potent symbolism. Banners, swords, coronets (that is, inferior crowns), caps of state, rings and sceptres found their way during the period of this study into the hands and on to the heads of the greatest of the great. These were not simply badges of social status. They were tangible symbols of an invisible world; the world of power and dominion which has no other existence but in the minds of men. In this part of the book I will look at these symbols and their history, and point to a certain fastidiousness within the aristocracy about the use of them. We can learn a lot about the aristocratic mentality of the High Middle Ages from its use of insignia.

It is not always possible to be precise about the origins of such aristocratic insignia. It is not always possible to date their first appearance, which is why I take 1000 as my nominal starting point, a date by which most of the repertoire of insignia was in use. I will be considering in turn the use of banners, swords, coronets, caps and sceptres as insignia by men below the rank of king. From what we can know and observe about their use, and the way contemporaries regarded them, it is possible to say that they had one thing in common: they were all in their ways thaumaturgic, or incantatory. They were meant to conjure up an image of power greater than the man who bore them. Some summoned up the giants of Antiquity: caesars, patricians, consuls and the triumphal general. Others invoked the bearded prophets and kings of the Old Testament. Others again sought to call up more contemporary avatars: the power embodied in the vested king in majesty, as Byzantium and the Ottonian monarchy had between them made him to be understood in Western Europe; and perhaps also the bishop, seated as magistrate and pastor above his people. There was little in the insignia of aristocratic power in the High Middle Ages that was intrinsic to it. It was almost all a matter of borrowed state. Exceptions are few, but such as they are, they are significant, as will be explained in due course.

THE BANNER AS INSIGNIA

The banner (Lat. *vexillum, signum*; Fr. *banière, gunfanun*) was – the pun is unavoidable – one of the earliest true ensigns of aristocracy. The banner was essentially a military device, a method of distinguishing bodies of troops and their commanders. Banners stood above the heads of men, on poles, and therefore could be seen at a greater distance than the faces of the men beneath them. It is important to bear in mind that this military purpose always remained the chief secular use of banners in the medieval period. To ride out with banners flying in Normandy in 1091 meant you intended no good to your enemies, according to the customs of the duchy written down for the Conqueror's sons.[4] Banners were the rallying points of companies of troops, and when a figure is depicted as bearing one in sculpture or illumination there may well be no other intention in it than to say to its audience 'Here is a military commander', as for instance in the depiction of 'Arthur of Brittany' (King Arthur) leading his troops in an assault on a castle, carved on the Porta de Pescheria of the cathedral of Modena. In the ninth century, as in the thirteenth and fourteenth centuries, the banner's military use continued to be paramount in a military society. In a Burgundian capitulary of AD 865 King Charles the Bald instructed his envoys that they should ensure that contingents of troops sent to the royal army by bishops, abbots and abbesses should be up to quota

---

4 *Consuetudines et Iusticie*, c. 8, in C.H. Haskins, *Norman Institutions* (Cambridge, Mass., 1925), 283.

and led (in default of the prelate) by a gonfanonier (... *cum guntfanonario, qui de suis paribus cum missis nostris rationem habeat*).[5] Over three centuries later the banner was the insignia of the constable of Leinster in Ireland because the chief purpose of his office was to lead the knights of Leinster into battle.[6] In the fourteenth century the banners of the Scottish provinces were in their earls' custody, because they still led the provincial levies into battle.

Such was the overall utilitarian purpose of the banner, but there was more to it than that. If banners were used by powerful men in the High Middle Ages, they had also been used by the giants of the past. An aura of antiquity clung about them. The Roman past provided more than just the Latin words to denote the medieval banner. *Vexillum*, the most commonly used word to describe the flags of the medieval period, was once used for one of the chief of the legionary ensigns, a painted linen banner used for signalling movements on the march and in the field.[7] But Roman ensigns gave out more esoteric signals. The pre-Christian Roman army had invested its banners and other ensigns, notably its famous eagles, with a religious significance; something that made their loss a national humiliation. A religious, or at least magical, significance clung about the later history of banners too. The Frankish kingdom of the Merovingians and Carolingians drew on the Roman tradition. The early French word, *enseigne*, was derived from the Latin *signum*, a word that comprehended miscellaneous Roman banners and standards. Eagles were adopted as imperial symbols by the Carolingians, and in the time of the Staufer the eagle made its way on to the heraldic shield of the king of Germany. The same spirit of imitating the Roman past is to be found in England, where King Edwin of Northumbria (died 632) rode about in wartime or peace preceded by a banner-bearer, or

---

5 *Monumenta Germaniae Historica [M.G.H.] Capitularia*, ii, 331, no. 272 c.13. This passage is discussed by J. Nelson, 'The Church and Military Service in the Ninth Century', in *Politics and Ritual in Early Medieval Europe* (London, 1986), 123 and n. She sees the use of a gonfanon to ensign companies raised by prelates as evocative since they were not specifically required for counts' contingents, but does not consider that the counts themselves would lead their own companies, and the gonfanonier stood in the prelate's place.
6 *The Song of Dermot and the Earl*, ed. G.H. Orpen (Oxford, 1892), 220.
7 G. Webster, *The Roman Imperial Army of the First and Second Centuries* (3rd edn., London, 1985), 138–9.

walked about with a Roman-style banner called a *tufa* carried before him.[8]

The Church also took up the banner from the Late Empire as a potent symbol, and in doing so restored and adjusted its religious meaning. Its use in processions following after the cross is mentioned as early as the seventh century. The famous, early ninth-century mosaic once in the Lateran palace, commissioned by Pope Leo III to celebrate the alliance between the Franks and the Papacy, is very keen to make the point of the banner as a symbol of dominion, as later borne by Christ in depictions of him as the Paschal lamb. The mosaic showed St Peter conferring a banner on Charlemagne, as a symbol of worldly power, got, naturally, through the favour of Rome. It was this conjunction between spiritual and secular power that made the banner something more than a military device. Sacred banners were part of the treasure of kings. The royal saint, Oswald of Northumbria (died 641), was laid in a tomb at Bardney abbey, Lincs, beneath his banner of gold and purple.[9] Much later, Hugh the Great, duke of France, sent to King Athelstan of England early in the tenth century the banner of the legendary St Maurice, amongst several other sumptuous gifts designed to entice the king to marry his sister to the duke.[10]

Banner-bearing was not unknown amongst pre-Conquest English earls, as well as kings. A twelfth-century source refers to Earl Siward of Northumbria having, over a century before, a particular magical banner called the 'Ravenlandeye', which was eventually left to the city of York, where he died in 1055, and hung there in the minster.[11] The Bayeux Tapestry shows the English bearing banners much as the French did. When, in an earlier scene, it shows Duke William investing his visitor, Earl Harold, with arms after a successful

8 *Bede's Ecclesiastical History of the English People*, ed. B. Colgrave and R.A.B. Mynors (Oxford, 1969), 192. The *tufa* is mentioned by the late Roman military writer, Vegetius, as a species of *signum*. Henry of Huntingdon, in setting out his own version of Bede's story, adds the information that 'the English call it a "tuf"'. In the fourteenth century a 'tuff' signified a plumed helm. see references collected in *Glossarium Mediae et Infimae Latinitatis*, vi (Paris, 1846), *s.v. tufa*.
9 Bede, *Ecclesiastical History*, 246.
10 In William of Malmesbury, *Gesta Regum Anglorum* (2 vols, Rolls Series, 1887–9), i, 150, Duke Hugh is mistakenly called a king in the passage, derived from a lost encomium of the king; see M. Wood 'The Making of King Athelstan's Empire', in *Ideal and Reality in Frankish and Anglo-Saxon Society*, ed. P. Wormald et al. (Oxford, 1983), 265–7.
11 *Vita et Passio Waldevi comitis*, in *Chroniques Anglo-Normandes*, ed. F. Michel (Rouen, 1836), 106–10.

campaign in the west of Normandy, Harold is depicted as holding a gonfanon. Presumably the designer of the tapestry believed that such a man would not have been embarrassed to be seen with such a foreign accessory.[12]

By the late tenth century there were in use in the Church ritual blessings for military banners: this sacral element may well have made the counts of eleventh-century France the more avid for such symbols, and the power they lent their user. Count Geoffrey Martel of Anjou in the middle of the century, engaged in conquering the Touraine, solicited the banner of St Martin of Tours from the abbey there, and lacing it to his own lance bore it into battle against his enemy the count of Blois.[13] His victory confirmed his relationship as 'advocate' or 'protector' of the abbey, and the banner of St Martin became part of the comital regalia of his house. The famous example of the papal banner supposedly sent to William the Conqueror on the eve of his expedition to England in 1066 demonstrates just as powerfully how sacred or sanctified banners were considered useful accessories before going on campaign. There was a similar relationship between the counts of the Vexin and the great abbey of St-Denis. The banner of St-Denis was believed in later times to have been borne by Charlemagne, and its special royal dignity led King Louis VI of France (1108–37), a king greatly in need of support to his royal dignity, to adopt it. This was the origin of the oriflamme, the national banner of France.[14]

The banner in such a context might very easily become regarded as insignia, weaving into its web strands of royalty, antiquity, command and ritual. There is plenty of evidence that banners were being used in the investitures of princes in the twelfth century. Within the realms of the Angevin king of England this was certainly the case.

---

12 This little scene has been supposed to show the English Harold being subjected to the foreign rite of knighting, but I wonder if more can be read into it than that rather insular point. After all, no gonfanon is ever recorded as part of the knightly regalia. The duke himself, when depicted receiving a messenger in his quarters during the Hastings campaign, is shown seated on a chair of state, a gonfanon (the papal banner?) in his left hand. Was this banner supposed to be a symbol conferred by the duke on Harold to show he held his authority from him after his submission? Or more, was Harold to regard himself now as one of Duke William's counts? If so, we have in this cartoon the earliest depiction of the investiture of a count-earl.
13 Rodulfi [Ralph] Glaber, *Historiarum Libri Quinque*, ed. J. France (Oxford, 1989), 242.
14 R. Barroux, 'L'Abbé Suger et la vassalité du Vexin en 1124', *Le Moyen Age*, lxiv (1958), 1–26.

By 1200 a banner played an important part in the investiture rituals of the duchies of Aquitaine, Normandy, and probably also Brittany. The earliest traces of the practice are in Gascony, where in the second half of the fourteenth century it was regarded as an ancient custom going back to legendary times that the count of the province should receive his banner and sword from the altar of the collegiate church of St-Seurin-de-Bordeaux.[15] When we combine this belief with the fact that in 1172 the young Duke Richard of Aquitaine was indeed invested by banner and sword by the archbishop of Bordeaux, we can give the canons of St-Seurin some credit, the only reservation being that the ceremony of 1172 took place not at Bordeaux but at the church of St Hilary of Poitiers. Perhaps the canons' assertion had been a cry for the defence of what they saw as the more ancient rights of their home as an investiture church.[16] The dukes of Brittany were being invested with sword and banner at Rennes in the early thirteenth century, when it was said to be 'customary' to do so. The similarities to the earlier Aquitainian investiture make it most likely that the Breton custom was an imitation of the practice of their southern neighbour during the period of Angevin overlordship of both in the late twelfth century.[17]

The Norman ducal investiture of John in 1199 involved the handing over to him by the archbishop of Rouen of a banner. John, busy chatting to his cronies, dropped it. The account of the incident, in the life of St Hugh of Lincoln – as well as making the obvious deduction about the fate of Normandy under John – tells us that it was customary for the dukes of Normandy to receive a banner on their investiture.[18] How far back this custom went can only be a matter of conjecture. On the one hand, there is the evidence of the great seal of William the Conqueror as king of England and duke of Normandy. As king of England he is seated crowned in majesty, but on the reverse, ducal side he is mounted

15 *Cartulaire de l'église collégiale-de-St-Seurin de Bordeaux*, ed. J-A. Brutails (Bordeaux, 1897), 6–7; see commentary in H. Hoffmann, 'Französische Fürsten-weihen des Hochmittelalters', *Deutsches Archiv für Erforschung des Mittelalters*, xviii (1962), 103–4.
16 The custom of St-Seurin was a hardy one. It was still being honoured nearly two centuries later, when, in 1355, Edward of Woodstock, prince of Wales and Aquitaine, arrived in Bordeaux as its new sovereign. He dutifully received investiture by banner and sword from the altar of St-Seurin, *Cartulaire de St-Seurin*, 4–5.
17 Hoffman, 'Fürstenweihen', 111 and n.
18 *Magna Vita Sancti Hugonis*, ed. D.L. Douie and H. Farmer (2 vols, London, 1961–2), ii, 144: *vexillum . . . quo duces Neustrie honoris sui investituram solebant percipere.*

Figure 2 Seal effigy of Earl David of Huntingdon (*c.* 1113–24) showing his gonfanon. The seal is evidently modelled ultimately on the reverse of the seal of the Conqueror. The earliest seal of Count Stephen of Aumale is akin to it in design.

as a warrior, bearing a gonfanon.[19] Here we have the problem of intention I mentioned earlier: is the Conqueror to be interpreted in this case as war-leader, or warrior and duke? If we go by the Bayeux Tapestry, and Norman written sources, the preferred focus of ducal power in the eleventh and twelfth centuries was the sword. But it is not unlikely that the duke may have taken up the banner too – he appears on one occasion on the tapestry grasping a banner instead of a sword (although he was on campaign at the time, even if not in armour). I would admit that the antiquity of the banner investiture in England and Normandy will always remain an uncertain area, but some comparison with German evidence hints that it may have been widespread in northern Europe at an early date.

The banner as attribute of a sovereign prince is much in evidence in twelfth-century Germany. Otto of Freising in 1156, following

19 T.A.M. Bishop and P. Chaplais, *English Royal Writs to 1100 AD* (Oxford, 1961), p. xxviii.

the settlement of the succession dispute to Bavaria, describes the emperor investing Henry the Lion with the duchy by means of seven banners. What these banners represented is made clear when Otto talks of the other claimant, Henry Jarmingott, being invested in compensation with Austria by means of two banners and another territory 'the Three Counties' with three banners. Each *comitatus* had its banner, and a grant of the county was represented by a banner investiture.[20] There is further evidence. The coinage of the German princes not infrequently features portraits of the man in whose name it was issued. Some of these portraits make pointed use of insignia. Two successive landgrafs of Alsfeld, Ludwig III (1172–90) and Hermann I (1190–1217) are depicted holding aloft banners, the former also with a sceptre, the latter with a sword. The margrafs Albrecht of Aschesleben (*c*.1170) and Otto I of Brandenburg (1170-84) are also distinguished by banners, the former receiving it from St Stephen, the patron of his *Stift* (monastery).[21] Seal evidence also indicates the association of banners with twelfth-century German princes, the most famous being that of Henry the Lion as duke of Saxony and Bavaria. Although an argument can be made for deriving the banner investitures of the Angevin empire from a common source in Aquitaine, this cannot apply to the German examples. Bearing in mind the investiture of Charlemagne portrayed in the Lateran mosaic (depicting him in effect as a duke of St Peter) a retrospective case can be made for the banner investiture being common to the lands of the old Frankish empire, and having a common antiquity.

Within the insular and continental realms of the king of England, men of a lower rank than the sovereign affected to use banners. As early as 1070 a Norman count, Robert of Mortain, was carrying a sacred banner. He bore in battle the banner of St Michael from the abbey of Mont St-Michel, of which he had been the principal patron since around 1060.[22] In the twelfth century, certain other Franco-Norman earls and counts acquired sacred banners. Robert,

20 Otto of Freising, *Gesta Frederici seu rectius Cronica*, ed. A. Schmidt (Ausgewählte Quellen zur Deutschen Geschichte des Mittelalters, xvii, 1965), 388. I owe this reference to the generosity of Maurice Keen.
21 *Die Zeit der Staufer: Geschichte, Kunst, Kultur* (4 vols, Stuttgart, 1977–9) i, nos. 187.27–8, 189.34, 193.30; ii, pls 101, 108, 113. H. Dannenberg, *Die deutschen Münzen der sächsischen und fränkischen Kaiserzeit* (4 vols in 5, Berlin, 1876–1905), i, 399; ii, pl. 39, no. 887.
22 *Cartulary of St Michael's Mount*, ed. P.L. Hull (Devon and Cornwall Record Soc., new ser., v, 1962), 1.

earl of Gloucester declared in 1133 to a Norman inquest that he was 'a baron of his lady, the blessed Mary [of Bayeux] and by hereditary right her banner bearer (*signifer*)'.[23] This arrangement between the earl and the bishop of Bayeux was part of a pact by which the earl took a substantial amount of land from the Church and in return sent it a certain number of knights and undertook this much honourable service. There was a similar arrangement between the Norman count of Aumale and the archbishop of Rouen. Earl and count gave knights and the protection of their local power to the bishops, and in return bore the cathedral's banner in the field. In England in the 1170s the earls of Arundel, Hertford and Norfolk disputed the right to carry the prestigious banner of St Edmund, and be recognised as a particular patron of the abbey of Bury.[24]

Banners as symbols of secular dignity were well established by the early twelfth century amongst the earls and counts of England and Normandy. The seal of David, earl of Huntingdon (1113–24), one of the earliest of English earls' seals to survive, has him on horseback with a banner draped across his right shoulder (Fig. 2).[25] A somewhat worn impression of the seal of Stephen, count of Aumale (*c.*1090–1128), which is earlier than Earl David's, also depicts the count with a banner.[26] The sculptors of both seals must have taken their inspiration from the reverse side of the Conqueror's seal, which they resemble. The tradition of magnates bearing banners on their seals continues through the century. At a later date, in the 1150s, the most potent of all Anglo-Norman counts, William son of King Stephen, count of Boulogne, Mortain and Warenne, still made a point of bearing a banner on his seal.[27] French counts and German princes were also being portrayed in this style on their seals in the second quarter of the twelfth century. It seems

23 H. Navel, 'L'Enquête de 1133 sur les fiefs de l'Eveché de Bayeux', *Bulletin de la Société des Antiquaires de la Normandie*, xlii (1935), 15. Earl Robert succeeded Robert fitz Hamo his father-in-law in his holdings from the bishopric, and he must have been the original *signifer*.

24 *Annals and Memorials of St Edmunds Abbey*, ed. T. Arnold (2 vols, Rolls Series, 1890), i, 261–2; *Jordan Fantosme's Chronicle*, ed. R.C. Johnston (Oxford, 1981), 74; *The Chronicle of Jocelin of Brakelond*, ed. H.E. Butler (London, 1949), 57.

25 See Durham D & C, misc. charters 759, 762, for two good impressions.

26 Count Stephen's seal is attached to a Cluny deed of 1096, see *Recueil des chartes de l'abbaye de Cluny*, ed. A. Bruel (6 vols, Paris, 1876–1903), v, 63–4, n. 3717, described and wrongly identified as a seal of William II of Nevers in *Inventaire des sceaux de la Bourgogne*, comp. A. Coulon (Paris, 1912), no. 110. A picture of another impression of this seal is to be found in B. English, *The Lords of Holderness, 1086–1260* (Oxford, 1979), pl. 2.

27 Brit. Libr., Harley Charter 83 A 25.

likely to me that they were drawing their inspiration here from the Anglo-Normans.

By the twelfth century banners and aristocratic status were already inextricably linked. The aura of the sacred banner and the humdrum practical point that only a man great enough to command a company of men would need such a thing combined to make banners social as well as military accessories. Hence the rise of a military and social dignity in England and France: the 'banneret' (see Chapter 3). In the mid-twelfth century the historian Wace could describe an army mustering and state that 'there was there no great man or baron who had not his banner (*gonfanon*) or other ensign (*enseigne*) with which to mark out his company (*maisnie*)'.[28] We occasionally hear of the banner-bearers who had the honour of carrying these aristocratic accessories for their lords. Sometimes they were men of substance. Such a man was Robert de St-Pierre, *vexillarius* of Count John of Eu (1140–70), and his chief officer. Others were humbler, such as the squire, William Mallard, who was the banner-bearer of William Marshal, earl of Pembroke (died 1219), and who was rewarded with an estate in Ireland (Mallardstown, co. Kilkenny).

By the 1180s an untitled magnate with the means to recruit a company of knights, a man who might earlier have been called a baron, was being called in the vernacular a knight *portant banière*. It is difficult to see such a man actually carrying his own heavy banner himself, except in a ceremonial context, so the jump from the awkward vernacular phrase to the neat Latin word *banerettus* was no long hop. We first find the banneret in the second decade of the thirteenth century. By the late thirteenth century in England the word 'banneret' did not just comprehend a military rank, it described a social level superior to the simple knight, the bachelor. The banner was therefore a social indicator. Since it was an item of insignia which did not lend itself to imitation by a common knight (whose task it was to follow banners) the banner was used as an effective definition of magnate status, and it is as such that we find it in the inquisitions carried out by the government of Philip Augustus (see Chapter 3). Although the knight became regarded as aristocratic by the mid-thirteenth century, the

28 *Roman de Rou*, ed. A. Holden (3 vols, Société des anciens textes français, 1970–73), ll. 3923–6.

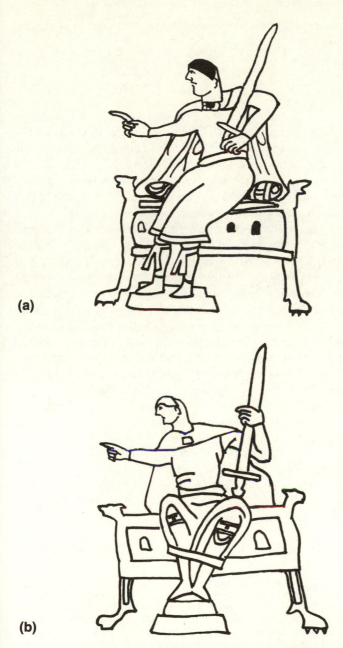

(a)

(b)

Figure 3   Varieties of comital poses on the Bayeux Tapestry: (a) Duke
William (b) Count Guy of Ponthieu.

banner made sure that his status within the aristocracy was strictly limited.

THE CEREMONIAL SWORD

The sword as an all-purpose symbol of lay power had a long history. In the royal coronation rituals of Carolingian times it was a symbol of the king's duties to protect the good, and confound the evil; the symbol of his power to use force to impose order. Jean Flori tells us that in Germany in the tenth century the sword was considered a symbol appropriate also to the powers of the secular princes under the king, and the idea spread to France (if it was not already there). Flori has as evidence a German ritual for the blessing of a sword, known as the *Benedictio ensis noviter succincti*, which for him is clearly intended as part of an investiture ritual of a prince. His reasoning relies partly on the fact that the consecration borrowed from royal coronation *ordines* the formula: *accingere gladio tuo super femur tuum potentissime* (Psalm xliv 4); partly it has to do with the fact that the man being girded with the sword is charged, as kings were charged, to protect the Church and the weak and to combat the heathen. He also points to the known contemporary examples of the delivery of arms from kings to princes, a ceremony in which this benediction might well have featured.[29]

Pre-Conquest England was also influenced by this idea of the sword as a symbol of power. Just before 1000 an ealdorman or thegn called Aelfric had made for himself a seal matrix. It depicted him grasping an upright sword facing to the right. Here again the model is a royal one. It has been suggested that Aelfric's designer was copying the armed image of Aethelred II found on his coins. A thegn called Godwin had a seal with a comparable image in the mid-eleventh century. Such a tradition of English aristocratic seals survived the Conquest. The impression of the seal of a North Country thegn called Thor the Long is to be found in

29 J. Flori, 'Chevalerie et liturgie', *Le Moyen Age*, 84 (1978), 272–3; idem, *L'Idéologie du glaive préhistoire de la chevalerie* (Geneva, 1983), 96. For the text of the benediction, C. Vogel and R. Elze, *Le Pontifical Romano-germanique du xe siècle* (2 vols, Vatican, 1963) ii, 379. An early instance of a ceremonial sword delivered to a duke may be that inscribed sword of purest gold which the Emperor Henry sent with many other precious gifts to William the Great, duke of Aquitaine, early in the eleventh century; see Adémar de Chabannes, *Chronique*, ed. J. Chavanon (Paris, 1897), 163.

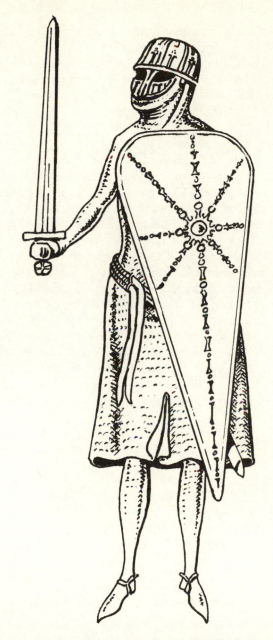

Figure 4   William Clito, count of Flanders (killed 1128) from his tomb effigy, once in the abbey of St-Bertin. The effigy dates to a time some forty years after the count's death.

the archives of Durham Cathedral, and it dates from the early twelfth century. Thor is shown seated cradling in both hands his upright sheathed sword. Flori's German model seems therefore to have spread wider than he realised. Since the depictions of Edward the Confessor on his seal were ultimately inspired by images of Emperors Otto III, Henry II and Conrad II, we should not be surprised at this.[30]

The Normans had embraced the same image of power as the earls and thegns of England. The Bayeux Tapestry displays Duke William of Normandy in three of its cartoons sitting on a chair of state, distinguished by a sword held in the manner of sceptre in either his right or left hand (on two occasions it seems to be unsheathed, on another sheathed).[31] The duke is not otherwise armed in these seated images. As we will see, the tapestry's designer, in the early 1070s, thought this the proper way to depict a ruler below the rank of king, whether he was a duke or a count. If he were English, native tradition would have transmitted to him the same image. Take away from the eleventh-century depictions of a king in majesty his crown and orb and you have an image precisely like that of the duke and count on the Bayeux Tapestry. The seat itself was an evocation of royal state, for King Edward sat on just such a throne in the tapestry. Moreover, the seat was flanked by lions, a Biblical allusion to the throne that King Solomon set up in his house in Jerusalem.[32]

Other and later images of non-royal rulers parallel those of the tapestry. On an enamel plaque on his tomb in Le Mans cathedral, nearly a century later, Geoffrey Plantagenet, count of Anjou (but also at one time duke of Normandy), was depicted standing, with a sword held the same way (see Fig. 6). The symbolism is to be found, unsurprisingly, in Germany, for Henry the Lion, duke of Saxony (died 1195), was depicted on his mid-thirteenth-century tomb effigy in Brunswick cathedral, bearing a sheathed sword

---

30 T.A. Heslop, 'English Seals from the Mid-Ninth Century to 1100', *Journal of the British Archaeological Association*, cxxxiii (1980), 1–16.

31 *The Bayeux Tapestry: a Comprehensive Survey*, ed. F.M. Stenton *et al.* (London, 1957), pls. 14, 29, 50.

32 I Kings xi, 18–19: *Fecit quoque rex Salomon thronum de ebore grandem: et vestivit eum auro fulvo nimis, qui habebat sex gradus: et summitas throni rotunda erat in parte posteriori: et duae manus hinc atque inde tenentes sedile: et duo leones stabant iuxta manus singulas.* Solomon's throne in turn seems to have been inspired by Egyptian models.

(point upward) in his left hand.[33] Duke Geoffrey and Duke Henry were both portrayed in civilian dress. It was not as yet thought *de rigueur*, as it would begin to be in the next century, for a magnate to be seen armed as a knight in order to express his power – this use of the sword was drawn from images of the king, not the soldier.

In Normandy by the early twelfth century the sword had undoubtedly the same significance with regard to the duke as a crown did to a king. In verses addressed around 1100 to the Conqueror's daughter, Adela of Blois, Baudrey de Bourgeuil referred thus to her father: 'As king he wore a crown, as duke he bore the arms of a duke'.[34] As early as the 1140s criminal cases in the duchy were 'pleas of the sword', just as 'pleas of the crown' were criminal cases in England.[35] Girding the new duke with a sword was part of the investiture of the dukes of both Aquitaine and Normandy before the end of the twelfth century. For Normandy an investiture *ordo* was in use from at least 1189, the *Officium ad ducem constituendum*.[36] Using prayers adapted from the English coronation order, the archbishop of Rouen conferred on his duke both a ring and a sword. In the case of both Normandy and Aquitaine an archbishop had the responsibility of girding the sword to the duke, whether in Limoges in 1172, or in Rouen in 1189, and the very presence of such a prelate on such an occasion makes it all but certain that benedictional *ordines* were being observed, in Limoges as much as Rouen. We do not know when the ritual investiture was first carried out in either duchy (although the Aquitainians claimed some antiquity for it), but people had seen the sword as the particular attribute of ducal power in Normandy for well over a century before 1189, and

33 *Die Zeit der Staufer*, i, no. 447; ii, pl. 248. The sheathed sword seems to be met with more in Germany than in the western lands. The same manner of sword-carrying is to be found in late thirteenth-century depictions of the dukes of Austria in the cartulary of St Florian, see G. Schmidt, *Die Malerschule von St Florian* (Forschungen zur Geschichte ober Osterreichs, no. 7, 1962), 55–6, pl. 3(a). I owe this and several more references to Julia Walworth of the University of London Library, who has been most kind in sharing her considerable knowledge with me.

34 *Adelae Comitissae*, trans. Herren, in S.A. Brown, *The Bayeux Tapestry: History and Bibliography* (London, 1988), 177.

35 *Regesta regum Anglo-Normannorum*, ed. H.W.C. Davis *et al.* (4 vols, Oxford, 1913–69), iii, no. 381; C.H. Haskins, *Norman Institutions* (Cambridge, Mass., 1925), 152.

36 *The Benedictional of Archbishop Robert*, ed. H.A. Wilson (Henry Bradshaw Society, xxiv, 1903), 157–9.

that in itself is grounds for placing some sort of ducal investiture with sword in Normandy back before the Conquest.

If we look lower in the scale of status than sovereign duke, the example of pre-Conquest England shows how men of the status of thegn were associated with swords at an early time. In France, a range of (somewhat later) examples can be offered to demonstrate how the less exalted counts had also taken it up. To begin with, the Bayeux Tapestry depicts Guy, count of Ponthieu, in the same way as it depicts Duke William, seated on a chair of state and holding a sword (Fig. 3).[37] The now lost seal of Robert, count of Meulan and Leicester (1107–18), is known to have displayed on one of its faces the count in civilian dress bearing a sword, point down in front of him (Fig. 5). He is depicted in the same manner on his tomb effigy at the abbey of St Peter of Préaux, commissioned by his son, or other later member of his family, at some time towards the end of the twelfth century.[38]

Such an image is by no means confined to the counts and thegns of England and Normandy. A precisely similar image to that of the count of Meulan lay on the contemporary tomb of Fulk Nerra count of Anjou in the abbey of Beaulieu-lès-Loches (Fulk in fact died in 1040, a century and more before his tomb was thus refurbished).[39] The copper coinage of Count Baldwin II of Edessa, issued before 1118, has the count full face, dressed as a knight but bearing the sword unsheathed and upright. There is a remarkable English parallel to this Palestinian issue in the silver penny struck for an earl, possibly Patrick of Salisbury, in Wiltshire in the later 1140s: here again a helmeted figure holds an upright sword in his right hand; doubtless it is meant to be the earl, identified by the symbol of his status.[40] The military effigy of William Clito, count of Flanders

37 *The Bayeux Tapestry: a Comprehensive Survey*, ed. Stenton pl. 11.
38 For a surviving drawing of the seal of Robert I of Meualan and Leicester, see J. Nichols, *The History and Antiquities of the County of Leicester* (4 vols in 8, London, 1795–1815), i, appendix I. (The original of the seal was until recently in the University Library, Keele, but has been lost); for the Meulan tombs at Les Préaux, J. Mabillon, *Annales Ordinis Sancti Benedicti Occidentalium Monachorum Patriarchae*, v (Paris, 1738), 329 (no. 4). Some of the figures on these important, and now lost tombs, are difficult to attribute to particular persons, but another bearing a sword in the Bayeux Tapestry pose (Mabillon's no. 2) must be Count Robert's brother, Henry, earl of Warwick (1088–1119).
39 For Count Fulk's tomb, J. Adhémar and G. Dordor 'Les Tombeaux de la Collection Gaignières', in *Gazette des Beaux-Arts*, 6th ser., lxxxiv, 1974, 17, no. 40.
40 D.M. Metcalf, *Coinage of the Crusades and the Latin East* (London, 1983), pl. 4, no. 63; *English Romanesque Art, 1066–1200* (Arts Council, 1984), 331, no. 443.

(died 1128), placed on his tomb in the abbey of St Bertin at St-Omer in the 1160s or 1170s, has him in just such a pose: helmeted and with shield along his body, the sword held (unsheathed) upright in his right hand (Fig. 4).[41] It is interesting that around 1200 the comital pleas of Cheshire and Lancashire, where the earl was particularly powerful and filled the place of the king, were called 'pleas of the sword', just like the ducal pleas in Normandy.[42]

In England we hear of a ceremonial investiture of a new earl by the girding of a sword by the king's hands in the reign of Henry II – and this may well have been an adaption from one of the known rituals involved in the ducal investiture in Normandy. One wonders if this ceremonial aspect of the sword and its relationship to secular dignities might in part be the origin of the processional duties of four earls to precede the king bearing aloft swords, which we hear of as early as the reign of William Rufus (1087–1100). But some measure of the difficulty in disentangling the meaning behind the symbol can be found in the famous (and probably apocryphal) story of Earl John of Warenne's resistance to the *quo warranto* inquisition of 1288. The earl was supposed to have responded to the impertinence of a request for the warrant for his possessions by producing an ancient and rusty sword before the king and his barons, asserting: 'Look, my lords! This is my warrant!' Was he alluding to the sword of his county, or the means by which his ancestors had won such wealth at the Conquest?[43]

The non-royal image of power was a long-lasting one. The prince seated or standing with unsheathed sword in hand, point upward,

---

41 The effigy is known from at least two independent seventeenth-century antiquaries' drawings, see F. Sandford, *A Genealogical History of the Kings of England and Monarchs of Great Britain* (London, 1677), 17; and an earlier drawing from a MS in the Royal Library, Brussels, reproduced in E. Warlop, *The Flemish Nobility before 1300* (4 vols, Coutrai, 1975–6), i, pl. fac. 139. The effigy can be dated to the period of the third quarter of the twelfth century (perhaps the 1170s) by details of the armour, notably the early form of closed helm (fully developed by c.1190) and the shape of the shield (still embracing most of the body). The effigy as it was in the seventeenth century shows some evidence of later accretions, notably the angels who sit at the count's feet, which appear stylistically different, from the drawings at least.

42 For Earl Ranulf III's pleas in Cheshire, see *Charters of the Anglo-Norman Earls of Chester*, ed. G. Barraclough (Record Soc. of Lancashire and Cheshire, cxxvi, 1988), no. 282; for Count John of Mortain's pleas in Lancashire, see *The Coucher Book of Furness Abbey*, ed. J.C. Atkinson (3 vols, Chetham Soc., new ser., ix, xi, xiv, 1886–7), pt 3, 468.

43 *The Chronicle of Walter of Guisborough*, ed. H. Rothwell, (Camden Soc., 3rd ser., lxxxix, 1957), 216n. The same story is told of Earl Gilbert of Gloucester in the entry for the year 1295.

remained a basic image of secular power throughout the Middle Ages, although other precious items of regalia were later added to the picture. When French princes took to having themselves portrayed in state on their seals and coinage in the early fourteenth century, this is the image they chose.[44] It appears on the coins struck between 1362 and 1372 in the duchy of Aquitaine when Edward of Woodstock was its prince. On his gold coins Prince Edward is found either standing or seated, and in the majority of the depictions he has an unsheathed sword in his hand and a coronet of roses on his head.[45] In the fifteenth century, the clerk and panegyrist of the earls of Warwick, John Rous, still found it appropriate to depict many of the historical earls of Warwick bearing swords upright and unsheathed to depict their particular state (although by his time the prevailing artistic fashion meant that they had to be in plate armour too). Nonetheless the same basic image is there in Rous's Roll as may be found in the depiction of Geoffrey of Anjou, centuries before.[46] What had changed was that Rous only used this pose for earls. He distinguished dukes not by a sword, but by the sceptre and coronet that had since become part of their regalia.

However, the use of the sword in the language of symbols was rather more complicated than might so far seem. Although it is clear that by 1000 the sword had become a particular attribute of princely power, its use as an image was rather wider, and older. The Germanic past laid a foggy mystique over the importance of the sword. English, Franks, Scandinavians and Germans had long been given to consider that there was a magic in the blade. Swords were given names in *Beowulf* and in the German epics.[47] In the first French epic, the 'Song of Roland', Roland's sword had

44 The counterseal of Hugh V, duke of Burgundy, affixed to a deed of 1313 shows him precisely thus, including the seat flanked by lions, *Inventaire des sceaux de la Bourgogne*, 15, no. 64.
45 *Age of Chivalry: Art in Plantagenet England*, ed. J. Alexander and P. Binski (Royal Academy of Arts, 1987), nos. 618–21.
46 *The Rous Roll*, ed. C. Ross (Gloucester, 1980), particularly no. 54, Henry de Beauchamp, duke of Warwick. Two windows of *c*.1340–44 in the choir of Tewkesbury abbey depict eight of the abbey's greater advocates who had been buried within its walls: the founder, Robert fitz Hamo; Robert son of Henry I, earl of Gloucester; various earls of Gloucester of the Clare family; and Hugh Despenser. All hold spears in their right hands. The spear obviously has some significance, but since not all of those depicted were earls, it may be an allusion to their status as advocates of the abbey. The tombs of the advocates of Valle Crucis abbey also bear spears.
47 H.R. Ellis Davidson, *The Sword in Anglo-Saxon England* (Oxford, 1962), 146–55.

the name Durendaal. The mid-twelfth-century William of Orange cycle has Charlemagne give its hero his sword Joyeuse. The naming of swords gave them a personality, and not always a pleasant one. The 'Sword with the Strange Baldric' given Perceval by the Fisher King was destined to betray him in battle. It could be suggested that the naming of swords might have grown out of the manufacturers' names and other inscriptions which were being tempered into the fullers (central troughs) of blades by the early eleventh century.[48] Later owners of a good blade perhaps took the maker's name for the sword's own. But Durendaal's magical quality was attested by the fact that Roland's dying efforts were expended in attempting to shatter the blade so it might not fall into pagan hands. Interestingly, the statue of Roland incorporated into the orders of a door at Verona cathedral has the name +DVRINDARDA inscribed up the blade of his naked sword, as if it were the maker's name. Legend, as ever, had a way of intruding into real life. When John of Marmoutier in the 1160s gives an idealised account of the knighting of Geoffrey of Anjou by Henry I of England at Rouen in 1128, he notes that the sword the king gave the count had been made by the legendary smith, Weyland, whose workmanship was ascribed to tenth- and eleventh-century coats of mail and swords.[49] By the thirteenth century two of the royal swords of state in England had acquired names: Caliburn (that is, Arthur's Excalibur) and Curtana (the blunted sword of mercy).

But such mystique could not be confined to just kings and magnates. From the pages of Tacitus we know that young German warriors in the second century AD had marked their coming of age by publicly receiving shield and spear from a respected elder. This is the first reference to the 'delivery of arms', a descendant of which ceremony can be found amongst Frankish warriors in the ninth century. By then, at least, 'arms' had become 'horse and arms', and the particular equipment that distinguished the properly inducted mounted warrior of the eleventh and twelfth centuries were his sword, lance and shield. Peasants of that time, by contrast, were assumed never to carry weapons such as swords. Along with monks,

---

48 For names inlaid in blades see R.E. Oakeshott, 'An *Ingelri* Sword in the British Museum', *Archaeological Journal*, xxxi (1951), 69; Davidson, *The Sword in Anglo-Saxon England*, 45–8; I. Pierce, 'Arms, Armour and Warfare in the Eleventh Century', *Anglo-Norman Studies*, x (1987), 250–57. The suggestion about sword-names is mine. Twelfth-century romances refer to 'inscribed swords' as a commonplace.
49 Davidson, *The Sword in Anglo-Saxon England*, 155.

clerks and women, they were the 'unarmed masses' (*inermis plebs*).[50] In mid-twelfth-century England the phrase 'belted knight' implied a certain distinction in society.[51] But so far the symbolic accent is not on the sword, despite the importance of its belting to the knight in the ceremony of dubbing. The root of the phrase is to be looked for in the military belt (*cingulum militiae*), the golden belt that was the mark of a Roman soldier or civil servant. It was a phrase beloved of Carolingian and later writers to describe the state of a fully invested warrior. When such men retired to the cloister they are said to have done something like 'thrown off the military belt and taken on with joy the monastic habit'.[52] Conversely, if a noble clerk wished to leave his clerical orders, the ceremony of knighting was held to invalidate them.[53] The sword signified the calling of a soldier. The Bible provided a number of examples of this image. Did not the Evangelist preserve the promise that all who took up the sword should perish by it?[54] But we cannot see the sword as ever signifying the state of knighthood in such a particular way as it signified the state of a prince.

THE CORONET AND CAP

Headgear of one sort or another was being employed by princes as early as the ninth century. Some form of cap or circlet was universal amongst them throughout our period, although the use of these became more standardised towards the end of it. It is not always clear to me from where these princes took their inspiration, particularly in the use of gold circlets. The temptation is to see the use of a circlet as a borrowing from the royal crown, but I think

---

50 P. Guilhiermoz, *Essai sur la noblesse du moyen âge* (Paris, 1902), 185–7, 226, 380–1, 467n.

51 S. Harvey, 'The Knight and the Knight's Fee in England', *Past and Present*, no. 49 (1970), 29, 34.

52 Guilhiermoz, *Essai*, 446–9. See in particular the description of the entry of Herluin of Bec into the monastic life by Robert de Torigny, *Chronica*, in *Chronicles of the Reign of Stephen, Henry II and Richard I*, ed. R. Howlett, (4 vols, Rolls Series, 1884–9), iv, 26: ... *hoc anno*, cingulo militiae deposito, *ad Christi paupertatem tota devotione se contulit ... habitum monachalem cum gaudio suscepit*. Compare the words of a royal letter concerning the coming of age of Maurice fitz Gerald in 1217 who was 'girded by the belt of a knight' (*cingulo militis cinctus est*), *Rotuli Litterarum Clausarum*, i, 314.

53 J. Dunbabin, 'From Clerk to Knight: Changing Orders' in *The Ideals and Practice of Medieval Knighthood*, ii, ed. C. Harper-Bill and R. Harvey (Woodbridge, 1988), 26–39.

54 Matt. xxvi, 52.

this would be simplistic. Tellenbach was more inclined to look to Classical models, to the garlanded heads of Roman patricians, and this must certainly be one of the directions to consider, although not the only one.[55] A complicating observation is that crowns (*coronae*) were never perceived as for kings alone in the Middle Ages. Both the Bible and Roman Antiquity could give examples of their wider use. The twenty-four crowned elders of the Apocalypse were a vivid example, frequently before the eyes of literate and illiterate alike.[56] A garland and circlet played their part in the Triumph awarded to victorious generals of the Republic and Empire. This use of the crown was absorbed by early Christian society, the 'crown of life' awarded to the elect of Christ after conquering temptation and evil. A further influence was from Roman military life, where various 'military crowns' were awarded to soldiers for exploits of bravery or enterprise.[57] It is no surprise therefore to find the Latin word *corona* used for the headgear of rulers other than kings. In 876 the annals of St Bertin record that Charles the Bald paused at Pavia on the way back to France, and there he nominated his brother-in-law, Boso, as duke of Italy and placed a 'ducal crown' on his head (*duce ipsius terrae constituto et corona ducali ornato*).[58]

The precise nature of the ducal crown conferred on Boso is unknown. Indeed, we have no clear idea of what any princely gold circlet looked like until the very end of the twelfth century. Tellenbach, however, favoured the idea that princes and dukes of the Carolingian period, and later, would wear filets or garlands fashioned in metal, modelled on the Classical wreath worn by a military *imperator* or caesar. He based his conclusion on illustrations depicting a king in state in Carolingian bibles. To right and left of the diademed king stand the nobles, adorned in just such a Classical manner.[59] Otherwise, indications are very few. There are persistent eleventh-century hints that the rulers of Brittany had pretensions to quasi-royal insignia. One eleventh-century Breton writer pictured the ninth-century Breton ruler Salomon, called variously prince or

55 G. Tellenbach, 'Uber Herzogskronen und Herzogshüte im Mittelalter', *Deutsches Archiv für Geschichte des Mittelalters*, v (1942), 59–61.

56 Rev. iv, 4 .. *et super thronos viginti quatuor seniores sedentes, circumamicti vestimentis albis, et in capitibus eorum coronae aureae.*

57 Webster, *Roman Imperial Army*, 132–3: the *corona muralis, corona vallaris, corona obsidionalis* and *corona aurea.*

58 *Annales Bertiniani*, ed. G. Waitz (M.G.H., Scriptores rerum Germanicarum in usu scholarum, 1883), 128.

59 Tellenbach, 'Herzogskronen', 57–8.

duke (or sometimes king) of the Bretons, in royal state, and felt called upon to apologise for it: 'Salomon was called king, not because he was really a king, but because he wore a golden circlet and purple, by permission of the Emperor Charles (the Bald)'.[60] This pointed allusion to imperial consent for the use of regalia must have had a contemporary relevance for the writer. Referring back to the end of the tenth century, Ralph Glaber talks scathingly of the arrogance of Conan of Rennes, who assumed to himself a crown 'in the manner of a king'.[61] Sico, duke or prince of Benevento in the second quarter of the ninth century, was apparently accustomed to wear what a near-contemporary source called 'a sumptuous crown (*corona*) of fine gold and most precious gems', which he offered on the altar at his translation of the body of St Januarius to Benevento.[62] This sounds more like a royal diadem than anything else, but the princes of Benevento may have been a special case: Sico's predecessor, Arachis, had contemptuously defied Charlemagne in the late eighth century by having himself anointed and then wearing a crown, apparently intended to be royal rather than ducal.[63]

The eleventh and twelfth centuries do not give us many examples of princes and dukes wearing circlets. The sudden silence of the sources may be eloquent. Tellenbach amply illustrates that the German emperors at this time were still conferring crowns on inferiors, but the inferiors now were called kings, whether of Poland, Bohemia or Denmark, and not patricians and dukes.[64] By 1100, and for some time before, the gold crown can be regarded as we regard it today, as an exclusively royal attribute. The Breton examples rather stand alone. Both writers who mention them treat them gingerly. Ralph Glaber was scandalised that a Breton prince of the previous generation had assumed a diadem, and his anonymous contemporary at Rennes felt called upon to apologise for such a use. Banners and swords had become the attributes of counts, dukes and

---

60 *Vita Connuoionis*, in *The Monks of Redon*, ed. C. Brett (Woodbridge, 1989), 243; A late ninth-century Breton writer asserts that the Breton prince, Nominoe, sent a gold crown encrusted with gems as a gift to St Peter of Rome, *Gesta sanctorum Rotonensium*, ibid., 111.
61 *Historiarum Libri Quinque*, ed. J. France (Oxford, 1989), 58: *Nam more regio imposito sibi diademate . . .*
62 *Translatio SS. Januarii, Festi et Desiderii*, in *Acta Sanctorum*, Sept., vi (Antwerp, 1757), 490.
63 Hoffmann, 'Fürstenweihen', 94–5.
64 Tellenbach, 'Herzogskronen', 61–2. One should compare the comments of the Breton writer on Salomon, noted earlier. An eleventh-century writer by now assumed that the wearing of a crown was a claim to kingship.

princes. Such few exceptions as there are, are to make a point. A depiction of Duke Henry the Lion and his wife, Mathilda, daughter of Henry II of England, in a gospel book executed for him *c*.1188, shows both him and his wife receiving crowns from heavenly hands. That this indicates a coronation in progress is unlikely; commentators see it as a borrowing from the dedicatory pages of royal bibles of previous centuries, and the MS explicitly links these crowns with those awaiting the elect in Heaven.[65] Elsewhere however, Henry the Lion and his wife were depicted on their tombs in a demurely ducal style, Henry clasping the appropriate symbol of an upright sword.

The first firmly recorded use of a coronet, a lesser crown, in the period after 1000 by a lay magnate below the rank of king came in 1199 when John (not yet king) was crowned duke of Normandy in the cathedral of Rouen. The description by Roger of Howden pictures a whole coronation order for this occasion; doubtless the core of it was the *ordo* by which Richard was invested as duke ten years earlier. It was held only two weeks after news of the Lionheart's death reached the city, so an existing *ordo* would have met the need for haste. But to the conferring of a ring (and, according to another source, a banner), and the girding of a sword was added the coronation by a golden circlet (although without anointing). It is most likely that John was the first, as well as the last, duke of Normandy to be crowned in Rouen cathedral. The ducal investiture at Rouen in 1199 was held under the joint threat of Arthur of Brittany's pretensions and Philip Augustus's claims. It was most necessary at this time to reinforce the image of the duke of Normandy: a golden coronet would have met the need neatly. Of course, for most of the past 130 years the duke of Normandy had also been a king. This would allow such a duke a certain latitude in matters of trappings that other princes might not attempt.

Even though the duke of Normandy permitted himself a circlet in 1199, this did not mean that he did so too brazenly. It is significant that the word used for the bauble in question was 'garland' (Lat. *garlanda*, Fr. *gerlaunde*), not *corona* or *diadema*. The description of it leaves no doubt that the coronet of 1199 was devised in a fashion

---

65 F. Mütherich, 'Das Evangiliar Heinrichs des Löwen und die Tradition des mittelalterlichen Herrscherbildes', in *Das Evangiliar Heinrichs des Löwen und das mittelalterliche Herrscherbild* (Munich, 1986), pl. 28. Tellenbach, 'Herzogskronen', 63 does, however, point out the gem-encrusted circlet worn by Duke Wittukind on his tomb in the cathedral of Enger.

similar to a royal crown; both William of Newburgh and Roger of Howden describe it as 'a golden circlet having along the crest (*in summitate per circulum*) golden roses'.[66] This makes it resemble more the contemporary royal crown with its high points fashioned into lilies. For this reason, more than anything else perhaps, it was necessary that contemporaries should draw a delicate distinction between the royal crown and lesser diadems. The rose flower was not directly associated with royal power, in the way that the lily was by 1200.

The use of a coronet by the duke of Normandy was soon being emulated. An *ordo* for the investiture of a duke of Aquitaine was composed in 1218 by the precentor of the cathedral of Limoges.[67] The *ordo* was probably never used, and may never have been more than a bid by the chapter of Limoges to stress its status as a ducal investiture church in the aftermath of the destruction of the integrity of the duchy by the Capetians. It is nonetheless significant. As in the ducal investiture of Richard in 1172, there is the conferring of a sword and banner, and a ring, the ring of St Valeria (although the part played by the clergy of Poitiers in 1172 is edited out in 1218). But the writer of the Aquitainian *ordo* adds from the Norman *ordo* the coronation with what is again called a 'garland', a golden *circulus*.

Brittany was another eventual imitator of Normandy. The surviving Breton coronation order from Rennes cathedral is of fifteenth-century date, but it incorporates some features, including the use of a circlet, which might well date back through the centuries in a number of recensions.[68] Certainly, as discussed above, the Bretons were employing a sword and banner in investitures by the time of Duke John I (who succeeded to the duchy in 1237). Otherwise, if we are to link the Breton dukes with coronets we must leap back to Conan of Rennes in the late tenth century, as we have seen. Conan's use of a circlet may have been, however, a survival of a Carolingian privilege accorded to the prince, Salomon. The use of a coronet by

66 William of Newburgh, *Historia rerum Anglicarum*, in *Chronicles of the Reigns of Stephen, Henry II and Richard* (4 vols, Rolls Series, 1886), ii, 504.
67 *Recueil des historiens des Gaules et de la France*, ed. M. Bouquet *et al.* (24 vols, Paris, 1869–1904), xii, 451.
68 F. Fery-Hue, 'Le Cérémonial du couronnement des ducs de Bretagne au xve. siècle édition', in *Questions d'Histoire de Bretagne* (Paris, Comité des Travaux historiques et scientifiques, 1984), 252–3. The earliest chronicle reference to a duke of Brittany's coronation is to that of Francis I in 1442. The Breton *ordo* does however contain several resemblances to the prayers of a French royal *ordo* of the thirteenth century, and in the coronation itself to the Aquitainian *ordo*. I must thank Professor Michael Jones for his help in this.

the fourteenth-century dukes must be a distinct development, owing nothing to that remote custom; an imitation of the ducal insignia of Brittany's neighbours.[69]

Of all places, Gloucester in the mid-thirteenth century has some significance in the history of the ducal coronet. At some time around 1250 the abbey of St Peter there had a wooden effigy carved to place over the tomb of its then most distinguished corpse, the remains of Robert Curthose, duke of Normandy (1087–1106). The duke had died in prison at Cardiff in 1134 and been entombed in a site fitting to his rank, before the high altar, where his remains still lie. The effigy executed over a century later is a typical military one, except that around the flat helmet is a coronet, as one would by then expect for a duke. Opinion is divided as to the original form of this coronet, because the effigy was broken up in the Civil War and later reassembled, then restored at various times. But that there was a coronet around the helmet before the seventeenth century is clear.[70]

Gloucester saw another episode in the history of the coronet when, in 1240, Henry III bestowed on his nephew, Dafydd ap Llywelyn, prince of Gwynedd, what was called the 'lesser diadem', the *garlanda*, described by the Tewkesbury annalist as 'the insignia of the principality of Gwynedd'.[71] This episode has already been discussed in Chapter 1, where it was interpreted as a recognition by the king of the superior status of the princes of Gwynedd. He raised them publicly by the employment of the same regalia as the duke of Normandy had used to the position of *dux et princeps*. The

69 It is worth noting that the tomb effigy of Duke John V of Brittany (1364–99) in the cathedral of Nantes depicted the duke in armour, a coronet around his bascinet, see Adhémar and Dordor, 'Les Tombeaux', i, 173, no. 970. Furthermore, the pretender, Duke Charles (1341–64) pointedly included coronets on his copper and gold coinage, whether ensigning a monogram of *Bretannia* or adorning a depiction of himself, see F. Poey d'Avant, *Monnaies Féodales de France* (3 vols, Graz, 1961), i, no. 415 (pl. 12, no. 17), no. 463 (pl. 14, no. 16). Two imaginary fifteenth-century portrayals of Count Alan of Brittany, receiving the earldom of Richmond from the Conqueror, and receiving his barons, signify him by a golden coronet and banner, Register of the Honor of Richmond, Brit. Libr., ms Cott. Faustina, B vii, fo. 72v. This probably tells us more about the state of a contemporary fifteenth-century earl than a twelfth-century Breton duke.

70 For contrasting views on the coronet see *Age of Chivalry*, no. 2 (an anachronism of the restoration), and no. 390 (altered). As it is now, the coronet has alternate roses, pearls and fleurs-de-lis. Anachronism is no ground to dismiss the placing of a coronet on a ducal head in the thirteenth century.

71 *Annales de Theokesburia*, s.a. 1240, in *Annales Monastici*, ed. Luard, i, 115: . . . *et ibidem portavit praedictus David diadema minus quod dicitur garlande, insigne principatus Northwallia.*

use of the same word, 'garland', in 1240 as Howden fixed on when talking of John's coronation in 1199 is significant also. Again there was a scrupulous insistence that a crown was not being conferred, but something inferior. Crown-wearing in the house of Gwynedd may perhaps have been older than the 1240 episode. That a coronet was seen as the 'insignia of the principality of Gwynedd' at that time implies that it had already been used by at least one earlier prince. It may be significant that amongst the fragments of sculptured stone found amongst the ruins of Prince Llywelyn ab Iorwerth's early thirteenth-century castle of Degannwy was one depicting a head surmounted by a coronet of fleurs-de-lis and high points. Similarly, the artist who embellished the Latin text of the Welsh Laws in the early thirteenth century saw nothing odd in depicting a Welsh ruler crowned and enthroned. Perhaps we should see Prince Dafydd's father, the great Llywelyn, as the originator of the coronet of the house of Gwynedd; he was also probably the first Welsh prince to embrace heraldry, and the first to build castles on a princely scale (see below, pp. 241–2, 227–8).

Crown-wearing continued within the dynasty of Gwynedd. When Edward I seized the treasury of his fallen enemy, Llywelyn ap Gruffudd, a golden circlet (*aureola*) was amongst the jewels. Welsh poets tell us that Llywelyn had worn just such an object on occasions of state. The king offered Llywelyn's jewels to the shrine of the Confessor at Westminster in 1284 as a thank offering for his conquest of Wales.[72] When, half a century later, Edward of Woodstock was invested as prince of Wales before

72 *Annales de Waverleia, s.a.* 1284, in *Annales Monastici*, ed. Luard, ii, 401; *Annales de Wigornia, s.a.* 1284, ibid, iv, 490; *Flores Historiarum*, ed. H.R. Luard (3 vols, Rolls Series, 1890), iii, 61. Llywelyn's gold circlet (*talaith*) was also referred to in the elegy composed after his death by the poet, Gruffudd ab yr Ynad Coch:

    Bright gold was bestowed by his hand,
    He deserved his gold diadem.

1282: A Collection of Documents, ed. R. Griffiths (National Library of Wales, 1986), 32.The dispersal of Prince Llywelyn's treasure is discussed by R.R. Davies, *Age of Conquest* (Oxford, 1991), 355–6. The head of Llywelyn was spiked at the Tower of London, it was mockingly, but significantly crowned with a wreath of ivy, to fulfil a prophecy of Merlin that one day a prince of Wales would be crowned in London, *Annales Monastici*, ii, 398; iv, 486. A later (early fourteenth-century) source, Walter of Guisborough, has Llywelyn's head paraded on a spear down Cheapside 'crowned with a silver circlet in the manner of a prince (*apposita serta argentea in signum principis*)'. According to Walter, Llywelyn had consulted a witch, who told had him that one day he would ride crowned along Cheapside, and Llywelyn had taken this as a sign he would one day be king of England, see *The Chronicle of Walter of Guisborough*, ed. Rothwell, 221.

Parliament in 1343, a chaplet (*sertum*) was employed along with a golden ring and a silver rod, and it is an intriguing suggestion that the chaplet might have been the very *aureola* of his predecessor, Llywelyn, recovered from Westminster abbey. For the investiture was said to have been made 'according to custom'.[73]

What was the shape of these British princely coronets? The use of the word *sertum* in 1343 to signify a coronet recalls the 'garland' of a century before and the ninth-century *Patrizienszirkelen* of Tellenbach. In 1199, the garland used by the duke of Normandy is described in terms reminiscent of a royal crown, with high points of roses rather than lilies. The coronet adorning the helmet of Robert Curthose's effigy at Gloucester, as it now is, looks much the same. In the case of the Norman garland of 1199, it is undeniable that some allusion to royalty was intended; it looked like a royal crown and was bestowed by an archbishop in a recognised investiture church to the chanting of clerks. Henry III did not think it beneath his dignity to wear a lighter circlet called a *garlanda* in his private chambers at Westminster, when he took off his royal crown.[74]

It is interesting to see just how careful lesser princes were in the portrayal of their headgear on their coins and seals. A good example can be found in the coin issues of numerous Continental princes of the Low Countries between the 1270s and the 1300s. Westphalia, Holland and Flanders formed part of a sterling currency area at that time; the result of the thriving English wool trade.[75] The dukes of Hainault, Lorraine and Brabant, the counts of Flanders, Luxembourg, Loos and Holland, and the castellans of Herstal, Agimont and Hornes, all issued pennies modelled on those of Henry III and Edward I. But whereas Henry and Edward wore standard issue royal crowns with trefoils, all the Continental princes took care to appear either

---

73 *The Fifth Report from the Lords Committees touching the Dignity of a Peer of the Realm* (London, 1829), 43–4.

74 The point is reinforced by Matthew Paris, *Chronica Majora*, ed. H.R. Luard (7 vols, Rolls Series, 1872–83), iv, 644. He describes Henry III retiring after a solemn celebration at Westminster to a side chamber, and changing into a rich brocade robe 'and the coronet (*coronula*) which is commonly called the garland (*garlanda*)' in order to knight William de Valence, his half-brother, and other aspirants.

75 N.J. Mayhew, 'The Circulation and Imitation of Sterlings in the Low Countries', in *Coinage in the Low Countries (880–1500): The Third Oxford Symposium on Coinage and Monetary History*, ed. N.J. Mayhew (British Archeological Reports, International Series, no. 54, 1979), 56–7.

Figure 5 Antiquary's sketch of seal of Robert, count of Meulan and earl of Leicester (died 1118). The original was until recently in Keele University Library.

bare-headed, or to wear a wreath or band, decorated with roses (Fig. 7).[76]

By the fourteenth century, there had been a slow but steady elaboration in the depiction of princely state. If we contrast the eleventh-century image of non-royal state as exemplified by Duke William or Count Guy of Ponthieu on the Bayeux Tapestry with the corresponding fourteenth-century image, we see the degree of change. Duke William in the 1070s was shown bare-headed when he was not in his military gear. It is quite otherwise with his seven-times great-grandson, Edward of Woodstock, three centuries later. The gold coins struck in the name of Prince Edward (the Black Prince) in Aquitaine between 1362 and 1372, and his great seal in use after 1362, show him indeed in something the same princely state as his ancestor; as does also the obverse 'majesty' side of his great seal

76 J. Chautard, *Monnaies au type esterlin frappées en Europe pendant le xiiie et le xive siècle* (Nancy, 1871), pls. 2, 4–5, 8, 11–14, 16–17, 31.

as prince of Wales and Aquitaine. The basic pose is still there, but there have been additions. Coins and seal alike have the prince with a coronet of some sort, whether a plain circlet or one formed of four flowers, probably roses, that is, the garland. Such, according to Walter of Guisborough, was the proper sign of a prince.[77] The prince also bears on seal and some coins a new piece of insignia for England, a ducal sceptre, topped with a fleur-de-lis.[78]

If we are to find the origins of this elaborate Anglo-French image of the Black Prince, it must be compared to contemporary and earlier ducal images from the great French principalities. A gold *écu* of Duke Eudes IV of Burgundy (1315–50) and a gold *royal* of Charles de Blois, pretender to Brittany (1341–64) bear similar (standing) images. Duke Eudes has a chaplet of roses much the same as that later attributed to the Black Prince, and bears a sceptre topped with a fleur-de-lis. Duke Charles wears a coronet of four high points of fleur-de-lis, and also has a sceptre.[79] If we look further back, the late thirteenth- and early fourteenth-century civilian effigies on tombs of younger members of the royal house of France once in the churches of St-Louis and Notre-Dame at Poissy demonstrate that insignia of a sceptre and chaplet, or coronet with high points, was thought not inappropriate to a king's son around 1300. And Philip and John, sons of Louis VIII (1223–6) and Robert, son of Philip IV (1284–1314), did not live to be duke or count.[80] These juvenile Capetians had the excuse of royal blood, but the same was not true of the many dukes, counts, dauphins and even castellans of France who affected the chaplet before 1300.

In Britain, before 1300, only the prince of Gwynedd had been in a position to assume a princely coronet, and the dynasty had gone down in war in 1282. But the creation of dukes in England in the fourteenth century changed this situation. In 1362, at the

77 *Chronicle of Walter of Guisborough*, ed. Rothwell, 221.
78 W. de Gray Birch, *Catalogue of Seals in the Department of Manuscripts in the British Museum* (6 vols, London, 1887–1900), ii, 221, no. 5551; Sandford, *Genealogical History*, 125.
79 Poey d'Avant, *Monnaies* i, no. 463 (pl. 14, no. 16); iii, no. 5686 (pl. 131, no. 19). Other contemporary seal-effigies of French dukes approximate the Black Prince's image, as on the great seal of John, duke of Berry of c.1377–80 (standing under a canopy wearing chaplet and bearing a sceptre) and Louis II, duke of Bourbon of c.1380 (standing and bearing an unsheathed sword upright in his right hand), see *Les Fastes du Gothique: Le siècle de Charles V* (Paris, 1981), nos. 352, 353, pp. 411–12.
80 Adhémar and Dordor, 'Les Tombeaux', i, 53, no. 28 (Philip and John of France); 102, no. 543 (Robert son of Philip IV).

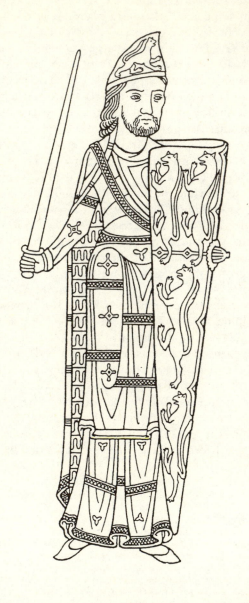

Figure 6 Drawing from the funeral enamel of Count Geoffrey of Anjou (died 1151).

Figure 7   Varieties of coronet as depicted on thirteenth-century coins and tomb effigies. Such coronets are probably what were meant by the 'garland' of Normandy or the 'talaith' of Gwynedd.

investitures of his sons, John of Gaunt as duke of Lancaster, and Lionel of Antwerp as duke of Clarence, Edward III established that English dukes were thereafter to have caps and coronets as their permitted regalia, and creations later in the century added golden sceptres to this insignia. When the first English marquis was created in 1385, he too was allowed the insignia of a gold circlet, although not a cap.[81] As we can now see, the 'custom' by which both English dukes and marquises were being invested with such insignia was an older, Continental model (something that has not been evident to English writers on the subject).

The cap, the *pileus*, often called the 'cap of maintenance' was not a new element in the ducal insignia. The inspiration seems to have been ultimately ecclesiastical, although I am uncertain whether some reference was being made to the episcopal and abbatial mitre, or to the *pileus* of a lesser dignitary, *magister* or canon. Geoffrey of Anjou's funerary enamel shows him wearing a rich embroidered cap, rather like a Phrygian cap. Embroidered and gemmed caps, not unlike mitres, were commonly to be found on the heads of German princes in the twelfth and thirteenth centuries.[82] Something of the same thing can be found in France. The civilian tomb effigy of Count

81 For ducal and marchisal investitures in England in the fourteenth century, see W.H. St John Hope, 'The Cap of Maintenance' in *English Coronation Records*, ed. L.G. Wickham Legg (Westminster, 1901), pp. lxxxii–lxxxviii.
82 Tellenbach, 'Herzogskronen', 65–8; Schmidt, *Malerschule von St Florian*, pl. 3(a).

Robert III of Dreux (died 1233) at St-Yved-de-Braine showed him wearing a cap similar to a canon's; but as yet I have not found other such French images.[83] Caps of state are rarely to be met with in England before 1300. A mid-thirteenth-century effigy found in the ruins of Ramsey abbey, which may represent either St Aethelbert or St Aethelred, martyred members of an Anglo-Saxon royal family, is carefully portrayed bearing a rod and wearing a round cap.[84] But tall caps formed of rich cloth, lined with ermine, were very much the fashion amongst the great of England by the mid-fourteenth century. The inspiration seems to have been Continental, perhaps an importation from the Low Countries. Insignia of combined hat and coronet such as the dukes of Clarence and Lancaster had bestowed upon them by Edward III compare directly with the headgear affected by the dukes of Austria as early as the late thirteenth century.

In the absence of dukes in England before 1337, earls seem to have felt entitled to take up coronets upon their own account; their dignity may well have seemed enough to them to do so. Until the second quarter of the fourteenth century the title of count was considered sufficient for a king's son in both England and France. The first English earl to be found with a gold circlet was Aymer de Valence, not a member of the royal family, simply a son of the uterine brother of Henry III. In the inventory of his chattels submitted by his treasurer to the Exchequer after his death in 1324 (a document seen by Selden in the seventeenth century) is a reference to 'a gold crown' (*corona aurea*). It might possibly have been a piece of Earl Aymer's wife's jewellery, but it is far more likely to have been his own coronet.[85] The tomb effigy in Westminster abbey of John of Eltham, earl of Cornwall and son of Edward II, constructed a year or two after the earl died in 1336, has him as a knight with a jewelled circlet of roses and trefoils around his helmet.[86] On his seal, the helm of William Montagu, earl of Salisbury (1337–44) was depicted topped by a coronet of flowers between pearls; William had no connection whatsoever with the royal family.[87]

83 Adhémar and Dordor, 'Les Tombeaux', i, 36, no. 151.
84 *Age of Chivalry*, no. 22.
85 J. Selden, *Titles of Honor* (2nd edn, London, 1631), 680.
86 L. Southwick, 'The Armoured Effigy of Prince John of Eltham in Westminster Abbey and some closely related Military Monuments', *Church Monuments*, ii (1987), 9–21. His tomb set a fashion, but none of its derivatives is adorned by a coronet.
87 W.H. St John Hope, *Heraldry for Craftsmen and Designers* (London, 1913), pl. xii(a).

By the mid-fourteenth century it seems to have been common for English earls to possess one or more golden coronets. By his will of 1375 Richard fitz Alan, earl of Arundel, left his best coronet to his son, to descend successively to the earls after him. But he had another two circlets, which he left to his daughters.[88] In 1380 the earl of March left to his daughter 'a coronet (*coronal*) of gold with jewellery and 200 large pearls, and also a coronet with roses in emeralds, and rubies of Alexandria in the roses'.[89] Michael de la Pole, earl of Suffolk, in his testament of 1415 mentions that he possessed a coronet (*diademata*) which had belonged to his father-in-law, the earl of Stafford, who had died in 1386.[90] Yet these earls' coronets could only have been worn in private state. It was not until Henry VI created Henry de Beauchamp premier earl of England that an earl was allowed the privilege of wearing a coronet alongside the dukes (and marquises) in the king's presence.[91] In Scotland there is, as ever, little evidence. However, it is interesting to find that Agnes, countess of Dunbar and Moray, had depicted on her seal (affixed to a deed of 1367) a design of coronets interspersed with shields.[92]

THE SCEPTRE OR ROD

When English princes and dukes appeared in the fourteenth century, they acquired as part of their insignia a silver or golden rod (*virga*), as we learn from the descriptions of their investitures and the depictions of dukes in the late fifteenth-century roll of John Rous. The use of the sceptre was in imitation of the sceptres in much earlier use by Continental dukes and princes, and indeed by the prince of Wales. The earliest written description associated with the Anglo-Norman world that I have noted was the rod (*virga*) borne in 1128 by Sybil, wife of the Norman prince of Tarragona, Robert Burdet, as token of her lordship over the city in her husband's absence.[93] A casual mention by Chrétien de Troyes of one of his counts carrying a *verge* as he rode about his city may indicate that some form of rod was a recognised item of insignia of counts in the

88 W. Dugdale, *The Baronage of England* (3 vols, London, 1675–6), i, 317–18.
89 J. Nichols, *A Collection of all the Wills now known to be extant of the Kings and Queens of England* (London, 1780), 114.
90 *The Register of Henry Chichele, Archbishop of Canterbury, 1414–43*, ed. E.F. Jacob and H.C. Johnston (4 vols, Canterbury and York Soc., 1937–47), ii, 58–9.
91 St John Hope, *Heraldry for Craftsmen and Designers*, 273–5.
92 W.R. Macdonald, *Scottish Armorial Seals* (Edinburgh, 1904), 284, no. 2251.
93 Orderic Vitalis, *The Ecclesiastical History*, ed. M. Chibnall (6 vols, Oxford, 1969–80), vi, 404.

1170s.[94] It depends how *verge* is translated (might it not in this case
– as one translator has suggested – have been just a riding-switch?).
Elsewhere I have mentioned the depiction of a late twelfth-century
German landgraf with a trefoil-headed sceptre in his hand. There
is also the example of the investiture by King William of Sicily of
his son Bohemond with the duchy of Apulia in 1182 with a golden
sceptre (*per aureum sceptrum quod in manu gerebat*).[95] Later on, in
France, we find Alice, duchess of Brittany, depicted with a sceptre
in her hand on her tomb at Villeneuve-lès-Nantes, which appears
to have dated to the later thirteenth century (although in fact she
died in 1221).[96] The effigies of the early fourteenth-century Capetian
cadets buried at Notre-Dame-de-Poissy bear sceptres topped with
a fleur-de-lis. Coin evidence of the early fourteenth century, which
has already been referred to, shows that the use of sceptres was by
then widespread amongst French and German princes. Edward III
in 1343 could consider that it was customary that his son, the prince
of Wales, as a prince, should bear a silver rod, and depictions of it
on coins and seal has it too topped with a lily. The rod conferred on
John of Gaunt in 1390 on his investiture as duke of Guyenne was,
however, gold, as was the rod given his son Henry of Bolingbroke
on his investiture as duke of Hereford in 1397.[97]

It is a little difficult to know what word to use for this particular piece of insignia when carried by princes: sceptre or rod?
Contemporaries themselves are unresolved in their usage. But
in royal coronation *ordines* of the tenth century and later the
rod (*virga*) and sceptre (*sceptrum*) are distinct regalia with their
individual significance and place in the ritual.[98] Indeed the sceptre
is referred to explicitly in the English *ordo* of the twelfth century
as 'the sign of royal power' (*regie potestatis insigne*). An occasional,
and rather literary, Latin synonym for 'king' in medieval writings is
sceptifer. A view of the superiority of the sceptre to other forms of

---

94 *Erec et Enide*, ed. M. Roquez (Classiques francaişes du moyen âge, 1952).
ll. 801–4.
95 Robert de Torigny, *Chronica*, in *Chronicles*, iv, 303.
96 Adhémar and Dordor, 'Les Tombeaux', i, 65 no. 323.
97 St John Hope, 'The Cap of Maintenance', pp. lxxxiii–lxxxiv.
98 P.E. Schramm, *A History of the English Coronation*, trans. L.G. Wickham
Legg (Oxford, 1937), 20. Compare the views on the coronation of the Conqueror
expressed in *The Carmen de Hastingae Proelio of Guy, Bishop of Amiens*, ed. C.
Martin and H. Muntz (Oxford, 1972), ll. 783–6: 'After the diadem he prepared
the sceptre (*sceptrum*) and the rod (*virga*) which alike symbolise the weal of the
realm; for by the sceptre the tossing reins of the kingdom are controlled, and the
rod gathers and recalls.'

insignia is to be found in the writings of Geoffrey Gaimar in the 1140s. When he describes the crown-wearing of William Rufus at Westminster in 1099, he has a charming story of the earl of Chester grandly declining to carry a sword before the king, as beneath his dignity, but being satisfied with the higher status of carrying the royal sceptre. The sceptre-bearer in twelfth- and thirteenth-century coronations was selected on the grounds of particular royal favour; it was not awarded as a hereditary privilege. The eminent warrior, William Marshal, bore the sceptre at the coronation of Richard in 1189; in 1236 another famous soldier, Sir Richard Siward, bore the sceptre for Queen Eleanor.

The object carried by princes is sometimes called sceptre although more frequently it is a rod (*virga*). Its status is even more confused in that its origins might well be independent of the royal rod, in a staff of some sort, supposed to represent the power of a Germanic elder or magistrate. A duke of Bavaria, Henry the Wrangler (died 995), is depicted with such a staff on the dedicatory page of a contemporary bible.[99] The later twelfth-century Beaumont tombs once in Préaux abbey in Normandy depicted similar staffs in the hands of the patriarch of the family Roger de Beaumont and his brother. The batons of Roman tribunes and centurions was another source of inspiration for *virgae*, along with the Biblical God-given staffs of prophets and elders such as Moses and Aaron.[100] But there was also, inevitably and unmistakably, an element of borrowing from – and confusion with – the royal sceptre. The depictions of such objects in the hands of twelfth- and thirteenth-century princes give them heads of fleur-de-lis just like royal sceptres. *Virgae* in royal regalia, on the other hand, were longer objects, and if they were headed at all, they were topped by a bird, to represent the Holy Spirit.

Although the royal sceptre was then the clear model for princely rods, the word *sceptrum* was, it seems, generally and coyly avoided for the object if it was not in the hands of a king. The use of the Latin word *virga* (Fr. *verge*) in the description of the investiture of the Black Prince in 1343, rather than *sceptrum*, must be deliberate;

99 *Evangeliar Heinrichs des Löwen*, pl. 5.
100 Exod. iv, 17: *Virgam quoque hanc sume in manu tua, in qua facturus es signa.* Num. xvii, 2, also had some significance for the use of *virga*. The Lord commanded Moses to take *virgae* from each of the twelve *principes* of the houses of Israel. However, there is an ambiguity in this passage if it is taken to demonstrate *virgae* as symbols of princely authority, for God meant them to be used as a means of selecting a priestly caste. The royal coronation order evoked a more pointed passage from Ps. xliv, 7: *virga directionis virga regni tui*.

for when we see executions of it, it is indistinguishable from the royal sceptre. Like *garlanda* in relation to *corona*, *virga* was a word which did not directly invoke royal state (indeed, the same word was used for the baton which was the badge of office of officers such as seneschals and marshals).

THE IMAGE OF THE PRINCE

Out of this glittering, medieval confusion of gold, gems, silver and silk emerges, in the end, a remarkably consistent image of princely power: the prince seated above his men, invested with robes, cap or coronet, sceptre or sword. It was a European image as much as a British one. In England, France and Germany artists and writers all paid homage to the idea of the prince, the duke or the count exalted above his men as a great lord above other men.

It is to contemporary writers that we turn for the rounded and expounded explanation of the enthroned prince. Understandably, kings and bishops occupy them more, but occasionally they can oblige. The romance 'Guy of Warwick' depicts the legendary Earl Roalt of Warwick holding high feast at Whitsun in the castle from which he took his name. Here came earls, barons, lords and ladies of many lands about his own. With them he heard mass in his great church and processed back to his great hall to hold a banquet, seated above the rest, apart from them on his dais. Gold, silver, silk, castles, cities and knights were his in abundance. Of Roalt you could say, as the same romance says of another of the counts it depicts in state, Florent of Brabant: 'full well did he seem the lord of a great land'.[101]

The prince in state was as seductive and useful an image as the king in state. Indeed, since in France patronage was in the hands of princes as much as the king, it was as well for writers to have a stock image by which to glorify the lesser potentate. Baudrey de Bourgeuil, archbishop of Dol, in writing verses around 1100 describing scenes on an embroidery very like that known as the Bayeux Tapestry, depicts Duke William in state in Normandy.

> William himself sitting in an exalted place,
> Orders the court to sit, as was proper according to
> custom.

101 *Gui de Warewic, roman du xiiie siecle*, ed. A. Ewart (2 vols, Classiques français du moyen âge, 1932), i, pp.2, 6–7; ii, p.7.

> After the throng of elders and youths fell into a
>   hushed silence,
> Speaking as befitted a ruler he said . . .[102]

The duke sat alone, his men about him. As we know from the
tapestry, its designer thought that it was proper for a chair of state
to be set aside for him above the others, complete with footstool.
Every time such a chair appears in the tapestry, whether a king, duke
or count is occupying it, it features lions' heads, recalling the lions
of justice which flanked the seat of Solomon. Intimate counsellors
might, sometimes, be allowed to seat themselves on the chair beside
him (in fact this may indicate that what we are seeing is not so much
a throne as the bed of state, as set up in the palaces of the kings of
France and England in the mid-thirteenth century). Others stood
until informed they might sit; all fell reverently silent as the duke
spoke. For he too was a man consecrated into his position, solemnly
invested in his state. Until at least the time of Philip Augustus it was
not unheard of to acknowledge that such and such a man was duke
or count *dei gratia*, by God's grace.[103]

So the basis of a universal image formed, which was slowly
elaborated over our period. Before 1300 such rulers would occasionally be depicted as seated on their thrones wearing coronets,
and wielding sceptres as often as swords. By at least 1400 canopies
of state of brocade and cloth-of-gold were erected above great dukes
and their thrones, as in the depictions of the dukes of Brittany and
Bourbon in King René's tournament book, and their servants are
depicted kneeling, hats doffed, before them.[104] Three centuries after
the Bayeux Tapestry, after the end of our period, Froissart preserves
a vivid picture of the court of Gaston-Phoebus, count of Foix at
Orthez in 1388, and it is not so very different from that we find
in the stylised scenes of the tapestry and the writings of Baudrey
de Bourgeuil. Again, the solemn celebration of the great feasts, the
count seated apart from his retinue and only addressed by them

---

102 *Adelae Comitissae*, trans. Herren, 169, ll. 262–5.
103 Dr Maurice Keen has pointed out to me that a duke like John IV of Britanny
took up the style *dei gratia* once again in the fourteenth century in order to stress
his independence from the crown of France, see J. Le Patourel, 'King and Princes
in Fourteenth-Century France', in *Europe in the Late Middle Ages*, ed. J.R. Hale
et al. (London,1965), 165.
104 F. Avril, *Le Livre des tournois du Roi René* (Paris, 1986), pls. 1–2. Perhaps
some of the inspiration for these canopies was the Gothic niches in which crowned
and sceptred dukes might be depicted on their great seals.

when he began the conversation, his prestige so great that many of his court believed he had supernatural powers.

More non-literary evidence of such scenes of princely state is to be found in the earlier time. We know of the grand progress which a Norman count, Waleran of Meulan, made about his estates in 1155, attended by bishops and abbots and by lesser lords who were allied with him (although they were not his dependants). He was received and fêted in the abbeys that his family had founded, and held the great feasts of Easter and Whitsun at his own castles. In the next century we can assume there was a scene of comital state at Hanley castle in 1250, when Earl Richard de Clare knighted two of his tenants; it was sufficiently splendid for the neighbouring abbey of Tewkesbury to note the event in its chronicle.[105] Some years later, we hear of the chair that was set aside for the great earl, Simon de Montfort, in the hall of his chief seat, Kenilworth castle: the chair in which he would have sat in judgement or in state.[106] Almost in passing, an early fourteenth-century inquest tells us that the earl of Warwick had been long accustomed to celebrate the high feasts of the church at Christmas, Easter and Whitsun at his castle of Warwick, his hunting lodge of Sutton Coldfield or his halls of Claverdon or Tanworth-in-Arden. The earl would summon to these occasions his great officers and followers to wait and attend on him, just like the legendary Roalt, his predecessor.[107] So much was expected of the great man. At such occasion earls and counts could be seen acting out the part that society prescribed for them: living up to the image.

This chapter has dealt with the choice pieces of insignia which were generally reserved for the great man. As such they were tools of social definition. No knight would wear a coronet or wield a rod (save if he were a steward or officer of a great man's hall). Banners defined the magnate, as I have already noted. Coronets were appropriate only to the highest of the titled aristocracy (it was

105 *Annales de Theokesberia*, in *Annales Monastici*, ed. Luard, i, 142.
106 *The Chronicle of William de Rishanger of the Baron's War* ed. J.O. Haliwell (Camden Soc., xv, 1840), 87. One of the miracles of Simon de Montfort was the curing from a nasty case of gout of the rector of Sapcote who sat in this seat a short time after the earl's death at Evesham. My thanks to Dr David Carpenter for this reference.
107 *Calendar of Inquisitions post mortem, 1216–1307* (4 vols, PRO, 1898–1913), vii, no. 417. The reference comes in a record of the service owed by the earl's hereditary butler: because of the places it names, and the family history of the butler in question, the service can be dated back to the twelfth century.

not until the seventeenth century that the English baron obtained a coronet of his own). Rods of precious metal were reserved for even higher ranks; denied to the English earl by the fourteenth century, and eventually denied the English duke also in the sixteenth. The sword, held *so*, was reserved for the count, earl or duke before the end of the twelfth century.

Here we invoke again the name of Georges Duby, whose essay on cultural diffusion has created a useful scalpel in the historical laboratory. I have no intention of disputing Duby's chief argument that in medieval society many of the attributes of the aristocratic life-style derived ultimately from the king, and that they travelled down the social scale.[108] One only has to look at the late eleventh-century princely image, as I have presented it, to see that much of it was an adaptation of the image of tenth-century Germano-French kingship. The Byzantine orb was the only item of regalia that was not borrowed or somehow modified for princely use. Moreover, in the case of the use of coronets, it is demonstrable that at least in England their use descended in the classic mechanism described by Duby, from the ultimate model, the diadem of the king, to the prince, to the duke and to the earl. At the end of the seventeenth century, coronets would descend even further down the scale, to viscounts and barons. No wonder that kings were forced to further elaborations of their regalia to accommodate the pressure from below. The royal crown of England under Henry V (1413–22) was enclosed by arches, in imitation of that of the emperor, to produce the so-called 'imperial crown'. Was this a propaganda coup to boost the image of English monarchy by indulging in a little downward diffusion from the model of the emperor? Or was it also the adoption of a form more easily distinguished from the open crowns of earlier centuries which were then being affected by princes, dukes, and even counts?

The proof that what we are witnessing amongst the aristocracy is a result of social aspiration (rather than the result of what a widening variety of sources reveals to us of contemporary attitudes) lies in the *language* of the change. A good example is the downward progress of the use of heraldry through the ranks of the aristocracy. It was characterised by the visual language of punning and flattery. Men took such aristocratic symbols often in a joking fashion, or in

---

108 G. Duby, 'The Diffusion of Cultural Patterns in Feudal Society', in *The Chivalrous Society*, trans. C. Postan (London, 1977), 175-6.

imitation of a great local lord. They edged into the use of them defensively and uneasily. Similarly, the downward progress of the sceptre and the coronet has something of the same uneasiness: from the twelfth century onwards words like 'sceptre' and 'crown' were avoided by the imitators because they had unambiguous royal associations. Instead titled magnates had 'coronets', 'garlands' and 'rods' (some effort – albeit inconsistent – was made to make aristocratic coronets look different from royal crowns, giving them the appearance of garlands of flowers). Sometimes, as in the case of the use of a ducal coronet, we can find the source of a new practice in one particularly adventurous prince (in this case the duke of Normandy), whom others then copied, once he had got away with it. The peculiar timidity with which symbols of power might be taken up may well stand as a moral exemplum on the fragility of the ambitions to which these potentates were victim.

However, it is necessary to inject some caution into the use of Duby's model. I said at the beginning of this chapter that the use of aristocratic insignia was incantatory. Princes copied the image of kings because the depiction of a king was a recognisable icon of power. There were, however, other icons of power. There was the insignia of the Roman world, and of the Church. It seems to me in the case of certain items of insignia that the European aristocracy had originally looked rather wider than their royal master's court for inspiration. The use of rods by magnates, for instance, does not seem to be demonstrably any later than the use of them by the king (however much the royal sceptre influenced their making and depiction). The use of caps of state is wholly independent of the royal image, and may have an ecclesiastical inspiration. Furthermore, the use of insignia to evoke an appearance of power was not something that could travel down to a class that did not exercise significant jurisdiction. The use of coronets (at least as worn by men) stopped in England and elsewhere even before it reached the lowest titled rank in society, and went no further. It did not embrace the whole range of the grades of the peerage until the early modern period. Sceptres in England were put into the hands of men of a rank no meaner than dukes, and were wrested even from them by the time of Henry VIII. The style *dei gratia* accorded to dukes, counts and earls from the tenth century onwards, was no longer given to them or assumed by them much after the end of the twelfth century. It was later said that it could only be accorded with propriety to kings and bishops, who had received grace through the rite of anointing. Similarly, banners were always the prerogative of the upper aristocracy, and never penetrated to the simple knight or squire, who had to be satisfied with cut-down pennants.

Where cultural diffusion works best is in aristocratic symbols which had little aura of power. The aristocratic image of the armed warrior that was examined in an earlier chapter was not ultimately royal, even though aristocratic seal effigies of the late eleventh and twelfth centuries drew their immediate inspiration from royal sources. Likewise the social use of systematic heraldic devices came from below, not above. It was not generated by kings, but by the greater aristocratic families, who took clan devices of an almost totemic type. Lesser families eventually copied the greater, as did kings themselves.

From all this we may draw two general morals about change within the aristocracy of England before 1300; morals which in fact chime quite neatly with what has been observed about it from other directions. Successive generations witnessed the slow widening of the use of some aristocratic trappings in society (like heraldry, the language of deference, private devotions and commemorative burial) and therefore, we must conclude, the number of people that might be considered aristocratic also grew with time. On the other hand, the limitation of other sorts of aristocratic symbols, the insignia related to power, tells quite a different story. Here we see exclusivity of practices within the levels of the aristocracy, not growth. This parallels what English historians have observed about the growth of a 'parliamentary peerage' in the fourteenth century. The closing off of the higher reaches of the aristocracy, the separation of lords and commons. There was even some violence in the process: the class of bannerets was literally destroyed in the process, some pulled into the peerage, others demoted to commoners. The watchfulness of kings and the fear of ridicule meant that the diffusion of some aristocratic models only went so far, and no further. Image must ultimately bend the knee to reality.

7

INSIGNIA DEFINING ARISTOCRACY

THE BANNER, THE FAMILY AND THE ORIGINS OF HERALDRY

We have been discussing so far the banner as a social indicator; a marker of magnate status. There is another side to the banner, however. It is on the banner that we first detect the practice of heraldry. What we call heraldry began at some time in the eleventh century as a means of expressing pride in high lineage through particular family devices. Initially, this 'proto-heraldry', as it has been called, was the preserve of the magnate group. Where it filtered down to knights was (to begin with) in the practice of their employer marking them by issuing them with distinctive garments and equipment of a particular colour, or with a particular badge. By the middle of the thirteenth century, knights and squires were both employing heraldry in the same way as magnates had employed it over a century before, as symbols of family pride and alliance. Heraldry therefore diffused more widely through society than the insignia discussed in the previous chapter. By 1300 the heraldic device was a mark of nobility, a claim to be part of the aristocracy.

A good place to begin – in fact the only place – is with the Bayeux Tapestry. It has been noted that the symbols depicted on the *shields* of the characters on the tapestry are random, and have no meaning. A character who appears twice on the tapestry does not have the same design on his shield the second time as he had when he was first shown. This is not the case with the *banners* on the tapestry. The 'standard' of the English is depicted more than once and each time it is the same, a dragon attached to a pole, a bit like a windsock.[1] The same applies to the banner that accompanies Duke William, which may be meant to be that sacred banner sent to him by the pope to sanction his expedition. Other sources of the late eleventh and early twelfth century confirm that by then particular great men were associated with individual banners. William de Poitiers refers to 'the well-known banner (*vexillum*) of Harold, bearing the woven depiction of a warrior in pure gold', as being part of the spoils of Hastings which the Conqueror sent as part of a thank-offering to Rome.[2] The contemporary histories of the First Crusade tell of particular banners associated with particular leaders: the golden banner of the duke of Normandy, the white banner of King Baldwin I of Jerusalem, the red banner of Bohemond.[3] The Turkish emir of Antioch in 1098 in surrendering asked for a Christian banner to display from his fortress. He was rather upset when he was sent the banner of the count of Toulouse, for there were men on hand able to tell him that the banner was not that of Bohemond, which he had particularly requested.[4]

We have a good idea of what such early banners looked like. Depictions of them on early magnate seals show a square of cloth, sometimes decorated with a cross, to which were stitched three or more streamers (*linguae*, or 'tongues'). These *linguae* were designed to whip out and flutter colourfully in the breeze of its bearer's passage; when Count Bohemond rode against the Turks in the Holy Land in 1097, the points of his banner coiled over the heads of the infidel line as he passed.[5] At much the same time, the writer of the 'Song of Roland' records his eponymous hero's gonfanon which he bore when he led the French rearguard; white, with its long golden streamers (*lingues*) flicking at his hands as he rode along. Contemporary illuminations and sculpture show the same sort of thing. A drawing of St Michael slaying the dragon from the Jumièges Gospels, a Norman work of the later eleventh century, shows the

1 The memory of this dragon-standard long survived the Conquest; in 1244 Henry III commissioned in some detail a red silk standard in the shape of a dragon, spangled with gold, to be kept for him in the abbey of Westminster, *Excerpta Historica*, ed. S. Bentley, (London, 1833), 404.
2 William of Poitiers, *Gesta Guillelmi ducis Normannorum et regis Anglorum*, ed. R. Foreville (Paris, 1952), 224.
3 Robert the Monk, *Historia Iherosolimitana*, in *Recueil des historiens des croisades: historiens occidentaux*, iii (Paris, 1886), 761; Fulcher of Chartres, *Historia Iherosolymitana*, ibid., 343, 414.
4 *Gesta Francorum*, ed. R. Hill (Oxford, 1962), 70–1.
5 ibid., 37.

warrior saint and his fellow-angels armed with lances to which similar, richly embroidered banners were laced, some with three, others four, streamers.[6] The banners of the Bayeux Tapestry look much the same as those of the Gospels, and with them we can begin to trace the rise of the wider phenomenon of heraldry, and through it a new awareness of the uses of symbols to advertise aristocracy.

As the twelfth century progressed, the use of symbols on banners was slowly refined. As William de Poitiers and the historians of the Crusades indicate, banners, whatever their source, were already regarded as the personal ensigns of great men in the eleventh century. Distinctive colours or designs identified the great man to whom the banner belonged. The next generation added to this idea by making devices not just personal but also indicators of lineage. In the 1130s the banner on the first seal of Ralph I, count of Vermandois, the greatest magnate in Picardy and a descendant of Charlemagne, bears a distinct design of checkers upon it. That this was a design particularly associated with his family is clear from the fact that his close cousins, the Franco-Norman counts of Meulan, and the English earls of Leicester, Warenne and Warwick, also, sooner or later, carried a checky device. Where the colours of these shields are later known, three of them (Meulan, Warenne and Warwick) were in the same colours: blue and yellow.[7] The Carolingian associations of the house of Vermandois may well explain the prestige of this device. In the Vermandois banner we have the first instance of a particular design being linked to a great man and his family, indeed to a wide kin group. The Vermandois–Leicester–Warwick–Warenne device is evidence of the 'horizontal' and 'vertical' perceptions of relationships by the magnate group (Fig. 9(a)). A vertical relationship is evoked, running back to Charlemagne, and a horizontal one too, a common cousinship linking twelfth-century families with interests

6 The banner lost its streamers in England and France by the end of the twelfth century, and became a simple square or rectangle. The reason seems to have lain simply in fashion. Streamers appear to have remained in fashion longer in Germany.

7 G.H. White, 'The Beaumont Seals in the British Library Catalogue', *Notes and Queries*, 11th ser., cli (1926), 112; A.R. Wagner, *Heralds and Heraldry* (Oxford, 1939), 14–15; G.E. Cockayne, *The Complete Peerage*, ed. V. Gibbs *et al.* (13 vols in 14, London, 1910–59), xii, pt 1, appendix D; D. Crouch, *The Beaumont Twins*, (Cambridge, 1986), 10–11, 211–12. Other families have been linked into this heraldic network. Although there is a good case for including the Norman family of Le Neubourg (cadets of the Warwicks), there is no warrant for adding, for instance, the Angevin family of Craon, which used different colours and lozenges, not a check device.

running from West Wales and Yorkshire to Paris and the frontier of the Empire. This may be a truer picture of contemporary attitudes to family than the 'vertical' scheme evoked by the study of toponyms (see Introduction).

The chevrons (inverted 'V's) used on the seals of the various branches of the Anglo-Norman family of Clare soon provide us with another example, datable to a time as early as the 1140s: the Clare network eventually included the allied houses of Monmouth, fitz Walter and Montfichet (Fig. 9(b)).[8] Furthermore, another group of aristocratic clan devices was formed by the intermarried Mandeville, Vere, Say and Lacy families. In their case the design was a quartered shield of yellow and red. This particular network of kinship stemmed from the events of the reign of King Stephen, and it is not going too far to see the Mandeville quartered device as established (like that of the Clares) by the 1140s.[9]

By the mid-twelfth century, there is abundant evidence of the vogue for display of family power by family symbols. One obvious lead in the search for the origins of such symbolism of lineage is to test whether royalty used it too. But it very soon becomes apparent that the aristocracy was not in this case imitating royal trappings, rather the reverse. The case of the royal family of England has often been cited as one inspiration for heraldry, for as early as the reign of Henry I (1100–35) the king is said to have used a lion device.[10] The principal evidence for this is, however, retrospective, and derives from a common source, the court of Henry I's Angevin successors. Around 1170, the Angevin historian, John of Marmoutier, describes Henry I's knighting of Count Geoffrey of Anjou at Rouen in 1128, before Geoffrey married the king's daughter. Among the gifts were said to be shoes and a shield marked by little gold lions. These are said – in retrospect by modern heraldists – to have been the English royal device, and certainly the tomb of Count Geoffrey (died 1151) bore an enamelled plaque showing the count bearing a blue shield marked by little gold lions (he also had a cap of the same design). Yet this is evidence only for *Count Geoffrey's* choice of dynastic symbol; John of Marmoutier's source for his assertion about the count's dress and arms in 1128 might well have been no more than

8 J.H. Round, 'The Introduction of Armorial Bearings to England', *Archaeological Journal*, li (1894), 44–8.
9 J.H. Round, *Geoffrey de Mandeville* (London, 1892), 388–96.
10 A. Ailes, *The Origins of the Royal Arms of England* (Reading Medieval Studies, no. 2, 1982), 46–9, makes the best case.

the funerary plaque or some other depiction of the late count.[11] Writers at the court of Henry II (1154–89) were certainly taking the line that the Angevin lion device which came to their master was derived from that of his royal forebears. The *Chronique des ducs de Normandie*, composed at Henry's court, depicts William the Conqueror, a century and more before its composition, bearing a shield of blue marked with little golden lions, just like Count Geoffrey's. But there is no reason to believe that the author was doing more than stressing the legitimacy of Henry II's claim to England by retrospectively crediting his great-grandfather with the Angevin lioncels.[12]

The balance of evidence convinces me that the 'lions of England' were ultimately a French comital device. Too much can be made of Geoffrey of Monmouth's elliptical reference to Henry I as the 'lion of justice' in the 'Prophecies of Merlin'. The inspiration for the remark was more biblical than heraldic. Lions and *leunculi* (little lions) adorned the seat of justice of King Solomon. Only one piece of evidence is in favour of the supposed lion arms of Henry I, and that is that the seal of Earl William of Gloucester (1147–83), a grandson of Henry I, features a lion. This might be interpreted as some evidence that Henry I did indeed use a lion device, which passed to the earl through his father, a royal bastard. However, the seal might just as well have been designed to stress the cousinship of Earl William to the Angevin house, as his descent from Henry I: for Henry II did on occasion refer to Earl William as his cousin, as a way of flattering him.[13]

How about the French royal house as an exemplar of heraldry? It is in northern France, after all, that the earliest stirrings of the symbolism of lineage is to be found. Again, chronology is against the idea. The lily device of the king of France is evident on coins

11 John of Marmoutiers's description of Geoffrey of Anjou's get-up in 1128 does not tally exactly with the depiction of Geoffrey in the funerary plaque. This does not necessarily mean that description and depiction are therefore independent sources; but there may well have been other depictions, surviving robes and, indeed, memories of Geoffrey which made John describe him in 1128 clothed in lioncels as he was in his later days.
12 P. Adam, 'Les Usages héraldiques au milieu du xiie siècle', *Archivum Heraldicum*, lxxvii (1963), 19.
13 *Earldom of Gloucester Charters*, ed. R.B. Patterson (Oxford, 1973), 23–4, pl. xxxi(a). Professor Patterson sees the seal as a copy of the lost seal of William's father, but that can only be guesswork. The seal's earliest impression is on a charter of 1150 x 53, a time when Henry Plantagenet was the acknowledged leader of the opposition to King Stephen.

of Louis VI (1108–37) and moves on to the seal of his successor Louis VII (1137–80).[14] But in neither case is the emblem used in quite the way the Vermandois cousins of the Capetians used their checky device to mark their family pride. The lilies did not appear on shield or banner of a Capetian king until the time of Philip Augustus; a considerable lapse of time between aristocracy and monarchy. It is also noteworthy that the Vermandois did not allude to the lily when they were conjuring up a device as a sign of their dignity. If they were trying to evoke royal blood, one might have thought that an allusion to the lily would have been one way, if the lily was then seen as a Capetian symbol. It has been suggested as an alternative link that the blue and gold of the Vermandois device was an allusion to an early version of the blue shield scattered with gold lilies known to have been carried by the king of France after 1180.[15] However, blue and yellow (or gold) was not an unusual combination of colours. No one would suggest that the Vermandois were alluding to kinship with the Angevin house in their choice of colours for their shield, yet the Angevins began by using blue and gold too.

If anywhere, the origins of the symbolic expression of aristocratic lineage lie amongst the competitive nobles of north-eastern France in the eleventh century. Here, as Professor Pastoureau points out, we find the earliest examples of the taking of symbols of lineage. The intruding family of Candavène, which took as its base the county of St Pol in the mid-eleventh century, was using its distinctive device of a sheaf on its coins as early as 1100. The device was doubtless a punning one: Candavène translated into Latin as *campus avene* (field of oats). The seal of Count Enguerrand of St Pol (1141–50) actually showed him riding his horse through a field full of sheaves, and sheaves duly feature on the shield and horse-trapper of the seal effigy of his son, Count Anselm (1150–74). The same antiquity has been claimed by Pastoureau for the two fish back-to-back which were carried as arms by a whole group of great families descended from Thièrry II, count of Bar (died 1103). Other candidates for such ancient symbolism are the early counts of Boulogne, who affected a design of roundels.[16]

14 Ailes, *Origins of the Royal Arms*, 26; M. Pastoureau, 'La diffusion des armoiries et les débuts de l'héraldique', in *La France de Philippe Auguste: le temps des mutations* (Colloques internationaux CNRS, no. 602, 1981), 755–9.
15 M. Pastoureau, 'L'Origine des armoires: un problème en voie de solution?', in *Genealogica et Heraldica*, ed. S.T. Achen (Copenhagen, 1982), 249.
16 ibid., 246–51.

To find the inspiration for heraldry in the pre-heraldic, almost totemic, symbols taken up by eleventh-century counts and lords of the rising aristocracy of that quarter of France, is by no means unconvincing. They give us the clue to what sorts of design were appearing on the individualised banners about which the historians of the Crusades tell us. To do so also neatly explains how England was included so quickly in the process. Flemings and Picards played a full part in the Norman Conquest of England, and contacts remained close for a century and more afterwards. The Vermandois–Meulan–Leicester–Warenne–Warwick heraldic group is then easily understood as part of a cross-Channel cultural movement within a closely interrelated aristocracy. Another early example lies in the connection between the dukes of Lorraine and the Percy family. The later Percies of Topcliffe, Craven and Alnwick were descended from Joscelin of Louvain, son of Duke Godfrey, who crossed to England in 1122 with his sister Adeliza, second wife of Henry I. Joscelin stayed in England and married the heir of the first line of Percy, and his descendants took the Percy name. However, Joscelin's descendants retained the arms of Louvain, a blue lion on gold, alluding thus to their ducal lineage. Kings simply had to catch up with this process later, and such evidence as there is suggests it took them a full generation to realise that their dignity would be enhanced, not compromised, by the new aristocratic craze; a realisation to which they came rather more quickly than they did over their reservations towards another aristocratic craze, the tournament.

THE SHIELD OF ARMS

By the mid-twelfth century the display of the clan device had shifted off the banner on to the shield. Indeed when the Vermandois check was used by Waleran, count of Meulan, on his second seal, the fashioning of which can be closely dated to 1139–40, the design featured not just on the banner but on the count's shield, robe and horse-cloth.[17] The shield became the alternative place of display of the family symbol after the 1130s. Its convenient shape and smooth,

---

17 For the date of the seal, see E. King, 'Waleran, Count of Meulan, Earl of Worcester (1104–1166)', in *Tradition and Change in the Central Middle Ages: Essays in Honour of Marjorie Chibnall*, ed. D.E. Greenway, C. Holdsworth and J. Sayers (Cambridge, 1985), 167–8.

Figure 8 Seal of Waleran II, count of Meulan and Worcester (died 1166) showing heraldic checky device on surcoat, banner, shield and horse-cloth.

leather surface made it very suitable for the painting of designs. It became the chief vehicle of heraldry in the end. Banners, as we have seen in the treatment of the social rank of banneret, long remained an aristocratic attribute of the baron. Ordinary knights never bore banners; their lances were adorned with coloured pennants or pencils (*penoncel*).[18] When knights eventually took individual devices after 1200, their display had to be made on their shield, robes or horse-trappers, for a pennon was too small for identification over a distance, and it was impractical for every soldier in an army to carry a banner. Of these vehicles for display, the shield was most convenient because it did not bunch or ripple, and in that way distort the device.

The shield does not seem to have had any relation to heraldry in the beginning. The shield designs of the eleventh century show no consistent use of symbols. They are either depicted as plain, with metal studs or bosses, or with a random design of dots and beasts painted on them. By the early twelfth century things were changing. The shields of the knights depicted in the Cîteaux Bible of the 1110s, or in a manuscript of the chronicle of John of Worcester in the 1120s, show the first stirrings of the stock designs of later heraldry: chevrons, roundels, and stripes of various orientations (fess, bend and pale).[19] But by the 1140s, at the latest, the shields of the great were displaying coherent family devices, as also were their robes and their horse blankets, according to the images of these depicted on their seals.

By the 1160s other great men who were not of such high family, but were nonetheless powerful, had taken up their own family devices. They occasionally did it a little hesitantly. The twelfth century was the first great age of studied courtliness, and accomplished courtiers were schooled in self-deprecation: it did not do to be too pushy and stand out from the crowd. Richard de Lucy, a Norman raised from nothing by King Stephen who successfully transferred his service to Henry II and became chief justiciar of England, demonstrated this accomplishment when he commissioned a seal, probably in the 1160s, which was to show a family device. The device was chosen carefully, it was a fish, a pike to be more accurate. In Norman French this was a *luz*.

18 See above, pp. 114–15.
19 P. Gras, 'Aux Origines de l'héraldique: la décoration des boucliers au début du xiie siècle d'après la bible de Cîteaux', *Bibliothèque de l'Ecole de Chartes*, cix (1951), 198–208.

In other words Richard's assumption of this aristocratic attribute of family was carefully designed to be a joke, one of those word-plays of which medieval man was so fond, along the lines of the Candavène oat-stooks of a century before, although with a more serious intent. Richard smilingly insinuated himself amongst the earls by means of a pun. It may have been done with a simper and the shrug of a shoulder, but the intention was serious, and his family, beginning with his nephew Godfrey, followed suit on their seals and shields.[20] The Lucy pikes are still borne by Richard's descendants and collaterals to this day. The *eagles* of the Norman lords of *L'Aigle*, and the *lily* on the shield of Simon de Senlis, the bastard of Northampton, in the 1180s show how Richard de Lucy was by no means alone in his courtly presumption.[21]

But the common knight in the employment or following of a great man was not as yet permitted any use of individual family symbols; these were still reserved for the baron. However, there is evidence that certain symbols or colours were allotted them by their masters as a token of their service. The Rule of the Knights Templar, composed in 1128, expects the knights to be uniformly equipped in white robes, shields, spears and cloak; the lesser members of the order, the squires, were to be fitted out in black or brown.[22] Although the monastic habit might have been one of the inspirations for this 'uniform', it seems more likely that the Templars were doing no more than any other company of knights under a common employer at the time. In 1119, we are told, numbers of knights from the French army defeated by the Normans at Brémule threw away their cognizances (*cognitiones*) to deceive their pursuers, whose war-cry they copied in order to further confuse them.[23] Here again is evidence of knights kitted out in a distinctive and recognisable fashion; dressed to kill, so to speak. Epics and romances from the 'Song of Roland' to Chrétien de Troyes, tell us quite clearly what manner of cognizances these were. They were helmets, lances, pennons and shields painted in the colours, or with the simple badge, of the knights' lord.[24] Historical

20 D.L. Galbreath, *Manuel de Blason* (Lausanne, 1942), 27–9.
21 For L'Aigle, Brit. Libr., Additional charter 47388; for the bastard Senlis, London, Guildhall Libr., ms 25121/1228.
22 *Regula Pauperum Commilitonum sanctae Civitatis*, in *Patrologia Latina*, clxvi, 864–7, caps 20–2, 38.
23 Orderic Vitalis, *The Ecclesiastical History*, ed. M. Chibnall (6 vols, Oxford, 1969–80), vi, 242.
24 Adam 'Les Usages héraldiques', 20–1.

sources from England occasionally confirm this. Two intending assassins of King Stephen in the middle of the century exchanged not just shields but also saddles with collaborators in the royal army, so as to blend in and get near their victim.[25] Rather later, in 1176, Gerald of Wales records his cousin, Raymond fitz Gerald, greeting a royal representative landing in Ireland, escorted by a company of thirty knights, all his kinsmen, and all kitted out in shields bearing the same device.[26]

In the twelfth century the whole equipment marked the knight's allegiance, because in those days the household knight had his equipment from his lord and patron, who made sure that everyone recognised his man. A good example of this is to be found in the biography of William Marshal. In 1167, after his knighting and first experience of battle, the Marshal took time away from his then lord, his mother's cousin, William de Tancarville, to try his luck on the tournament field. In the style of true romance he carried all before him. An older knight, observing his success from the sidelines, asked a friend who the young wonder-boy was, and was told it was William Marshal *'his shield it is of Tancarville'*. The Marshal, common knight that he was, had no arms of his own yet; he wore the token of his then lord. His biography tells us how, at every change of employer – whether Patrick earl of Salisbury or Queen Eleanor – his new lord, or lady, would lavish on him horses, robes and arms, as well as gold and silver. He would not have taken his own device until he raised his own banner in 1180, at the tournament of Lagny near Paris, as the leader of his own company.[27] Even then the device he chose reflected that of his patron, the Young King of England, the Angevin lion in red, on a field of yellow and green. Nor was he alone in this; as we have seen, Earl William of Gloucester (died 1183) took a lion on his seal to advertise his cousinship with the Angevin house. Two great ministers of the Angevin dynasty, Geoffrey fitz Peter and Hubert de Burgh, were using seals in the 1190s which had on them

25 H. Cam, 'An East Anglian Shire-Moot in Stephen's Reign', *English Historical Review*, xxxix (1924), 569-70. Chrétien de Troyes in the 1170s describes the same stratagem: knights of King Arthur twice penetrate a rebel camp by exchanging their own *conuissances* for the lances and shields painted in the rebel count's colours, *Cligés*, ed. A. Micha (Classiques français du moyen âge, 1957), ll. 1305–6, 1815–17.
26 Gerald of Wales, *Expugnatio Hibernica*, ed. A. Scott and F.X. Martin (Irish Academy, 1980), 168.
27 *Histoire de Guillaume le Maréchal*, ed. P. Meyer (3 vols, Paris, 1899–1909), i, ll. 1474–8, 4607–19.

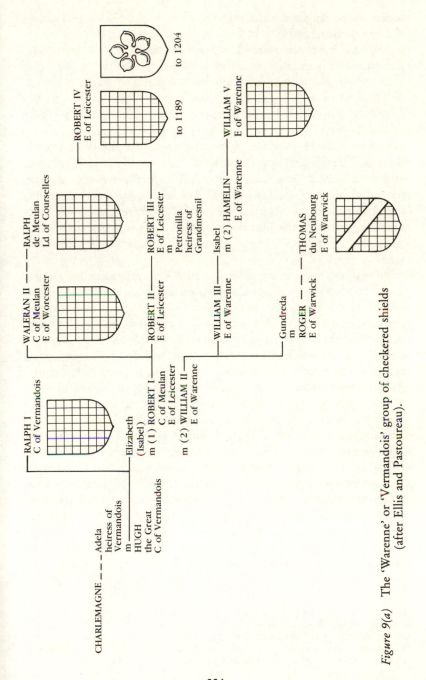

CHARLEMAGNE – – – Adela
heiress of
Vermandois
m
HUGH
the Great
C of Vermandois

RALPH I
C of Vermandois

Elizabeth
(Isabel)
m (1) ROBERT I
C of Meulan
E of Leicester

m (2) WILLIAM II
E of Warenne

WALERAN II – – –
C of Meulan
E of Worcester

ROBERT II
E of Leicester

WILLIAM III
E of Warenne

Gundreda
m
ROGER – – –
E of Warwick

RALPH
de Meulan
Ld of Courselles

ROBERT III
E of Leicester
m
Petronilla
heiress of
Grandmesnil

Isabel
m (2) HAMELIN
E of Warenne

THOMAS
du Neubourg
E of Warwick

ROBERT IV
E of Leicester

to 1189

to 1204

WILLIAM V
E of Warenne

Figure 9(a)   The 'Warenne' or 'Vermandois' group of checkered shields
(after Ellis and Pastoureau).

231

a lion or lions: plainly the recognised badge of the *realx* (men of the royal household).[28]

Maurice Keen has pointed out to me that William Marshal also indicates another influence on early heraldry. The two old knights viewing the tournament in which the Marshal distinguished himself in 1167 looked first to his equipment to discover who he was, but found from that only his household device. The tournament, being a more frequent occurrence than a pitched battle, must have played a part in moulding contemporary attitudes to military and noble devices. Twelfth-century heraldic devices, which identified lords and their men, were naturally useful in the great tournaments patronised by dukes, counts and barons. In the more frequent lesser tournaments, such as that of 1167 where there were only knights present, household devices were less useful. Because of this there was a reason for common knights to aspire to an individual iconography.

As the twelfth century drew on, the display affected by knights began to change. In England and northern France, as knighthood began to be perceived as a claim to be considered aristocratic, knights began to affect the symbols previously used by their betters. One of the first of these was the shield of arms. It was a natural attribute to copy. Magnates had long rejoiced in arms, and had chosen to be depicted on their seals as knights since the late eleventh century. As a matter of course, their family emblems had appeared on their military equipment, as we have seen in the case of the counts of Vermandois and Meulan. When devices were to be seen on the battlefield, and performed there a clear and useful military function, it was natural for knights to seek to take their own, in due course.

The evidence from seals charts this social and military aspiration very neatly for us. Shields with individual designs begin to appear on knightly seals in the 1180s and 1190s (earlier knightly seals tend just to show the knight himself, as a stock effigy). From these tentative first appearances the shield of arms became universal on knightly seals by the 1230s.[29] The chronology throughout appears to be the same in both England and France, which is not surprising. French and English nobles and knights met each other so regularly on

---

28 For Geoffrey, see Oxford, New College charter 13018; for Hubert, Brit. Libr., ms Stowe 955 fo. 86r.
29 B. Bedoz-Rizak, 'L'Apparition des armoiries sur les sceaux en Ile-de-France et en Picardie (vers 1130–1230)' in *Les Origines des Armoiries*, ed. H. Pinoteau *et al.* (2me Colloque International d'Héraldique, Bressanone, 1981), 23–41.

tournament and battlefields that in many ways they operate as a single class in the twelfth and early thirteenth centuries, whatever the new national frictions between them.

The mode in which many of these knights took on personal devices, however, has something of the courtly caution of Richard de Lucy earlier. Knights had long been accustomed to carrying their lord's colours, or some form of uniform badge, to mark them out as his men. When the time came when individual knights felt it was safe and appropriate to take up their own devices, many insinuated themselves into this aristocratic network by assuming variants of the device associated with their lord. They stepped gingerly from complete dependence into iconographic individuality; an essay on protective social colouring. So it was that the Martinwast family of Noseley, Leicestershire (which we have already met), long attached to the retinue of the earls of Leicester, assumed around 1200 a shield bearing the cinquefoil (a five-leaved flower), the device particularly associated with their lord Earl Robert IV (died 1204). The difference was that the earl's shield was a white flower on red, and the Martinwasts had a black flower on white. Seals and the later thirteenth-century rolls of arms tell us that several other men and institutions in the Midlands closely associated with Robert IV took the same device, again changing its colours, or multiplying the number of flowers: the famous Astley family of Warwickshire (Thomas of Astley was the earl's steward) and the Motuns of Peckleton, Leicestershire, as well as the family abbeys of Leicester and Garendon.

The process can be observed happening at the same time all over England. Followers of Ranulf III, earl of Chester, took up wheatsheaves, his own particular device. Followers and lesser relatives of the Clares, earls of Hertford, took up combinations of the Clare chevrons. Several followers of the earls of Warwick affected the checky shield of their lord (probably not realising that their lord too had earlier taken the shield for social purposes, to allude to his connection with the counts of Vermandois and beyond them, Charlemagne). Three leading knightly families of the honor of Striguil (Chepstow) – Bloet, Durnford and Seymour – all assumed shields carrying linked wings. Since this cannot be connected with the arms of the Marshal earls, and since these three families were more closely associated with the Marshal's predecessors, the wings may allude to a badge device of an earlier period, perhaps the equipment issued them by the great earl Richard Strongbow (died

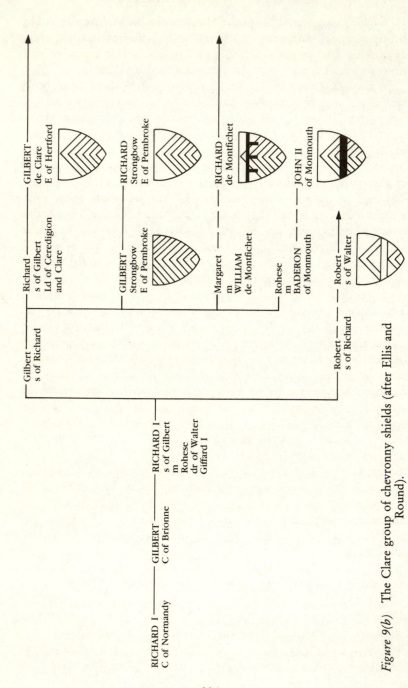

Figure 9(b) The Clare group of chevronny shields (after Ellis and Round).

1176) who conquered Leinster. Many more such examples could be given, easily sufficient to prove that the assumption of heraldic devices by the knightly families of England was a tentative and nervous social climb during the decades flanking 1200.

By the 1250s the numbers of heraldic shields affected by most of the 1,500 or so knights of England (the actual number is debatable, but I give Jeremy Quick's) were so great that lists were made to register them. In the beginning these lists must have been products of leisure; the result of individual enthusiasm. Such must have been the numerous sketches of shields that pepper the margins of the works of Matthew Paris, the monk-historian of St Albans. The earliest purpose-made heraldic roll survives from some time around 1250. It is called 'Glover's Roll' after a later owner; the true author is unknown. What is known is that, unlike Matthew Paris, its author described the shields he had collected in words, not pictures. In doing so, he reveals that a standardised format had evolved for describing coats of arms; there was by 1250 a sufficient community of afficianados of heraldry to have created a jargon. The author also demonstrates an exquisite social sensitivity. He commences his list of 215 shields with the king's arms, moves on to the king's brother (Cornwall), then to the king's brother-in-law (Montfort) and then to the other earls. From the earls he moves to the king's Poitevin relations, and then to the holders of baronies. Earls and barons take up 105 of the items he describes. He finishes up with a significant group of knights, all major county figures but not holders of baronies. Moving on a generation, we find that the next significant roll of arms, the 'St George's Roll' of *c*.1285, is three times as long, describing 677 shields. It comprehends within its catalogue the greater part of the substantial county families of England.[30] This roll and its successors and contemporaries were striving to be inclusive of all current armorial devices. This very fact tells us that more was attached to the use of heraldry than its utility on the battlefield. It was now one of the means of demarcating the extent of the aristocracy. To be a knight was to enjoy the right to armorial bearings. However, as we have seen, there was a social group lower than the knights who were putting this distinction under pressure.

It was more or less impossible to stop squires assuming arms, though it is interesting to find that it was believed inappropriate

30 *Rolls of Arms: Henry III*, ed. T.D. Tremlett (Harleian Soc., 1967), 91–2, 115–59; *English Mediaeval Rolls of Arms*, i, *1244–1334*, ed. R.W. Mitchell (Peebles, 1983), 121–50.

that they should do so for many years, and some element of discouragement was put in the way of would-be armigerous squires (for the 'squire' see Chapter 5). Edward I's Statute of Arms of 1292 is very firm in stating that squires must not bear their own device but wear those of their respective master, as on a cap, for instance. This rebuke alone tells us that some squires were indeed assuming arms. The position of the squire in 1292 was the same as the position the knight was supposed to have occupied a century earlier. But theirs was a position of inferiority that could not be enforced. In thirteenth-century France a similar prohibition is evident. In France, where 'squire' was a dignity added as early as the 1200s by individuals to their name, like 'knight', we can watch the process better at this early time than in England. In France, squires were scrupulous in not placing arms on their seals for the first half of the century, but if a squire was knighted he would have a new seal cut, which did display an armorial shield. By the 1260s such a severe distinction had broken down, and squires in France were using arms indifferently.[31] Despite Edward I's prohibition there is every reason to think that the same happened in England if not precisely at the same time. It was unreasonable to expect that a thirteenth-century squire, whose father might well have been a wealthy knight with a heraldic device, should not attempt to use that device even if he did not take up knighthood. After 1370 the arms of squires begin to feature on rolls of arms in England, and in this way (the nearest there ever was to an edict on the subject) we could say that the squire was accepted within the pale of the aristocracy of England.

It would not do to suggest that the evolution of a heraldic system in society was a neat process of diffusion. There was undoubtedly a progression evident, but it was fitful. At some times the process worked quicker than others. The mid-thirteenth century was a time of particular mobility amongst the knights and squires. Also there were some reverses for which it is difficult to account. This is especially true around 1200 amongst the higher aristocracy. There are three well-attested examples of great men abandoning devices they or their family had held in the past for new ones. Robert IV, earl of Leicester (1190–1204) threw over the distinct Vermandois check he had used before succeeding to the earldom for a new design of a cinquefoil (five-petalled flower). Simon de Montfort (died 1218)

---

31 P. Adam-Even, 'Les Sceaux d'écuyers au xiie. siècle', *Archives héraldiques suisses*, lxvi (1951), 19–23.

Figure 10 Heraldic schema of Kirkham priory gatehouse (1) England
(2) Ros (3) Clare (4) Warenne (5) Espec (6) Greystoke (7) Scrope
(8) Aumale.

abandoned the ancient device of the Montforts of Yvelines, counts of
Evreux (*party indented argent and gules*) for a device of a white lion
with a forked tail, on red. In his old age, Ranulf III, earl of Chester
(died 1232), abandoned the device of a lion he had carried on his
shield in the twelfth century for that of three wheatsheaves. Some
suggestions have been made to account for these radical changes.
Robert IV of Leicester is said to have changed his arms in order
to allude to his mother Petronilla (Pernel), a great Norman heiress.
Ranulf III is said to have been alluding to his (somewhat remote)
kinship with the Candavène counts of St Pol. Whether or not these
suggestions are convincing, it is a salutary indication of the still fluid
nature of aristocratic symbolism that old established devices might
be dropped to make particular points. Heraldry was a new system in
the thirteenth century, and it was still possible for a strong-minded
individual to override it.

HERALDRY, RETINUES AND DOMINATION

The investment of family and personal prestige in heraldic bearings made them an obvious icon of power in society, and therefore desirable (indeed, arms are still as much concerned with pretension as family pride). For that reason, institutions that had little connection with the world of warfare and the court took up heraldry too; they did so because heraldic arms cloaked them with prestige. Shields of arms were being formulated for bishoprics, religious houses and towns by the end of the thirteenth century. Where religious houses took up arms, they often did so to allude to the families of their founders and advocates. Thus the abbeys of Leicester and Garendon in England and Lyre in Normandy all bore arms featuring the white cinquefoil on red associated with the twelfth-century earls of Leicester and their successors (varied with marks of difference). Here was a curious similarity with the way that early arms of knightly families alluded to the magnates under whose protection they were.

The late thirteenth-century great gate of Kirkham priory in Yorkshire gives us another illustration of this association of heraldry, power and protection. It bears ten shields: three show the water-bougets (conventionally drawn water-skins) of the house of Ros, its then advocates, and one shows the alleged (but anachronistic) arms associated with its founder, Walter Espec. Yet, just to proclaim the priory's place in the local structure of power, the gatehouse is also adorned with the arms of many of the greatest families in Yorkshire: Clare, Warenne, Greystoke, Aumale and Scrope.[32] The royal arms share the highest place with those of Ros, flanking the central mandala enclosing Christ in Majesty. As an evocation of a priory's conception of the world of power that surrounded it, Kirkham gatehouse could hardly be bettered (other, later, examples are known, such as the gatehouse of Butley Priory in Suffolk with thirty-five shields). Travellers who rode under that arch would know they were riding into the precincts of a house supported and protected not just by saints in niches, but by the greatest men of the region; it was both threat and boast. In associating heraldry, power and community, the gatehouse of Kirkham precedes and complements the example of the fourteenth-century heraldic glass

---

32 As far as is known, none of these magnate families actually made any grants to the priory. The priory was soliciting their protection, perhaps, rather than acknowledging it.

at Etchingham church, ably explored by Nigel Saul. Here too local patron and royalty shared the place of honour, in this case about the altar; the arms of earls filled the windows of the chancel, gentry the windows of the nave; status was linked with closeness to the sacrament, and the place of its transformation.[33]

The badge of service, as it began to evolve in the thirteenth century, is another aspect of power expressed by heraldry. Badges were not a feature of the personal heraldic achievement of the magnate or knight; they were subsidiary devices, designed to mark dependants and property belonging to the great man. Great magnates of the thirteenth century were beginning to realise that a whole range of devices might be as beneficial to their dignity as just one. One of the earliest symptoms of this can be found in the remarkable seal of Margaret de Quincy, countess of Winchester (died 1236). Countess Margaret was one of England's great heiresses. She was daughter and co-heir of Robert IV of Leicester and one of the last representatives of both the Leicester family and the Norman house of Grandmesnil. Her seal depicts her standing in a gown figured with the newer device (seven mascles) of her husband, Earl Saher de Quincy. On a tree to one side hang shields with both coats of arms of her husband: the chevrons which record his connection with the Clare clan and the mascles, his individual shield. A castellated canopy above her records the other great connection, the cinquefoil of Robert IV of Leicester, allusion to the ancient Norman blood of Grandmesnil. The countess's younger son later chose to take up the cinquefoil device of his mother's line.[34]

A further addition to the Quincy repertoire of badges was a wyvern, taken up by Earl Roger, the second earl of Winchester (died 1263); it decorates both the base of his seal and the top of the great helm shown in his seal-portrait.[35] Other magnates were also appropriating a range of symbols. Robert II de Vere, earl of Oxford (died 1296), had a pair of boars' heads depicted on his counterseal.[36] This corresponds nicely with the evidence of his surviving tomb effigy at Bures, Essex, where the feet rest on

33 N. Saul, *Scenes from Provincial Life: Knightly Families in Sussex, 1280–1400* (Oxford, 1986), 140–52.
34 For the seal, see *Age of Chivalry: Art in Plantagenet England*, ed. J. Alexander and P. Binski (Royal Academy of Arts, 1987), no. 141; for the Quincy seals, G. Henderson, 'Romance and Politics on some English Seals', *Art History*, i, (1980), 32–8.
35 Brit. Libr., Harley charter 83 B 42.
36 Cambridge, Queen's College, muniment Box 63 no. 7.9.

a boar. These may be references back to his ancestor, Aubrey, the first earl of Oxford, credited with the nickname *Aper* (the boar) by a Flemish chronicle.[37] Lower down the social scale, Peter de Montfort, the Midlands banneret who was one of the chief allies of Simon de Montfort in the 1250s, had seal and counterseal which repeated motifs of cinquefoils and fleurs-de-lis: part allusion to his service to Leicester, part personal livery badge. The cinquefoils recall Leicester, the fleurs-de-lis his links with the Cantilupe and Corbezun families of south-west Warwickshire.[38]

In the thirteenth century we can therefore see the development of the livery badge alongside the development and extension of heraldry proper. We know from fourteenth-century evidence that the use of badges by magnates to mark their retainers was by then well entrenched; the indications given here are that the practice began earlier.[39] If knights and squires were assuming arms across England and France, magnates and bannerets still retained a range of family symbols that could be used to mark their retainers and servants. In the Quincy wyvern and the Vere boar are the thirteenth-century predecessors of the magnificent fourteenth-century Dunstable brooch, which depicted the swan badge of the Bohuns, and was worn by one of their noble retainers. Such symbols were valuable reminders that there was a group in society which could buy followers and mark them as their own, even though such followers might be men who had taken up coats of arms in their own right.

HERALDRY IN SCOTLAND AND WALES

The subject of Welsh and Scots heraldry is worth more than a cursory look before the end of this chapter. The case of Scotland is closely parallel to that of England. Because the interests of many Anglo-Norman families spanned the border, heraldry must have developed simultaneously in both kingdoms. The fact that native magnates were boasting heraldic designs on their seals early in the thirteenth century shows how open they were by then to the trappings of aristocracy. Alan, lord of Galloway (died

---

37 Lambert of Ardres, 'Historia Comitum Ghisnensium', in *M.G.H. Scriptores*, xxiv, 583; William of Ardres, 'Chronica', ibid, 701.
38 Brit. Libr. Cotton charter xi, 28.
39 A. Payne, 'Medieval Heraldry', in *Age of Chivalry*, 58–9, argues that badges were a fourteenth-century phenomenon.

1234), and Patrick III, earl of Dunbar (1182–1232), took the lion later associated with their dynasties; Gilbert, earl of Strathern (1171–1223), had an armorial privy seal before his death. The Scottish kings came to heraldry relatively late, if the seal evidence is to be trusted. The great seal of Alexander II (1214–49) is the first to feature the lion which became the centrepiece of the royal arms of Scotland.[40] Nor was the Scottish royal family consistent in its use of symbols, unlike the English royal family (which used lions in all its branches). King Alexander's uncle, Earl David II of Huntingdon (1185–1219), employed after 1185 a device of three piles on his seal and was succeeded in it by his son Earl John.[41] Apart from the great Scottish magnates, at least one Scottish knightly family is found with a hereditary device in the mid-thirteenth century: the Anglo-Scottish Grahams, with their design of scallops.[42] This gives some exiguous evidence that all levels of Scottish aristocratic society were following a broadly similar heraldic chronology to that of England.

Welsh heraldry appears at much the same time as that of Scotland, although it was nowhere near as widespread. We see here again the resistance of the Welsh aristocracy to outside influences. There were Welsh knights in the twelfth century, but they did not tourney, and as a result the need for the trappings of heraldry was not obvious. Similarly, pride of family was expressed differently in Wales. A Welsh aristocrat would, like Gruffudd ap Cynan (died 1137), cite his descent through innumerable generations of kings as a bolster to his family pride: a painted shield and banner would seem an alien method of doing the same thing. Nonetheless, to move in aristocratic circles dominated by French fashion meant that the international Welshman would ultimately need a device. It is not therefore surprising to find that the house of Gwynedd was the first to have its heraldry noticed. Matthew Paris noted both sons of Llywelyn ab Iorwerth (died 1240), Dafydd and Gruffudd, as having a quartered shield of yellow and red, with four interchanged lions.[43] That both sons were following their father's arms is very likely. The heraldic reference contained in the arms of Gwynedd to those of England is clear: Llywelyn had married an illegitimate daughter

---

40 J.H. Stevenson, *Heraldry in Scotland* (2 vols, Glasgow, 1914), i, 17–18; ii, 390–1.
41 K.J. Stringer, *Earl David of Huntingdon: A Study in Anglo-Scottish History* (Edinburgh, 1985), 215–16; *Rolls of Arms: Henry III*, ed. T.D. Tremlett (Harleian Soc., 1967), 39.
42 Stevenson, *Heraldry in Scotland*, i, 18.
43 *Rolls of Arms: Henry III*, 69–70, 71.

of King John, and indeed Llywelyn's uncle and predecessor had married a sister of Henry II. But other examples of Welsh heraldry are few and far between. At the end of the thirteenth century the south Welsh knights Lleision of Afan and John Abadam both used arms, but they were enthusiastic Anglicisers, so that much was to be expected. Evidence for erratic use of heraldry amongst the Welsh gentry does not come before the mid-fourteenth century, and it remains eccentric, with sons not always following their fathers in their arms.

THE SEAL

Seals are another indication that society was changing the ground-rules of aristocracy. The great round seal (60–80 mm. in diameter), impressed on wax of a variety of colours, and applied to a document by a variety of means, appeared in the early eleventh century.[44] It was then used by kings and emperors, but some examples of similar seals of counts datable to the last years of the eleventh century have been found. Barons came to use them not long afterwards, perhaps even simultaneously.[45] The kings of England after 1066 impressed both sides of the wax, having themselves depicted in majesty on one side, and armed as a warrior on the other. Other sovereigns copied them in this.

Earls and barons in general started by using only one side of the round seal, although there are exceptions, such as Robert I, count of Meulan and earl of Leicester, the intimate of William Rufus and Henry I, and husband of a Capetian lady.[46] Comital and baronial seals as found in the early twelfth century usually show their owners on horseback and armed. The earliest known example in England or France appears to be that of Count Stephen of Aumale, an Anglo-Norman magnate, whose seal was being used in the 1090s. There may well be older examples: antiquaries' sketches survive of a two-sided military/episcopal seal of Odo of Bayeux, alluding to

---

44 A rare exception to the round seal is the seal of Richard de Clare, earl of Hertford (1173–1217) which was distinctive in being octagonal, see Brit. Libr., Additional charter 47953.

45 In the Seine valley, the viscount of Mantes declares that he has sealed a grant to Bec abbey made by his sister, who had no seal, in 1083, L.A. Gatin, *Un village: St-Martin-la-Garenne* (Paris, 1900), 235; unfortunately this grant is known only from a copy of the copy.

46 Other early two-sided seals are those of Waleran, count of Meulan and earl of Worcester, and Alan, count of Brittany and earl of Richmond; the possession of more than one title seemed to invite obverse and reverse dies.

his double status as bishop and earl. Such effigies often flourish a sword (as with Bishop Odo) or a lance, but sometimes they have a banner draped over their shoulders: copying the military effigy of William the Conqueror's great seal, as did Count Stephen's.

It can only be significant that lesser men begin to imitate the great seals of kings and magnates around the 1140s. They are men who can be identified as lords of only one or two villages, or even part of one. However, since they have themselves depicted on horseback and armed and armoured, they must have considered themselves knights. It is part of the subtle momentum we have already noticed that was impelling lesser men to imitate the trappings of the great: aristocratic clothes, the delivery of arms, and as we will see in a later chapter, upgraded aristocratic housing. However, in the case of their use of seals there is proof that their encroachment on the dignity of the great produced some reaction.

Counts and dukes took their seals seriously as an expression of their power and status, and were adorning them with family symbols as early as the 1120s. Early in the 1120s, Count Hugh of Champagne affixed his seal to a charter, proclaiming it to be the mark of his dignity (*virtus*) and power (*potestas*).[47] The clerks of John, count of Eu and lord of Hastings (1140–1170) expressed the view that the impression of their lord's seal gave the full weight of their lord's protection (*patrocinium*) to a document.[48] Richard de Lucy, justiciar of England, all but foamed with rage when confronted by a knight with just such a seal. It had not been, he said, the custom for every petty knight (*militulus*) to have such a thing (see above, p. 139). So it seems that contemporaries were not blind to changes in social aspirations, and were ready to resent and chastise what they saw as usurpations. The irony was that Richard's beginnings were as not much more than a petty knight, a member of King Stephen's military household.

Knightly seals are indeed much in evidence by the end of Stephen's reign. It is true that the great increase in surviving documentation from that period partly accounts for the surge in their survival. Monasteries were being founded in great numbers and therefore new archives were being created and preserved. Yet it is unlikely that seals began to be used for the first time by lesser men at this time; informed opinion seems to be that their use had long been

---

47 M. Bur, *La Formation du comté de Champagne, v. 950–1150* (Mémoires des annales de l'Est, liv, Nancy, 1977), 469.
48 Archives départementales de la Seine Maritime, 8 H 8.

general in society.[49] Nonetheless, the appearance of the knightly effigy on the seals of lesser men than barons at this time is new. These seals were generally smaller than those of magnates, although not universally so. The mid-twelfth-century equestrian seal of Geoffrey l'Abbé, steward of Earl Robert II of Leicester and sometime sheriff of Leicestershire, was the same diameter as that of his master, about 60 mm.[50]

The knightly seals may account for some new fashions in magnate seals. Perhaps even more pressing a reason was the affectation of business seals in the later twelfth century by such humble people as common foresters and Jews.[51] There is a trend for barons in the last quarter of the twelfth century to commission dies for great seals which had their shield of arms on them, not an equestrian image. The point they may have been making was that they were armigerous and had family symbols while knights, as yet, did not. But once common knights assumed arms, as they did early in the thirteenth century, this stratagem would have lost its point.

Another development which emphasised the difference between magnate and knight was the growing fashion in the later twelfth century for magnates to use more than one seal. This could not have been the original intention of the followers of the fashion. In fact this trend began in the Church, where functionaries bought personal seals which featured cut intaglio gems; often imported Ancient Roman intaglios, occasionally home-produced. Thomas Becket, while archdeacon of Canterbury, used just such a seal. It was a mannered fashion, alluding to the Classical world in the literature of which such men were learnèd. The intellectual snobbishness of twelfth-century laymen meant that they found this desirable too. The earls of Chester and Leicester were using intaglio lesser seals in the late 1140s (Leicester at least was a literate and educated man). Later generations made such lesser seals more personal to themselves by having their family devices executed on them. Robert IV, earl of Leicester, was using such an armorial counterseal before he succeeded his father in 1190.[52]

---

49 Heslop, 'English Seals from the Mid-ninth Century to 1100', *Journal of the British Archaeological Association*, cxxxiii (1980), 14–16.
50 Durham D & C muniments, Charter 2.3. Ebor. 14.
51 Foresters with seals occur in the Charter of the Forest (1217), c. 16; seals of Jews are noted in a receipt of 1182, PRO, E210/10868.
52 C.R. Cheney, *English Bishops' Chanceries* (Manchester, 1950), 50–1; T.A. Heslop, 'Seals', in *English Romanesque Art 1066–1200* (Arts Council, 1984), 299, 317; Crouch, *Beaumont Twins*, 210–11, 211n, 212.

The earl of Leicester's lesser seal was used in his acts as a counterseal, applied to the back of impressions of his great seal perhaps to indicate his personal approval of the transaction. Count John of Mortain (later king) notes such a practice in one of his acts dated 1192: 'So that this grant and concession of mine may be forever kept firm and unchallenged, I have strengthened it by the impression of my seal, *and the setting* (appositione) *of my own ring*'.[53] Such seals were very personal; they were often carried on finger-rings. They were sometimes known (as was Count John's) as 'secret' seals, and it was such seals that gave rise to the office of 'secretary' (after the royal official who kept the royal 'secret' seal). It seems likely that lesser seals were a response to the growth of the custom amongst magnates of confiding the great seal to a clerk of the household. Therefore the possession of a lesser, secret seal, in addition to a great seal, would have been seen as a declaration of status: the owner was a man of affairs, he had a clerical office, he had both public and private correspondence. Naturally, as a matter of course since they declared status, lesser men would have imitated such seals; numerous small knightly seals of the thirteenth century are copies of armorial magnate counterseals of the later twelfth century.

The subject of Scottish seals needs little exploration here. As has already been said in this chapter, the social distribution and style of Scottish seals more or less respected that of the Anglo-French world. The native Welsh were also by no means slow to adopt seals. Welsh society was as literate as English society in the eleventh century, perhaps more literate, but there is no evidence of the use of seals by Welsh individuals or religious communities until the Norman period. The use of personal seals must soon have become known to the Welsh in the 1090s. If we are to believe a story of Gerald of Wales, Welsh enemies of his grandfather, Gerald the constable of Pembroke, were able to recognise sealed letters of Gerald, which were deliberately faked and dropped where they could be found, in order to mislead the Welsh.[54] There is a hiatus in the survival of Welsh acts between the 1070s and 1130s which makes it impossible to say to what extent the use of seals caught on amongst Welsh

---

53 Cartulary of Lichfield, Brit. Libr. ms Harley 4799, fo. 38v.; just such a Classical intaglio ring is set to the back of seals of original acts of Count John of the 1190s, it bore the legend + SECRETVM IOHANNIS, Berkeley Castle Muniments, Select Charter 47; BL Harley Charter 83 A 27; PRO C109/86/4; Archives départementales de la Seine-Maritime, 13 H 14; Durham D & C muniments, Charter 1.3. Ebor. 12.
54 Gerald of Wales, *Itinerarium Kambriae*, in *Opera* (8 vols, Rolls Series, 1861–91), ed. Dimock, vi, 90.

magnates themselves in that period. However, there is no doubt, from the language of Welsh charters of the 1140s, that it was then normal for them to possess seals.

What such early seals looked like has recently become clear with the identification of a charter and seal in the Devon Record Office as belonging to Cadell ap Gruffudd, king of Deheubarth, dating to late in the reign of King Stephen of England (1135–54). Cadell's seal has no pretensions to royalty. On its one face it has a military equestrian effigy, looking no different to that of a contemporary English earl.[55] The message is clear. Welsh magnates were affecting the style of contemporary English magnates, and seals were one other means to do so. Later twelfth- and thirteenth-century lay Welsh seals were commissioned in the same tradition. Apart from the names on the legends and the absence of heraldry, there is nothing to distinguish native Welsh from English seals.[56] Llywelyn ab Iorwerth, prince of Gwynedd, responded to the challenge of lesser men taking up seals in much the same way as the English magnates. He too had a secret seal, distinct from his public great seal. On two known occasions he issued letters under his lesser seal, saying on one occasion to the recipient (William Marshal II of Pembroke): 'Do not be concerned that this letter has been sealed by our secret seal; we do not have our great seal with us here.'[57] The seal of Dafydd, son of this Llywelyn, needs mentioning here, although it only survives now in an antiquary's sketch. Unlike any other known Welsh lay charter it was double-sided. As well as the usual equestrian effigy, it also had a 'majesty' side. The pretensions of the house of Gwynedd are well known, so in itself this affectation of royalty is not unexpected. The example is rendered more curious when it is noted that the effigy of the enthroned prince is in fact from dies copying the seal of his uncle King Henry III; the equestrian face apparently had the royal arms of England removed and replaced by a single lion rampant.[58] It may be possible to see this seal as a diplomatic gift from his uncle, perhaps on Dafydd's investiture at Gloucester in 1240. King John is known to have made such gifts, to the king of Norway, for instance.[59]

55 D. Crouch, 'Earliest Original Charter of a Welsh King', *Bulletin of the Board of Celtic Studies*, xxvi (1989), 125–31.
56 M.P. Siddons, 'Welsh Equestrian Seals', *National Library of Wales Journal*, xxiii (1983–4), 292–317.
57 *Royal and other Historical Letters illustrative of the Reign of Henry III*, ed. W.W. Shirley (2 vols, Rolls Series, 1862–6), i, 369.
58 Siddons, 'Welsh Equestrian Seals', 305–6.
59 Personal communication by Dr T.A. Heslop.

DRESS

The subject of aristocratic dress is a most involved and complicated one. I do not intend here any thorough treatment, which would require an analysis of a corpus of manuscript illustration, sculpture and painting so comprehensive as to defy the confines of one or, more likely, several volumes. But some things can be said on the subject of elaboration of dress and its relation to aristocracy. Rich and elaborate dress was an easy way for the wealthy to advertise social superiority. Silks, brocade, fine linen, gold and silver embroidery were only affordable in any amount by the wealthiest. Silks were greedily collected by magnates. Their private chapels were well stocked with copes and chasubles of figured silk for the use of their chaplains. Vestments and lengths of unworked silk lay in their treasuries and feature in stock descriptions of great wealth. For instance, when describing the unequalled power of Robert of Meulan, earl of Leicester (1080–1118) Henry of Huntingdon talks of his ability to advance and destroy careers. 'And so a mass of treasure, gold and silver, gems and lengths of cloth, streamed to him in unbelievable quantities from all sides.' Henry also talks in Byzantine terms of William Atheling, son of Henry I (died 1120), 'clothed in silk embroidered with gold, surrounded by a throng of servants and guards, glittering in a glory all but heavenly'.[60]

Silks were part of the currency of power and patronage. When William de Mandeville, earl of Essex (1167–90), returned from a pilgrimage to the Holy Land, he brought with him a great quantity of oriental silk, lengths of which he gave to all the churches under his patronage for working up into vestments. The best of these he conferred on his priory of Walden as a peace-offering to make up for past differences.[61] If he was like William Marshal, who also returned from the East with luxury silks, he would have deposited the rest of the cloth in one of his castle treasuries. William Marshal kept one great silk cloth for over thirty years, intending it to be a magnificent pall over his bier when the time came.[62] There is no knowing for certain how much silk was in circulation in England in the twelfth and thirteenth centuries, but one measure of its relative abundance

60 *De contemptu mundi*, in Henry of Huntingdon, *Historia Anglorum*, ed. T. Arnold (Rolls Series, 1879), 303, 306.
61 *Liber de fundatione abbathiae de Walden*, in *Monasticon Anglicanum* ed. J. Caley *et al.* (8 vols, London, 1817–30), iv, 144.
62 D. Crouch, *William Marshal: Court, Career and Chivalry in the Angevin Empire* (London, 1990), 187.

in aristocratic households is the fact that little bits of silk were not infrequently used by clerks to make bags to protect great seals after they were set to documents.

Fur too had its aristocratic cachet. Vair (squirrel fur) and ermine were particularly prized; so much so that in the late twelfth and early thirteenth centuries they were translated into heraldic bearings. Vair had its heraldic manifestation as a pattern of blue-grey and white (representing pelts sewed alternately back and front); ermine was represented by a white field spotted with black (to represent the unfortunate creatures' tails). Heraldic furs were not uncommonly used as an alternative to the heraldic metals and tinctures: in fact the arms of the dukes of Brittany were a plain shield of ermine. Nothing could be more aristocratic.

Ostentation through dress had a very long history by 1000; one only has to recall the richness of the surviving ornaments from Sutton Hoo. Even in that remote period (c.AD 625) ostentation was not merely barbaric splendour. The personal trappings and weapons of the East Anglian king buried at Sutton Hoo deliberately alluded to such figures of power as the Imperial Roman officer and the Frankish prince. It was by dressing up in such a way that men expressed then and later their own power in its most immediate form. However, there was in place by 1000 a tradition of austerity which began to affect lay dress in a surprising way. The Church, remembering Christ's injunctions against luxury clothes in the Sermon on the Mount, was one agency in society which was inclined to look askance on ostentation. The Church had moved Carolingian kings to issue edicts against luxury. This seems to have had a lasting effect, for eleventh-century magnates had developed a sophistication in attitudes to dress. Guibert de Nogent records the eleventh-century Count Everard of Breteuil who 'had so little concern for being well-dressed, that he did not resemble a man of wealth at all'. Guibert says that the count was much amused by men who dressed to impress in purple cloaks and fashionably cut leggings, and who wore their hair long, with a central parting 'like women'.[63] Of course, Everard became a monk, and so Guibert may have been crediting him with premature monkish sentiments, but it is quite likely that society had become sufficiently sophisticated by 1100 for there to be aristocrats who indulged in ostentatious moderation; the sort of moderation that was a component of

63 *De Vita Sua*, ed. E.R. Labande (Paris, 1981), 54–6.

twelfth-century 'courtliness'. Herluin, a leading knight of Count Gilbert of Brionne in mid-eleventh-century Normandy, was another such. Long before he renounced his lord's service for an eremitical cell, Herluin practised public austerities in the matter of dress and diet.[64]

The stringencies of the Church indicate that the majority of people were not averse to luxury and fashion, however. Indeed, an aristocracy, like that of Scotland, which failed to dress up to the contemporary standards of luxury and ornament was looked down on as lacking elegance (*decus*). Margaret, queen of Malcolm III (1058-93), bullied her court into adopting the appropriate standards of luxury.[65] Writers of around 1100 felt called to remark upon the luxury of the dress of the Anglo-Norman courts of the time: scandalously cut shirts and tunics, long and rich mantles. The fashion of wearing the hair long and of wearing long and pointed toes to the shoes had come to the Normans after the Conquest of England. The canons of the Council of Rouen of 1096 attacked the fashion for long hair with no little asperity. Churchmen were apt to link bizarre fashions in dress at court with perverted sexual practices.[66] By the time of Henry I long hair was so universal that Bishop Serlo of Séez felt called upon to preach against it in 1105 before the king himself and his court. Since the king was about to embark on a critical campaign and needed all the support he could get, the bishop achieved a degree of success which may have surprised him.[67] The success was only temporary, and William of Malmesbury mentions the same fashion for long hair at Henry's court towards the end of the reign, adding the significant information that court fashion was being affected by county knights; those whose natural hair was too thin went so far as to wear wigs![68]

Edicts against elaborate dress in the twelfth century continued

---

64 *Vita Herluini*, in, J. Armitage Robinson *Gilbert Crispin, Abbot of Westminster* (Cambridge, 1911), 88–90; translated by P. Fisher, in S. Vaughn, *The Abbey of Bec and the Anglo-Norman State, 1034–1136* (Woodbridge, 1981), 68–70.

65 *Vitae sanctae Margaretae reginae*, in *Symeonis Dunelmensis Opera et Collectanea*, i, ed. J. Hodgson Hinde (Surtees Society, li, 1867), 241–2; translated in A.O. Anderson, *Early Sources of Scottish History AD 500 to 1286* (2 vols, Edinburgh, 1922), ii, 68.

66 F. Barlow, *William Rufus* (London, 1983), 102–6.

67 Orderic Vitalis, *The Ecclesiastical History*, ed. Chibnall, vi, 64–6. The disjointed observations of the anonymous justice who wrote the 'Laws of Henry I', in the middle of the reign of that king, show strong traces of lasting unease on the subject of dress (c.15.9).

68 *Historia Novella*, ed. K.R. Potter (London, 1955), 6.

to have a penitential rather than regulatory purpose. St Bernard of Clairvaux preached long and hard against the luxury of 'worldly knights'; the Rule he sponsored for the Knights Templar stressed simplicity of dress and knightly equipment (see Chapter 2). This insistence on simplicity of dress is nowhere more evident in England than in the ordinances associated with Crusades. The Crusade of 1147, which ended in Portugal fighting Moors, assembled at English ports and had a large English contingent. Its ordinances 'forbade the wearing of all manner of luxury clothing'.[69] Forty years later the ordinances issued by Henry II of England for the Crusade he never undertook are more specific. Squirrel fur and sable were forbidden, as was the high-quality cloth known as 'scarlet'. All the potential Crusaders were to eschew clothes which were ornamentally slashed or dagged.[70]

The image of the twelfth- or thirteenth-century aristocracy involved rich clothing, but there was not as yet any clear conception of suitable clothing for the evolving ranks within it. Conceptions of levels within society were too ill formed to lead to ideas of *degrees* of richness in dress. The stock picture of a rich and famous knight, such as Chrétien's picture of Erec riding forth with Queen Guinevere, would do as well for knight, or for baron, count or king: ermine-trimmed mantle, tunic of diapered oriental silk, brocaded hose and golden spurs.[71] Nonetheless, there was in the late twelfth and early thirteenth century at least one fashion in dress which could only have applied to magnates and their wives: the wearing of civilian clothes and military tunics embroidered with family bearings (as seen on the seal of Margaret de Quincy). By the mid-thirteenth century, however, this fashion would have been general once knights embraced heraldic arms, and is seen in the early fourteenth-century psalter of the knightly Luttrell family.

Sumptuary legislation as a definition of degrees of status in English society was a feature of the fourteenth century. Yet some moves towards it are evident in the thirteenth century, and these all revolve around the need to be economical. It was the custom in at least one, and probably most, noble households to buy cloth for garments and match the quality to the importance of the recipient. The squires of Bishop Richard Swinfield of Hereford (1283–1317), according to

69 *De Expugnatione Lyxbonensi*, ed. C.W. David (New York, 1936), 56.
70 *Gesta Henrici Secundi*, ed. W. Stubbs (2 vols, Rolls Series, 1867), ii, 32.
71 *Erec et Enide*, ed. M. Roques (Classiques françaises du moyen âge, 1952), ll. 97-102.

his account roll of 1289–90, were clothed in cloth worth 2s.11d. a yard; *valetti* were dressed in cloth of 2s. a yard, and lesser servants cloth of 1s.7d. value.[72] Austerity and economy in the matter of dress and status had begun to have a significance more than penitential in the France of Philip III (1270–85). In 1279 the Parlement of Philip III had issued ordinances to regulate the dress and diet of the different degrees of society, lay and ecclesiastical. The intention was apparently that private economy in such matters would boost public wealth. There is some evidence that before the end of the century Edward I of England was being briefed on these measures, and perhaps contemplated similar edicts. A letter addressed to the king from Paris discusses such proposals. It talks (amongst other things) of limiting the robes of knights to cloth worth 3s. a yard, squires to cloth worth 2s.; nor should a member of the household receive more than one robe a year from his lord.[73] Whatever the sense, or lack of it, behind these measures, they reflect an undeniable view that the degree of ostentation and quality in dress should be attuned to rank within society, a view which would be more closely defined in the next century.

72 Dyer, *Standards of Living in the Later Middle Ages: Social Change in England, c. 1200–1520* (Cambridge, 1989), 78.
73 C.V. Langlois, 'Project for Taxation presented to Edward I', *English Historical Review*, iv (1889), 517–21. I owe this reference to Dr Trevor Dean.

8

CASTLES AND HALLS

THE HALL

Housing was an area in which you might suppose that the aristocracy would rejoice at the opportunity to display wealth and exclusivity. Yet the march of sophistication was not at such a quick step here as elsewhere. Reviewing developments over the period from 1000 to 1300 we find one obvious change of great consequence: the move from wood to stone as a building material for lordly residences; but this was a slow shift, spanning two centuries. It was not until the end of the twelfth century that poets and writers assumed as a matter of course that the aristocratic house would be built of stone. It is at this point that there is at least one example which confirms the lesser standing of wood. The timber hall of the bishop's palace at Hereford (one of the few such to survive to be recorded) was built late and copied the form of contemporary stone halls. It declared by this affectation that it was the hall in stone which was taken to have prestige. Earlier generations thought differently, seeing length and size in a timber hall as a sufficient declaration of wealth and status. Such seems to be the message of *Beowulf*. What its poet saw as most impressive about the timber hall Heorot that Hrothgar built was its hugeness: 'greatest of houses'. After that came the rhapsodies on the plates of gold nailed to its beams, the carved drinking benches, the tapestries and trophies. There was also some idea in the ninth century that growing sophistication demanded bigger and better residences: the greater the man, the more he excelled his forebears in the elaboration and magnificence of his hall. Asser observes of Alfred that amongst all his tribulations, the king was able 'to erect buildings to his own new design more stately and magnificent than had been the custom of his ancestors'.[1]

With the mind of early medieval man dwelling on the size (and decoration) of halls, it may not be surprising that there was little attention to spare for the elaboration of domestic planning. There may have been many good reasons for this. The first was the lack of obvious prestige models to take; aristocratic titles might hark back to Roman and Carolingian times, but there were no standing Roman palaces or villas in France or Britain for the socially ambitious nobleman to imitate. A small exception, but a magnificent one, was the model of Byzantium, which lent itself as the inspiration for the Carolingian palace at Aachen, which in turn has been seen as a model for at least one English royal hall complex, at Abingdon.[2] Abingdon was also notable for the erection of a private house in the mid-eleventh century, which took as its model the monastic enclosure (its plan derived ultimately from the Mediterranean country villa).[3] This may be seen as an unusual source of inspiration, even though the cloistered enclosure was well-enough known, and has been found as far north and as early as Bede's Jarrow.

Another obstacle to the rapid development of the domestic building would have been the itinerant life of the king and magnate in the High Middle Ages. Earls and barons travelled far, often across the seas, touring their estates. The twelfth-century earls of Leicester had castles and halls at Leicester, Hinckley and Groby, Leicestershire, and Brackley, Northamptonshire, and a hall in the Strand in Westminster. In Normandy they had castles at Breteuil and Pacy-sur-Eure, and a hall besides at Rugles (Eure). It would have been beyond their resources for them to have afforded luxurious and elaborate homes on each and every one of their many estate centres. Technology might have been another drag on architectural display, in stone at least. The heaviness of early Romanesque masonry, and the thickness of walls, seems to bespeak a lack of confidence, and a fear of the weight of roofs. Even so casual tourist as I am is struck

1 Translation from *English Historical Documents*, i, c. AD 500–1042 ed. D. Whitelock (London, 1955), 267.
2 R. Gem, 'Towards an Iconography of Anglo-Saxon Architecture', *Journal of the Warburg and Courtauld Institutes*, xlvi (1983), 8–9.
3 *Chronicon monasterii de Abingdon*, ed. J. Stevenson (2 vols, Rolls Series, 1852), i, 474; ii, 283.

by the laboured masonry of the eleventh century, as rare as it is heavy.

From the beginnings of our period, castle and hall were aristocratic buildings with several purposes, some rather contradictory. The heavily defended enclosure that is the castle was designed to overawe the subject population and neighbours, to state a degree of power, and keep the lord secure; its military function was to keep people out. On the contrary, the hall was a public stage for the lord to display his greatness, whether in entertaining or in doing justice; therefore the hall should be open to all. A hall can sit ill within a castle, especially when the later domestic range was added to an existing and constricted castle bailey.[4] One only has to look at the palatial quarters erected by Earl Roger Bigod in the lower bailey of Chepstow castle to realise how castle and hall contradicted each other's purposes. The Bigod hall-complex is tucked away awkwardly in a corner, on the edge of a cliff, all but invisible from the main gate of the castle, its fine porch and oriel dwarfed by the great towers and walls around it. The dimensions of the castle make the earl's hall into a something no more impressive than a huddle of farm buildings. Yet if it had been built alone in the fields it would have been rather more impressive than a contemporary manor house, like Stokesay, and quite as impressive as the great royal country houses. The grand domestic ranges at Ludlow and Nottingham received the same unhappy treatment from their surroundings.

Yet both castle and hall did answer one need: the need for a magnate to impress and overawe. In fact the castle and hall express very neatly, and in a material way, the complicated nature of the sources of aristocratic power. Magnates imposed their will on the localities in a range of ways. To seduce people into their obedience (their *ditio*, as their clerks occasionally put it in Latin) they offered generous hospitality, places and offices in their large households, money, presents and (as an ultimate reward) land. They also had jurisdiction over their own manors and followers; a court in which justice was done in their name. In all these activities, the hall played its part, as a stage for ceremonial, feasts and court. But aristocratic power also operated on a degree of menace. Geoffrey of Monmouth put it well when describing the power of his patron, Waleran, count of Meulan and earl of Worcester (died 1166): 'you have learnt,

---

4 M.W. Thompson, *The Decline of the Castle* (Cambridge, 1987), 55.

under your father's guidance, to be a terror to your enemies and a protection to your own folk'.[5] To be feared where he was not loved was the ambition of an eleventh- or twelfth-century magnate.[6] The brooding power of a castle, and its garrison of knights and serjeants, was one means for him to achieve this. The association of castle and aristocratic power had begun in the 1030s in Normandy.[7] Throughout northern France around this time and a little before we find references to such characters as *castellani*, magnates who based their power on the possession of castles, and the garrisoning of them with *milites castri*, knights of their military household.

Of the two forms of aristocratic building, the hall has the most relevance to display and prestige. This had long been the case. One ancient Latin word for 'courtier' was *aulicus* ('hall-person' from *aula*: 'hall'). *Aulicus* had an Anglo-Saxon parallel, *healthegn*, showing that the idea was a common European one. The idea of the hall was an ancient one, indeed it must be prehistoric. Its power over the early medieval mind is nowhere better (or more famously) demonstrated than in Bede's remarkable passage comparing the hall with life itself. Within, the king and his men sit at the feast, the fire burning merrily on the central hearth, while a winter storm of rain and snow howls in the blackness outside. The individual soul is like a sparrow that flutters momentarily into the warmth through one door and soon flies out the other and is lost in the dark. Anglo-Saxon literature was saturated with remembrances of the hall. It was an image of light and peace; the hall and its enclosure (*beorg, burh*) was a haven from discomfort and danger. More than that, it was the seat of power where the lord distributed patronage and gifts. It is likely that contemporary Franks saw the hall in exactly the same way; not just a building but the warm centre of their social and political life. The lord sitting in the hall was one of the oldest and most potent images of royal and aristocratic power. It sufficed for an Anglo-Saxon when he tried to picture God sitting in Zion.[8]

5 Geoffrey of Monmouth, *Historia Regum Britannie*, ed. N. Wright (Cambridge, 1985), p. xiv, translation by Lewis Thorpe.
6 See a discussion of this in D. Crouch, *William Marshal: Court, Career and Chivalry in the Angevin Empire* (London, 1990), 150–7.
7 See for Normandy, D.R. Bates, *Normandy before 1066* (London, 1982), 114–15, and references there given; and for France, J. Dunbabin, *France in the Making, 843–1180* (Oxford, 1985), 144–50.
8 K. Hume, 'The Concept of the Hall in Old English Poetry', in *Anglo-Saxon England* iii, ed. P. Clemoes *et al.* (Cambridge, 1974), 63–74.

Nor was the image confined to Anglo-Saxons. St Anselm, when a boy in Savoy in the mid-eleventh century, had a dream in which his mind pictured God the king in much the same way, in a mountaintop hall (*regia aula*) seated, and attended by his steward.[9]

From the archeological evidence there seems little to distinguish the English from the Norman hall in 1000. The hall-complex at Cheddar, much frequented by the kings of the Wessex dynasty, may have been typical. In the early eleventh century, it boasted a well-built timber hall, 54 × 22 feet, alongside a stone chapel of similar dimensions. A private chamber (bower) stood isolated within the enclosure, offering the king the possibility of withdrawal from the common gaze. Latrines and craftsmen's buildings were laid out more or less at random within the fenced and ditched *burh*.[10] The contemporary hall of Richard II of Normandy at Fécamp was not very different in general appearance. Within a large enclosure stood the rectangular ducal hall (called a 'palace' in imitation of the royal residences) in stone about 70 feet long, with a large stone collegiate church not far to the north. A kitchen and what might have been a private apartment (both in wood) adjoined the hall, but stood apart from it.[11] Such were the modest domestic models the king or prince could offer to his aristocracy at the beginning of the eleventh century.

What little evidence there is suggests that princely residences were in fact little different from those of the aristocracy in the early eleventh century. We hear of the estate of Ealdorman Aethelwine of East Anglia (died 992) at Upwood, which he had from King Edgar. There in his lifetime he had a hall and court 'suitable to a man of such nobility', a residence made attractive by the vicinity of moors and fens for hunting and hawking.[12] Upwood may have been similar to what has been found by investigation of the site of an aristocratic residence at Goltho, Lincolnshire. Around 1000 it consisted of a complex of hall, kitchen, bower and industrial buildings very like that at Cheddar, although enclosed within a smaller, more stoutly defended enclosure. It lacked the chapel

9 Eadmer, *The Life of St Anselm*, ed. R. Southern (repr. Oxford, 1972), 4–5.
10 *The History of the King's Works: The Middle Ages*, ed. H.M. Colvin *et al.* (2 vols, HMSO, 1963), ii, 908–9.
11 A. Renoux, 'Recherches historiques et archéologiques sur le château de Fécamp, ancien palais des ducs de Normandie', *Château Gaillard*, vii (1975), 183–6.
12 *Chronicon abbatiae Rameseiensis*, ed. W. Dunn Macray (Rolls Series, 1886), 52.

which was so important a part of the princely residences of England and the Continent.[13] Across the Channel, a comparable and contemporary Norman site at Le Plessis-Grimoult also had a strong ditch and rampart enclosing a hall-complex of a similar type.[14]

These were primarily domestic structures, the enclosure designed to restrict access to the lord within. That they also offered a measure of security is clear, the offence of *hamsocn* (housebreaking) under English law was a serious offence, and apparently a not uncommon one.[15] It was as well for an earl or thegn, as much as a Norman seigneur, to have a residence fortifiable against a marauding rival. In dealing with 'hall-complexes' and 'castles' we have to remember that the distinction between them may not have been very clear at the time. Indeed buildings we would call 'castles' are sometimes called by contemporaries *domus* (houses). Halls within enclosures were defensible, and intended to be defended. English halls often included a wooden tower (or belfry). Nonetheless it is usually possible to discern if a building's principal purpose was domestic, and intention is the guideline followed here.

THE CASTLE AND STATUS

The structures I have so far considered can all be described as halls or hall-complexes. They were domestic sites, lightly defended, if at all, by bank, ditch and palisade. The tradition of erecting such structures was ancient and remained vigorous; they are the physical ancestors of the English country house and the French *manoir*. A complicating development well under way by 1000 was the erection by individuals of more deliberately fortified structures: castles. Fortifications and common defence had originally been a monopoly of the Carolingian dynasty in Francia, and there seems

13 G. Beresford, 'Goltho Manor, Lincolnshire: the Buildings and their Surrounding Defences', in *Proceedings of the Battle Conference*, iv, ed. R.A. Brown (Woodbridge, 1982), 27–30; idem, *Goltho: the Development of an Early Medieval Manor, c. 850–1150* (English Heritage Archeological Report, iv).
14 E. Zadora-Rio, 'L'Enceinte fortifiée du Plessis-Grimoult', *Château Gaillard*, v (1970), 237–9.
15 A. Williams, 'A Bell-house and Burh-geat: Lordly Residences in England before the Norman Conquest', in *The Ideals and Practice of Medieval Knighthood*, iv, ed. R. Harvey and C. Harper-Bill (Woodbridge, 1992). I am much obliged to Dr Williams for allowing me to see a typescript of this important article before publication.

to have been a similar situation in England.[16] In both kingdoms these were often the surviving walled circuits of Roman towns, or newly-embanked sites (like the Wessex *burh* at Wareham) or simply ancient hilltop or island strongpoints. In the tenth century, however, there was a new development in France. Royal fortresses fell into private hands, and became the bases of semi-autonomous lordships. New castles multiplied as other lords protected themselves, or simply emulated their neighbours. Technology improved in this competitive environment. The great stone keep or *donjon* – something quite unknown in England – appeared in Central France just before 1000.[17]

Normandy had fortifications of a sort in the early eleventh century. They were, however, few, and confined to the ownership of the duke and his close kin, the counts. The greatest of them seem to have been promontory-forts like Ivry, Falaise and Domfront: sites defended by nature as much as art. It was in the 1030s and the 1040s, when the young Duke William was under the tutelage of his aristocracy, that castles multiplied, built by men other than members of the ducal family. These men were all, apparently, men of higher status and heads of wealthy families; some had been ducal officers and some claimed a blood connection with earlier dukes. It does not seem that their new castles were particularly numerous. Some of them were strongly sited, like Pont Audemer on its riverside bluff, and Tancarville on a peninsula protected by the Seine, but few betray any major advance in military architecture. The strongest, such as Grimboscq in central Normandy, featured the new development of a *motte*, a tall, artificial mound surmounted by a wooden tower. It gave the lord and his men an inner stronghold to which to retreat, and doubtless added a much-needed impression of height and power to the simple enclosure-fort. Individual Norman magnates occasionally took the names of these new fortresses as surnames, identifying themselves intimately with the structure that expressed their status.

Such structures stood apart from the palisaded halls in which other landowners dwelt. They expressed power and enabled jurisdiction

---

16 C. Coulson, 'Fortress-Policy in Capetian Tradition and Angevin Practice: Aspects of the Conquest of Normandy by Philip II', in *Anglo-Norman Studies*, vi, ed. R. Allen Brown (Woodbridge, 1984), 14–16; Dunbabin, *France in the Making*, 40–2; for England, Williams, 'A Bell-house and Burh-geat'.
17 A development summarised by Contamine, *War in the Middle Ages*, trans. M. Jones (Oxford, 1984), 44–7.

to be claimed over a surrounding area. Recent studies of Norman society have emphasised how these exceptional castles were the points around which great lordships rapidly grew. Lesser men around about the new castle submitted to its lord, coming to arrangements by which they and their men enlisted in his military retinue, and frequented his hall. In this way, by the 1050s, when William of Normandy managed to impose his will on his principality, its aristocracy had been made sharply aware how the *turris* or 'tower' not merely demonstrated status but could transform the political balance of any area in which it was planted.[18]

It is not easy to say when lesser Norman landowners erected structures that we call castles.[19] In 1091 a Norman inquisition recalled that in the days of the Conqueror a structure might have been considered a fortification subject to ducal control if a height of nine or ten feet separated the top of the rampart from the bottom of the surrounding ditch. Some degree of scientific fortification was also expected at that date: a castle should have salients and outworks, and a sentry walk. By implication therefore, the simple palisaded hall in which most Norman landowners lived was beneath ducal notice and could not have been considered to have shared the exclusive cachet of the 'tower' of the counts and *grands seigneurs* of the duchy.[20] The same must be true of many of the enclosed dwellings built by the Normans in Britain. Many of the 'ring-works' built in the years after 1066, whether in England, Scotland or Wales, are often classified in modern works as castles, but excavation reveals them as not much more than enclosed halls strengthened occasionally with a wooden turret placed beside a gate, bearing a strong resemblance to the pre-Conquest thegnly residence of hall, *beorg* and *burh-geat*. It is unlikely that such

18 Summarised from J. Yver, 'Les Châteaux forts en Normandie jusqu'au milieu du xiie siècle', *Bulletin de la Société des Antiquaires de la Normandie*, liii (1957 for 1955–6), 52–7; B.K. Davison, 'Early Earthwork Castles: a New Model', *Château Gaillard*, iii (1966), 37–47; Bates, *Normandy before 1066*, 111–28; J. Le Maho, 'De la *Curtis* au château: l'exemple du Pays de Caux', *Château Gaillard* viii (1977), 171–83.
19 In 1051 the Anglo-Saxon chronicle, written by men who knew little of the Frankish castle with tower, called the fortifications built by French settlers in their kingdom under the Confessor, *castel* – a loan word from the French *chastel* (or possibly the Latin *castellum*). In English usage, therefore, it is permissible to use the word 'castle' for the intrusive French fortification, new and alien to England; see Williams, 'A Bell-house and Burh-geat'.
20 See remarks in C. Coulson, 'Structural Symbolism in Medieval Castle Architecture', *Journal of the British Archeological Association*, cxxxii (1979), 82.

works would have come within the purview of the prince, by the criteria given by the Norman inquisition of 1091. Some, like the early twelfth-century ring-work at Llantrithyd in South Wales, were wretched indeed, with an ill-built hall on the lines of an oversized peasant cot. Llantrithyd could not by any means have been considered a prestigious dwelling, and its owner seems to have abandoned it rather than go to the expense of upgrading it.

Castles – deliberate fortifications of some strength and a degree of sophistication – were not very common structures in post-Conquest England. We should treat with care the comment of the Anglo-Saxon chronicle under the year 1067 that the Normans 'built castles (*castelas*) widely throughout the country, and oppressed the poor people'. However, few though they were, they were unprecedented structures in most of England, sited prominently in great towns, and had a dramatic visual impact. We can therefore excuse some overstatement, and associate the 1067 remark, perhaps, with a spate of new and small fortified halls built by the intruding *castelmenn*, resented for that reason. If we take the county of Warwickshire to illustrate this point, we find only three fortifications of any size which could be confidently assigned to the period immediately after the Conquest: Warwick, Oversley and Brinklow, which commanded respectively a major town and two important roads. All three were earthworks, and it is unlikely that these, or the castles that were erected subsequently to mark the establishment of new lordships in the reign of Rufus, were graced with masonry works till at least the early years of Henry I. The first major stone-built castle in the county did not come about until Henry I's minister, Geoffrey de Clinton, commenced the erection of a magnificent square keep at Kenilworth around 1125, thus advertising both his own status and the insignificance of the castle of his close neighbour and social superior, Earl Roger of Warwick (Warwick apparently had only a stone shell-keep on a mound).[21] There were rather more castles proportionally in the counties of the Welsh and Scottish Marches, but the situation in most English counties paralleled that of Warwickshire, as a consideration of the material in Cathcart-King's *Castellarium Anglicanum* demonstrates.

It was in Henry I's reign that we find castle-building being used and generally perceived as a social statement by rising men in both

---

21 P.B. Chatwin, 'Castles in Warwickshire', *Birmingham Archeological Society Transactions*, lxvii (1951 for 1947–8), 1–34.

Normandy and England. Geoffrey de Clinton is an example of this. Like another of his colleagues at court, Bishop Roger of Salisbury, he was willing to invest his new wealth in masonry as a demonstration that he had arrived at the top of society. Geoffrey had begun as a minor Norman landowner of the Cotentin; Bishop Roger began as a poor priest in the diocese of Avranches.[22] By the 1120s both were the king's intimates, both had great lands and to advertise their new power and wealth they built castles in stone, bigger and better than those that most of the great magnates had yet built. For example, the great earl of Warenne, in pursuit of control over Norfolk in the 1140s, discovered that he had no suitably impressive fortification at the centre of his extensive Norfolk estates, just a stone hall within an enclosure at what was later called 'Castle' Acre, once he had erected a stone castle to remedy the deficiency in prestige. Geoffrey de Clinton built in stone at Kenilworth and Brandon in Warwickshire, and possibly also at the Château de Semilly in the Cotentin. As William of Malmesbury says of the bishop of Salisbury, one of his patrons, 'wishing to seem magnificent in the buildings he [Bishop Roger] erected . . . [he] raised masses of masonry, surmounted by towers, building over a great extent of ground' at Old Sherborne and Devizes.[23] Nor is this an isolated statement; according to Orderic Vitalis another Norman parvenu, Richard Basset, made his fortune at Henry I's court, and 'swollen with the wealth of England, had made a show of superiority to all his peers and fellow countrymen by the magnificence of his building in the little fief he had inherited from his parents in Normandy. He had therefore built a very well-fortified castle of ashlar blocks at Montreuil.'[24]

The pursuit of magnificence in the shortest time possible was common to all three of these men, and others of their colleagues at the court of Henry I. For them the building of such a 'tower' as the count or great baron should possess was one way to assert themselves and give material form in the country to the status they enjoyed at court. No wonder therefore that their pushiness caused resentment, and both Geoffrey and Bishop Roger fell victim to the envious intrigue of more truly noble factions at court. His castles did nothing, in the end, to help Bishop Roger. But Geoffrey de Clinton's son, Geoffrey II, may have had his father's desire for

22 For their origins and careers see Green, *Government of England under Henry I*, 239–41, 273–4.
23 *Historia Novella*, ed. K.R. Potter (London, 1955), 25.
24 *The Ecclesiastical History*, ed. M. Chibnall, (6 vols, Oxford, 1969–80), vi, 468.

grandeur to thank for his survival, when he came under the attack of his father's enemy, the earl of Warwick, late in the 1130s.[25] There is good evidence that it was possession of Kenilworth which allowed young Geoffrey to maintain himself and his family against their enemies: a salutary reminder that castles had other uses than prestige for men at the mercy of the unstable fortunes of the court.

After Henry I's reign the process of social climbing by castle-building went on. Stephen's reign produced a number of castles built with social elevation partly in mind. Castle Rising (how aptly named!) in Norfolk was rebuilt in stone to commemorate the fact that its owner, William d'Aubigny of Buckenham, a royal butler, had married the widow of Henry I and been raised to the rank of earl. What is most interesting at Castle Rising is that the keep was designed consciously to impress. It is of the type sometimes known as the hall-keep, a type first raised in Britain by Earl William fitz Osbern at Chepstow in the late 1060s, but that at Castle Rising is far more elaborate, and resembles the impressive keeps that Henry I had raised some years earlier at Norwich and Falaise. The visitor approaching it is faced by the walls of a forebuilding which carry much ornament, blank arcades and roundels, a wealth of elaboration sited in order to impress. A stately staircase – which appears designed to allow the sorts of procession which might be marshalled by ushers with their wands – leads to an antechamber, and from this an impressive, tall door leads into the hall. There one would turn to face the earl; the place for his chair is framed by a tall alcove in the wall behind. To one side (duplicating within the keep the arrangements of the hall-complex) were a kitchen and domestic offices. A door behind the lord's place allowed withdrawal to a private chamber, and the possibility of a grand entrance to give audience.

Castle Hedingham in Essex is a similar sort of statement. It was erected in the 1140s by Aubrey de Vere, count of Guines and later earl of Oxford, and in this case the inspiration would seem to have been the keep at Rochester built a score or so years before. Aubrey was the son of a royal chamberlain, and indeed of no mean family. But his elevation to comital rank (as much as the instability of Stephen's reign) demanded something new. What the demand produced was one of the most elegant keeps in

25 D. Crouch, 'Geoffrey de Clinton and Roger, Earl of Warwick', *Bulletin of the Institute of Historical Research*, lv (1982), 120–2.

England, with apartments that seem to defy the heaviness normally associated with Romanesque. Both Hedingham and Castle Rising conspicuously share the finely joined ashlar blocks Orderic remarks upon at the Basset castle of Montreuil. Well-squared masonry was obviously more expensive, and had more aesthetic appeal. The diagonal-tooled blocks were indeed harder to produce in quantity with only the crude tools available before the mid-twelfth century. Where squared masonry was used, contemporary writers felt called on to mention it.[26] At castles such as Hedingham and Castle Rising a new intensity of thought was being given to aristocratic display and exclusivity. This is not to say that either castle was revolutionary in basic design, it is just that there was an overt intention by their designers to impress contemporaries with their wealth and importance, as much as to build a fortress. For displays of status to take a military direction was hardly surprising in view of the prevailing ethos of the magnates. Such a display was the noble castle *mout riche et fort* in which a writer like Chrétien de Troyes could rejoice in the 1170s, the keep springing up from the foundations, the curtain wall of (again) those high-status squared blocks, with turrets and a barbican overlooking the approach by a bridge (itself closed by a tower).[27]

The castle had taken on a symbolic dimension before the end of the twelfth century. A great count or baron must have a castle or castles; it was part of his prestige. At least one count carried this need for prestige to an extreme. On one known occasion in 1165 Waleran of Meulan and Worcester chose to have his clerk refer to his Norman fortress of Beaumont-le-Roger as his 'palace'. When he did so, he was imitating royal state quite deliberately; his daring example seems to be unique.[28] Other counts were content with taking pride in their castles, without going so far as Waleran. In the early thirteenth century, the anonymous author of the successful English romance 'Guy of Warwick', when describing the wealth and power of the

---

26 Lambert of Ardres, describing the erection of the castle of Guines by Count Baldwin, mentioned its keep 'a round building with squared masonry (*domum rotundam lapidibus quadris*)', Lambert of Ardres, 'Historia Comitum Ghisnensium', in *M.G.H. Scriptores*, xxiv, 596.

27 *Le Conte de Graal*, ed. F. Lecoy (2 vols, Classiques français du moyen âge, 1972–5), i, ll. 1317–46.

28 Paris, Archives nationales, K24 no.10.4. Waleran's clerk did so when dating a charter, and in this he was copying the way Capetian *mandements* were phrased. Nonetheless, the choice of example to emulate, as much as the word *palatium*, is significant.

legendary Earl Roalt of Warwick, described his 'strong castles and rich cities' as much as his silks, precious vessels and many knights.[29] Since the form of the castle had status, the possession of crenellated (battlemented) buildings was a social statement. Charles Coulson has pointed out that many licences to crenellate buildings were obtained for buildings of little military importance, even monastic precinct walls. The intention was to impress, little more.[30] The best example of such a building is the mid-thirteenth-century outer court of the priory of Ewenny in Glamorgan. Massive, expensive and businesslike walls and towers dominate the road that approaches the convent from the west. On the eastern side, the precinct is, and always was, entirely undefended.

The later Middle Ages added a dimension of romantic grandeur to the show castle. Noble piles like Bodiam, Tattersall, Herstmonceux and Raglan in the late fourteenth and fifteenth centuries chiefly advertised grandeur. They were devised to impress, like the castles in contemporary illuminations. Bodiam had a kitchen door dressed up as a gatehouse, randomly sited arrow-slits, gun-loops designed to be seen at their best from a hillside viewing platform, and intended as porters' view-holes. The builders of such castles were often new men, like the new men of Henry I, creating a set for their social ambitions.[31] They had nothing to do with blank, frowning inaccessibility. That they were handsome residences possessing some practical defensibility is true, but there is more than something of machicolated, finialed and turreted confections about them; they were the end product of the idea of the status castle, which we first find dawning in Henry I's England.

STATUS AND DOMESTIC PLANNING AFTER 1100

As with the castle so with the hall. It underwent a change in emphasis after 1100; scale was part of this. Aisles added spaciousness to the height and length of the older form of hall. The great hall raised by William Rufus at Westminster in the 1090s seems to have inspired several aristocratic imitators. One obvious imitator is the great hall

29 *Gui de Warewic roman du xiiie siècle*, ed. A. Ewert (2 vols, Classiques français du moyen âge, 1932), i, ll. 27–43.
30 C. Coulson, 'Hierarchism in Conventual Crenellation', *Medieval Archeology*, xxvi (1982), 69–71.
31 See for this, Thompson, *The Decline of the Castle*, 72–96. For Bodiam and its pretensions, see C. Coulson, 'Bodiam Castle: Truth and Tradition', *Fortress*, x (1991), 1–7.

at Leicester castle dating, apparently, from late in the reign of Stephen. It was of considerable proportions. It had a stone shell and gables, with a timber arcade of six bays, fit for a session of the court and exchequer of the great Earl Robert II (died 1168).[32] Other halls arcaded in either stone or timber were erected on the Westminster model. The most famous of them survive at Oakham, Farnham and Winchester. These halls, particularly those arcaded in stone, were new in their ambitious scale and ornament, if not in form. In the amount of space included under their roof timbers we see what it was that impressed the twelfth-century mind. The long, vaulted spaces of the Romanesque abbeys and cathedrals of England confirm this. Such halls were, as they ever had been, public stages for holding court; as such they tend to appear in royal, comital and episcopal residences. The public shire-halls were of similar form, for they had a similar function. Such halls continued to be built, draughty and cold as they must have been, because they met this idea of grandeur.

Stone construction was also something which was new in halls. The hall-cum-keep at Chepstow, built before 1071, is a fine example of this. Very much a frontier castle when first built, it still contained elements designed to impress: the first-floor entrance was richly ornamented and reached by a stately flight of steps. Two other early examples are in houses associated with the earl of Warenne. One was in his great town house in Southwark, at the south end of London bridge; the other was at his (originally lightly fortified) rural residence of Castle Acre, the centre of his Norfolk estates. Both are of the hall (or chamber) over undercroft variety. Boothby Pagnell, Lincolnshire, and Burton Agnes, Yorkshire, are other later examples. Again, both are associated with magnates (the Paynel and Stuteville families). Both are well built and impressive enough in their ways, and contain the luxury of a fireplace and chimney built into the wall. The important thing about all of these, one suspects, was that they were tall buildings of stone. Timber halls continued to be built (although few survive), but the rising trend was for stone during the twelfth century.

Something else that was new in domestic buildings in the twelfth century was the growth in facilities offered the great man to withdraw modestly from the public gaze. They did not seek privacy

32 N.W. Alcock and R.J. Buckley, 'Leicester Castle: the Great Hall', *Medieval Archaeology*, xxxi (1987), 73–9.

here, just a retreat into the company of a more intimate group of servants and counsellors, chamberlains and confessors. On the rare occasions that we have accounts of lords within their chambers (as when Becket was confronted by his intending assassins) they are not alone, but in the company of numerous intimates. It is also worth noting that Becket's assassins had first to be announced to him by the steward of the archiepiscopal hall, before they were admitted to the inner chamber, where he was sitting on his bed. By the early 1240s, the preference for the inner chamber had become so marked that lords (and ladies) were being advised to resist the temptation of closeting themselves away, and make a point of visiting the hall for their meals.[33]

Withdrawing chambers are to be found early, as early indeed as the 'bowers' of Anglo-Saxon halls, so there was nothing new about this idea. Part of the charisma of greatness must be periods of inaccessibility. The lord closeted in a withdrawing chamber was difficult to approach, and by making approach possible he could show favour to a particular man; it created intimacy between them. Also, leaving the private chambers to appear in the public hall was an occasion of state; the earliest function of the Anglo-French herald was to announce such an entrance, and kings and all great men employed ushers to clear their way to their chair of state. Welsh magnates had related officials, the *gostegwr* (crier) and *gwas ystafell* (chamberlain), and this demonstrates how universal in medieval society was the need to display status by the control of access and space. What was new in the later twelfth century was the idea that complexity of domestic plans related to status. The twelfth-century historian of the counts of Guines rejoiced in the 'many and various chambers, rooms and resorts, like unto a labyrinth' when describing the comital mansion.[34]

It was when magnates had domestic ranges built for them which combined both great hall *and* chamber block – often built at right angles to each other, or the one tacked on the end of the other – that we begin to see the more intensive exploitation of the two lives of the great man; a new sophistication in the material expression of rank.[35] This development had certainly happened by the end of the twelfth

33 *Walter of Henley and other Treatises on Estate Management*, ed. D.M. Oschinsky (Oxford, 1971), 407. I owe this reference to Mr Richard Eales.
34 Lambert of Ardres, 'Historia Comitum Ghisnensium', 596.
35 P.A. Faulkner, 'Domestic Planning from the Twelfth to the Fourteenth Centuries', *Archaeological Journal*, cxv (1958), 180–3.

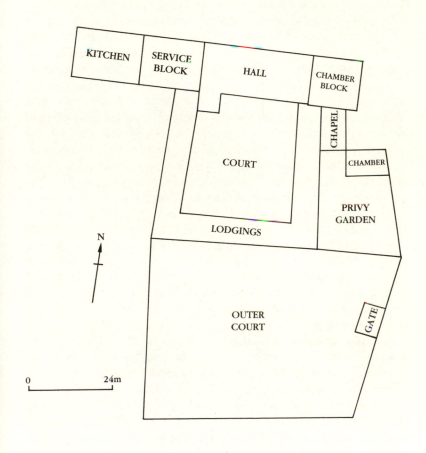

KITCHEN

SERVICE BLOCK

HALL

CHAMBER BLOCK

CHAPEL

COURT

CHAMBER

PRIVY GARDEN

LODGINGS

N

OUTER COURT

GATE

0   24m

Figure 11   Winchester Place, Southwark, *c.*1250 (after Carlin, 1985).

century. A further contemporary elaboration was the provision of service rooms at the end of the hall: butteries and pantries from where the officers of the hall could assemble and supervise the processions of servants arriving from the exterior kitchen with food for the hall, carve the meat, and fill the cups. The presence of such service rooms has been detected at a structure as early as Henry II's hall at Clarendon, near Salisbury, built in 1181–3. It may be that King Henry imported the idea from France for his magnificent refurbishment of the hilltop palace in the 1170s and 1180s.[36] Magnates visited Clarendon regularly in the reigns of the Angevin kings, it was the site of three of the major assizes of his reign: its great enclosure, expensive buildings with flint walls and freestone dressings, the panelled and plastered king's chamber, the queen's chamber and private chapel, the great chapel with marble columns, the barns, wine-stores, kitchens and service rooms may well have been taken as a model in its day for those ambitious to impress.

One late twelfth-century aristocratic complex which had echoes of Clarendon and other of Henry II's palaces was the episcopal palace at Hereford. An aisled timber hall of four bays has attached to it a chamber block of three floors and an undercroft, with a chimney stack. North of the hall was a magnificent episcopal chapel in stone, and to the east of it, attached by a passage, was the bishop's great chamber; his place to withdraw. There is no evidence of a service block, but the chambers attached to the end of the hall may represent early moves in that direction. Whatever the case, service blocks appear associated with halls as a matter of course in the thirteenth century, a fine example attached to the bishop's palace at Lincoln dating to some time between 1200 and 1220.[37]

Royal residences tell us that in the thirteenth century interior decoration had come into its own.[38] The novelty of plastered, painted rooms seems to have reached England (from France) during the reign of Henry II, for he had chambers at Winchester painted with allegorical scenes in the 1180s. Whitewashed chambers would frequently be painted with red lines to represent the high-quality

36 *History of the King's Works*, ii, 910–11; M. Wood, *The English Mediaeval House* (repr. London, 1983), 124; T.B. Jones and A.M. Robinson, *Clarendon Palace* (Society of Antiquaries Report xlv, 1988).
37 J. Blair, 'The Twelfth Century Bishop's Palace at Hereford', *Medieval Archaeology*, xxxi (1987), 59–72.
38 Wood, *The English Medieval House*, 394–402.

squared stonework that was so much valued at the time. Sometimes such rooms would be panelled with wainscot, fashioned from Scandinavian fir. A king might aspire to a coherent scheme of decoration. That favoured by Henry III was green, spangled with gold stars. The king seems to have employed it at most of his palaces, and it has been suggested that green was chosen as being the most expensive pigment. Otherwise paintings of heroes and Biblical scenes seem to have been common enough in the chambers of royal palaces. It is a pity that evidence about the interior decoration of baronial residences is so much lacking. Baronial household accounts do not survive for the period in anything like the fullness of those of the English monarchy. Nonetheless, it is likely that a degree of decoration must have been affected by the aristocracy before 1300, if only from a comparison with the residences of contemporary prelates.

Rambling country houses were coming to be fashioned into a new ideal of prestige around 1200. It was becoming possible to impress without building a castle, for there was an acceptable royal model of a noble dwelling which was hedged off from the world by ditch, bank, wall or moat, but not fortified – a hall, chambers, and, most importantly, a private chapel. An example is the manor house of Noseley, Leicestershire, where in the late 1220s its owner, Sir William de Martinwast, a prominent county knight and a retainer of the chief justiciar, Stephen of Seagrave, arranged the licensing of a private chapel with two bells in the court of his manor, south of the hall. Here Sir William, his wife and household might hear mass sung by his own chaplain, being constrained to mingle with common folk at the parish church only at the great feasts, if he was in residence.[39] Sir William was neither alone in doing this, nor the first to do it. The records of Leicestershire and Warwickshire are particularly rich in mentions of similar chapels being built at the manor houses of Market Bosworth, Leicestershire, Asthill, Bishopton and Pinley, Warwickshire, around this time, all for the benefit of rising county knights.[40] Chapels in castles had been a matter of course before 1200, and followed naturally from the

39 H. Hartopp, 'Some Unpublished Documents relating to Noseley, co. Leics.', *Associated Architectural Societies: Reports and Papers*, xxv pt 2 (1900), 433–4; D. Crouch, 'The Family of Martinwast of Noseley', *The Harborough Historian*, viii (1989), 9–10.
40 J.R.H. Moorman, *Church Life in England in the Thirteenth Century* (Cambridge, 1946), 15–16, notes licences of such chapels in early registers of the bishops of Lincoln from the 1220s onwards.

collegiate chapels in royal and ducal halls of the tenth and eleventh centuries. When private chapels begin to appear in England within knightly residences (despite the proximity of a parish church) it is clear enough that they are structures that declare status.[41] The lord of the village might still be buried in his parish church, but he would only be seen dead in it. In 1292 the parishioners of Crawthorne, Kent, were complaining that the lady of their manor would neither contribute to their church nor come to it. Her chaplains said mass in her own chapel, even baptising her children there, using a bucket for a font.[42]

A number of excavated examples are revealing the slow elaboration of the magnate and gentry residence of the thirteenth century. The survival of the thirteenth-century accounts of the bishops of Winchester means that the development of their large and partly excavated palace in Southwark can be monitored over the period (Fig. 11). The small twelfth-century hall-complex survived into the thirteenth century, but was then falling into disuse. It was dismantled and superseded by larger and finer quarters and the remains of the original hall converted into a wood store. The new palace had been built for Peter des Roches by 1220, and was to be a place fit for the residence of a royal justiciar, adviser of popes and emperors, and wealthiest bishop on the English bench. A great gatehouse (doubtless on the model of that of an abbey precinct wall) was in existence early in the thirteenth century, to overawe visitors from their first approach to the house. The gate opened into an outer court ranged about with offices and stables. Above this rose the high roofs of the inner court. The hall was joined to a kitchen-complex and service rooms at one end with a withdrawing chamber at the other. The whole range formed the north side of the court, around the other sides of which were a chapel, and lodgings for knights,

---

41 There is evidence that private oratories in the big enclosures of the early London city-magnates were the basis for some of the later network of parish churches of the city; and a large number of early country manor houses are built adjacent to parish churches, which at some time, maybe, were house-chapels preceding parochial status. But I feel that, nonetheless, the licensing and building of chapels *in addition to neighbouring parish churches* amongst the barns and service buildings of country knights and squires after 1200 was a significant step in the expression of a feeling of aristocratic exclusivity, see *Annales de Theokesberia*, in *Annales Monastici* ed. H.R. Luard (5 vols, Rolls Series, 1864–9), i, 147–8, for the way that rectors acted to safeguard what rights they could in the face of this new trend.

42 C.E. Woodruff, 'Some Early Visitation Rolls at Canterbury', *Archaeologia Cantiana*, xxxii (1917), 151, quoted by Moorman, *Church Life in England in the Thirteenth Century*, 16.

clerks and servants. The whole court was raised on undercrofts, thus allowing lean-to pentice passages around a courtyard which would have resembled a cloister. There were fireplaces and glazed windows throughout. A handsome walled garden opened from the bishop's private chambers. Even at the beginning of the century the bishop paid an ample salary to a gardener, who tended both kitchen and ornamental gardens. There were vines, fruit trees, lawns and herb beds.[43] The great complex formed three distinct rings of intimacy – the outer court for suppliants (for there was an almonry) and tradesmen; the inner court for the retinue and servants, with the public stage of the hall, with its dais; inmost of all was the bishop's chamber, with its access on one side to the little paradise of the bishop's garden, and on the other to the spiritual refuge of his chapel.

We can see the same elaboration of accommodation in the house of a lay magnate. The house of the Cardinan family at Penhallam, Cornwall, was originally a ring-work enclosure with, presumably, timber interior buildings. In the late twelfth century it acquired a stone first-floor hall, to which was added after some years a chamber block and garderobe at one end (Fig. 12). As with Winchester Place in Southwark, Penhallam saw considerable elaboration in the early thirteenth century. The owner at this time was Sir Andrew de Cardinan, a leading Cornish magnate, with a castle elsewhere at Restormel. A courtyard house was developed with a much larger stone hall added on at right angles to the existing range. Service rooms (buttery, pantry, kitchen, bakehouse and brewhouse) formed the third side of a court, while a chapel connected to the twelfth-century range. The withdrawal from the public gaze at devotions is noticeable here as it is at contemporary Noseley (see also below, p. 320). A wall and gatehouse, with drawbridge, completed the four sides of the court. Fireplaces, garderobes, large glazed windows, and even a wattle hood over the open fire in the hall, tell of high standards of comfort, even in this, the far south-west of the realm.[44]

The same process can occasionally be glimpsed at a lower social level. At some time on one side or other of 1200 at Glottenham in Sussex, the lord of the manor rebuilt his ancient (and one assumes

43 M. Carlin, 'The Reconstruction of Winchester House, Southwark', *London Topographical Record*, xxv (1985), 33–57.
44 G. Beresford, 'The Medieval Manor of Penhallam, Jacobstow, Cornwall', *Medieval Archaeology*, xviii (1974), 90–127.

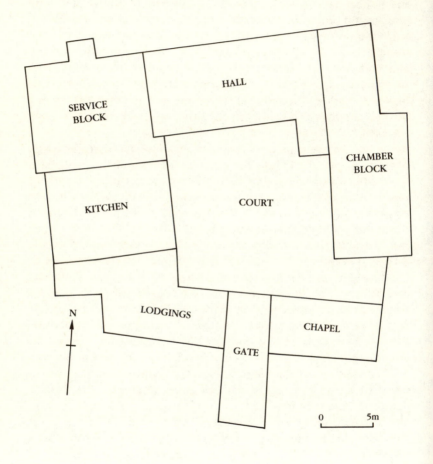

Figure 12   Penhallam, Cornwall, *c*.1300 (after Beresford, 1974).

inadequate) seat as a sizeable, ditched residence with a stone hall and kitchen, perhaps to advertise his status as a knight of the county court. Soon after 1300, the then owner, a rising knight and Despenser retainer, Robert of Etchingham, having acquired the manor rebuilt it in what he considered a fitting style. The new manor house had a moat, big gatehouse, perimeter wall and appropriate domestic range and offices.[45] Rebuilding succeeded rebuilding as its owner's expectations and fortunes improved. The example above all examples for the gentry residence built from the ground in the later thirteenth century, is Stokesay, Shropshire. This house is more important than others for, like the Clinton work at Kenilworth, it was the work of a newcomer amongst the county families, Lawrence of Ludlow, who made his money as a merchant. Moreover, it still stands much as it was built. Here, as at Glottenham, are moat, gatehouse (timber this time), hall, chambers and kitchen. The whole is given a more military air, in that there is also a refuge tower (but Stokesay lay in the Marches).[46] Something of a pattern had been established for the prestige residence by the end of the thirteenth century, and it is interesting to see how even some men of not much more than yeoman class attempted to follow elements of it.[47] Things had, it is true, not moved far in essentials from 1000: the hall–bower–chapel complex was still there in the centre of it. But it had been elaborated both at the top and in the middle reaches of society, which had laid claim to it. Most importantly, a more artful use had been made of barriers, of obstacles to progress towards the lord himself. New generations had made suitable theatres for the intricacies of parade and pomp out of the barns with which their ancestors had been content.

HALL AND CASTLE IN WALES

The Welsh too had an ideal of the hall. They had a name for a lordly residence, a *llys* (Lat. *curia*). What the twelfth-century Welshman understood the ideal *llys* to be is clear from the recensions of Welsh customary law, which survive in Latin and Welsh from

45 D. Martin, N. Saul *et al.*, 'Three Moated Sites in North-East Sussex. Part 1: Glottenham', *Sussex Archaeological Collections*, cxxvii (1989), 89–122.
46 J.D. La Touche, 'Stokesay Castle', *Transactions of the Shropshire Archaeological Society*, i (1878), 311–32.
47 J.B. Whitwell, 'Excavations on the Site of a Moated Medieval Manor House in the Parish of Saxilby, Lincs', *Journal of the British Architectural Association*, xxxi, 3rd ser. (1969), 128–43.

the early thirteenth century. In fact the material in the Laws is older than that, and the first (lost) versions must belong to the twelfth century. The Welsh put great store by residences as centres of lordship. The Laws mark out three royal seats: Dynefwr for Deheubarth, Aberffraw for Gwynedd, and Marthrafal for Powys. This was not merely legal antiquarianism: Gruffudd ap Cynan's principal seat was recorded in his *marwnad* as being at Aberffraw; 'prince of Aberffraw' was one of the titles of Llywelyn the Great (died 1240) in the latter part of his career, at the time when he had achieved overlordship of all the Welsh magnates. At the other end of Wales, the royal dynasty of Glamorgan made much of their association with Caerleon, made world-famous as a legendary Arthurian 'city' (complete with fantastical abbey and cathedral) by their neighbour Geoffrey of Monmouth.[48] Successive princes, Hywel ab Iorwerth and Morgan ap Hywel, took Caerleon (*de Karliun*) as their surname. This was something which was very unusual for Welshmen to do, and they would not have done it at all unless there were a measure of prestige to be drawn from the name of the place.

The first thing that a *llys* required would have been the bank and ditch universal in contemporary English and Norman homes; 'enclosure' is in fact what the word *llys* means. In this respect the royal residence paralleled another Welsh seat of power. The great churches of Wales before the mid-twelfth century were the communities of canons known as *clasau*. The *clas* also lived within an enclosure (Wel. *llan*, Lat. *atrium*). The canons of the *clas* lived, like the king and his officers, in a scattering of buildings around the enclosure.[49] To the Welsh mind of the eleventh century, it may be that the bustling little royal and ecclesiastical towns within banks and ditches, devoted either to lordship or worship, represented an ideal of a seat of power. Certainly, there was an association between centres of lordship and spirituality in Wales. Close to Gwynedd's royal centre of Aberffraw was the ecclesiastical centre of Llangadwaladr, and this is matched by the proximity of Mathrafal

48 It has been suggested that the revival of royal status in south Wales and Geoffrey of Monmouth's choice of Caerleon as a centre for Arthur's power were intimately linked, J. Gillingham, 'The Context and Purposes of the History of the Kings of Britain', *Anglo-Norman Studies*, xiii, ed. M.M. Chibnall (Woodbridge, 1990), 113–16.
49 See the idealised description of Llancarfan in *Vita sancti Cadoci*, in *Vitae Sanctorum Britanniae et Genealogiae*, ed. A.W. Wade-Evans (Cardiff, 1944), 120–2.

to the royal *clas* of Meifod, and Dynefwr to the ancient *clas* and cult centre of Llandeilo Fawr.[50]

Earthwork enclosures of rectangular form can still be seen, or have been discovered, at the royal seats of Aberffraw and Marthrafal, and at a number of other sites which may be lesser *llysoedd*. Within these courts, according to the Laws and other sources, should be found a chapel, as in contemporary English royal residences, and the contemporary courts of the *clasau*. The biography of Gruffudd ap Cynan, king of Gwynedd (died 1137), mentions the great churches he had built within his chief residences; and indeed the existence of one such medieval palace chapel is known at Gruffudd's royal seat of Aberffraw.[51] The chapel (*kapel*) and the hall (*neuadd*) were doubtless the most impressive buildings within the court of the *llys*, but they formed only part of a cluster of buildings; the Laws give nine as the required number, although some may well have been adjacent in reality, like the hall and the chamber (*ystafell*). Besides these there were kitchen, stable, barn, kennels, latrines and an oven. All the buildings of the *llys* were expected to be of timber. The Laws mention obliquely that there would be clusters of lesser buildings too, stores, lodgings for household staff, forge and cellars. Such is said to have been a royal or princely hall, but the lesser lord too had his *neuadd*. It expressed an idea of status appropriate to his level. The Laws mention the division of his three-bayed hall into an upper and lower hall, by means of a central hearth. Additional chambers would be attached to the hall, maybe a porch and a lean-to shed.[52]

Although excavations still have to be made to discover the reality lying behind the ideal, the evidence (even when allowance is made for the artificiality of the picture sketched out by the Laws) leads to a conviction that the Welsh did have an idea of aristocratic domesticity. Within that idea was room for gradation by rank in society. The *llys* of the king, like a little town of functionaries and offices, was clearly differentiated from the *neuadd* of the lord, in its farmyard setting. Just as in England, the well-ordered hall was a

---

50 *Early Medieval Settlements in Wales AD 400–1100*, ed. N. Edwards and A. Lane (Cardiff, 1988), 62.

51 *The Life of Gruffudd ap Cynan*, ed. D. Simon Evans (Lampeter, 1990), 50, *A Gruffudd ynteu a wnaeth eglwysseu mawr yn y llysoedd pennaf idaw e hun* . . . . For the 'palace chapel' Eglwys y Beili (church of the enclosure) see *Early Medieval Settlements in Wales*, 19–21.

52 For the use of the Laws to reconstruct the Welsh royal or noble residence, see L.A.S. Butler 'Domestic Building in Wales and the Evidence of the Welsh Laws', *Medieval Archaeology*, xxxi (1987), 47–51.

metaphor of peace and prosperity; the empty, dark hall an expression of desolation.[53] The shabby hall, dusty and cold, reeking with urine and infested with fleas, was a place to avoid; such a place as Rhonabwy, the companion of the outlawed Iorwerth ap Maredudd of Powys, was forced into for refuge in one of the tales of the *Mabinogion*. A different hall was the hall which the poet Cynddelw conjured up to please Rhys ap Gruffudd of Deheubarth (died 1197). It was guarded by doorkeepers and heralds, crowded with attendants and the gentry dependent on the prince, a place to hear bards and drink good mead. In such a way was the ideal of good order and lordship made real in Wales, and in not too dissimilar a way from eleventh-century England; by succession of porch, hall and chamber, by successive barriers of functionaries, partitions and steps.[54]

The introduction of the castle into Wales by the Normans brought new ideas of a high-status residence. The Welsh cottoned on to the ideas of Anglo-Norman fortification remarkably quickly; indeed they must have had some ideas of fortification already.[55] A magnate of Powys, Uchdryd ab Edwin, was the first named Welshman to build a Norman-style castle, at Cymer in Meirionydd in 1116; a motte still remains to mark the site. It did not do him much good, his lands were overrun anyway, but the step was a significant one. Other Welsh princes simply settled into fortresses taken over from the Normans. Cardigan, Carmarthen, Llandovery and Caerleon were all castles which changed hands at intervals between English and Welsh. After his reconquest of southern Ceredigion in the 1140s, Cadell ap Gruffudd, king of Deheubarth, settled himself at the ringwork in Lampeter, probably built in the reign of Henry I by Stephen the constable of Cardigan. There, in the company of his family, his *distain*, and his household clerks, he confirmed to the monks of Totnes the church of Lampeter in a charter describing itself as given at 'the house of Lord Cadell on the river Teifi next to the church of St Peter'. Although Cadell was residing in a Norman hall within the banks of a ringwork neighbouring what seems to have been a speculative borough foundation, his clerk might have been describing a Welsh *llys* next to an ancient *clas* church.[56] At this

53 W. Davies, *Wales in the Early Middle Ages* (Leicester, 1982), 29–30.
54 J. Vendryès, 'Trois poèmes de Cynddelw', *Etudes celtiques*, iv (1948), 20–3.
55 The *Historia Brittonum* in the ninth century refers to King Benlli dominating his people from a fortress (*arx*), see W. Davies, *Patterns of Power in Early Wales* (Oxford, 1990), 10.
56 D. Crouch, 'The Earliest Original Charter of a Welsh King', *Bulletin of the Board of Celtic Studies*, xxvi (1989), 125–31.

stage of the game, the step from *llys* to castle would sometimes have been barely noticeable. However, the introduction of great towers to Wales would have changed the rules, for they were alien expressions of prestige.

Fortification in stone by Welsh lords followed remarkably soon after the adoption of earthwork castles. The earliest Welsh masonry castle so far identified is that of Plas Baglan, the chief residence of the Welsh lords of Afan in western Glamorgan. Excavation has revealed a substantial rectilinear keep probably of several floors with a garderobe turret, dating to the mid-twelfth century. It was comparable to keeps of the same region built by the Normans, bigger indeed than the Norman keep at Ogmore, residence of a prominent Marcher baron. Appropriately for a *llys*, albeit one fortified in an alien tradition, it neighboured the ancient mother church of the lordship. Plas Baglan marked the residence of a Welsh lord of high status, overlord of most of the uplands of Glamorgan in the twelfth century. Its stone tower and curtain wall also marked it as the centre of power of a lord adopting new ways of competing with his Anglo-Norman neighbours. The same Afan family which built it was in due course to integrate thoroughly with the English gentry of the region, and put its Welshness behind it. Plas Baglan is the weathercock that points to changing Welsh ideas of the material expression of lordship.

The princely houses of Powys, Deheubarth and Gwynedd soon saw the way that the wind was blowing. By the early thirteenth century they were all provided with stone-built fortress residences rather different from the ideal *llys* of the lawyers. The Lord Rhys of Deheubarth indeed converted the *llys* of Dynefwr into a stone fortress as the centre of his dominion in west Wales, the seat of the justiciarship he held from King Henry II. The princes of Powys shifted their seat from Madog ap Maredudd's *llys* of Marthrafal to Castell Coch (the Red Castle) above Welshpool (now Powis Castle). A square keep and high stone hall within a circuit wall gave them a residence indistinguishable from that of a Marcher baron. But greatest of all the Welsh castle-builders were the princes of Gwynedd: rather suitably, for they were the Welsh princes with the greatest pretensions to dominion. The first generation of the Venedotian dynasty which built in stone seems to have been the sons and grandsons of Owain ap Gruffudd (died 1170) in the last decades of the twelfth century. A couple of unimpressive stone towers can be associated with them.

It was Llywelyn ab Iorwerth, known as the Llywelyn the Great (died 1240), who was the first Welsh prince to develop a fortress policy. Llywelyn's individuality here, as elsewhere, set him apart from his fellow princes in his ideas of lordship. Castles at Castell-y-Bere, Castell Carndochan and Ewloe are convincingly attributed to the early period of Llywelyn's rule (before 1215). All have characteristic apsidal keeps (that is, towers with the outside face curved) which are seen as a development indigenous to north Wales. They are sited on the edge of Llywelyn's principality facing his rivals of Powys and Chester. Llywelyn's later castles show direct borrowing from his Marcher neighbours in the use of round keeps. He erected such a 'great tower' at Dolbadarn in Snowdonia in the heart of his principality. Another Marcher castle, Beeston, provided the model for one of Llywelyn's fortresses, Cricceith. All Llywelyn's castles were built in military earnest, to buttress his power against hostile neighbours, both Welsh and English. However, in Dolbadarn and Cricceith the investment in stone and the models taken show Llywelyn responding wholeheartedly to English comital and baronial castles of the March. He was declaring that his dignity was no less than those of the earls of Chester, Kent and Pembroke, his great neighbours.[57]

Llywelyn was not following here anything related (at least at first sight) to older Welsh forms of residence. But the presence of great towers in the centre of his castles may be a little misleading. It is noticeable that within the curtain walls, notably at Castell-y-Bere and Dolbadarn, there was nothing that resembled the hall–chamber–service block complex of the English magnate's castle. Internal buildings there are, but they are built at odd corners of the circuit, seemingly where the ground was more level or convenient. Moreover, the buildings outside the keep towers were frequently slight in construction, and unmortared. It must be significant that this random plan of internal buildings echoes the circuit of houses within the *llysoedd* of the Laws. Their construction may have been less robust because they were seen as expressions of the noble household offices rather than as part of a castle. The great towers appear in this light to be additional buttresses to the prince's dignity, grafted on as being necessary to impress the wider world, ambassadors of which frequented his court. Such perhaps was the way that Welsh magnates came to a compromise between

57 R. Avent, *Castles of the Princes of Gwynedd* (HMSO, 1983), 7–20.

domestic and alien models of a prestigious residence. They found here a compromise that was lacking elsewhere in their relations with the intruding Anglo-French world.

CASTLE AND HALL IN SCOTLAND

Lack of written sources and a dearth of excavations mean that very little can be said about ideas of status as they relate to residences in Scotland. It would be surprising if the Scots had not shared the general European idea that a lord should have a suitable hall, but the archeological work to investigate it still needs to be undertaken. Certainly the eleventh- and early twelfth-century Scottish kings had the ceremonial households with which to celebrate great occasions in the sort of style which would have needed a public space. Turgot's 'Life' of Queen Margaret hints at places for royal assemblies, however unsophisticated they were before his heroine got to work on them. What we know of the youth of St Ailred, brought up in the 1120s at the court of King David, tells us as much. His *Vita* talks (conventionally) of King David's 'palace' and the host of officials thronging it, over whom Ailred came to exercise jurisdiction. It pictures King David at table waited on by a multitude with cups and dishes.[58] There were recognised royal seats at Edinburgh, Stirling, Roxburgh, Forfar and Scone; but what they looked like is quite unknown.

What can be said with some confidence is that castles were adopted with enthusiasm by the Scots in the course of the twelfth century. Their first acquaintance with castles would have come from the Norman-built castles in Cumbria and Northumbria occasionally to be found on the Scottish side of the fluctuating frontier with England. The erection of mottes and ringworks was undertaken in large areas of Scotland in the century's later decades. Certain areas of Scotland are liberally dotted with them. The mottes of Galloway and Dumfriesshire have been related to the policy of Kings Malcolm IV and William to secure Galloway more closely to their kingdom, and to the Anglicisation carried out by the native lords of Galloway themselves. They seem to have been constructed both by Anglo-French incomers and at the residences of the lords

---

58 Walter Daniel, *The Life of Ailred of Rievaulx*, ed. F.M. Powicke (repr. Oxford, 1978), 3–6.

of Galloway.[59] Elsewhere mottes are to be found in Fife, the Clyde Valley, Menteith, and in lesser numbers in Angus and Moray. Lothian, nearer England, has relatively few of them. As many as 250 have been identified overall. It has been plausibly suggested that castles are thickest on the ground (as in Galloway) where native lords were encouraging settlement and granting fees in the twelfth century, or where (as in Clydesdale) the king was planting incoming Anglo-French aristocrats. Castles are less in evidence in Lothian, where the castle sites expressed dominant royal power and are located at the seats of sheriffs, besides royal burghs.[60] Wherever new lords went, castles and burghs were planted. When King William granted the lordship of Garioch to his brother, Earl David, in about 1180 the earl set up his chief seat at Inverurie, where he had erected a motte and planned a burgh by 1199. Another administrative centre was developed at Dundee. Other subsidiary castles marked the colonisation of the surrounding lordship.[61]

Whether Garioch or Galloway, the indications are that castles came late to Scotland, although they came in great numbers when they did come. As in Wales, native lords and intruders alike built similar earthwork and timber structures derived from Anglo-French models. But unlike Wales, the two sets of builders were not generally in competition. Stone castles were also built later in Scotland; it seems unlikely that there was much building in stone before 1200. There was, however, a series of impressive masonry castles by the mid-thirteenth century, notably Dirleton, Dunstaffnage and Bothwell. These seem to be developments of earlier ringworks, or mottes: substantial mural towers set about stone enceintes.[62] Such examples as there are compare favourably with the castles built by the Welsh princes, although the lack of keeps divides the Scottish castle from the English. There are no great towers to compare with that at Newcastle upon Tyne built by Henry II to strengthen English royal power in the north.

59 S. Cruden, *The Scottish Castle* (London, 1960), 9; C.J. Tabraham, 'Norman Settlement in Galloway: Recent Fieldwork in the Stewartry', in *Studies in Scottish Antiquity presented to Stewart Cruden*, ed. D.J. Breeze (Edinburgh, 1984), 117–22.

60 G.G. Simpson and B. Webster, 'Charter Evidence and the Distribution of Mottes in Scotland', in *Essays on the Nobility of Mediaeval Scotland*, ed. K.J. Stringer (Edinburgh, 1985), 1–11.

61 K.J. Stringer, *Earl David of Huntingdon: A Study in Anglo-Scottish History* (Edinburgh, 1985), 68–79, 91.

62 W.M. Mackenzie, *The Mediaeval Castle in Scotland* (London, 1927), 40–57.

9

THE NOBLE HOUSEHOLD

'Counts get their name from "accompanying" because it is right that they be accompanied by many men,' says Gerald of Wales. In this Isidorean exercise Gerald isolates the nub of aristocratic dignity. A magnate shows his power in many ways, but in no way more expressively than by acting the great man amongst a band of inferiors. Followers were his necessary accomplices in the conspiracy of power. A man might posture in gold and fine clothes and be detected as no more than a charlatan, like Guibert de Nogent's fake count of Breteuil. It was followers that most truly marked the great man. Some of those followers go beyond the scope of this book, for the most prestigious of them were men of power themselves, political allies at court or in the country. The study of such men does not belong in a work devoted to the *trappings* of power; such men were the reality of power itself. But there were other followers, retainers, men who sought places in the household and offered their skills and hands to the lord, rather than their own modicum of power, as their side of the bargain. It is these who are the concern of this chapter.

THE MODEL HOUSEHOLD

The retained household can be regarded as an aristocratic trapping for one good reason: the manner of its organisation became a matter of emulation and prestige. In this case the ultimate model was clear: the household of the Carolingian kings of the Franks. The starting point of a study of the formal noble household is the remarkable tract which is the first surviving description of its ideal layout: the *De ordine palatii* of Hincmar, archbishop of Reims, written for the instruction of a minor Carolingian king just before 880.[1] The essentials of the organisation of the royal household were far older than that; officers named in Hincmar's treatise occur in diplomata of the seventh century. However, Hincmar presents us with a rounded and coherent picture of the model royal household in a way which tells us that it was now a comprehensible and recognised institution. It was so much an institution that Hincmar might tell us how an ideal version of it must be organised.

To Hincmar, there were two manifest divisions of the household: the clerical and lay, and the head of the clerical household, the *apocrisarius* or *capellanus*, stood immediately after the royal family in prestige. Next to him in dignity was the chancellor (*cancellarius*). Both clerics kept the king's secret counsel along with his records. The running of the sacred palace after these dignitaries lay in the hands of their two lay equivalents: the count of the palace (*comes palatinus*) and chamberlain (*camerarius*); the highest of the laymen at court. After them came the seneschal (*senescallus*), butler (*buticularius*), constable (*comes stabuli*), under-chamberlain (*mansionarius*) four huntsmen and a falconer. Beneath these was a lesser cadre: usher (*ostiarius*), treasurer (*sacellarius*), dispenser (*dispensator*), under-butler (*scapoardus*) and others. The count of the palace saw to justice about the court; the chamberlain to the fabric and regalia of the palace (as the queen's deputy), and also to receipts from some public levies. Of the upper cadre of officers about the palace the seneschal was chief 'because every matter is his concern excepting drink and provisioning the horses' (these two were the business of the butler and the constable). The under-chamberlain saw to the preparation of the royal lodgings whenever the king was on the road.

Hincmar uses a number of words that imply that many of the household he describes were unfree servants: *pueri* and *ministeriales*. Indeed the Latin form of seneschal *senescalcus* contains the Frankish element *-scalc*, meaning a slave. The name of another minor court functionary (not mentioned by Hincmar but well attested elsewhere in contemporary documents), the marshal (*marescallus*), contains the same element. The picture we get from Hincmar – despite the element of theory in his work – is of a teeming crowd around the king. Presiding over the multitude are a select group of four

1 *De ordine palatii*, ed. T. Gross and R. Schieffer (M.G.H. Fontes Iuris Germanici Antiqui, iii, 1980). Hincmar refers (p. 54) to an earlier treatise on the same subject by Adelhard, abbot of Corbie (died 826), which he had read and copied.

pre-eminent royal servants: the chaplain, chancellor, count of the palace and chamberlain. Beneath these the status of the second cadre of servants is less clear; that many were unfree ministerials for all their authority over the royal hall and court is clear: Hincmar calls them *capitanei ministeriales*. The Carolingian capitularies mention that such *ministeriales*, seneschals, butlers, huntsmen and falconers might be sent out of the court on royal business to the provinces.[2] But men close to the king, free and unfree, were likely to have power and respect, so there is little odd in such trust. One only has to recall the power of the Imperial slaves and freedmen of the Julio-Claudians. The lower orders of the palace are also evident in Hincmar's treatise, the *discipuli* who serve the greater officers, the slaves (*pueri*) and the military household, all clamouring for food, robes, horses, trappings and money.

By 1000 the model of the Carolingian household had been taken up all over Europe, and not always by kings. Prominent in imitating Carolingian state were the count-dukes of Normandy. Duke Robert I in the 1030s bestowed the titles of seneschal, chamberlain, butler and constable on several members of his entourage, a group of court intimates. Magnates of Normandy were amongst those who took up the titles: these were no ministerials. Osbern fitz Herfast, a lord of the southern March, and Humphrey de Vieilles, the greatest lord in central Normandy, both assumed the title of seneschal. Apart from the appearance of these titles in the ducal household, we know little about the duties of these new officers. It may well be that Normans were quite vague themselves about duties. William fitz Osbern was variously described as 'seneschal' and 'count of the palace' of Duke William II.[3] Yet these offices were originally quite separate. To Hincmar (and royal diplomata bear him out) the count of the palace was an officer separate from and outranking the seneschal. The confusion of the eleventh century about William fitz Osbern must tell us that the important thing about these officers was not what they did, but their place next to the duke. Their status was thus enhanced by attending on their prince, while his security was enhanced by such great men serving him. Exact use of titles was unimportant.

The known composition of the Norman ducal household bore a

---

2 *M.G.H. Legum*, ii, pt 1, 84. On the other hand the status of another Carolingian royal steward, Isengrim, mentioned in 898, cannot have been other than free, for he was also a count: *M.G.H. Diplomata regum Karolinorum*, ii, no. 251.
3 D.R. Bates, *Normandy before 1066* (London, 1982), 116–17, 155.

resemblance to Hincmar's idealised royal household of 150 years before in titles, but not in numbers; however, there is not much evidence as to how closely Hincmar's household mirrored the reality of his own day. What we can say is that in scattering Carolingian titles around his court Duke Robert was making a number of political points. He was wrapping himself up in quasi-royal state by surrounding himself with such a household, pretensions given a cutting edge by the fact that the Capetian king at this time was apparently doing without such officers himself. But more than that, he was securing to himself prominent men by their undertaking of the honour of service to him. This development, visible here in early eleventh-century Normandy, will be a potent force in the elaboration and workings of the noble household over the succeeding centuries.

THE IDEA OF THE HOUSEHOLD IN BRITAIN BEFORE THE NORMANS

The Carolingian model had a much wider influence than merely in France. Kings (and queens) in England before 1066 had long been followed by a household (*hirede*) made up of thegns (in Latin, *ministri* or *pediseci*). It is in the tenth century that we begin to find something approaching the organisation of the Carolingian royal household. This does not mean that before AD 900 there were no titled officials busy about the hall and king's person, but it was in the century after that date that the Latin continental titles were generally appropriated to English officials. In diplomats, chronicles and wills we find Englishmen going under the names of seneschal, butler and chamberlain. The twofold division of the Frankish court was also there, English kings had their chaplains and, by the 1060s at least, an officer called a chancellor. Tenth- and eleventh-century English writers clearly accepted the Frankish idea of a structured and compartmentalised royal household, and it is likely that they got such an idea from Hincmar and his like.

It does not seem to have been difficult for writers to translate most of the existing English officers into their Continental equivalents. But it would not do to ignore the fact that there were underlying differences. The English vernacular gave the *discthegn* a leading place in the English court. This made it natural to make him the equivalent of the Frankish 'seneschal', but other Latin words like *discifer* or *dapifer* ('dish-bearer' and 'feast-bearer') were also used as equivalents. The situation was clouded further in Cnut's reign by the importation of the title of the Scandinavian chief court officer, the staller. The staller (Old Norse: *stallari*, Lat. *strator* or *stabulator*) also corresponded in many ways to the contemporary seneschal. He was a leading official of great power, perhaps closest in essence to the Frankish count of the palace. But since the countship of the palace had been subsumed in function into the seneschalship by 1000 in France then the staller too might be considered a seneschal, if equivalents were looked for. When the Normans came to England they solved the problem by arbitrarily making a staller the equivalent of the constable (presumably because the Latin *conestabularius* sounded a little like one of the Latin equivalents for staller, *stabulator*). The Normans could do this because 'constable' was not one of the Frankish Latin titles which had been taken up by the English royal household. But the fact that the Normans had to go to such shifts indicates that the structure of the pre-Conquest English royal household was not always easy to translate into familiar terms.[4]

Laurence Larson made the illuminating observation that, although the Frankish model of the royal household was attended to and borrowed from by the Old English monarchy, it nonetheless had itself a distinct sphere of influence in Britain and even further afield in the Scandinavian world.[5] This is nowhere clearer than in Wales. The Welsh king was used to being followed by a substantial household. The ancient documentation to be found in the Book of Llandaff consistently depicts the kings of south-east Wales as the centres of groups of followers. One narrative of the mid-eleventh century talks of Caradog ap Rhiwallon,

> one of the followers (*comites*) of Meurig, king of Glamorgan [who] broke the sanctuary of SS Dyfrig, Teilo and Euddogwy while in the following and bidding of King Meurig (*in comitatu Mourici regis et uerbo*) by bearing off by force the wife of Seisyll from the church door.[6]

Despite such riotous scenes, Welsh kings set some store by their dignity. One of the ways this was expressed was in imitating the

---

4 For the English royal household before 1066 the classic study remains L.M. Larson, *The King's Household in England before the Norman Conquest* (Madison, 1904), particularly chs 5–7, 9.
5 ibid., 196.
6 *The Text of the Book of Llan Dâv*, ed. J. Gwenogvryn Evans (Oxford, 1893), 261–2.

state in which the English kings lived, and bestowing household titles on their men.

Descriptions of Welsh royal households first occur in the legal texts of the early thirteenth century, and these derive from twelfth-century exemplars. The twelfth-century compilations in turn looked back to organised Welsh royal households which had been operating since (at least) the eleventh century. We know this because Welsh treatises on the royal entourage describe a few of its members whose titles would not have been adopted *after* the conquest of England by the Normans. The three in question are the *edling*, the *distain* and the *medyd*.[7] The *edling* was the designated heir of the king, a borrowing from the English word 'atheling'.[8] The *distain* was none other the the English 'discthegn', the major-domo of the hall. The *medyd* was the preparer and dispenser of mead. Mead played the same part in Welsh poetry as it did in English, as the drink offered by the lord in his hall to his men. The *medyd* may be compared to the 'mead-wright' of the court of Edward the Confessor, or the *medarius* of the abbot of Ely.[9] None of these English titles would have been adopted by Welsh kings for their households after 1070, because by then the vernacular titles of the officers of the English royal court had lost prestige: no Welsh ruler concerned about his dignity would imitate a discredited court. The prestige model was by 1070 the new Norman court with its Frankish titles.

By the mid-eleventh century the greater Welsh kings can therefore be proved to have borrowed the model of the royal court from England. Along with this model, they would of course have acquired at second hand the Carolingian idea of a structured and compartmentalised court. Some early Welsh court offices seem directly related to the ideal Carolingian household. The biography of Gruffudd ap Cynan of Gwynedd refers back to the eleventh century and the existence of the chamberlain and treasurer (*guas ystavell a thrysoryer*) of King Gruffudd ap Llywelyn (killed 1063), its hero's predecessor.[10] This worthy had passed down in his

---

7 *The Latin Texts of the Welsh Laws*, ed. H.E. Emmanuel (Cardiff, 1967), 109, 111–12. For the Welsh *edling*, J. Beverley Smith, 'Dynastic Succession in Medieval Wales', *Bulletin of the Board of Celtic Studies*, xxxiii (1986), 199–206.

8 For the atheling in England, D.N. Dumville, 'The Aetheling: a Study in Anglo-Saxon Constitutional History', *Anglo-Saxon England*, viii (1979), 1–33.

9 Larson, *King's Household*, 181; *Inquisitio comitatus Cantabrigiensis; subjicitur Inquisitio Eliensis*, ed. N.E.S.A. Hamilton (London, 1876), 115.

10 *The Life of Gruffudd ap Cynan*, ed. D. Simon Evans (Lampeter, 1990), 29, 101.

family a shirt cut from the royal robes of the late King Gruffudd; plainly this man had at least kept the wardrobe of his master, and the term 'treasurer' united in his title implies he had all the royal treasure confided to him.[11] Both of these Welsh terms seem to have derived ultimately from Latin originals: *camerarius et thesaurarius* (although the 'guas ystavell' would relate nicely to the vernacular English 'burthegn', keeper of the royal chamber or 'bower'). Here at least, in the king's chamber, the Carolingian model would seem to have been followed (if only at second hand) by eleventh-century Welsh kings. The appearance in the Welsh laws of other figures hints at further infiltration of Frankish ideas. Along with other officers we find in the idealised Welsh court of the Laws the presence of court priests, and some redactions of the Laws talk of a *cyngelor* (chancellor) presiding over them. A number of twelfth-century Welsh acts confirm that Welsh kings and magnates employed chaplains and clerks at an early date, but there is no way of knowing if the Welsh royal chancellor of the past (as opposed to the genuine princely chancellor of Llywelyn the Great's day) was anything more than a fantasy of a thirteenth-century clerk.[12]

What sort of household served the Scottish kings in the eleventh century is difficult to say, because the sources are so slight compared to those of Wales. What little evidence there is is retrospective. That there was some influence from England and perhaps Scandinavia at the time seems likely, but is hard to prove. The English lady, Margaret, queen of Malcolm III (1058–93), is said to have carried out a wide-ranging reform of her husband's household. She introduced foreign fashions, fine ornaments and 'a more elevated conduct' (whatever that meant) towards the king.[13] But the fact that officials with Gaelic names survived in both Scottish royal and comital courts well into the twelfth century tells us that there was in Scotland as

---

11 *Latin Texts of the Welsh Laws*, ed. Emmanuel, 109, 117, uses both the vernacular *guas ystavell* and the Latin *camerarius* for this officer. It says of him that 'he should have the king's old clothes when he casts them off . . . he has no house of his own in the court, for he keeps the king's chamber and controls access from the hall to the chamber'.

12 *Guffus clericus noster* attests an act of King Cadell of Deheubarth of 1146 x 54, D. Crouch, 'Earliest Original Charter of a Welsh King', *Bulletin of the Board of Celtic Studies*, xxvi (1989), 131; Hywel ab Iorwerth ab Owain of Caerleon issued a charter attested by *Urbano clerico meo et canonico Landauensi*, Cambridge, Trinity College ms R.5.33, fo. 107r.

13 *obsequia . . . sublimiora*, Vita sanctae Margaretae reginae, in *Symeonis Dunelmensis Opera et Collectanea*, i, ed. J. Hodgson Hinde (Surtees Soc., li, 1867), 242.

in Wales an indigenous household tradition. An officer called a *rannaire* (Lat. *rennarius*) had a traditional responsibility for the distribution of food in the royal household until as late as the 1170s.[14] A Henry *rennarius meus* occurs in an act of Gilbert, earl of Strathern (1171–1223), dated 1218.[15] The Gaelic lawkeeper, the *brithem* (Lat. *judex*), occurs frequently in royal and comital courts throughout the twelfth century, but it is a moot point whether such an officer can be classed within the household, particularly as the office of the Scottish *brithem* tends to be associated with named provinces. The *brithem* was more of an officer at large than a courtier.

One possible contact between the early Scottish and English households is in the appearances of officers called *dapiferi* in twelfth-century deeds of native magnates of Lothian. A charter of one Thor son of Swein to Holyrood, dating to before 1162, has as witness Gillandres his *dapifer*. Two charters of Gospatrick earl of Dunbar (1138–66) are attested by *dapiferi*, one called Haldain, the other Lambekin.[16] The stolid Englishness of Gospatrick and his servants encourages one to believe that we see here men following in a long line of *discthegnas* or *stigweardas*, going back well into the eleventh century. But that, of course, is no more than supposition.

FROM ROYAL TO NOBLE HOUSEHOLD

I have so far been dealing for the most part with royal households, to get some idea of how the idea of a structured formal household permeated both Continental and insular society by the mid-eleventh century. The significant development of the later eleventh century was that such households began to be perceived as appropriate to men who were not of sovereign rank, mere magnates.

In the period before 1050 it was not usual to find the chief servants of great men other than sovereign princes being dignified with the titles of the royal court. When there are indications of magnate households in the early eleventh century in central France, we find an

14 *Regesta Regum Scottorum*, ed. G.W.S. Barrow *et al.*, 5 vols (Edinburgh, 1960—), i, 33.
15 *Liber Insule Missarum*, ed. H. Drummond (Bannatyne Club, 1847), 12.
16 *Early Scottish Charters prior to AD 1153*, ed. A.C. Lawrie (Glasgow, 1905), 175; *Charters of the Cistercian priory of Coldstream*, ed. C. Rogers (London, 1879), 6, 8.

unspecialised vocabulary to describe them. Officers of a whole range of magnates from the greater to the lesser were *prepositi* (*prévôts*). According to one analysis of early French administration these were a variety of men, often of some substance in society, administering the affairs of magnates. By the twelfth century such French *prévôts* often came from families who specialised in administration.[17] The use of a loose vocabulary for servants of magnates may long have been general in France. Dr Janet Nelson has pointed out to me the comments on the households of ninth-century great men by Walafrid Strabo, abbot of Reichenau, and adviser to Charles the Bald. Walafrid deliberately refrains from using the vocabulary of the Frankish royal household to describe the household followers of men below royal rank, and uses all sorts of vague phrases, one at least with Biblical antecedents.[18]

Normandy can show at least one dynasty of early *prévôts* in the service of a magnate family. This was the family of Glos, for at least three generations hereditary *prévôts* of the lord of Breteuil, and themselves men of some substance. The earliest of them appears in the 1040s, but the second had adopted or been given a much more evocative title by 1050. This was William fitz Bjarni *dapifer* of the great Norman magnate William fitz Osbern, lord of Breteuil and earl in England later.[19] Another such example from the fringes

17 K.F. Werner, 'Kingdom and Principality in Twelfth-Century France', in *The Medieval Nobility*, trans. T. Reuter (Amsterdam, 1978), 256–9.
18 *Patrologia Latina*, ed. J-P. Migne *et al.* (221 vols, Paris, 1844–64), cxiv, cols 964–5. *Habent et potestates saeculi consiliaros in domesticis et liberorum paedagogos suorum, habent ipsi* procuratores *rei familiaris: similiter in quibusdam ecclesiis archidiaconos, quos familiae respicit gubernatio . . . Habent aulae potentium janitores, habet et domus dei ostiarios. Habet mundus veredarios, commentarienses, ludorum exhibitores carminum pompaticos relatores.* Compare the biblical use of *procurator*, Luke, viii, 3, *Joanna uxor Chusae procurator Herodis et Susanna et aliae multae quae ministrabant ei de facultatibus suis*; Matt., xx, 8, *cum sero autem factum esset, dicit dominus vineae procuratori suo.* In the passage quoted, Walafrid was comparing the dignitaries of lay households to the functionaries of the Church. It is notable that talking of royal officials he uses the language of the capitularies: *duces, comites, centenarii, vicarii* and *collectores.*
19 D. Crouch, *The Beaumont Twins* (Cambridge, 1986), 106–7; for fitz Bjarni as *dapifer*, *Recueil des actes des ducs de Normandie* (911–1066), ed. M. Fauroux (Caen, 1961), 285. J.F.A. Mason, 'Barons and their Officials in the Later Eleventh Century', *Anglo-Norman Studies*, xiii, ed. M. Chibnall (Woodbridge, 1991), 259, notes a charter to Marmoutier (dating to *c*.1060) of Nigel, vicomte of the Cotentin, which mentions a seneschal, Ingulf, and a chamberlain, Ralph; Ingulf was probably Nigel's seneschal (from his position after Nigel's sons) but we cannot be so sure of Ralph, for he might have been the abbey's chamberlain, see *Calendar of Documents preserved in France*, i, *918–1206*, ed. J.H. Round (London, 1899), no. 1166 (I see no warrant for dating the charter, as did Dr Mason, to *c*.1048).

of Normandy can be found in the case of Count Hugh of Meulan. In a charter dated 1056, he is attended by a prominent officer called John the *prévôt*, but John's son, Odo or Odard, was a *dapifer*.[20] It is impossible to say how widespread amongst magnates was the practice of retaining titled officers in Normandy before 1066. But a certain Azo, lord of Bizy, near Evreux, whose economic standing cannot have been very high, had a *dapifer* called Urse in the years immediately before the Conquest.[21] Furthermore, Norman abbots and priors were employing lay seneschals before 1066, which might have some relevance to their proliferation in lay society generally.

What we see in the mid-eleventh century are the first hesitant attempts of magnates to bolster their dignity by bestowing titles drawn from the royal household on their leading followers. We cannot make too much of the pre-Conquest examples, even while we acknowledge their significance. The word *dapifer* might have been meant loosely. Certainly the French equivalent, *senescal*, had a general application to any household officer in the twelfth century. Men who were in fact royal chamberlains and marshals had the word applied to them. But in the decades after 1066, when magnate households appear with the *full* range of household officers, then something clearly had happened to perceptions of aristocratic state. What were the Anglo-Norman magnates up to? On one level they were doing what the duke of Normandy had done at the beginning of the century; binding useful men to them by forging links of honourable service. But on another level they were doing rather more; endeavouring to raise their standing by comparing themselves to the great of the world, the kings and princes. In France, it is not easy to find out how widespread the affectation (for such it was) had spread by the end of the century. In England, on the other hand, the Domesday Survey occasionally records the titles borne by some followers of the great magnates of 1086. Most frequently (and unsurprisingly) we find people called *dapiferi* (seneschals or stewards). Very great people had them, such as Geoffrey, bishop of Coutances (one of the greatest landowners in England), Count Robert of Mortain, Count Alan of Brittany, and Countess Judith (widow of Earl Waltheof of Northampton

---

20 See charters in *Cartulaire de St-Père de Chartres*, ed. B.E.C. Guerard (2 vols, Paris, 1840), i, 178; *Chartes de l'abbaye de Jumièges*, ed. J-J. Vernier (2 vols, Rouen, 1916), i, 78.
21 *Recueil des actes des ducs de Normandie*, 420.

and Huntingdon). Barons, both great and small, had them too: Hugh de Grandmesnil, Henry de Ferrers, Hugh de Port and Harduin de Scalers. But Domesday Book records other titled officers belonging to magnates: Count Alan and Odo of Bayeux had chamberlains; the count of Mortain had a constable and a butler.[22] The greater number of seneschals than other sorts of officer is most likely to be because such men would customarily have been regarded as the chief representatives of their lords. Being in the public eye in their lords' stead, these seneschals would find their office becoming part of their name, and it is as 'William the steward' or 'Payn the steward' that they appear in the survey.

When charter evidence is brought into play, it is occasionally sufficient to show that in Normandy, England and elsewhere – whatever Domesday Book says of the prevalence of stewards – magnates were boasting nearly the complete set of officers of the model household. In 1096, for instance, Eustace, count of Boulogne (who was also a great magnate in England), was attended by his constable, butler and chamberlain.[23] At some time in the same decade, Gibert de Clare appears attended by butler, chamberlain and chaplain in a grant to the abbey of Bury St Edmunds.[24] The household of Adela of Blois, the daughter of William the Conqueror, at this time included such officers as a pantler, master-butler (*archipincerna*) and marshal.[25] In Normandy, a solemn charter of the great magnate, Roger de Beaumont, father of both an earl of Leicester and an earl of Warwick, was attested in 1090 by seneschal, chamberlain and doorkeeper; another charter of the same year mentions a butler.[26]

Occasionally the sources are such that we can get a very good picture of a late eleventh-century household. The household of the earls of Shrewsbury (a title suppressed in 1102) has been reconstructed by J.F.A. Mason. Here we find steward, butler,

22 Domesday Book i, fos. 59v, 60r, 92r, 206v, 207r, 210r, 216r, 218r; *Inquisitio comitatus Cantabrigiensis* ed. Hamilton, 4, 99; Mason, 'Barons and their Officials in the Later Eleventh Century', 245–6.
23 *Les chartes de St-Bertin*, ed. D. Haigneré (4 vols, St-Omer, 1886–90), i, 38.
24 *Feudal Documents from the Abbey of Bury St Edmunds*, ed. D.C. Douglas (British Academy, 1932), 153.
25 *Cartulaire de Notre-Dame de Chartres*, ed. E. de Lépinois and L. Merlet (3 vols, Chartres, 1862–5), i, 107-8.
26 Cartulary of St Peter of Préaux, Archives départementales de l'Eure, H 711, fo. 125r; *Cartulaire de l'église de la sainte-Trinité de Beaumont-le-Roger*, ed. E. Deville (Paris, 1912), 6.

constable, huntsmen (at least two), and cook; and on the clerical side, a large number of chaplains and clerks.[27] A great magnate whose household is even better known is Robert, count of Meulan and earl of Leicester (1080–1118); the greatest nobleman of his age, according to some contemporary writers. Accompanying Count Robert we find not just one, but two stewards, two butlers, constable, chamberlain and marshal; and in the clerical entourage once more, several chaplains and clerks.[28]

There cannot be much doubt that by 1100 the greatest barons of the realm were being followed about by impressive entourages of men bearing the titles of the royal court. How far down the social scale did this practice go? The number of appearances of people called seneschals (*dapiferi*) in Domesday Book makes it likely that seneschals at least were to be found in the households of barons, greater or lesser, by 1086, and Mason gives an example of a Domesday sub-tenant – Robert de Curzon – with a steward.[29] Whether other officers were to be found in lesser baronial households at the time is more difficult to prove. I would think it is likely that chaplains, at least, were to be found as denizens of most baronial entourages at this time. The autobiography of Guibert de Nogent tells of his mother, a noble lady of modest resources, who asked for advice about her son's education through certain clerks '. . . called chaplains who celebrated divine office for her in her household (*familiariter*)'.[30] This was in northern France in the later eleventh century, and a woman to boot. The cartulary of Colchester contains some confirmation of the proliferation of household clerks in the household of the lesser baronage. It refers to the Norman baron, Hubert de Ryes (father of Eudo, steward of the Conqueror), employing an English clerk Ailward, first as clerk (*notarius*) and then chaplain (*capellanus*), who had from Hubert the rectory of St Mary Newchurch (or Woolchurch) for his support.[31] By the time that the so-called 'Laws of Edward

27 J.F.A. Mason, 'The Officers and Clerks of the Norman Earls of Shropshire', *Transactions of the Shropshire Archaeological Society*, lvi (1957–60), 244–57.
28 Crouch, *Beaumont Twins*, 139–40, 148–53.
29 Mason, 'Barons and their Officials in the Later Eleventh Century', 248–9, makes some interesting points about the distribution of officers, drawn from Domesday evidence.
30 *De Vita Sua*, ed. E.R. Labande (Paris, 1981), 26.
31 *Cartularium monasterii sancti Johannis de Colecestria*, ed. S.A. Moore (2 vols, Roxburghe Club, 1897), i, 6, 15, 50, 82. This Ailward is also referred to in records of Westminster abbey, which had a rival claim to St Mary Woolchurch, Cartulary of Westminster, Brit. Libr., ms Cotton Faustina A iii, fo. 64r–v.

the Confessor' were compiled, in the latter years of the reign of Henry I (1100–35), it was assumed (apparently as a matter of course) that all barons would have in their following a number of titled household servants: stewards, butlers, chamberlains, cooks, bakers, as well as a party of squires and lesser attendants.[32] This being so, I would place the spread of the noble household amongst the baronage, great and small, early in the reign of Henry I, once it was accepted (as I think it had been by 1086) that the greatest counts and earls should have such a household as a matter of course.

That the noble household, like castles and seals, was viewed as a baronial essential at this time may be seen, I think, from the behaviour of baronial parvenus in Henry I's reign. That weathercock, Geoffrey de Clinton, is a case in point. He had become a leading courtier only in 1120, yet by the middle of the decade, we find from his charters that his following featured a steward, Anschetil, a butler, Ralph, a chaplain, Osbert of Kenilworth, and a clerk, Roger. A royal administrator like Geoffrey might be expected to ensure that such officers he had would work for their fees. We find indeed that his steward, Anschetil, was active in collecting money from his master's clients. Furthermore Anschetil received on one occasion a writ from his master ordering the return of some property. The Clintons patronised at least one ministerial family: Ralph the butler's son, William, was acting as steward for Geoffrey II de Clinton in Stephen's reign.[33] Noble women at this time must also have their appropriate household. Adeliza, widow of Gilbert de Clare, and mother of Earl Gilbert of Pembroke, had in her service in the 1140s a steward, a chaplain and a household knight, as well as a maid-in-waiting (*puella*).[34]

NUMBERS AND ELABORATION

It would not be too far from the truth, I would guess, that the full household of a magnate of around 1130 (such as that of

32 *Leges Edwardi Confessoris* c. 21, in W. Stubbs, *Select Charters and other Illustrations of English Constitutional History*, ed. H.W.C. Davis (9th edn, Oxford, 1913), 128.
33 For the Clinton household, Cartulary of Kenilworth, Brit. Libr. ms Harley 3650 fos. 2r–v, 2v–3r, 3r, 6r–v, 12v–13r; for the doings of Anschetil, the Clinton steward, ibid, 69v–70r.
34 *Monasticon Anglicanum*, ed. J. Caley *et al.* (8 vols, London, 1817–30), ii, 603.

Waleran count of Meulan, or Ranulf II, earl of Chester) would total about a dozen titled officers, maybe half a dozen to a dozen retained knights, half a dozen clerks or chaplains and an indeterminate number of lesser servants, scullions, carters, attendants, messengers and grooms; maybe as many as forty in all, perhaps more.[35] Looking ahead, the surviving day-roll of Earl William de Warenne of Surrey and his wife, which survives for 1230, speaks of a travelling household of thirty-five. It seems very likely that average numbers within magnate households had remained constant between the mid-twelfth and mid-thirteenth century, and it seems that numbers were to rise in or soon after the late thirteenth century.[36] The descent of a hundred barons and their households on a royal centre for a great council in the early thirteenth century might well have meant the gathering of some four to five thousand people; maybe more if they brought their wives and children. No wonder that twelfth- and thirteenth-century literature is so forthcoming on details of life in tents and lodgings.

It might be assumed that lesser barons had smaller households than those of the earls and greater magnates, but this may not necessarily have been the case. The last testament of Agnes, lady of Clifford, which dates to the second decade of the thirteenth century, carries bequests to many household functionaries: a dispenser, clerk, baker, two baker's boys, a cook and his boy, a packman, huntsman, four male servants she says are her own, and her serving maid (to whom she left a robe and wimple). These do not include the officers proper to her husband (then still living) whose titles we know from other sources: seneschal, chamberlain, chaplains and clerks. There must have been more servants besides these in the Clifford household.[37] The Cliffords were Marcher lords, but not by any means lords of the highest rank; indeed they generally followed greater men: the earls of Hereford or Pembroke. At the

---

35 See for Waleran, ibid., and for Ranulf II of Chester, Crouch, 'The Administration of the Norman Earldom', in *The Earldom of Chester and its Charters: a Tribute to Geoffrey Barraclough*, ed. A.T. Thacker (Chester Arch. Soc., lxxi, 1991), 73–94, *passim*.

36 K. Mertes, *The Noble Household, 1250–1600* (Oxford, 1988), 14–15; C. Dyer, *Standards of Living in the Later Middle Ages: Social Change in England, c. 1200–1520* (Cambridge, 1989), 50–1.

37 *Testamenta Vetusta*, ed. N.H. Nicholas (2 vols, London, 1826), i, 45–6; for a glimpse of her husband's household see charters in Cartulary of Godstow, PRO, E164/20, fo. 152r–v.

other end of the thirteenth century, a surviving list tells us that the lord of Erdesby, Lincolnshire, in 1284 employed a household staff of twenty-five, not including his squires and other retainers.[38] Erdesby did not even rate as a barony, yet its lord had a household which could only be called noble.

With numbers like this, the twelfth- and thirteenth- century nobleman had every reason to measure out his largesse with care, especially as servants of the day were notorious as thieves from their masters' larders. Like Sir Walter Scott's old laird of Milnwood, Gerald of Wales and Walter Map believed that lower servants should be treated economically. Map, moreover, believed that the dishonesty and laziness of servants was incorrigible.[39] This suspicion is another aspect of the contemporary paranoia of the higher social levels towards the lower (we have already noted other occurrences of it in Map's writings). Walter of Henley's late thirteenth-century treatise on estate management puts this view succinctly, as if it were a proverb: 'Since servants are by nature remiss in their work, you must be alert to their tricks.'[40]

Generally, noblemen of the time were careful men with their resources, and their household stewards were urged to keep a keen eye on consumption. Day-rolls (the earliest English examples survive from the later twelfth century) speak of a need to monitor the expense of at least the feeding of the mobile communities represented by the noble household, especially as bed and board was one means of rewarding adherents. Certainly clerks were there to provide the specialist skills to do so at an early period. The most heedless lord of the twelfth century, the Young King Henry (died 1183), son of Henry II, still employed a clerk of the kitchen, whose main responsibility could only have been the compilation of day-rolls (however, he made extra money by freelance work, keeping a tally of

---

38 N. Denholm-Young, *Seigniorial Administration in England* (London, 1937), 7 and n.

39 For a prolonged discussion on that point (dating from 1181 x 82), and a despairing verdict that economy was impossible to achieve in the face of the deviousness of the servants, see Walter Map, *De Nugis Curialium*, trans. M.R. James (revised edn, Oxford, 1983), 16–18. Gerald of Wales has a supernatural story of the household steward of a Welsh magnate with precocious Leveller tendencies, *Itinerarium Kambriae*, in *Opera* (8 vols, Rolls Series, 1861–91), vi, ed. Dimock, 96–7. Map tells a similar, but incomplete, story of a sinister red-headed servant, this time of the hereditary seneschal of France, ibid, 206–8

40 *Walter of Henley and other Treatises on Estate Management and Accounting*, ed. D.M. Oschinsky (Oxford, 1971), 316. Walter was urgent in believing that servants 'often' defrauded their masters, *De Nugis Curialium*, 340.

ransoms won by the Young King's tutor-in-arms, William Marshal and his partner).[41]

The sophistication in monitoring expense was matched by an elaboration of the noble household as consumption became more discriminating, and display more orchestrated. Cooks were important members of the household from the eleventh century, often to be rated alongside the greater officers. The cook of Hugh the Fat, earl of Chester, held two manors of the earl at the time of the Domesday Survey. Earl Hugh took his stomach seriously. The hereditary cook of the earl of Warwick was lord of the hamlet of Woodloes outside the town, as well as substantial properties within it. In the thirteenth century, the then cook, Alan II, doctored his family's archive so as to secure substantial perquisites from the earl: the robes, horses and fees of a household body-squire.[42] But as well as these landed gentleman-cooks we begin to find other officers as the twelfth century progresses.

The royal kitchen seems to have been taken as a model. The picture of the kitchen of William the Conqueror to be found in the legend of Hereward the Wake, composed in the later twelfth century, has it bustling with Norman attendants (*clientes*) and grooms (*garciferi*), arguing, working and jostling.[43] The kitchen, pantry and larder of Henry I, as described by the *Constitutio Domus Regis* was already compartmented. Its staff was around forty men, and included ushers of kitchen, larder and roasting house; carters; a napier in charge of linen and a waferer to bake mass-bread.[44] Magnates had therefore a well-organised royal model to imitate. Already by the mid-twelfth century titles had appeared in magnate households which indicate the same departments: larderers (who assisted the cook), and pantlers and bakers (whose domain would have been the pantry, one of the new service rooms of the hall). The thirteenth century brought further elaboration: a saucer (sauce-cook) and poulterer feature in the Erdesby household list of

41 *Histoire de Guillaume le Maréchal*, ed. P. Meyer (3 vols, Paris, 1899–1909), ll. 3395–408. A *computator* monitored the consumption of bread in the household of Henry I, and he may have been a forerunner of the royal kitchen clerk, *Constitutio Domus Regis*, in *Dialogus de Scaccario*, ed. C. Johnson *et al.* (revised edn, Oxford, 1983), 129.
42 Warwick Record Office, CR26/1(1)/Box 1/W2, an original deed, of which an altered copy is to be found in Oxford, Bodleian Libr., ms Dugdale 13, pp. 521–2.
43 *Liber Eliensis*, ed. E.O. Blake (Camden Soc., 3rd ser., xcii, 1962), 184.
44 *Constitutio Domus Regis*, 129–33.

1284, and Erdesby was not a major baron. This more than hints at elaboration and growing hierarchy in the service rooms of the period.

Ushers (*hostiarii*) mark another important elaboration. Theirs was a post whose only justification was to keep order in the hall, to marshal processions and control access. Ushers could be men of status; knight-ushers appear in the marshalsea of King Henry I.[45] Walter, usher of the chamber of Henry II, came by the manor of King's Stanley, Gloucestershire.[46] Charters prove that ushers featured in baronial households in the first half of the twelfth century. The usher of a magnate might be as important a servant as a royal usher. Ranulf of Merton, the hereditary usher of the household of the earl of Chester in the early thirteenth century, held the manor of Merton, Cheshire. He received fees of two horses and three oxen, and had a subordinate page (*valettus*).[47] What made such men important was their function. We have a glimpse of this from Geoffrey Gaimar in the 1140s. He depicts the ushers of William Rufus (said to be 300 in number) clothed in rich cloth or fur, escorting in procession the magnates of the court into the royal presence, their rods of office keeping back the swarm of commoners. Parties of them also flanked the royal plate and the steward of the hall.[48] Apart from the matter of numbers, the role that Geoffrey gives the ushers in preserving and enhancing the high dignity of a hall can probably be trusted. Royal ushers were a manifestation of public dignity, and the fact that magnates wanted them too means that they had the same concern to marshal and stage-manage occasions of high festivity.

Quite how formal the hall could be can be seen in the 'Rules', a treatise on the management of a household attributed to Bishop Robert Grosseteste of Lincoln and dated to the early 1240s. It was written with the running of the household and estates of a countess in mind, but may have as much reference to that of the bishop himself. The Rules assume that the household will be peripatetic, staying a number of weeks at each manor house. When staying at a hall, the doorkeepers, ushers and the marshal await the arrival of

45 *Constitutio Domus Regis*, 133.
46 PRO, JUST1/275 m.41.
47 *Charters of the Anglo-Norman Earls of Chester, c. 1071–1237*, ed. G. Barraclough (Record Soc. of Lancashire and Cheshire, cxxvi, 1988), no. 270.
48 *L'Estoire des Engles*, ed. A. Bell (Anglo-Norman Text Soc., xiv–xvi, 1960), ll. 5975–6020.

guests, who are to be received with elaborate politeness by these and the seneschal of the hall. The knights and other noblemen of the household are to be attired in the proper livery robes when in attendance. Dinners are to be carefully choreographed. The gentlemen of the household are first to be seated, at which point the servants who are to eat are to enter demurely and take their places in concert. The lord or lady is to be seated centrally so that all can see him or her. Bread and wine are to be brought into the hall by the appropriate officers, side by side, pacing themselves. Squires are to be nominated to serve the high and side tables with wine. The marshal is to escort the seneschal of the hall in with lord's meal, and then station himself so that servants entering and leaving the hall do so in silence and serve in the proper order.[49]

THE INNER HOUSEHOLD

Further development of the noble household can best be seen, for our present purposes, in the intimate officers: chamberlains and confessors. These were the men who created privacy and exclusive space around their masters; guardians and inhabitants of the chamber. The chamberlain had a special place within the noble household. Kings, both English and Welsh, had need of analogous private servants before 1066: *burthegnas* and *gweision ystafell*. Their intimacy with their lords is well attested. Henry II's chamberlain guarded his dozing master from interruption in his chamber at Westminster in 1174, when a messenger with news of the defeat of the rebellion against him tried to get in.[50] His eldest son, the Young King Henry, we are told loved above all his chamberlain, Ralph fitz Godfrey 'The most courteous servant of his household, and the most valiant'.[51] When it came to confidential missions, the chamberlain was the officer trusted above other intimates. In 1203 William fitz Alan sent post-haste his chamberlain to warn Gerald of Wales in secret to get out of Worcestershire quickly, because the men of the county were out against Gerald on royal orders.[52] In romances, chamberlains flit around and about the heroes and

---

49 *Walter of Henley*, ed. Oschinsky, 401–5.
50 *Jordan Fantosme's Chronicle*, ed. R.C. Johnston (Oxford, 1981), 144.
51 *Histoire de Guillaume le Maréchal*, ll. 6528–32.
52 'De iure et statu Menevensis ecclesie', in *Opera* (8 vols, Rolls Series, 1861–91), iii, ed. Brewer, 227.

heroines, taking messages, and minding hats and coats; a necessary literary lubricant. In the 'Eliduc' of Marie de France, for instance, the *chamberlenc privé* of Guilliadun, the king of Devon's daughter, was the girl's main support in her dalliance with Eliduc: the chamberlain was her sole confidant and served her loyally (rather than her father, the king).[53]

The importance of chamberlains lies in more than just their use as a literary device. It can be related to the growing detachment between the hall and chamber of the aristocratic house. As the twelfth century progressed, the growing size and complexity of the chamber block rather transcended the 'bower' of the early eleventh century, and increased the possiblity for isolation. This gave the chamberlain no small influence, for he had the power to limit access to his lord. Other officers – hall-stewards, butlers, dispensers and pantlers – inhabited the hall outside, or the new service rooms at the opposite end to the chamber block.

The Rules of Bishop Robert, dating to the 1240s, show that the household had already fragmented. The Rules look on the public theatre of the hall as important to the exercise of lordship, but see its importance as having been eroded. It is as if the great days of the hall were already seen as lost in the past. The Rules enjoin a lord to make a point of eating publicly in the hall *devaunt voz genz* (except if sick or tired) because of the 'great benefit and honour' which they will acquire; that is, one supposes, the reputation for public splendour and generosity. Serving dinners in corners and private rooms is to be strictly avoided; it brings 'no honour' to lord and lady.[54]

There was also a spiritual withdrawal by the lord as the twelfth century wore on; a magnate's closest counsels would be reserved for his confessor, an attendant selected as the sole repository of his master's miseries and guilt. In earlier days, spiritual counsel would have been available to a magnate too, but from a number of clerical attendants who rode and ate with him. The first royal confessor we hear so named was that of Henry I, Aethelwulf, prior of Nostell, 'to whom he was wont to confess his sins'. Aethelwulf was rewarded with the new bishopric of Carlisle in 1133.[55] He was an Augustinian; later kings favoured Cistercians. In the middle of

---

53 *Les Lais de Marie de France*, ed. J. Rychner (Classiques français du moyen âge, 1983), ll. 271–326.
54 *Walter of Henley*, ed. Oschinsky, 407.
55 Robert de Torigny, *Chronica*, in *Chronicles of the Reigns of Stephen, Henry II and Richard I*, ed. R. Howlett (4 vols, Rolls Series, 1884–9), 123.

the twelfth century we hear of the noble lady Euphemia, countess of Oxford, whose chaplain, Robert, served as her confessor.[56] Noble ladies seem to have been then already vulnerable to the charms of the intimate spiritual adviser. Gilbert Foliot, himself much favoured by aristocratic ladies, wrote to the countess of Leicester of 'the worthy fathers you have about you, faithfully administering comfort to you'.[57] But such influence was not just exerted over females. The grip of Gerold, the charismatic chaplain of Hugh, earl of Chester, on the minds of his lord's knights was so close that he was able to turn a number of them to the cloister.[58]

For the most part we do not know the names of these spiritual comforters and directors. Some magnates had particular friends amongst the higher clergy. William Marshal, earl of Pembroke, for instance, was close with the bishop of Ossory, and the abbots of Bristol and Notley.[59] The latter abbot was certainly prominent in the confession of the dying earl, and may well have served as his confessor on other occasions. Doubtless, private spiritual counsellors were recruited from amongst the numerous chaplains in the households of greater and lesser men. The thirteenth century, however, saw new fashions. The arrival of the Franciscans in England caused much interest amongst the aristocracy. Early Franciscan history makes it clear that the brothers found much support from the magnates of the realm and their wives. Loretta, countess of Leicester, living as a recluse at Hackington, exerted much influence on the order's behalf 'like a mother for her sons'. This influence was extended through confession. Brother Solomon, a Franciscan based in London, was such a fashionable confessor amongst courtiers that he was able to ignore the bishop of London's attempts to regulate his activities. The Dominicans likewise attracted much support from barons, earls and princes, and probably for the same reason.[60]

---

56 *Cartularium prioratus de Colne*, ed. J.L. Fisher (Essex Archaeological Society, Occasional Publications, no. 1, 1946), 30.
57 *The Letters and Charters of Gilbert Foliot*, ed. A. Morey and C.N.L. Brooke (Cambridge, 1967), 160.
58 Orderic Vitalis, *The Ecclesiastical History*, ed. M. Chibnall (6 vols, Oxford, 1969–80), iii, 144, discussed in C. Harper-Bill, 'The Piety of the Anglo-Norman Knightly Class', in *Proceedings of the Battle Conference, 1979*, ed. R.A. Brown (Woodbridge, 1980), 75.
59 D. Crouch, *William Marshal: Court, Career and Chivalry in the Angevin Empire* (London, 1990), 142–3.
60 *Tractatus de adventu fratrum minorum in Angliam*, ed. A.G. Little (Manchester, 1951), 20, 62; W.A. Hinnebusch, *The Early English Friars Preacher* (Rome, 1951), 86–102.

Friars were associated as spiritual advisers with the greatest men of thirteenth-century England: Simon de Montfort (Adam Marsh) and William de Valence (Peter de la Roch).[61] Occasionally, the chamber must have been the place for high spiritual discourse and comfort, and the intimacy between lord and spiritual director must have seemed a threat to the lay retinue which surrounded the magnate. It would certainly account for the anticlericalism evident amongst the knights of the late Earl William Marshal (died 1219) when they recalled the deathbed scenes between their lord and his chaplains and confessors.[62]

The development of the household through the eleventh and twelfth centuries has its significance for our understanding of aristocracy, and how it was to be expressed. The development follows a pattern of diffusion which was strictly *au Duby*. In its first manifestations, the noble household was a matter of casual dignity. Names were transplanted from the royal household, to the princely household and into that of the magnate. The precise meaning of the titles conferred was probably unimportant; seneschalcies, marshalseas and constabularies were scattered about, regardless. Although the seneschal was supposedly the highest of the royal servants, it is noticeable that in certain households other officers occupied that place: the constable in the Chester household, the butler at Leicester. Having the full complement was what counted, not what they did.

During the twelfth century (leaving aside genuine developments in administration in the household, which are not our concern here) the magnate household began to express a concern for that aristocratic dignity which we have already considered. Standards of public display and entertainment meant an elaborate kitchen staff, swarms of liveried squires and servants, a dignified usher and his underlings to control the throng and marshal processions. Yet at the same time, the magnate continued to make himself less visible; the elaboration of the hall-complex, chamberlains and discreet confessors allowed him a private world into which to withdraw; not just a side-chamber in which to sleep. The magnate might ration his appearances, increasing the impact of his presence by its comparative rarity, raising the value

61 For Valence and Roch, see H. Ridgeway, 'William de Valence and his *Familiares*, 1247–1272' (forthcoming).
62 Crouch, *William Marshal*, 135; see also Morris, '*Equestris Ordo*: Chivalry as a Vocation in the Twelfth century', *in Studies in Church History*, xv (1978), ed. D. Baker.

of intimacy with him, and limiting the possibility for patronage. It is this context of formal public parade and strategic withdrawal which the noble household contributed to the aristocracy of the twelfth and thirteenth centuries.

KNIGHTS AND THE NOBLE HOUSEHOLD

The progress of the noble household down the social scale is a tricky process to try to chart. Dispersed and fragmentary evidence is, of course, the major hindrance. In the twelfth century, when the magnate class generated few enough surviving records, the lower groups generated even fewer. By the reign of Henry II it is clear that *some* knights were affecting to appoint at least a steward, but how many? And if we accept that many lesser landowners were appointing stewards, does this have any real significance in exploring changes within the aristocracy? To take some solid examples: William Burdet, a substantial tenant of several manors in the earldoms of Huntingdon and Leicester (and indeed steward of Huntingdon) had his own steward, Hamund, by 1163. William was the ancestor of a prominent Midland knightly family, so it is appropriate here to call him a knight.[63] In the Pembrokeshire of the later twelfth century, Gerald of Wales tells us of the household steward of Elidor, lord of Stackpole.[64] Nigel de Mondeville (*viv.* 1203), who held the two manors of Berkswell and Lighthorne in Warwickshire for one knight's fee of the earl of Warwick in the late twelfth century, had a *dapifer*, one Richard of Kington, a substantial free tenant and local man of affairs.[65] We can

---

63 Brit. Libr., Additional Charter 48086. For William Burdet see Crouch, *Beaumont Twins*, 156–7; Stringer, *Earl David of Huntingdon: A Study in Anglo-Scottish History* (Edinburgh, 1985), 159.
64 Gerald of Wales, *Itinerarium Kambriae*, in *Opera*, vi, ed. Dimock, 96–7.
65 For Nigel's *dapifer*, Cartulary of Kenilworth, fo. 27r–v. For Nigel's lands, see also, Shakespeare Birthplace Trust DR18/1/181; DR98/665; Bodl. Libr. ms. Dugdale 12 p. 269. For his knight service, see *Red Book of the Exchequer*, ed. H. Hall (3 vols, Rolls Series, 1896), 326. Richard of Kington, or possibly Kineton, appears in several contemporary deeds. He had interests in the manor of Alspath, neighbouring Berkswell. He is noted as sometime owner of a half-virgate there, which later came to the priory of Thelsford, see E. Bernard, *Catalogi librorum manuscriptorum Angliae et Hiberniae in unum collecti* (2 vols, Oxford, 1697), ii, 206; he or a son of the same name also had an assart in the same manor, and a number of properties held in demesne, or rented out, which came to his wife Mathilda on his death, see Birmingham Central Reference Library Archives Chs 608881, 608882. There is also a reference to Richard's enjoyment of the overlordship of one twentieth of a knight's fee held by Alexander of Bickenhill in Alspath, see PRO, JUST1/614B m. 16. He or his son served as bailiff of Hemlingford hundred in Warwickshire in 1232 and was still alive in 1247, PRO, JUST1/951A m. 22.

see Richard as the progenitor of what late medievalists call the 'parish gentry'. When such men as Elidor and Nigel were employing officers called stewards, the process of diffusion of the noble household through society had gone nearly as far as it could. (Dr Paul Brand has, however, pointed out to me an example of a steward of a single manor, Melchbourne, Bedfordshire, in 1262.[66]) Nigel de Mondeville, whom we might call a man of knightly class (since his descendants were prominent county knights) was at the lowest level of society which could support a steward, or might conceivably need one.

But if we are willing to accept on limited evidence that there was a multiplication of stewards at a lower level of society in the twelfth century, is this the same as the diffusion of the noble household? I do not think that it is. The appointment of stewards or seneschals really tells us little about ideas of status. As has already been mentioned, the vernacular word *senescal* was annoyingly unspecific, it had a general application to any servant; it could be used of a marshal or a chamberlain (as it was of the marshal of England and the chamberlain of Normandy). The Latin word *senescallus* too is suspiciously general. The way that early thirteenth-century legal and fiscal records attach it liberally to representatives of other men in legal cases seems to indicate a word detached from status and office. It was a word like bailiff, free to be used for any man's representative or attorney. For instance, the prominent Midlands knight, Arnold du Bois, employed the rector of the church of his estate of Ebrington, Gloucestershire, as his representative before the royal justices between 1200 and 1203, and as a result the rector is in 1203 termed his 'seneschal'.[67] Furthermore, the appearance of a seneschal of the lord of Bizy in Normandy before 1066 makes it likely that the title was being given to the officers of lesser landowners before the twelfth century. If diffusion of the noble household can be said to have happened on the basis of the spread of the title 'seneschal', then it happened early on. The choice of application of the word is another problem. It might apply to a landlord's estate manager and deputy; it might apply

---

66 PRO, JUST1/5 m. 19.
67 The pledge of *Beniamini senescalli Ernaldi de Bosco* is noted in a suit involving Arnold in 1203, see PRO, JUST1/799 m. 6. In 1200 *Beniaminus persona de Edbricton'* was attorney of Arnold in the curia regis, see *Curia Regis Rolls of the Reigns of Richard I, John and Henry III* (16 vols, HMSO, 1922–79), i, 239. *Beniamin de Ebricton'* was a witness to a charter of Arnold to St Andrew, Northampton, see Cartulary of St Andrew Northampton, Brit. Libr., ms Cotton Vespasian, E xvii, fo. 68v.

also to the presiding servant in his hall. The steward of Stackpole was such a man, feared and suspected by his lower servants. Richard of Kington, on the other hand, was a landowner himself and it is a reasonable assumption that he was employed outside the hall.

For my purposes here, the noble household must be considered to be that household which aspired to counterfeit the established households of kings and magnates. Earls and barons had such things by the end of the eleventh century; lesser barons, noblewomen and parvenus had them by the mid-twelfth century. That knights may well have had seneschals is not enough to justify the belief that they had noble households. Knights can, on occasion, be proved to have attempted more in the way of dignity than a seneschal. Sir Maurice Butler of Oversley (died 1243), a prominent Warwickshire knight and local justice, had both seneschal and chamberlain in the second quarter of the thirteenth century. His chamberlain went by the name of Lawrence Mauduit; 'Mauduit' was the traditional nickname for a chamberlain, applied to the chamberlain of Henry I of England, and the legendary chamberlain of King Arthur.[68] But Butler was a knight whose status bordered on that of the banneret, indeed two of his grandsons had summonses to Parliament.

At the very end of our period, the last testament of the Leicestershire knight, John de Charnelles of Muston (dated 1301), mentions bequests to his old nurse, his son's then nurse, his cook, groom and butler.[69] Since John's landed endowment was limited to a modest estate in Muston and Howes, Leicestershire, it is unlikely that his little household could have included men of substance, but the use of the title 'butler' within it is interesting and relevant to our purpose. Even the households of gentry families could be large by the fourteenth century. Working from the few surviving day-rolls of the period, Dr Mertes demonstrates that Roger Holm, a Norfolk knight, had a household of some eighteen persons in 1328–9. She concludes from this and other evidence that the gentry were under pressure to increase their numbers of servants by the end of the thirteenth century.[70]

68 Cambridge, Trinity College mss Box 45, no. 44.
69 *The Manuscripts of his Grace the Duke of Rutland, G.C.B., preserved at Belvoir Castle* (4 vols, Historical MSS Commission, 1888–1903), iv, 14.
70 Mertes, *The Noble Household*, 14–15.

THE LORD, HIS MEN AND THE HUNTING FIELD

One of the rarer sort of magnate seals of the thirteenth century is that represented by the fine great seal of Earl Simon de Montfort (died 1265). Surprisingly, its obverse shows this eminent soldier-earl riding through a wood blowing a horn, in hunting garb, a dog running at his horse's side; he has not chosen the more common image of the galloping knight.[71] But the image of the hunter is also an image of aristocracy, and the Montfort seal (probably commissioned in the 1230s) is hardly the first time that it is to be found. The Bayeux Tapestry features an eleventh-century example when it shows Earl Harold riding along in civilian (if we can use the word) dress, his hawk perched on his wrist and with several dogs running on ahead. A later twelfth-century knightly seal from Lincolnshire preserved the selfsame pose.[72]

It would be to miss out an important aspect of aristocratic life, if I neglected its hunting activity, a pursuit in which the household took a full part. The pursuit of wild animals by lords, with their dogs and birds, was indeed a favourite recreation of the magnate group. It involved great expense, a subsidiary and intimate household of specialists; and, most exclusive of all, tracts of countryside reserved for the chase. Very little has been written about aristocratic hunting in the period covered by this book; sources are complicated and sparse, and I am not particularly well fitted to fill this gap in scholarship, but a few observations are both necessary and relevant to the purpose of this book.

Hunting was a particular royal pursuit, and kings of England from the Confessor onwards had rejoiced in it, as well as suffered from it; two sons of the Conqueror (Richard and William Rufus) and one grandson (Richard, son of Duke Robert) died in accidents on the hunting field.[73] As records of *royal* hunting and forests in England are fairly good for the twelfth century a reasonable amount has been written about the king and his pursuit of game. Rather less has been written about how earls and barons enjoyed the same pursuits as

---

71 A good example of this rare seal is to be found on Gloucestershire Record Office, D 225/T.7 (Denison-Jones Deeds). This charter also features the earl's small and conventional armorial counterseal, which is found alone on Nottingham University Library, Middleton ms. Mi.C.2.

72 The lost seal of Adam of Ewerby, preserved in a good sketch by the seventeenth-century antiquary, Randle Holme, Brit. Libr., ms. Harley 2044, fo. 153v.

73 F. Barlow, *William Rufus* (London, 1983), 123.

their royal master and exemplar; but that they enjoyed them is very clear. Orderic's famous description of Hugh I, earl of Chester (died 1101), has him making daily 'a waste' of his forest, and accuses him of loving his hunters and hawkers above all his companions. It is worth pointing out in support of Orderic that in the household of the earls of Chester, hunters, hawkers and falconers were both numerous and very prominent until the mid-twelfth century.[74]

The concentration on hunting and the forest as a royal prerogative in medieval England has obscured the fact that the magnates also possessed considerable tracts of reserved forest, under their own forest law. Another reason why this has been neglected is the anachronistic insistence that twelfth-century magnates did not control forests but 'chases' (with the implication of an inferior sort of place and right). In fact the practice of reserving the word 'forest' for exclusive royal hunting grounds does not begin until the thirteenth century.[75] In the twelfth century, the earl of Gloucester's game preserve at Malvern, Worcestershire, is called on several occasions *foresta (mea) de Malvernia*, and charters talk of its hereditary foresters, its bounds and the earl's rights of hunting there; however, in 1291 Earl Gilbert de Clare refers to it as *foresta et chacia nostra Malvern(ie)*.[76] The earl of Warwick has a *foresta de Suttona* (Sutton Coldfield) in the twelfth century and early thirteenth century, but in 1247 and 1294 it is *chacea nostra de Suttona*.[77]

Many of the earls had great forests. The earl of Chester had in fact much of his shire under forest law, with a master forester in the mid-twelfth century in at least one of the major forests, Leek and Macclesfield. In another forest in the twelfth century, that of Mara, his foresters kept up his hunting and had the keeping also of his pack.[78] Another great Anglo-Norman magnate, Robert II, count of Meulan (1166–1207), a man who controlled more forest land in Normandy than any other individual apart from the duke, also had master-foresters, master-hunters (of knightly rank) and a

74 Crouch, 'The Administration of the Norman Earldom', in *The Earldom of Chester and its Charters*, ed. Thacker, 73, 79.
75 The canons of the Council of Lillebonne (1090) refer to 'the forests of the king or his barons', Orderic Vitalis, *The Ecclesiastical History*, ed. Chibnall, iii, 28.
76 *Earldom of Gloucester Charters*, ed. R.B. Patterson (Oxford, 1973), 92, 113, 176, 180; Worcestershire Record Office, Lechmere Deeds 705: 134/65 (vi).
77 Bodl. Libr., ms Dugdale 13, p. 419; Birmingham Central Reference Libr. Archives, Ch. 348039; Brit. Libr., Additional Ch. 20468; Cartulary of Beauchamp of Elmley, Brit. Libr., ms. Additional 28024, fo. 108r; PRO, JUST1/952, m. 27.
78 *Charters of the Earls of Chester*, ed. Barraclough, nos. 163, 176.

pack of hounds at his castle of Vatteville.[79] The twelfth-century earls of Derby had large tracts of private forest at Needwood, Duffield and in Cannock (their 'forest of Arden').[80] I have already mentioned the earl of Gloucester's forest of Malvern; apart from his forests in the March of Wales, the earl also had a large forest area around his estate centre of Cranborne, Dorset.[81] The twelfth-century earls of Leicester had Leicester Forest and Charnwood in Leicestershire, and in Normandy the magnificent forest of Breteuil.[82]

These are sufficient examples to prove how most of the greater magnates found means to secure forest for their private hunting, and not inconsiderable areas at that. More could be quoted. How far down the economic continuum represented by magnates did the possession of forests stretch? Orderic Vitalis apparently considered that hunting rights in England in the reign of Henry I belonged only to the greatest magnates and the king's friends.[83] In practice he was doubtless correct (if we relate hunting to the possession of a forest), in that there had to be a limit to the size of territory which could bear the name of 'forest' without seeming ridiculous, and needing lesser words like 'wood', 'park', 'frith' or 'hay' to better describe it. We hear of at least one lesser baron, Walter of Clifford, who in 1256 had what he called a 'forest', that of 'Northclye' in Shropshire, where he maintained a riding forester and staff, as his predecessors had also done since the reign of Henry II.[84] Another lesser magnate, Philip Marmion, lord of Tamworth, in 1247 would call his hunting preserve a wood (*boscum*), like Middleton Wood 'where he and all his ancestors had been wont to hunt'. Philip's right had been challenged by the countess of Warwick when Philip had drawn the wood to the sound of horns and dogs, riding with pack of brachets and greyhounds, and a large party of huntsmen and mounted archers.[85]

Iconography and history agree in depicting great aristocrats riding about with packs of greyhounds and brachet-hounds loping and snuffling alongside their horses. The packs (motes) of the count

79 Crouch, *Beaumont Twins*, 170 and n., 189–90.
80 Coucher Book of Lancaster, PRO, DL42/2, fo. 7v.; Bodl. Libr., ms. Dugdale 13, p. 315; *The Cartulary of Darley*, ed. R.R. Darlington (2 vols, Derbyshire Archaeological Society, 1945), ii, 582–3.
81 Cartulary of Mortimer, Brit. Libr., ms. Harley 1240, fo. 90r.
82 Crouch, *Beaumont Twins*, 191.
83 Orderic Vitalis, *The Ecclesiastical History*, ed. Chibnall, vi, 100.
84 PRO, JUST1/734, m. 9d.
85 PRO, JUST1/952, m. 27.

of Meulan and earl of Chester are mentioned in passing in pipe rolls and charters.[86] A connoisseur's interest in dogs and their behaviour occasionally comes through in the sources. William, earl of Gloucester (1147–83), went out of his way to acquire a greyhound whose particular virtue was that it had attempted (bravely but unsuccessfully) to defend its master, a Welsh magnate, from his assassins. The earl made a gift of the dog to his cousin King Henry II, a great man for the hunt. In describing the incident, Gerald of Wales himself displays more than a passing interest in dogs, their characteristics and breeds.[87] The most unlikely characters were associated with the paraphernalia of hunting. Eadmer notes in passing how greyhounds trotted along with the riding retinue of St Anselm of Canterbury, and were occasionally sent coursing after hares by his household squires as he rode along. Abbot Samson of Bury St Edmunds maintained parks, huntsmen and a pack for the use of his noble guests. Although he did not himself join the chase, or eat venison, the abbot and his chaplains sat in the shade of a tree in an elevated pleasance and watched the sport with interest.[88] Magnates doubtless were as intently interested in hawks and falcons as in dogs; hawkers and falconers are invariable, and sometimes high-ranking, members of baronial households. The British sources are generally uncommunicative on the subject, however, until later centuries.

To get the full savour of the medieval aristocratic passion for hunting, one example may be illuminating: Roger de Quincy, earl of Winchester (1235–64). Earl Roger was a man who was disappointed in life; although wealthy and influential, he never had the son he wanted to carry on his line, a misfortune which was said to have cast a gloom over the second half of his long life. It may be that he found consolation on the hunting field; certainly he was an avid conserver and hunter of game. He inherited with his earldom the large park of Bradgate, attached to his residence of Groby, near Leicester, which he considerably enlarged in the 1240s. He further developed waste land in the rugged district of Charnwood into what he called a 'forest' (probably to make up for the forest of Leicester which was apportioned to the Montfort family as its share of the

86 For the pack of Brotonne, Bibliothèque nationale, Collection du Vexin, viii, p. 625; *Magni Rotuli Scaccarii Normanniae sub regibus Angliae*, ed. T. Stapleton (2 vols., London, 1840–4) ii, 460.
87 Gerald of Wales, *Itinerarium Kambriae*, in *Opera*, vi, ed. Dimock, 69.
88 Eadmer, *The Life of St Anselm*, ed. R.W. Southern (repr. Oxford, 1972), 89; *Chronicle of Joscelin of Brakelond*, ed. H.E. Butler (London, 1949), 28.

earldom of Leicester). Elsewhere he developed a park on his estates at Stevington in Bedfordshire.[89] Some measure of his continuing enthusiasm for the hunt can be found in a Bedfordshire plea of 1262. The previous November, it appears that a prominent knight, John de Grey, had lent Earl Roger the use of his park at Silsoe; the earl had hunted it with a party of local gentry, some of whom had returned after the earl had left and done some hunting on their own account, without Grey's permission. The point we need to note is that Earl Roger was an enthusiastic sixty-seven years of age at the time when a day's hunting had been granted him by Grey.[90]

Sir John de Grey had his park stocked with deer at Silsoe in 1262. By that date it was becoming usual for any knight of pretensions, and one or two manors, to have enclosed an area for a diminutive hunting ground and stocked it with various beasts of the chase. Parks had been rare in the late eleventh century, but so widespread were they by the early fourteenth century that it has been calculated that there was one park to every four parishes in lowland England. The remarkable multiplication of emparked hunting grounds (which averaged out at 200 acres extent) in the twelfth and thirteenth centuries was a social process. It was social diffusion made manifest in the landscape. Kings and magnates had hunting forests in the eleventh century, knights aspired to miniature versions of the same in the later twelfth century. The introduction of the fallow deer to England in the twelfth century – which could be kept within palings – made the ambition of lesser men to have a hunting park easier to realise.[91] At what precise point (if any) the process got going is not known, but the Close Rolls preserve numerous copies of licences from the king to aspirant knights (and others) from the reign of John (1199–1216).

The park and its affectation by the knights brings us back to the subject of their inclusion within the aristocracy. Knights in the later thirteenth century were very alert to the possibilities of copying their betters. We see this most clearly with households and hunting. In both cases it was possible for knights to construct cut-down versions of what the magnate enjoyed. A 200-acre park may not have compared with Needwood forest in sheer size and

89 PRO, JUST1/454 m. 11d, CP25(1)/121/16/232, CP25(1)/121/17/265; Huntington Libr., Hastings deeds, nos. 129, 130; *Records of Harrold Priory*, ed. G.H. Fowler (Bedfordshire Historical and Records Soc., xvii, 1935), 41.
90 PRO, JUST1/5, m. 12.
91 O. Rackham, *Trees and Woodland in the British Landscape* (London, 1976), 143; idem, *The History of the Countryside* (London, 1986), 122–5.

variety of economic resources, but it adequately answered the social function of a place to hunt; answered it well enough for an earl like Roger de Quincy not to feel demeaned by borrowing it. A knight's household might not have been made up of the liveried noblemen who populated that of a magnate, but a seneschal for his manor, a butler for his hall, a body-squire, a chaplain and a chamberlain would have given enough retainers for an appearance of dignity. This parallels what was happening in the extension of heraldry, and the elaboration of knightly residences. Here Duby's process of social diffusion works best, and as far as can be seen, the chronology is the same throughout. The last decades of the twelfth century and the early decades of the thirteenth, some two generations, saw the self-transformation of the knights, and the consequent enlargement of the aristocracy.

10

PIETY AND STATUS

PATRONAGE, REPENTANCE AND RENUNCIATION

There were distinctly aristocratic ways of patronising the Church. A magnate did not lavish endowment on the Church solely to exalt himself in the eyes of the world; but the sincerity of his motives was consciously or unconsciously mixed with other, more worldly, concerns. It is that tinge of worldliness which concerns us here. Magnates were wealthy enough to be able to found entire abbeys unassisted, and indeed, in the eleventh and twelfth centuries were expected to do so. When and how they set up their monasteries could be questions of style and fashion, or family tradition, as much as piety and grace. The accumulation of resources that generations of aristocrats would plough into the Church can leave even the modern historian deeply impressed; and historians tend to be cynical, both by nature and training. The magnificence of the investment would hardly be less impressive to their contemporaries.

A glimpse of what just one family did for the Church (and that not the greatest of Norman families) is instructive. The family of Eu has certain advantages as an example. Eu was a county on the northern border of Normandy; the family that ruled it was a cadet branch of the Norman ducal house. There were six counts of Eu in the eleventh and twelfth centuries, but none of them were great intimates of the king-duke. After the Conquest, the counts of Eu were also (usually) lords of Hastings and its rape in Sussex. The second count, Robert (died *c.*1093), made the family's first foundation: the abbey of St Michael of Le Tréport (a *bourg* near Eu) for Benedictine monks, endowing it with the existing great church in the town, many urban properties and assorted revenues and tithes.[1] He eventually founded a corresponding spiritual centre for his lordship of Hastings in England; this was a college of secular canons in the church of St Mary.[2] He made further grants to the monastic houses of La Trinité du Mont, in Rouen, and Battle, in Sussex. Count Robert was a man whose emotional storms could take a religious turn; we glimpse in him the impulsive generosity and religious feeling of many of his fellow-barons. The funeral cortège of his wife, Beatrice, rested at the hamlet of Flamanville on its way to her burial at Le Tréport. Count Robert commemorated this by the erection of a church on the spot where her bier had stood. His son, Count William II (died 1095), did not feel called upon to add to his father's foundations; in any case he had fully participated in his father's donations. Furthermore, political misjudgement meant that he did not survive long as count. He added properties to Le Tréport and also (apparently) further patronised the college of Hastings, but did not make a foundation of his own.[3]

Count Henry I (died 1140), son of William II, dramatically increased the family's patronage. He was a man genuinely enamoured of the new monasticism of his day. Further grants came from him early in his career to the (by now) ancestral abbey of Le Tréport, but he made his own foundations too. In 1119 he refounded what was already an ancient college of secular canons at Eu as an abbey of Augustinian canons regular.[4] He seems also to have founded in his county the small abbey of Sèry for Augustinian canons (from references in his descendants' charters).[5] In 1105 he adopted the priory of the Benedictine abbey of Bec at St-Martin-au-Bois in the forest of Eu.[6] In 1130 Count Henry began a magnificent foundation; a Cluniac abbey on estates at the south-eastern end of his county at Foucarmont. He ended his days as a monk at the abbey of Eu.[7] Count John (died 1170), son of Henry, continued the patronage of his father's abbeys of Eu, Sèry and Foucarmont

---

1 *Cartulaire de l'abbaye de St-Michel du Tréport*, ed. P. Laffleur de Kermaingant (Paris, 1880), 1–19.
2 PRO, E210/1073.
3 *Cartulaire de St-Michel du Tréport*, 20.
4 Cartulary of the counts of Eu, Paris, Bibliothèque Nationale, ms Latin 13904, fos. 34r–36r.
5 ibid., fo. 81r–v.
6 ibid., fos. 77r–78v.
7 *Chronique des comtes d'Eu*, in *Receuil des historiens des Gaules et de la France*, ed. M. Bouquet *et al.* (24 vols, Paris, 1869–1904), xxiii, 439.

in grand style. He also patronised the priories of Lewes, Sussex, and Monks Horton, Kent; the cell of Criel, in his county of Eu, an outpost of his abbey of Eu; the abbeys of Battle and Briostel, and the cathedral of Chichester. The last of the counts of the old line, Henry II, patronised most of the above houses, and in addition the Cistercians of Robertsbridge in Sussex, a foundation made by his stepfather, Alfred de St-Martin.[8]

Five abbeys (if we include Robertsbridge), a major secular college and two priories owed their all to this one family. Many more besides benefited from their generosity. In this the house of Eu was not particularly remarkable. The families of Beaumont, Clare, Aumale, Chester, Warenne and Gloucester equalled or far excelled this total. Many other aristocratic families contributed two or more houses of religion. The inventory of magnate patronage of the Church in the eleventh and twelfth centuries was sumptuous in its scale.

What did magnates get in return? As I have said, this is not a study of aristocratic piety, but some reflection on it is not out of place. The particularly volatile mixture of violence and raw religion of the eleventh century inspired much frantic alms-giving. More, it inspired a good few remorse-racked warriors to reject the world for the cloister or a forest cell; Herluin of Bec and William of Llanthony are but two of the more notable examples. The twelfth century produced more subtle, more educated but no less enthusiastic patrons.

An early twelfth-century English sermon hammers home the message: 'Alms extinguish sin as water does fire.' The impenitent and impious would meet punishment. Orderic Vitalis conjures up the nightmare of Hellequin's Hunt: damned knights riding the dark of night, skin blackened and smoking, locked into red-hot armour.[9] The idea of spiritual consequences for wordly misdeeds found further elaboration and definition in his day. The idea of a 'third place' between Heaven and Hell entered the minds of the laity in the early twelfth century. The essential point about this place, Purgatory, was that the length of soul's stay there was negotiable.[10] The foundation of houses where perpetual prayer might be offered

---

8 Kent Record Office, U1475 (Delisle Deeds) T264/9.
9 C. Harper-Bill, 'The Piety of the Anglo-Norman Knightly Class', in *Proceedings of the Battle Conference 1979* ed. R.A. Brown (Woodbridge, 1980), 63–77, is a fine sketch of the tortured religious mentality of the noble of the period; he does not confine himself to knights however.
10 J. le Goff, *La Naissance du purgatoire* (Paris, 1981), 14–24, 436–9.

up for the departed soul of the founder and his family lent a new urgency to the process. Indeed it fuelled the aristocracy's appetite for new forms of religious life to sponsor. The promotion of new forms of holy life must increase the ration of grace extended in the next world to their supporter. For this reason, founders and patrons occasionally paused to reflect on the nature of the foundation they were making, and to congratulate themselves. Waleran of Meulan, when converting a college of secular canons into a priory of Bec-Hellouin said that he did so, 'in all good will, and to improve the standing of the church of Holy Trinity of Beaumont, aiming for the future increase of religious feeling amongst the souls in the same church'.[11] Gerald of Wales preserves what purports to be the debate of Ranulf de Glanville on the spiritual merits of the various orders of his day, when choosing the order in which to found the two houses he proposed to build on his estates (see below p. 328).

Extravagant penitence remained the fashion in the thirteenth century, and seems to have intensified under the influence of the friars. The romantic hero, Guy of Warwick, troubled (like the real-life hero William Marshal on his deathbed) by the hundreds who had fallen to his spear, resolved to throw over wife, family, rich county and honours, and seek instead exile and a hermit's cell. He had real-life counterparts, such as the world-weary *curialis* Sir Alexander of Bassingbourn, who resolved to throw over his career for a Franciscan habit around 1235.[12] The debate between Guy of Warwick and his wife about his dramatic decision is revealing. Why go into exile? 'All over your lands build churches and abbeys, which will pray for you forever, night and day without end![13] His passionate gesture of renunciation in the face of God is contrasted with her reasoned balance of materialism and spiritual investment. But it was not enough for Guy to give land. He had to give himself.

There is room for some reservation in our admiration for the spirit of twelfth- and thirteenth-century renunciation. We are being invited to admire Guy's austerity. Yet if we find ourselves too impressed by the renunciations of Guy of Warwick (and William Marshal) we

11 *Cartulaire de l'église de la sainte-Trinité de Beaumont-le-Roger*, ed. E. Deville (Paris, 1912), 10.
12 *Tractatus de adventu fratrum minorum in Anglia*, ed. A.G. Little (Manchester, 1951), 63–4.
13 *Gui de Warewic: roman du xiiie siècle*, ed. A. Ewart (2 vols, Classiques français du moyen âge, 1932), ll. 7663–6.

ought to bear in mind that their dramatic solutions left them still in a life that was aristocratic. They no more followed the advice of Christ to the wealthy young man who wanted to know how to have eternal life, than the original recipient of it.[14] Guy of Warwick's idea of an eremitical life was to settle at a well-appointed chapel at Guy's Cliffe, attended by servants and a staff of priests. The dying William Marshal expressed his renunciation by entering the order of Templars. But he did not become a 'poor knight' in the month or so left to him. He was still behaving as earl of Pembroke the day before his death, awarding robes to his retainers.

Imminent death could indeed bring on particular desperation; a number of religious houses owed their origin to a last frantic bout of alms-giving. Magnates in peril on the sea might vow to found abbeys if they survived. In this way began the Cistercian houses of Le Valasse in Normandy and Tintern Parva in Ireland. Other storm-driven magnates – such as was supposed of Count William of Aumale – might be comforted as their ships were tossed about by the thought of monks and canons in their patronage offering prayers for their safety. Coming to what was, or what seemed to be, the extreme end of life brought on remorse; and that remorse was worked on by the Church. Henry of Huntingdon describes the threats which could be brought to bear on a dying man. He pictures Robert, count of Meulan and Leicester (died 1118), on his deathbed, besieged by bishops: he must give up lands he had acquired through deceit or threat. The count, confronting the vision of Hell with which they threatened him, refused absolution on those terms. He counted on his sons, to whom he wanted his entire estate to go, to give alms from what they got from him to save his soul. Henry notes sardonically that up to the time he was writing it had slipped their minds; they were more interested in adding to what their father had given them.[15]

Other colleagues of the count at Henry I's court, men who had studied just as enthusiastically and dishonestly to extend their possessions, were more edifying examples. Thinking he was dying at Durham some time between 1109 and 1114, Nigel d'Aubigny had a stream of letters written to the king, various potentates and his brother, directing them to ensure that a whole catalogue of restorations of lands he had abstracted be made to those he had

---

14 Matt. 19, xxi–xxii.
15 *Epistola de Contemptu Mundi*, in *Historia Anglorum*, ed. Arnold, 307.

cheated. God had struck him down, as he said, and he knew not what was to become of him. As it happened, he survived his illness by a good number of years; one wonders how he accounted for this.[16] Richard de Beaumais, bishop of London, died in 1127 equally weighed down. The archbishop of Canterbury was present at his deathbed, and informed the necessary authorities that the deceased bishop had confessed, among other things, to attempting to defraud Shrewsbury abbey of an estate for the advantage of his nephew.[17]

ARISTOCRATIC CHANTRIES

The need for continual prayer to influence the fate of the deceased, as well as the imperatives of deathbed repentance, brought on a further trend in religious patronage as the twelfth century progressed; this was the chantry. As it was eventually to be understood, a 'chantry' was a priest or priests maintained and salaried for the purpose of saying numerous masses for the soul of a particular man, his family and friends (and in later days 'all faithful departed'). From that definition, of course, a priory or abbey could be seen in one of its aspects as a chantry; and indeed it is out of that aspect of monastic perpetual intercession that the later chantries come. What evidence there is suggests that we should look to the corners of monasteries for the chantry's first manifestations.

The first stirrings of such an idea of employing priests to offer up perpetual intercession for individual souls occurs in the reign of Henry I in England (as far as I am aware). It was, it appears, a decidedly baronial idea at the beginning. Before 1102, Count Roger of La Marche, lord of Lancaster and Eye, made a concession to Shrewsbury abbey and received in return an assurance that mass would be said daily in the abbey for him, his wife, son, mother and father.[18] Around the year 1125, Roger, earl of Warwick, granted two churches to Kenilworth priory: 'and for this concession of mine I should have for ever a canon in the priory'. The link between this canon and the earl is not made clear, but unless the canon in question were to offer up prayers for the earl, it is difficult to know what else

16 *Charters of the Honour of Mowbray, 1107–1191*, ed. D.E. Greenway (British Academy, Records of Social and Economic History, new ser., i, 1972), p. xxv, nos. 2–10.
17 *Cartulary of Shrewsbury abbey*, ed. U. Rees (2 vols, Aberystwyth, 1975), i, 23–4.
18 ibid., ii, 337.

the connection could be. It seems unlikely – although it was not impossible – that the earl was reserving the right to place a priest in the priory.

There are many twelfth-century examples of this association of an aristocratic house and nominated members of a community; nominated (as I am assuming) to assure the prayers of the community for individuals. One occurs early in the reign of Henry II when the baron, Robert of Stafford, granted fourteen acres to the Cistercian abbey of Bordesley so that the abbey received him within its fraternity: 'and conceded that two monks would be bound to him and his heirs for ever'.[19] In the reign of Stephen, there are more clear associations of grants for commemorative prayer. The wealthy aristocratic widow, Mathilda de Senlis, granted five acres to Dunmow priory in Essex for the soul of her late husband, Robert fitz Richard de Clare, for a mass on the anniversary of his death and on condition that prayers were said for him whenever any other mass for the dead was said in the priory. Her son, Walter fitz Robert, granted ten acres to the same priory for the soul of his cousin, Earl Roger de Clare 'so that the canons constitute one of their number in the church of Dunmow for the soul of Earl Roger'.[20] The practice of nomination was by no means solely an English one. In Normandy before 1170, Count John of Eu made a grant to the abbey of Eu with the intention that memorial prayers be said daily in the abbey at matins, high mass and vespers for himself, his parents, his sister and ancestors.[21]

The buying of perpetual prayer for individual souls seems therefore to have begun as a variant on the patronage of regular houses by magnates; a more specific targeting of a monastery's prayer on an individual benefactor's soul, and a specialisation within the community so that it might be carried out. In this respect there is a cousinship with the earlier idea, popular in the eleventh century, in some monasteries of *libri memoriales*, or *libri vitae*, books kept on altars recording the individual benefactors of abbeys, and members of their families to be kept in mind. Later twelfth-century examples are more informative about what such an

19 Cartulary of Kenilworth, Brit. Libr., ms. Harley 3650, fo. 12r–v.; Bodl. Libr., ms. Dugdale 13, p. 361. Some years later, Earl Hugh of Chester funded six monks at Bordesley for the souls of himself and family, *Charters of the Anglo-Norman Earls of Chester, c.1071–1237*, ed. G. Barraclough (Record Soc. of Lancashire and Cheshire, cxxvi, 1988), no. 148.
20 Cartulary of Dunmow, Brit. Libr., ms. Harley 662, fo. 9r–v., 57v.
21 Cartulary of counts of Eu, Bibliothèque nationale, ms. Latin 13904, fo. 43r.

intramural nominated 'chantry' involved. The Wigmore chronicle informs us of the terms of the endowment established around 1181 for the soul of Hugh II de Mortemer: a canon was to say daily mass for Hugh's soul, and celebrate the mass for the dead on the anniversary of Hugh's death with the whole community; bread and ale were to be distributed every week to the poor, and a hundred poor were to be fed on the anniversary (with bread, fish and soup, because Hugh had died in Lent).[22] In 1192 Count John of Mortain granted a church to the chapter of Lichfield on condition that a priest-canon would say mass daily for his health and well-being, and after his death, for his soul.[23] In 1227 Countess Alice of Eu stipulated that her chantry in the abbey of Eu should consist of two canons praying for her and her family in perpetuity; as soon as one died another should be appointed to fill the place of the deceased.[24]

It was natural that accommodation for the priest-monk or canon saying the mass for the dead should be found in an altar near the tomb of the deceased magnate. When this might have happened is difficult for a historian to say, but there seems little trace of such enclosed spaces or side chapels in the twelfth, or even thirteenth, century. In the twelfth century, when many magnates were buried under the floors of chapter houses or in the spaces of the choir, there could have been little scope for the reserved altars in the vicinity of the dead which we associate with the idea of a 'chantry'. However, the use of the word *cantaria* might well be relevant here. In its earlier manifestations *cantaria* (the Latin word from which we get 'chantry') was applied to any chapel where mass was licensed to be sung, and had nothing particularly to do with saying office for the benefit of a departed soul.[25] But early in the reign of Henry III, Countess Isabel of Arundel secured the acquiescence of her family's priory of Westacre to her arranging of a *cantaria* and

22 *Monasticon Anglicanum* ed. J. Caley *et al.* (8 vols, London, 1817–30), vi, 346.
23 Cartulary of Lichfield, Brit. Libr., ms. Harley 4799, fo. 5r.
24 Cartulary of the counts of Eu, Bibliothèque nationale ms. Latin 13904, fo. 67r–v.
25 The definition of the *cantaria* licensed by the rector of Noseley for the manor house there in the 1220s tells us that the word was meant to comprehend the building and fitting of a chapel and permission for a chaplain to sing mass there, H. Hartopp, 'Some Unpublished Documents Relating to Noseley Co. Leics', *Associated Architectural Societies: Reports and Papers*, xxv, pt 2 (1900), 433–4. This sense of the right to sing mass in a chapel appears early in the twelfth century, when the chapter of Salisbury tried to stop it in the chapel of Burton, Wiltshire Record Office, D1/1/1 (Register of St Osmund), p. 104.

burial at her foundation of Marham abbey.[26] *Cantaria* in this case was being associated with the daily sung office associated with her tomb, and implies – if not a chapel set aside – then nominated priests and altars.

The Marham example tells us how the word *cantaria* was associated with a burial and a daily commemorative mass by the early thirteenth century. Another Norfolk example (although the word *cantaria* is not used) confirms that there was by then a practice of reserving an altar at which a chaplain might say a commemorative mass. At some time in the reign of John (1199–1216), or soon after (certainly before 1221), a substantial county knight and baronial seneschal, Roger Rustein, granted land to Wymondham priory. In return, the priory was to nominate and pay a chaplain to say daily mass for Roger's soul at the altar of St James in the parish church of St Mary of Snettesham. Regulations were laid down by Roger for the replacement of his chaplain, so that the office would not lapse.[27]

The Rustein altar at Snettesham is highly significant. Wymondham priory had been set up by Rustein's employers, the earls of Arundel, as a community of prayer for their souls. Rustein could not or would not set up a chantry in their priory, but still used the priory as an intermediary for a chantry set up in one of his churches. The Rustein altar was therefore a significant foundation in which we see the nominated monastic chantry become extramural. It demonstrates that our concept of a 'chantry' had come about by the reign of Henry III in England. Moreover, the example of Roger Rustein indicates that what had till then been a magnate practice had been appropriated by the knights. For a knight, the foundation of a chantry was a satisfactory and economical way of achieving the same result as a baronial foundation of a monastery or secular college.

The association of the freestanding or annexed chapel and its *cantaria* (viz. licence to sing mass) with the commemorative office had brought about our idea of what a 'chantry' should be by the middle of the thirteenth century. One of the best examples of such an institution is the chantry founded in the 1240s at the Yorkshire abbey of Meaux by the magnate, Peter de Maulay, for his dead wife, Isabel of Thornham (she was a cousin of the then abbot

26 Cartulary of Marham, Norfolk Record Office, ms. Hare 1, fos 1v–2r.
27 Cartulary of Wymondham, Brit. Libr., ms Cotton Titus, C viii, fo. 48v. Roger Rustein occurs as seneschal of William III, earl of Arundel (1173–1221), Cartulary of Lewes, Brit. Libr., ms Cotton Vespasian, F xv, fo. 127r.

and had left her body for burial there). Peter erected at his own expense a freestanding chapel to house the chantry outside the monastic precinct in a nearby wood; Isabel herself was buried in the abbey's chapter house. He funded it by several generous grants of land, rents and mills. Later regulations (which are said to reflect conditions on its foundation) talk of two secular priests and two clerks resident at the chapel; one priest would sing the masses of St Mary, the other a daily mass for the dead. Other provisions related to the celebration of Isabel's obit and the provision of wax candles for the offices.[28] The last testament of the magnate, William de Beauchamp, dated 1268, provides another example of such an extramural chapel. He was to be buried in the church of the Franciscans at Worcester, leaving substantial properties to support a chaplain to say daily mass for himself, his wife, for Isabel de Mortemer, and 'all faithful dead' at (once again) an independent chapel he had built outside the Franciscan precinct in Worcester.[29] It must be that the appointment of secular clerks to such chantries moved the monks and friars to insist that they be situated outside their precincts. If so, it indicates that regular clergy were beginning to lose control of chantry endowments. The employment of secular clerks to serve chantries forced them out of the monastery. As the thirteenth century came to an end, such foundations – whether in monasteries or parish churches – would rapidly multiply until the majority of parish churches in England would contain a chantry of some sort, whether a single endowed altar, or, at the other extreme, a college of chantry priests with wardens, archpriests, sacrists and beadles.

The Rustein example proves how soon the knights copied the magnates in such endowments. The private manorial chapels being set up in or soon after 1220 might be easily converted to chantry purposes. The Martinwast chapel at Noseley, set up in the 1220s, was such an example. Sir Anschetil de Martinwast, the son of the founder of the chapel, a prominent county knight and royal justice, resolved on his deathbed in 1274 to convert it into an impressive collegiate chantry. He did not feel moved to build it outside a monastic precinct. As established by his son Roger (later bishop of Salisbury) Anschetil's chantry had a warden and several

28 *Chronica Monasterii de Melsa*, ed. E.A. Bond (3 vols, Rolls Series, 1866–8), ii, 59–62.
29 *Register of Bishop Godfrey Giffard, 1268–1301*, ed. J.W. Willis Bund (2 vols, Worcester Historical Society, 1902), 8.

chaplains generously endowed to do nothing but celebrate mass for the souls of this knightly family.[30] Wealthy burgesses were quick to set up such foundations in city churches and cathedrals. In the fourteenth century, the rise of fraternities meant that any moderately well-off citizen could aspire to have his or her name included in a chantry priest's daily office. The chantry is as perfect an example of downward cultural diffusion as one could hope to meet.

THE MATERIAL BENEFITS OF PATRONAGE

Magnates desired salvation, for themselves and their families; so did all in a position to make grants to the Church. In 1107, conceding an exemption to his abbey of Le Tréport, Count Henry I of Eu and his brother Robert said they did so, 'for the remission of our sins, for the health of the soul of Mathilda (the count's) wife, and we bind ourselves by the chain of eternal excommunication and invoke an eternal curse on those who gainsay it'.[31] But was there not more that the count and his family wanted from their foundations? A family abbey could be a dignified mausoleum. The family of Eu used their monasteries as burial places. A fourteenth-century chronicle gives us more detail on the burials of the Eu family than we have for most noble families. Count Robert and his wife Beatrice rested at Le Tréport; William II supposedly at Hastings. Counts Henry I and John were buried side by side in the chapter house at Eu, both portrayed in effigy in the robes of Augustinian canons, as a token that they were received within the fraternity of the order (the elegiac poem placed on the tomb noted how father and son had in this way become brothers). Count Henry II was laid before the high altar of Foucarmont. A dozen other members of the family, wives and children, were laid before the roods or high altars of Foucarmont and Eu, the preferred burial churches; a couple were buried at Hastings.[32]

The abbeys and churches of the counts of Eu gave their patrons dignified burial, and received benefactions in order that they might commemorate the anniversaries of their deaths with requiem masses

---

30 G. Farnham, 'The Manor of Noseley', *Transactions of the Leicestershire Archaeological Society*, xii (1922), 233–8. For observations on such foundations see J.R.H. Moorman, *Church Life in England in the Thirteenth Century* (Cambridge, 1946), 15–16.
31 *Cartulaire de St-Michel du Tréport*, ed. Laffleur de Kermaingant, 24–5.
32 *Chronique des comtes d'Eu*, 440–1.

and solemn feasts in the refectory. There was an element of commensalism between the monks and the living comital family too. This was as much neighbourliness as it was an evocation of the entertainments offered Christ and His disciples by the well-disposed of Palestine during His ministry. These were doubtless among the reasons why Count Henry I of Eu undertook himself to carry the cost of the banquet given at the abbey Le Tréport on its patronal feast of St Michael, which he, the countess and his retinue customarily attended.[33] There are other examples. Returning from the Holy Land, Earl William de Mandeville (died 1190) was received by his priory of Walden with a solemn procession, mass, and a plentiful feast in the abbey's guest house for himself and his retainers.[34] The tithes of the kitchens of numerous aristocratic households were made over to monasteries. In the mid-twelfth century the Mowbray household was regularly followed by a lay brother of Byland abbey, who received the portion of food allotted to the abbot and monks. If the household was in the vicinity of the abbey the food was sent direct to the abbey's table; if not, it was sold on the spot, and money sent instead.[35] In this way magnates sought to avoid the fate of Dives by serving from their tables the Lazarus at their gates.

Burial of the dead and fraternity with the living could be a powerful bond between the living family and their monks. Another early, Norman example shows this very well. The principal abbey of the counts of Meulan was the Benedictine house of St-Pierre-des-Préaux, near the Norman town of Pont Audemer. The stubborn Count Robert was laid in its chapter house, after supposedly refusing absolution (see above, p. 315). His father and uncle were already there before him, and the year after Robert's death his younger brother, Earl Henry of Warwick, was laid there too, coming home to Normandy for burial. Count Robert was followed in his Norman lands by his eldest son, Count Waleran. At some time between 1118 and 1120 the new count's vicomte of Pont Audemer ordered some houses of the abbey to be demolished and cleared.

The next day Waleran came (to the abbey) and Abbot Richard led him aside to the chapter house, to the foot of his father's tomb and the tombs of others of his relatives lying there. For

33 *Cartulaire de St-Michel du Tréport*, ed. Laffleur de Kermaingant, 21.
34 *Liber de fundatione abbathiae de Walden*, in *Monasticon*, iv, 144.
35 F.M. Stenton, *The First Century of English Feudalism, 1066–1166* (2nd edn, Oxford, 1961), 74.

the soul of his father, the abbot begged him to allow to stay standing the house of Eudo the smith, who shod the horses and asses of the abbey, and the house and barn of William Isoret, the tithe-collector, where was stored the abbey's tithes.[36]

The abbot made a calculated plea to the young count, and it paid off. He got what he wanted. Part of the reason why the abbot got his way was the solemn nature of his petition. He appealed to this emotional young man's filial piety, as well as his religious feeling, to his pride of lineage, and to the close fraternity of prayer and intercession which had linked family and abbey already for four generations.

There were other facets to that which earlier generations would have called the 'ghostly' link between patron and monastery. We have already looked at the way some magnates carried the banner of great abbeys or churches: Robert of Mortain and the banner of St Michael of Mont St-Michel; the count of Aumale and the banner of St Mary of Rouen; the earl of Gloucester and the banner of St Mary of Bayeux; the earls of Arundel and Norfolk competing for the banner of St Edmund of Bury. The fact that Louis VII of France displayed the oriflamme, lodged at St-Denis, led a contemporary (Jordan Fantosme) to call him 'the noble king of St-Denis'; a magnate protected his favoured cult centre, which offered him its own variety of protection in return.[37] This linking of lay and spiritual fortunes comes out in other ways. Stenton notes how several English honors were linked with the chief churches within them. Geoffrey de Mandeville's foundation at Hurley was to be ever in his protection and to be the head (*caput*) of his honour. The Busli honor in Yorkshire was known as the honor of Blythe, from its first lord's foundation there. Most revealingly, William de Warenne, earl of Surrey, had his clerk declare late in the eleventh century that he will take 'St Pancras' as his patron and the head of his honor of Lewes in Sussex: St Pancras was the dedication of the great Cluniac priory founded by his family at Lewes.[38]

Earl William may (for all we know) have carried a banner of St Pancras, but these passages taken together imply more than that. These magnates were serious in thinking that their lay honors needed a spiritual counterpart, and were sincere in

36 Cartulary of St-Pierre-des-Préaux, archives départementales de l'Eure, H 711, fo. 115v.
37 *Jordan Fantosme's Chronicle*, ed. R.C. Johnston (Oxford, 1981), 6, 122.
38 Stenton, *First Century of English Feudalism*, 62–3.

rating these centres equally. For this reason magnates might, as they occasionally did, hold sessions of their honor courts in the chapter houses of the associated abbeys and priories. It was not because these were buildings apt for the purpose, it was because in the mind of the founder the fortunes of monastery and honor were indistinguishable. For the same reason monasteries would suffer when the family of their patrons went into decline. The Clinton foundation of Kenilworth had its lands systematically wasted when war broke out in the late 1130s between the earl of Warwick and its patron, Geoffrey de Clinton.[39] One of the best statements of this need to identify secular with spiritual lordship is to be found in a description of the piety of the Anglo-Welsh magnate, Meilyr fitz Henry 'a knight of St David', who:

> invoked St David night and day, that he might aid him in doing deeds of valour; that he should give him praise and renown against all his enemies. Often he invoked St David, that he should not leave him in forgetfulness, but give him might and vigour in the midst of his enemies that day.[40]

Where the fortunes of a family were closely tied up with a cult centre, the protecting saint took on a significance that was other than religious. He became a symbol of the family pride which invested materially in his shrine. Meilyr's links with the royal family of Deheubarth brought him under the influence of St David, the dominant episcopal cult of West Wales. St David, the pacific water-drinking abbot, then became for Meilyr a martial cat's-paw; an unlikely but understandable association.

THE PATTERN OF PATRONAGE

The fashion amongst Normans for founding monastic houses began in the early eleventh century. Orderic Vitalis noticed its appearance and commented on it. He put down the initial impetus to the foundation of abbeys by the ducal house, notably the foundations (or refoundations) of the first two Dukes Richard: Fécamp, Mont St-Michel, St-Ouen of Rouen, St-Wandrille and

---

39 D. Crouch, 'Geoffrey de Clinton and Roger Earl of Warwick', *Bulletin of the Institute of Historical Research*, lv (1982), 120–1.
40 *The Song of Dermot and the Earl*, ed. G.H. Orpen (Oxford, 1892), 250.

Bernay. Orderic's comment neatly encompasses the mixture of religious feeling and aristocratic emulation that lay behind the movement. 'The barons of Normandy were inspired by the piety of their princes to do likewise, and encouraged each other to undertake similar enterprises for the salvation of their souls.'[41] Orderic's observation almost amounts to sociological analysis. It is an explicit statement of 'cultural diffusion' applied to religious patronage.

The fashion amongst Norman magnates for founding monasteries engendered many famous abbeys: all the great magnates sponsored at least one house, some founded more.[42] But as well as houses of regular clergy, Orderic fails to mention that magnates founded equally prestigious collegiate churches. His monastic prejudices are evident here. Some of the greatest and wealthiest Norman churches were staffed by secular canons throughout the eleventh and into the twelfth century; churches like the colleges of Auchy (Aumale), Lierru, Mortain, Eu, and Beaumont were stepsisters (occasionally elder stepsisters) of the monasteries founded by the same magnates.[43] The colleges also were churches under baronial patronage and statements of aristocratic prestige, although with a different emphasis.[44] Secular colleges were popular because they allowed the patron a measure of patronage amongst his clerks. Land and churches given to regular houses were lost for good (sharp practice aside); those given to colleges were still in the gift of the advocate, for he filled the vacant places in the chapter. From this loss stemmed a certain amount of anticlericalism amongst patrons.

The monks of Walden came in for the full weight of the displeasure of their estranged patron William de Mandeville, earl of Essex (1166–90) on the matter of over-generosity to monks: 'he was forever complaining that his father had confirmed all the churches of his domain to our house; he had not so much as one left to give

41 Orderic Vitalis, *The Ecclesiastical History*, ed. M. Chibnall (6 vols, Oxford, 1969–80), ii, 10.
42 For this see D.C. Douglas, *William the Conqueror* (London, 1964), 111–15.
43 Musset, 'Recherches sur les communautés de clercs séculiers en Normandie au xiie siècle', *Bulletin de la Société des Antiquaires de Normandie*, lv (1959–60), 5–27.
44 J. Yver, 'Autour de l'absence d'avouerie en Normandie', *Bulletin de la Société des Antiquaires de Normandie*, lvii (1965), 196–7, noted the failure to use the word *advocatus* for the patrons of colleges, but approximate terms do occur and Waleran of Meulan in fact is called in 1131 *advocatus* of the college of Beaumont, *Cartulaire de Beaumont-le-Roger*, ed. Deville, 10.

to his clerks'.[45] Earl William clearly regretted his father's generosity. Earl Robert II of Leicester (1118–68) had second thoughts about his over-generosity in his own lifetime. He had founded in 1138 or 1139 an Augustinian abbey to the north of his town of Leicester. He diverted to it as the core of its endowment the lands and churches till then enjoyed by the great collegiate church of Leicester castle, founded by his father in 1107 for a dean and thirteen canons.[46] Nearly thirty years later, a year or two before he died, Earl Robert had come to regret losing the college of St Mary in the castle, so he obliged the abbot of Leicester to refound it for a reduced establishment of a dean, sacrist and six canons. The abbey was to require an oath of loyalty from the canons, and nominate them, but the earl was the moving spirit in the business and he saw something to his own advantage in the reborn college.[47]

In patronising collegiate churches of secular clergy the Norman aristocracy demonstrated something in common with the aristocracy of pre-Conquest England. There were few regular monasteries in eleventh-century England, and it is true that those which did exist were mostly under royal protection. The most famous exception was Ramsey, founded by Ealdorman Aethelwine of East Anglia late in the 960s, and supported by his family. The monks of Ramsey remained stolidly loyal to his memory for long after the Conquest.[48] English earls and thegns were meticulous in making grants to regular houses, but they, like their Norman counterparts, vigorously supported secular colleges (generally but inaccurately known today as 'minsters'). In terms of numbers, the bulk of their patronage must have come to the minsters. England was still thickly populated with hundreds of such churches at the time of Domesday Book. Many were on or near royal estates, but the majority were not, and many of these must have had aristocratic patrons. The

---

45 *Liber de fundatione abbathiae de Walden*, in *Monasticon*, iv, 143. A similar case of a disgruntled patron can be found in the case of Manasser Arsic and his priory of Cogges, Oxons, who 'made no secret of his plan that all the patrimony of his predecessors should come back to him'. J. Laporte '*Epistulae Fiscannenses*: Lettres d'amitié, de gouvernement et d'affaires (xie–xiie siècles)', *Revue Mabillon*, xliii (1953), 29–30.

46 D. Crouch, 'The Foundation of Leicester Abbey and other Problems', *Midland History*, xi (1987), 2–4.

47 Register of Leicester, Bodl. Libr., ms Laud misc. 625, fo. 95r.

48 *Chronicon abbatiae Rameseiensis*, ed. W. Dunn Macray (Rolls Series, 1886), 11, has the Ramsey monks of the later twelfth century calling Aethelwine *advocatus noster*; a thirteenth-century effigy was placed above his tomb by the monks, thus emphasising the relationship.

eleventh-century earls of Mercia and Wessex can be shown to have patronised the greater minsters of their regions, and lesser aristocrats were also active.[49]

The Conquest does not seem to have changed the pattern of patronage of the English Church for at least a generation. Few new abbeys were founded, although a number of priories of French houses were planted in England. The minster-colleges seem to have survived quite happily for a while; hundreds were still around at the time of the Domesday Survey. The Normans added new ones too. Large and prestigious collegiate churches were founded (or refounded) by magnates at Hastings, Leicester, Warwick and St Martin-le-Grand. The great burst of the new monasticism took place during the reigns of Henry I and Stephen. Hundreds of new houses came into being, principally of the Cluniac, Augustinian and Cistercian orders. As we have seen, minster-colleges were occasionally converted at this time into regular houses. It was the aristocracy which funded and organised this great explosion of building and the regular religious life. By the time it came to an end (and the pace slackened rapidly early in the reign of Henry II) there were very few earls and barons who did not have at least one abbey or priory under their patronage.[50] It was at this time in the mid-twelfth century that we can begin to talk of advocacy as being general amongst the English aristocracy, and go on to consider its manifestations and diffusion.

ADVOCACY

The relationship between family identity and dignity and family monastic foundations was a close one. Magnates with monasteries in their advocacy would occasionally talk of their inmates as 'my monks'. There was also the matter of prestige. If it was generally understood that magnates had family monasteries, then it was important for a magnate to be 'advocate' of at least one. It has been calculated that over ninety religious houses were under the advocacy of earls, countesses or their heirs in England by the thirteenth century; over 200 more were in the advocacy of barons

---

49 J. Blair, 'Secular Minster Churches in Domesday Book', in *Domesday Book: A Reassessment*, ed. P. Sawyer (London, 1985), 121; J. Blair, 'From Minster to Parish Church', in *Minsters and Parish Churches: the Local Church in Transition, 950–1200*, ed. J. Blair (Oxford, 1988), 3–6.
50 D. Knowles, *The Monastic Order in England* (Cambridge, 1941), 100ff.

and greater knights.[51] The greater the monastery under the magnate's protection, the greater the magnate's dignity. The foundation of a monastery was consequently a necessity for the rising man in the twelfth century. Geoffrey de Clinton arranged the foundation of an Augustinian priory at Kenilworth in 1124 before he had even built the castle there to be the head of his honor. The foundation was a signal that he had arrived as a magnate in the West Midlands.[52] Augustinians and, by the end of the reign, Cistercians, were the lucky beneficiaries of the piety of courtiers in Henry I's reign. Clinton's colleague Walter Espec, a much-favoured royal justice who picked up numerous estates in the north of England, founded an Augustinian priory at Kirkham in the 1120s. He followed it up by the foundation of Cistercian abbeys at Rievaulx (1131) and Wardon (1136); indeed so taken was he with the Cistercians that he made moves to convert Kirkham to the newer order before his death.

The same need for the new man to found a prestigious monastery was true of other courtiers later that same century. Within a year of making his fortune at the court of King Richard, William Marshal celebrated his new status as landed magnate by founding an Augustinian priory at Cartmel, an estate he had picked up from Henry II a short time before.[53] His wealthy colleague at court, William Briwerre, founded three houses in quick succession: Torre (1196), Mottisfont (c.1200) and Dunkeswell (1201). Briwerre was catholic in his tastes; the three were respectively Premonstratensian, Augustinian and Cistercian.[54] Ranulf de Glanville, the counsellor and justiciar of Henry II, resolved, like Clinton sixty years before, on the foundation of an Augustinian priory (Butley in Suffolk) early in the 1170s. A decade later he erected another house, of Premonstratensian canons, at Leiston. In doing so he was endeavouring to signal to the gentry of his native East Anglia that he had become indeed a great man and risen above them. Gerald of Wales preserves what purports to be some of the thought behind Ranulf's actions. He had settled on the orders of canons as suiting his purpose because they were modest and unaggressive orders, unlike the gluttonous Cluniacs, and harsh and acquisitive

---

51 S. Wood, *English Monasteries and their Patrons in the Thirteenth Century* (Oxford, 1955), 7.
52 Crouch, 'Geoffrey de Clinton and Roger Earl of Warwick', 116–18.
53 D. Crouch, *William Marshal: Court, Career and Chivalry in the Angevin Empire* (London, 1990), 189–90.
54 R.V. Turner, *Men Raised from the Dust* (Philadelphia, 1988), 87–8.

Cistercians. The canons' respectability would be to his credit. He for his part did his best to bolster their modesty, forbidding those of Leiston to take land other than in free alms. He attempted to insulate Leiston from external control, by founding it from two other abbeys of white canons, not one, which might compromise his family's advocacy of Leiston by claiming privileges as mother house.[55]

It was the need for such an advocacy, for whatever reasons, that drove one of the greatest of all 'new men', Geoffrey fitz Peter, to bully and threaten the Benedictine monks of Walden into receiving him as advocate on his own terms. Geoffrey had received the estates of the Mandeville earldom of Essex from King Richard in 1189. To secure the grant he felt it necessary also to ruthlessly reduce the Mandeville family abbey to obedience and allegiance; this so that he might claim its spiritual protection and fraternity!

Geoffrey fitz Peter was not an acquisitive, insensitive brute. His motives in religious patronage were as complicated as those of any of his fellows. Once he had made his fortune, he devoted some of his wealth to the spiritual benefit of his dead relatives and wife. He had his first wife's body moved from Chicksands priory to his own foundation of Shouldham. In 1198 he arranged for his father's remains to be exhumed from the monks' cemetery at St Swithun's Winchester, and moved within the cathedral. He made a grant to Westminster abbey for an obit for his late mother.[56] For him, Walden was a problem. It had had itself promoted from a priory to an abbey immediately after the death of Earl William de Mandeville in 1190. It seemed as if Walden was attempting to escape the advocacy of the lords of Pleshey, becoming an abbey and accepting royal protection.[57] The abbey chose to interpret Geoffrey's anger as resentment at the legacy of land at Walden it had received in the testament of the late Earl William. The persecution of Walden which followed was in the tradition of Angevin methods of intimidation: petty harassment, removal of boundary stones and disseisins, coupled with difficulty for the abbey in gaining access to justice. King John's accession led to the abbey's abrupt surrender

55 R. Mortimer, 'Religious and Secular Motives for some English Monastic Foundations', *Studies in Church History*, xv (1978), ed. D. Baker, 77–81.
56 Turner, *Men Raised from the Dust*, 64.
57 This would account for the forbidding of Cartmel priory to seek abbatial status when William Marshal founded it, Crouch, *William Marshal*, 190 (I did not realise the significance of this clause at the time I wrote). See S. Wood, *English Monasteries and their Patrons in the Thirteenth Century* (Oxford, 1955), 26, 98–9.

when the new king publicly restored the advocacy of Walden to Earl
Geoffrey. This (rather than the return of the land at Walden) pacified
the earl, and a reconciliation was arranged. From their own account,
the monks were churlish in defeat, going through the motions of
meeting the earl as patron with less than joyful faces.[58]

Thirteenth-century sources occasionally reveal a degree of hostil-
ity between the descendants of the founders and the houses under
their advocacy. The reason was not always the alienation of churches
and lands by their ancestors (although there were many quarrels
about rights to present clerks to rectories). Often it was caused
by the resentment of houses themselves at the advocates' desire
to make a display of their rights. The example of the Beauchamp
family and its priory of Newnham, near Bedford, is particularly
well-documented. In 1247, the bailiff of William de Beauchamp,
attempting (as he said) to take seisin of the granges of the priory
during a vacancy in its priorate, was involved in an affray when
the canons' men resisted. In 1250 William's right to grant a licence
to elect and to present the new prior to the bishop of Lincoln was
denied, despite an abundance of evidence to the contrary. This
caused the exasperated baron to burst out in the royal court with
the telling assertion that,

> he had common wardship just as did earls and the other barons,
> his peers in England, who have abbeys and priories, whose
> lands they have in keeping during a vacancy.[59]

William won his case, but a few years later was obliged to fight it
all over again. His right to present a new prior to the bishop was
once more flouted, and as a result he rode in force to the priory and
forcibly installed the new prior by ordering him out to the gate and
then marching him back into the choir of the church.[60] In doing this
the Beauchamps were going beyond their rights, but it may be that
they had been sorely provoked.

Other relationships between houses and advocates were more
sedate and affectionate. The Benedictine abbey of Tewkesbury,
despite its wealth and greatness, seems to have enjoyed a fairly
even relationship with its aristocratic advocates. Since these were
the Clare earls of Hertford and Gloucester, the good relations are

58 *Liber de fundatione abbathiae de Walden*, in *Monasticon* iv, 145–8.
59 PRO JUST1/56 m. 33d; KB26/141 m. 25d.
60 *Annales de Dunstaplia*, in *Annales Monastici* ed. H.R. Luard (5 vols, Rolls
Series, 1864–9), iii, 191–2.

perhaps understandable. The Clares were ever in that century the greatest magnates in England and the March. Their protection was much to be valued. There were differences – over the abbey's right to a gallows and free election – but these were amicably settled. The annals of Tewkesbury are full of references to the Clares' doings: recording Clare births, marriages and burials; noting the investiture by the earl of an abbot with his pastoral staff; even the earl's decision to offer the abbey the services of his proctor at the papal curia. In return, the abbot was employed about the earl's business, settling as one of his justices a violent outbreak in Glamorgan in 1242.[61]

At what point on the scale of wealth did it become impossible to be an advocate? Small landowners compulsively patronised monasteries. Even where the foundation was a clear matter of the prestige of one magnate, lesser men from round about still sought the spiritual benefits to be gained from patronising his foundation. Usually in such a case they were his followers, and their small gifts may sometimes have been meant as much to seek favour with their lord as with God. But this was not always so: at least eight twelfth- and thirteenth-century Leicestershire knights made grants of virgates, mills, rents and rectories on becoming canons of Earl Robert's abbey of Leicester, seeking burial there.[62] Such grants were not political stratagems, these men were seeking the spiritual benefits of the abbey on their own account.

But could such men, substantial knights, ever attempt the unaided foundation of a monastery and uphold their rights to be considered advocates? This is a hazy area, and very little work has been done on it. Men who might be considered honorial barons (that is, men who were the principal tenants of a particular magnate) did found abbeys from time to time. Take the example of Hugh fitz Richard. Hugh was a major tenant of the earldom of Warwick, and in 1166 his estate was rated at ten knights' service. In Saumur abbey sources, Hugh is described as a *nobilis*, in those of Reading, a *dominus*; his grandson was a knight of the county court. His lands were concentrated in two parcels; west of the town of Warwick, and south-east of Tamworth. Hugh's generosity to the Church seems to have been compulsive. He made grants and confirmations of land to Oldbury, Warwick,

61 *Annales de Theokesberia*, in *Annales Monastici*, i, 70, 72–3, 76–7, 83–4, 106, 114, 115, 124, 137, 140, 147.
62 Register of Leicester, fos 7v–8r. *nomina eorum qui dederunt nobis certas terras etc. cum corporibus suis.*

Nuneaton, Kenilworth and Monmouth priories (his stepson was prior of Monmouth). But in addition to these grants – and they were certainly generous – he founded a house of Benedictine nuns at Wroxhall, Warwickshire. Wroxhall priory faithfully accorded him the rights of founder: he was buried in the centre of the choir of the priory; daughters of his family were nuns there; the family's obits were celebrated there; the family's legends and genealogy were kept on record for several generations after Hugh; and the family arms were in its windows.[63] It barely needs adding that his generosity wasted his estate. When he died he left his family with not much more than its two capital messuages (Hatton and Amington), and the advocacy of Wroxhall.

If Hugh fitz Richard was an extreme, he was not alone amongst men of his class in wishing to have a monastery in his advocacy. The substantial Midlands knightly families of Du Bois (Leicestershire and Gloucestershire) and Butler of Oversley (Warwickshire) also possessed the resources to found abbeys: Biddlesden (Cistercian) and Alcester (Benedictine).[64] Neither these nor Hugh were men with direct access to royal patronage in the twelfth century. Their descendants were county knights in the thirteenth century, and so it is reasonable to call them 'knightly'. They were certainly not the 'peers' of a man such as William de Beauchamp of Bedford. They were therefore men of no more than local significance, and yet all three endeavoured to found small monasteries, and these houses all continued to acknowledge the link with later generations of the families. So it is possible to say that there were men who could not be considered in any way to be barons who scraped together the resources to become advocates. Knights of such resources were aspiring to be seen as aristocrats in this way by the mid-twelfth century. But it was a rare event for men of less status than these to attempt it unaided.

What was advocacy, as it was understood in England and the Anglo-Norman realm? What did the patron get in return for his generosity? The ideal advocate and the model monastery were linked by a variety of rights and privileges, apart from the spiritual benefits

63 For Hugh and his family see generally, *Red Book of the Exchequer*, ed. H. Hall (3 vols, Rolls Series, 1896), i, 325; *Monasticon*, iv, 90–1; *Calendar of Documents preserved in France, i, 918–1206*, ed. J.H. Round (London, 1899), 412, 414.
64 D. Crouch, *The Beaumont Twins* (Cambridge, 1986), 80, 82, 143. It should be noted in the case of Alcester that, although it was founded on Butler land, the earl of Leicester, Butler's overlord, also claimed rights as advocate, *Monasticon*, iv, 175–6.

and commensalism we have already looked at. One of the chief of these was the right of the patron to be received by his monks or canons in procession. This may seem little enough, but the rare pictures that we get of such occasions are impressive. Earl William de Mandeville was received at Walden by the community in albs and embroidered copes chanting the *Benedictus*: 'Blessèd is he who comes in the name of the Lord'. He was led to the high altar and there blessed by the prior. In return the earl offered relics in ivory caskets which he had obtained in the Holy Land and been given by the Emperor of Constantinople and his friend, the count of Flanders. The *Te Deum* was then sung and all adjourned to the chapter house, where the earl gave the kiss of peace to every monk of the house, and compliments and news were exchanged in a very happy atmosphere. Thence to the guest house where a magnificent feast was prepared for the earl, his kinsfolk and retinue.[65] Monasteries were able to put on a very splendid reception when it suited them. The advocate would then get a taste of the splendour normally afforded to kings: cheering crowds, sounding bells, chanting clerks, music, ceremony and splendour. We should not wonder why the right was prized, nor why Geoffrey fitz Peter systematically broke down the resolve of the same monks of Walden, so that he too could enjoy the same grand reception. A procession also could mark a solemn family occasion. There is the Norman example of William de Tancarville II, who was received in procession at his family abbey of St-Georges-de-Boscherville on his coming of age and knighting late in the reign of Henry II. His reception by his monks was another rite of passage.[66]

The right of wardship has already been looked at. A number of circumstances limited its importance: to begin with, it did not apply to Cistercian, Premonstratensian, Carthusian or Gilbertine houses. Furthermore, since many vacancies in the headship of monasteries cannot have been very long, there may not have been much money to be made on this particular right. It may perhaps have become more important in the thirteenth century when alien priories were more decisively detached from their mother houses in Normandy and elsewhere in France. Generally, vacancies took place on the

65 *Liber de fundatione abbathiae de Walden*, in *Monasticon*, iv, 144.
66 Archives départementales de la Seine Maritime, 13 H 15. See the commentary on this occasion in J.C. Holt, 'Feudal Society and the Family in Early Medieval England: III. Patronage and Politics', *Transactions of the Royal Historical Society*, 5th ser., xxxiv (1984), 7–8n.

death or resignation of a head of a house. However, a house might also come into wardship when its head went overseas, as is made clear in a charter of Richard de Clare, earl of Gloucester, dated 1254 to St Neots priory. Since St Neots was a priory of the abbey of Bec-Hellouin in Normandy, and the priors of Bec's offshoots were called back every year to a chapter at the mother house, this was a convenient right for the likes of Earl Richard to enjoy.[67] By the end of the century, when war had broken out between England and France, advocates of alien houses might expect to receive more protracted custodies, as the communities in them were apprehended and their lands seized. Other than these somewhat special circumstances it was perhaps not much more than prestige that was involved in the right of custody. For a week or two the bailiffs of the house answered to the advocate's seneschal; his man was installed as gatekeeper and there was a flurry of activity as the chapter first asked the advocate's licence to elect and then considered the succession, with or without his advice. Once the decision was made, the advocate would have the right to present the head-elect to the bishop. Very little more was involved, and it is not surprising that in several cases the advocate's part was forgotten, and that several advocates surrendered their rights.[68]

Advocacy was a mixed bag of rights, some significant, others quite unimportant. The importance of advocacy was more marked for the advocate the higher up the social scale he was. Great magnates might make quite an occasion of the processions with which they were favoured. A magnate like the earl of Gloucester and Hertford in the thirteenth century could make something exceptional of the process of custody by taking the abbatial staff of Tewkesbury into his keeping, and then solemnly restoring it to the new abbot.[69] It is to be doubted that lesser patrons would have been so capable of extorting these grand rituals from their abbeys and priories.

THE WELSH AND SCOTTISH ARISTOCRACIES AND THE CHURCH

The relationship between aristocracy and Church in Wales had something in common with that between Church and aristocracy in pre-Conquest England. The coming of the Normans caused the

---

67 Cartulary of St Neots, Brit. Libr., ms Cotton Faustina, A iv, fo. 27v.
68 See in general, Wood, *English Monasteries and their Patrons*, 40–8, 75–100.
69 *Annales de Theokesburia* in *Annales Monastici*, i, 83–4.

Welsh and English societies to diverge by the mid-twelfth century; the Welsh aristocracy did not at once give up its old patterns of Church patronage. But the gradual filtering of Anglo-French ideas about aristocracy into Welsh society led English and Welsh to converge once more in the thirteenth century. We see here a similar pattern and chronology to developments about titles, castles and knighthood.

There were no regular monasteries in Wales in the eleventh century, and therefore there could not be the sort of advocacy found in contemporary Normandy, and later in England. Apart from this lack of monks, the Welsh Church was not wildly aberrant in its structure, compared with that of England, or even Normandy. By the eleventh century there were three or four bishoprics dominating the spiritual life of the country. Bishops operated from major churches where they were supported by communities of learned, often hereditary, priests. In the countryside the Church was organised around mother churches (*clasau*) staffed by communities of priests (*claswyr*). These had extensive *parochiae* in which – by the mid-eleventh century – small, local churches were being built by local lords (a development parallel to that of England). To that extent the picture was much the same as the organisation of the Church in England. Indeed it was to England that the episcopal church at Llandaff (for one) looked for training, ideas and, possibly, staff as well.[70]

There were broad similarities between the Welsh and the English Churches, but there were also more particular differences. The Church in Wales had no institutional integrity. Welsh bishops recognised no senior bishop within Wales, and had few links with the province of Canterbury. This was reflected in the strength of regional and episcopal cults. Teilo in south-east Wales, David in south-west Wales, and Deiniol and Beuno in north Wales commanded loyalties of whole provinces and were patrons of episcopal communities. The bishop of south-east Wales was known as 'Teilo's bishop' in the mid-eleventh century, as he had been for centuries, and the bishop of south-west Wales is still to this day St David's. David, Teilo and Beuno were consequently linked with the

---

70 For the native Welsh Church see W. Davies, *Wales in the Early Middle Ages* (Leicester, 1982), 141–73; C.N.L. Brooke, 'The Church in the Welsh Border in the Tenth and Eleventh Centuries', in *The Church and the Welsh Border in the Central Middle Ages*, ed. D.N. Dumville and C.N.L. Brooke (Woodbridge, 1986), 1–15; R.R. Davies, *The Age of Conquest* (Oxford, 1991), 172–9; D. Crouch, 'Urban, First Bishop of Llandaff, 1107–34', *Journal of Welsh Ecclesiastical History*, vi (1989), 1–9.

fortunes of the dynasties of the same area: Deheubarth, Morgannwg and Gwynedd. Powys had its chief church, Meifod, and its regional cult of St Tysilio, but no bishop. Besides these, there were also cults of local intensity, attached to particular mother churches. St Cadog, based at Llancarfan, was one of the most important of these, but there were many more, each fostered by its community. These communities of *claswyr* were not quite identical to the minsters of England or the collegiate churches of Normandy. Their heads might be called abbots, a relic perhaps of times when they had conformed to a more regular pattern of life. There is more than a suspicion that a good many of them had become quite secularised; landed, family concerns with barely a nod towards the maintenance of the church and its life (see p. 341).

The Welsh aristocracy of the eleventh and early twelfth centuries operated within this framework of bishops, cults and mother churches, as the Welsh Church did in a framework of predatory and violent kingdoms. Welsh religious poetry cast God, Christ and the saints in the same moulds as the heroes of the triads and epics. In the words of Rees Davies, 'rarely had a church so submerged itself in the social landscape as in Wales'.[71] That Welsh magnates were both intensely violent and devout is clear enough. The Book of Llandaff depicts several occasions when eleventh-century kings and magnates were brought abjectly to penitence after breaking the sanctuary of the episcopal church, or committing rape or murder.[72] This same conjunction of extremes long puzzled the more urbane (and slightly more controlled) Norman magnates. Walter Map repeats the story told him in bewilderment by the hard-bitten Marcher lord, William de Briouze, of a Welsh aristocrat of William's acquaintance. The Welshman's austerity and devotion was intense; he prayed passionately at unlikely hours, naked on a cold floor. You might have mistaken him for an angel on that account. But in battle no wild crime or bloodthirsty act was too diabolical for him to contemplate and execute.[73]

The evidence of the Book of Llandaff and the Llancarfan transcripts proves that the Welsh kings and lesser magnates of the eleventh century had offered patronage, and occasionally protection, to their

---

71 Davies, *Age of Conquest*, 175.
72 *The Text of the Book of Llan Dâv*, ed. J. Gwenogvryn Evans (Oxford, 1893), 255–73.
73 Walter Map, *De Nugis Curialium*, trans. M.R. James (revised edn, Oxford, 1983), 146.

chief churches. There was no question that Welsh magnates should found such churches, for the network of mother churches was static. There was no space in Wales for new cults to proliferate; they could only decline and be revived, like that of St Cennydd in Gower. The main aristocratic prerogative with regard to the Church seems to have been the right of the dominant king of the region to intervene in the election of new bishops and participate in major decisions within the episcopal *parochiae*. King Gruffudd ap Cynan of Gwynedd gave his consent to the election of David the Scot as bishop of Bangor in 1120. Some months later the same king approved the removal of relics from Bardsey island for export to south Wales.[74] This close connection between Welsh kings and bishops was later to be exploited by the Marcher lords in south Wales. The earls of Gloucester long maintained the unique right amongst English earls of the advocacy of a see, that of Llandaff. This involved the custody of the episcopal estates during a vacancy and the nomination to vacant prebends in the chapter. The final vestiges of this right were not eliminated until the reign of Edward I. Elsewhere in Wales, both Welsh and English magnates long aspired to control episcopal estates within their lordships at the time of a vacancy; there are examples in every diocese. The English crown was not able to fully suppress (or rather, arrogate to itself) this right until the end of the thirteenth century.[75]

The traditional structure of the Welsh church did not crumble at once at the onset of the Normans in the 1090s. Although many famous Welsh churches were granted away by the conquerors to English or French houses, there is some doubt as to how effective these grants were. Even in south-east Wales, where Norman lordships struck root, the great *clas* churches showed a surprising resilience and adaptability. The see of Llandaff was dominated by native Welsh clerks well into the thirteenth century. The great church of St Gwynllyw (now Newport) and the even more famous *clas* of St Cadog of Llancarfan seem to have survived their subordination to the abbey of Gloucester by many decades. A community can still be distinguished in residence under the mastership of the archdeacon of Llandaff in the 1160s. At St Gwynllyw, we hear of a 'dean' living in princely style as head of the church well into the twelfth century (despite the grant of St Gwynllyw to the abbey

---

74 *Text of the Book of Llan Dâv*, 84–5.
75 M. Howell, 'Regalian Right in Wales and the March: the Relation of Theory to Practice', *Welsh History Review*, vii (1974–5), 269–88.

of Gloucester), and a dean implies a community of which he was the head.[76] Some expulsions of *claswyr* were only temporary, like that of the community of Llanbadarn Fawr, which was temporarily displaced by monks from Gloucester around 1116, but restored under its hereditary abbots in 1136.

There were other ways in which the Welsh clergy were able to continue to assert themselves. Hagiography was a useful way to increase the glamour of their saints and patrons; the drama of their lives was retold, and collections of their miracles told of their continuing power. The episcopal communities of St Davids and Llandaff were prompt in producing lives of the greater saints of their churches, but other, lesser communities did so too. A remarkable collection of Welsh saints' lives survives, which was compiled (probably) at Monmouth priory around 1200. It features lives composed within the *clasau* at a time after 1120. It tells us that the communities were fighting back, composing and collecting material to testify to the continuing life and power of their holy patrons: Gwynllyw of Newport, Cadog of Llancarfan, Illtud of Llantwit and a number of others.[77]

Traditional Welsh lay patronage continued for a while, but was coming under Anglo-French influence before the end of Henry I's reign. This is nowhere seen better than in the singular biography of Gruffudd ap Cynan, king of Gwynedd (died 1137). The date of this work is disputed, but its concern to draw genealogical links between its hero and the Norman royal house indicates a time of composition not too long after Gruffudd's death. Gruffudd's career began before the arrival of the Normans in Wales, and he died during the great Welsh onslaught against the Normans, which re-established Welsh native power for over a century. The recorded bequests of his deathbed testament reveal some new influences as well as a concern to patronise the greater *clas* churches of north and west Wales: Gwynedd's episcopal church of Bangor got the largest cash bequest. Yet he also sent money to the Benedictines of Chester and Shrewsbury, and the prior of Chester was amongst the three prelates who attended him in his last hours. He was buried,

76 For the community of Llancarfan in the 1160s, see *Llandaff Episcopal Acta*, ed. D. Crouch (South Wales Record Society, v, 1988), no. 16; for St Gwynllwg's dean, mentioned as a leading ecclesiastic of Gwent in the 1120s, see *Vita sancti Gundlei*, in *Vitae Sanctorum Britanniae et Genealogiae* ed. A.W. Wade-Evans (Cardiff, 1944), 190–2.
77 D. Simon Evans, 'Our Early Welsh Saints and History', in G.H. Doble, *Lives of the Welsh Saints*, ed. D. Simon Evans (Cardiff, 1971), 12–14.

moreover, in the choir of the new Romanesque cathedral of Bangor, to the left of the high altar, rather in the manner of an Anglo-Norman baron.[78]

There are other indications of changing attitudes in the Welsh aristocracy of the mid-twelfth century. The first seems to have been in the proprietary way that some Welsh magnates were prepared to make use of the Church. This speaks of new and more direct notions of advocacy. Rhys ap Gruffudd, prince of Deheubarth (died 1197), provided for his son Maredudd in a rather Anglo-Norman way, by granting him the rectories of thirteen churches, and perhaps putting pressure on the bishop of St Davids (or using his own right of provision) to have Maredudd made archdeacon of Cardigan.[79] In doing this Rhys was doing little more than other *curiales* at the court of Henry II, as for instance Robert du Neubourg (died 1159), seneschal of Normandy. Robert granted the advowsons of all the churches in his *seigneurie* of Le Neubourg to his younger son, Robert, who was later made dean of Rouen by his uncle, Archbishop Rotrou.[80]

In some ways this Anglicisation of Welsh attitudes to the Church was unavoidable. Where Norman barons had taken areas from the Welsh, they had occasionally established houses of monks, or at least made grants of Welsh churches and tithes to monasteries in England. When in Stephen's reign the native Welsh magnates took back those lands they might sometimes oust the monks, but it was tempting for them instead to adopt the aliens and pose as advocates in the Anglo-Norman way; advocacy represented yet another way to imitate the attractive Anglo-French image of aristocratic power. For this reason Morgan ab Owain, who made himself king of Glamorgan after seizing much of lowland Gwent in 1136, assumed the advocacy of the Bec priory of Goldcliff, near Newport, which

---

78 *The Life of Gruffudd ap Cynan*, ed. D. Simon Evans (Lampeter, 1990), 50–1. Gruffudd's successor, Owain Gwynedd, was buried in the presbytery of Bangor, before the high altar, Gerald of Wales, *Itinerarium Kambriae*, in *Opera*, ed. Brewer *et al.* (8 vols, Rolls Series, 1861–91) vi, 133.

79 T. Jones, 'Cronica de Wallia', *Bulletin of the Board of Celtic Studies*, xii (1946), 41. Rhys's uncle, Cynan, was described late in the reign of Stephen as *decanus*, indicating that earlier generations of the family had made use of its advocacy over its greater churches, D. Crouch, 'Earliest Original Charter of a Welsh King', ibid., xxvi (1989), 131.

80 For Robert, see Cartulary of Bourg Achard, Bibliothèque Nationale ms. Latin 9212, fo. 4r. Davies, *Age of Conquest*, 177, sees the grant to Maredudd on the contrary as a Welsh practice. To me, the Welshness in the incident is that Maredudd passed on his churches to his two sons.

had been founded in the 1120s by Robert de Candos.[81] In west Wales, the restored power of the dynasty of Deheubarth brought Lampeter and the region of Mebwynion back under the control of King Cadell ap Gruffudd. The church of Lampeter had previously been granted by the intruding Normans to Totnes priory, but instead of negating the grant, Cadell decided to confirm it: 'for my own soul, and those of my father, mother and all my friends'.[82]

It was hardly to be wondered at that the Welsh magnates of the next generation should begin to assume conventional Anglo-French habits of church patronage. In the reign of Henry II in England all the royal houses of Wales had founded or acquired one or more major monasteries, either of Cistercian monks or Premonstratensian canons. The dynasty of Glamorgan added its own foundation of Llantarnam abbey (1179) to the priory of Goldcliff. The dynasty of Deheubarth acquired the patronage of Strata Florida in 1165 and added Premonstratensian Talley to its advocacy late in the 1180s. The house of Powys founded Strata Marcella in 1170, and that of Gwynedd founded Aberconwy in 1186. These houses became the places of Welsh aristocratic burial and commemoration, and centres of native learning. The thoroughness of the shift in patronage is best illustrated at Talley. When Rhys ap Gruffudd established his house of white canons there he found the resources by using the goods of the nearby ancient mother church and cult centre of Llandeilo Fawr. In this he was doing no more than the Anglo-Norman barons earlier in the century: converting secular colleges into regular houses. The comparison is worth making for other reasons, for Rhys's patronage was no more narrow than that of any English baron; he also made grants to the Benedictines of Cardigan and the Templars of Slebech.[83]

But just as some English barons continued to favour secular colleges, so Welsh magnates did not wholly abandon the heirs of the earlier Welsh communities of *claswyr*. Hywel ab Iorwerth of

81 Morgan and his brother Iorwerth confirm the grants of Robert de Candos, and confirm to the priory the right to hold a court in their lordship, PRO, C53/76 m. 10.
82 Crouch, 'Earliest Original Charter of a Welsh King', 130–1.
83 See the survey of these developments in H. Pryce, 'Church and Society in Wales, 1150–1250', in *The British Isles, 1100–1500: Comparisons, Contrasts and Connections*, ed. R.R. Davies (Edinburgh, 1988), 32–5. For Rhys's other grants and confirmations, see *Chertsey Cartularies*, ed. W. Hudson and M.S. Giuseppi (2 vols, Surrey Record Society, xii, 1915–63), i, 104–5; George Owen of Henllys, *The Description of Penbrokeshire*, ed. H. Owen (Cymroddor Record Series, no. 1, 1897), pt 2, 359, 362.

Caerleon (died 1216) patronised the Welsh-dominated chapter of Llandaff (he was its sole lay benefactor in the twelfth century), and indeed Hywel had a Welsh canon of Llandaff for his clerk. The community of Llanbadarn remained secular into the reign of Edward I, despite the claims of Gloucester abbey. Native usages survived long enough to amaze the mature Gerald of Wales. He tells the story of a Breton knight who had devoted his life to travel and the study of peoples who came at last to Wales while Stephen was king (1135–54). The Breton was astonished at the sight of the 'abbot' of Llanbadarn marching about his church bearing a spear, with an armed bodyguard in attendance: 'So much for new experiences and marvels!', declared the bemused Breton; he ended his travels there and then, and went home – he had now seen it all.[84] Gerald, as archdeacon of Brecon, must himself have seen sights to amuse and astonish him.

The Welsh aristocracy of the thirteenth century had acquired most of the habits of the Anglo-French aristocracy in church patronage. Llywelyn ab Iorwerth (died 1240) of Gwynedd demonstrated his sympathy with current modes of patronage by founding a Franciscan friary at Llanfaes. The courts of successive princes of Gwynedd in the thirteenth century reveal a relationship with the Church similar to that of any great Marcher baron. Monasteries in their advocacy provided clerks and were repositries of their treasure and goods. Bishops and archdeacons were amongst their intimates and counsellors. Doubtless they, like other magnates, used friars as their confessors; certainly Welsh friars were close in their attendance on their prince.[85] Gruffudd ap Gwenwynwyn, prince of Powys, no sluggard at taking up Anglo-French ideas, founded a chantry of some sort at an English manor of his in or around 1257.[86] In the way of religion, above all ways, the full measure of Anglicisation penetrated the Welsh aristocracy. It is difficult to think of anything in which the ecclesiastical patronage of the Welsh aristocracy differed from that of the English by 1240.

Scotland was in many ways similar to Wales. The situations of Welsh and Scottish churches were very similar at the end of the eleventh century. Scotland was a kingdom without a metropolitan

---

84 Gerald of Wales, *Itinerarium Kambriae*, in *Opera*, vi, 121. Pryce, 'Church and Society in Wales', 40, points out the conjunction of temporal, military and spiritual power manifest in abbots of mid-twelfth-century *clasau*.
85 Stephenson, *Governance of Gwynedd*, 33–9.
86 Cartulary of Lichfield, Brit. Libr., ms Harley 4799, fo. 27v.

bishop within its borders, a land also without a regular Benedictine house. As in Wales, the Scottish church was organised around strong episcopal communities, but in Scotia itself the dioceses had firmer boundaries, respecting the strong provincial structure which also accommodated the mormaers.

The royal house was the first to introduce regular communities of monks into Scotland. Queen Margaret installed Benedictines at Dunfermline and Coldingham in Lothian. Her son, King Alexander I, brought Augustinian canons from Nostell in Yorkshire to Scone, the centre of Scottish royalty (and planned further Augustinian houses). Alexander's brother, David I, brought English Augustinians to Holyrood, near Edinburgh, Jedburgh and Cambuskenneth, Cluniacs to the Isle of May, Tironensians to Selkirk, and Cistercians to Melrose, Kinloss and Newbattle. Here is quite a different story of native assimilation of foreign forms of ecclesiastical patronage from what went on in Wales. Melrose was founded in 1136; it would be over thirty years from that date before a native Welsh ruler undertook a regular foundation (Strata Florida), and even that was a refoundation of an English baronial venture. The monastic enterprises of the Scottish royal family preceded even Scotland's colonisation by Anglo-Norman barons. The influence of Queen Margaret's English background was obviously responsible for this. Her joint patronage of Benedictines and the major native churches has something essentially English about it, particularly as she looked for support to Durham and Canterbury. Her sons simply followed her lead, widening the patronage as new orders became available.[87]

The native aristocracy participated remarkably soon in the monastic colonisation of Scotland. Fergus, lord of Galloway, founded a Cistercian abbey at Dundrennan in 1142, only six years after David I founded Melrose. Fergus took his initial colony of monks for Dundrennan from Rievaulx in Yorkshire, the same source as Melrose. Fergus certainly was not copying incoming Anglo-Norman barons at this point, as he was when he erected castles over his lordship. It may well be that Fergus (who was occasionally styled 'king') was partly inspired in his foundation by King David, seeing

---

87 Some comparison might be made with one of the few wealthy English families which survived Hastings, the Midlands family of Arden. Immediately after the Conquest, Thurkil and Siward of Arden continued to patronise the traditional great English houses: Abingdon, Coventry and Thorney. The Ardens of Stephen's reign turned to the Augustinians of Kenilworth and Leicester, and the Cistercians of Combe.

such foundations as a suitably kingly act. If so, he became enthusi-astic about the new orders, introducing Premonstratensian canons to Saulseat and the cathedral chapter of Whithorn. By this time (the mid-twelfth century) Anglo-Norman barons were becoming entrenched in Scotland, and an avalanche of new priories and abbeys was transforming the pattern of Scottish religious patronage into something close to that of England in all respects. Native aristocratic patronage naturally followed suit, and Scottish nobles reached the stage of conformity with those of England more than a generation before the Welsh princes.[88]

88 Most of the matter of these paragraphs is derived from G.W.S. Barrow, *Kingship and Unity: Scotland, 1000–1306* (London, 1981), 61–83; idem, *The Kingdom of the Scots* (London, 1973), 165–211.

CONCLUSION

At the beginning of this book – which seems a long way away – we looked at two observations made by Génicot. Having now travelled through a colourful landscape of evidence and speculation we should be in a position to look back and reflect upon them from a distance. Study of the use of trappings and titles has shown us that there was indeed a contemporary awareness of aristocracy. At the beginning it was an awareness of a dominant magnate class, but later it comprehended various levels of status both within it and associated with it. The use of trappings and titles tells us of shifts in status, some striking and others subtle, within the aristocracy between 1000 and 1300.

A count in 1000 would have presided over a territory from a wooden hall set in a fortified enclosure. He would have been surrounded by a crowd of undifferentiated followers, knights and servants. His clerks would have preserved a memory of Classical and Carolingian grandeur in applying to him antiquated imperial formulae. He might have sat in some sort of state on an elevated seat and used a ceremonial sword, or a staff, to distinguish himself, but otherwise distinction would have lain in the weight of riches with which he surrounded himself. The count or earl of 1300 would have presented in some ways a similar picture. But his hall would have been of stone with glazed windows, leaded roofs and noble proportions, set within a castle or an embattled court. It would have had private chambers guarded by marshals and ushers in livery, bearing staffs. Etiquette guided a household of pages, squires, seneschals, butlers and household knights as it revolved around the count and his lady sitting under canopies, their heads crowned. The count's heraldic device and badge adorned the glass and masonry of his hall, his banners

344

and household, and the abbeys, priories and chantries within his advocacy.

In 1000 a count in state would have proclaimed himself by a rude sort of grandeur, but by 1300 the grandeur had become well articulated. It spoke a sophisticated language alluding to the greater glories of royalty; yet its vocabulary also contained a heraldry of family pride and lineage which was all its own. There was a symbolism of exclusiveness expressed through domestic planning, etiquette, and circles of servants, which hedged the count's dignity and marked him as above and beyond others admitted to be aristocratic. If we think in terms of society having learned a new language of the symbolism of power in the intervening centuries then we may have got close to the truth of what had happened. It was by that language that aristocracy had learned to express itself and become more self-conscious. In England, even spoken language was part of the process. The aristocracy spoke French, and so did all the socially ambitious: 'unless a man speak French, then he is thought of little account,' said a clerk of the later thirteenth century.[1]

This comment is part of the corollary to the definition of what is aristocratic. When the signs and marks of aristocracy are universally recognised, and more sophisticated than simple economics, then they become imitable. When there is a language of social distinction, it can also express social pretension. It is no coincidence that the new eleventh-century definitions of magnate attributes (the castle, the sub-royal household, heraldry, the great seal and monastic advocacy) were used by an increasingly wider group of people in the early twelfth century. This in turn led to a third stage in the process at the end of the twelfth century. Levels of status began to firm up within the group using aristocratic insignia. Titles and certain insignia assisted in the process. Although the practice of heraldry and the use of banners were initially associated, heraldry rapidly penetrated the middle gound of society while the use of banners did not. Coronets and rods, like banners, were never appropriate to any other than the greatest magnates, and were never diffused. The middle ground of society using aristocratic insignia, and living in recognisably aristocratic style, evolved recognisable ranks out of formerly shapeless terms: the knight and the squire. In the meantime, the terms 'baron' and 'banneret' evolved to distinguish

1 Robert of Gloucester, quoted in M.T. Clanchy, *From Memory to Written Record* (London, 1979), 153.

the magnates who possessed no comital style. In this period of social definition (the two significant generations on either side of 1200) the aristocracy of England and France was both enlarged and subdivided, and assumed a basic shape which was to be slowly refined in the fourteenth century. Indeed the shape has been refined and redefined to the present day as the language of attributes has altered and shifted its meanings.

This model of a three-stage formation of modern aristocracy needs to be modified for Wales and Scotland, although it is still applicable. In the case of Wales, the royal houses had been imitating recognised attributes of Anglo-French royalty early in the eleventh century, and it is possible that this was true also in Scotland. In the twelfth century the Welsh royal houses and the lesser Welsh magnate houses came closer together, as both imitated the repertoire of Anglo-French aristocratic attributes: the knightly image, heraldry, the castle and ecclesiastical patronage. This led also to a definition within the Welsh aristocracy; the new rank of prince defined the élite few families and excluded the rest, the *uchelwyr*. But in Wales the process was complicated. Native culture and organisation retained an influence; the *teulu*, its myths and key political importance inhibited the penetration of knighthood and squirehood until the fourteenth century. The chronology does not therefore match that of England and France, but native Wales certainly was influenced thoroughly by Anglo-French ideas from an early period, and was continually responding to them. Scotland is a far easier case. Determined Anglicisation early in the twelfth century and the importation of foreign aristocrats had produced an aristocratic society closely matching that of England in almost all respects by the end of the century.

I feel almost obliged to end this book on a grand statement, a piercing insight designed to sum up its argument and lay open the heart of a social process. But the whole concern of the book has been to show how complicated the developments in the aristocracy were between 1000 and 1300; I had best avoid statements that simplify them. Yet the metaphor of society learning a new language of power comes nearest to the point of the book. In a sense, these three centuries saw the discovery of aristocracy – although not its invention. Aristocracy became a matter of self-conscious expression, particularly around 1200. The language of prestige and symbols allowed the beginning of a new debate, the general (as opposed to the intellectual) discussion of social degrees, and ultimately of class. I do not think it is too much to claim that in writers like Andrew the Chaplain, Gerald of Wales and the anonymous author of 'Bracton' we see the stirrings of a debate to which *The Wealth of Nations* and the *Communist Manifesto* gave a new intensity over six centuries later.

BIBLIOGRAPHY

References are to printed works only. References to manuscript sources are given in full in the relevant footnote.

1282: A Collection of Documents, ed. R.A. Griffiths (National Library of Wales, 1986).

The Acts of the Parliaments of Scotland (12 vols, London, 1845–75).

Adam, P., 'Les Usages héraldiques au milieu du xiie siècle d'après le Roman de Troie de Benoît de Sainte-Maure et la littérature contemporaine', *Archivum Heraldicum*, lxxvii (1963).

Adam-Even, P., 'Les Sceaux d'écuyers au xiiie siècle', *Archives héraldiques suisses*, lxvi (1951).

Adémar de Chabannes, *Chronique*, ed. J. Chavanon (Paris, 1897).

Adhémar, J., and G. Dordor 'Les Tombeaux de la Collection Gaignières', in *Gazette des Beaux-Arts*, 6th ser., lxxxiv, 1974.

Ailes, A., *The Origins of the Royal Arms of England: Their Development to 1199* (Reading Medieval Studies, no. 1, 1982).

Alcock, N.W. and R.J. Buckley, 'Leicester Castle: the Great Hall', *Medieval Archaeology*, xxxi (1987).

Alexander, J. and P. Binski, *Age of Chivalry: Art in Plantagenet England* (Royal Academy of Arts, 1987).

Ancient Laws and Institutes of England, ed. B. Thorpe (2 vols, Record Commission, 1840).

Anderson, A.O., *Early Sources of Scottish History, AD 500 to 1286* (2 vols, Edinburgh, 1922).

Andrew the Chaplain, *Amoris Tractatum*, ed. P.G. Walsh (London, 1982).

The Anglo-Saxons, ed. J. Campbell (London, 1982).

Annales Bertiniani, ed. G. Waitz (M.G.H., Scriptores rerum Germanicarum in usu scholarum, 1883).

Annales Cambriae, ed J. Williams 'Ab Ithel' (Rolls Series, 1860).

Annales Monastici, ed. H.R. Luard (5 vols, Rolls Series, 1864–9).

Annals and Memorials of St Edmunds Abbey, ed. T. Arnold (2 vols, Rolls Series, 1890).

Avent, R., *Castles of the Princes of Gwynedd* (London, 1983).

Avril, F., *Le Livre des tournois du Roi René* (Paris, 1986).
Baldwin, J., *The Government of Philip Augustus* (Berkeley, Calif., 1986).
Barlow, F., *William Rufus* (London, 1983).
Barnwell, P.A., '*Epistula Hieronimi de gradus Romanorum*: an English School Book', *Historical Research*, lxiv (1991).
Barroux, R., 'L'Abbé Suger et la vassalité du Vexin en 1124', *Le Moyen Age*, lxiv (1958).
Barrow, G.W.S., *The Kingdom of the Scots* (London, 1973).
Barrow, G.W.S., *The Anglo-Norman Era in Scottish History* (Oxford, 1980).
Barrow, G.W.S., *Kingship and Unity: Scotland 1000–1306* (London, 1981).
Barthélemy, D., *L'Ordre seigneurial, xie–xiie siècle* (Paris, 1990).
Bartlett, R., *Gerald of Wales* (Oxford, 1982).
Bates, D.R., *Normandy before 1066* (London, 1982).
The Bayeux Tapestry: a Comprehensive Survey, ed. F.M. Stenton and others (London, 1957).
Bean, J.M.W., '"Bachelor" and Retainer', *Medievalia et Humanistica*, new ser., iii (1972).
Bede's Ecclesiastical History of the English People, ed. B. Colgrave and R.A.B. Mynors (Oxford, 1969).
Bédier, J., *Les Chansons de croisade* (Paris, 1909).
Bedos Rezak, B., 'Les Sceaux au temps de Philippe Auguste', in *La France de Philippe Auguste: le temps des mutations* (Colloques internationaux, C.N.R.S., no. 602).
Bedos Rezak, B., 'L'Apparition des armoiries sur les sceaux en Ile-de-France et en Picardie (v. 1130–1230)', in *Les Origines des armoiries* (IIe Colloque international d'Héraldique, 1981).
The Benedictional of Archbishop Robert, ed. H.A. Wilson (Henry Bradshaw Soc., xxiv, 1903).
Bennett, M., 'The Status of the Squire: the Northern Evidence', in *The Ideals and Practice of Medieval Knighthood*, i, ed. C. Harper-Bill and R. Harvey (Woodbridge, 1986).
Bennett, M., 'Wace and Warfare', *Anglo-Norman Studies*, ed. R.A. Brown, xi (1988).
Beresford, G., 'The Medieval Manor of Penhallam, Jacobstow, Cornwall', *Medieval Archaeology*, xviii (1974).
Beresford, G., 'Goltho Manor, Lincolnshire: the Buildings and their Surrounding Defences', *Proceedings of the Battle Conference*, iv, ed. R.A. Brown (Woodbridge, 1982).
Beresford, G., *Goltho: the Development of an Early Medieval Manor, c. 850–1150* (English Heritage Archeological Report, iv).
Bernard, E., *Catalogi librorum manuscriptorum Angliae et Hiberniae in unum collecti* (2 vols, Oxford, 1697).
Bernard, J.H., 'The Charters of the Cistercian Abbey of Duiske', *Proceedings of the Royal Irish Academy*, xxxv (1918–20).
Beverley Smith, J., 'Dynastic Succession in Medieval Wales', *Bulletin of the Board of Celtic Studies*, xxxiii (1986).
Binchy, D.A., *Celtic and Anglo-Saxon Kingship* (Oxford, 1970).

Bishop, T.A.M. and P. Chaplais, *English Royal Writs to 1100 AD* (Oxford, 1961).

Blair, J., 'Secular Minster Churches in Domesday Book', in *Domesday Book: A Reassessment*, ed. P. Sawyer (London, 1985).

Blair, J., 'The Twelfth Century Bishop's Palace at Hereford', *Medieval Archaeology*, xxxi (1987).

Blair, J., 'From Minster to Parish Church', in *Minsters and Parish Churches: the Local Church in Transition, 950–1200*, ed. J. Blair (Oxford, 1988).

Bloch, M., *Feudal Society*, trans. L.A. Manyon (2nd edn., 1962).

Bradney, J., *History of Monmouthshire* (4 vols, London, 1904–33).

Brenner, R., 'Agrarian Class Structure and Economic Development in Pre-Industrial Europe', *Past and Present*, lxx (1976).

Brooke, C.N.L., 'The Church in the Welsh Border in the Tenth and Eleventh Centuries', in *The Church and the Welsh Border in the Central Middle Ages*, ed. D.N. Dumville and C.N.L. Brooke (Woodbridge, 1986).

Brown, R.A., *English Castles* (London, 1954).

Brown, R.A., 'The Status of the Norman Knight', in *War and Government in the Middle Ages*, ed. J.C. Holt and J. Gillingham (Woodbridge, 1984).

Brown, S.A., *The Bayeux Tapestry: History and Bibliography* (London, 1988).

Brown, S.D.B., 'Military Service and Monetary Reward in the Eleventh and Twelfth Centuries', *History*, lxxiv (1989).

Brut y Tywysogyon: Red Book of Hergest Version, ed. T. Jones (Cardiff, 1955).

Bur, M., *La Formation du comté de Champagne, v.950–1150* (Mémoires des annales de l'Est, liv Nancy, 1977).

Bush, M., *The English Aristocracy: a Comparative Synthesis* (Manchester, 1984).

Butler, L.A.S., 'Domestic Building in Wales and the Evidence of the Welsh Laws', *Medieval Archaeology*, xxxi (1987).

Calendar of Charter Rolls preserved in the Public Record Office (6 vols, PRO, 1903–27).

Calendar of Documents preserved in France, i *918–1206*, ed. J.H. Round (London, 1899).

Calendar of Inquisitions post mortem, 1216–1307 (4 vols., PRO, 1898–1913).

Calendar of Patent Rolls preserved in the Public Record Office, 1216–1509 (PRO, 1906–16).

Cam, H., 'An East Anglian Shire-Moot in Stephen's Reign', *English Historical Review*, xxxix (1924).

Campbell, J., 'Bede's *Reges* and *Principes*', in *Essays in Anglo-Saxon History* (London, 1986).

Cân Rolant: The Medieval Welsh Version of the Song of Roland, ed. A.C. Rejhon (Berkeley, Calif., 1983).

Carlin, M., 'The Reconstruction of Winchester House, Southwark', *London Topographical Record*, xxv (1985).

The Carmen de Hastingae Proelio of Guy, Bishop of Amiens, ed. C. Martin and H. Muntz (Oxford, 1972).

Carr, A.D., 'An Aristocracy in Decline: the Native Welsh Lords after the Edwardian Conquest', *Welsh History Review*, v (1970–1).

Cartulaire de l'abbaye de Notre-Dame des Vaux de Cernay de l'ordre de Cîteaux au diocèse de Paris, ed. L. Merlet and A. Moutié (2 vols, Paris, 1857).

Cartulaire de l'abbaye de St-Martin de Pontoise, ed. J. Depoin (Pontoise, 1895).

Cartulaire de l'abbaye de St-Michel du Tréport, ed. P. Laffleur de Kermaingant (Paris, 1880).

Cartulaire de l'église collégiale de St-Seurin de Bordeaux, ed. J-A. Brutails (Bordeaux, 1897).

Cartulaire de l'église de la sainte-Trinité de Beaumont-le-Roger, ed. E. Deville (Paris, 1912).

Cartulaire de la Maladerie de St-Lazare de Beauvais, ed. V. Leblond (Paris, 1922).

Cartulaire de Marmoutier pour le Perche, ed. L'abbé Barret (Mortagne, 1894).

Cartulaire de Notre-Dame de Josaphat, ed. Ch. Métais (2 vols, Chartres, 1904–8).

Cartulaire de Notre-Dame de Chartres, ed. E. de Lépinois and L. Merlet (3 vols, Chartres, 1862–5).

Cartulaire de St-Aubin d'Angers, ed. A. Bertrand de Brousillon (Paris, 1903).

Cartulaire de St-Père de Chartres, ed. B.E.C. Guerard (2 vols, Paris, 1840).

Cartulaire du prieuré de St-Leu d'Esserent, 1080–1538, ed. E. Müller (Pontoise, 1901).

Cartularium abbathiae de Rievalle, ed. J.C. Atkinson (Surtees Soc., lxxxiii, 1889 for 1887).

Cartularium monasterii sancti Johannis de Colecestria, ed. S.A. Moore (2 vols, Roxburghe Club, 1897).

Cartularium prioratus de Colne, ed. J.L. Fisher (Essex Archaeological Society, Occasional Publications, no. 1, 1946).

The Cartulary of Darley, ed. R.R. Darlington (2 vols, Derbyshire Archaeological Soc., 1945).

The Cartulary of Haughmond Abbey, ed. U. Rees (Cardiff, 1985).

The Cartulary of Shrewsbury Abbey, ed. U. Rees (2 vols, Aberystwyth, 1975).

The Cartulary of St Michael's Mount, ed. P.L. Hull (Devon and Cornwall Record Soc., new ser., v, 1962).

The Cartulary of Worcester Cathedral Priory, ed. R.R. Darlington (Pipe Roll Soc., lxxvi, 1968).

Chandler, V., 'The Last of the Montgomerys: Roger the Poitevin and Arnulf', *Historical Research*, lxii (1989).

Chandos Herald, *Life of the Black Prince*, ed. M.K. Pope and E.C. Lodge (Oxford, 1910).

Charles-Edwards, T.M., 'The Heir Apparent in Irish and Welsh Law', *Celtica*, ix (1971).

Charles-Edwards, T.M., 'Honour and Status in some Irish and Welsh Prose Tales', *Ériu*, xxix (1978).

Charters of the Anglo-Norman Earls of Chester, c. 1071–1237, ed. G. Barraclough (Record Soc. of Lancashire and Cheshire, cxxvi, 1988).

Charters of the Cistercian Priory of Coldstream, ed. C. Rogers (London, 1879).

Charters of the Honour of Mowbray, 1107–1191, ed. D.E. Greenway (British Academy, Records of Social and Economic History, new ser., no. 1, 1972).

Chartes de l'abbaye de Jumièges, ed. J-J. Vernier (2 vols, Rouen, 1916).

Les Chartes de St-Bertin, ed. D. Haigneré (4 vols, St-Omer, 1886–90).

Chartularium Monasterii Sanctae Trinitatis de Monte Rothomagi, ed. A. Deville, in *Cartulaire de St-Bertin*, ed. B. Guerard (Paris, 1841).

Chatwin, P.B., 'Castles in Warwickshire', *Birmingham Archeological Society Transactions*, lxvii (1951 for 1947–8).

Chautard, J., *Monnaies au type esterlin frappées en Europe pendant le xiiie et le xive siècle* (Nancy, 1871).

Cheney, C.R., *English Bishops' Chanceries* (Manchester, 1950).

Chertsey Cartularies, ed. W. Hudson and M.S. Guiseppi (2 vols, Surrey Record Soc., xii, 1915–63).

Chew, H.M., *The English Ecclesiastical Tenants-in-Chief* (Oxford, 1932).

Chrétien de Troyes, *Le Conte de Graal*, ed. F. Lecoy (2 vols, Classiques français du moyen âge, 1972–5).

Chronica monasterii de Hida iuxta Wintoniam, in *Liber monasterii de Hyda*, ed. E. Edwards (Rolls Series, 1866).

Chronica monasterii de Melsa, ed. E.A. Bond (3 vols, Rolls Series, 1866–8).

The Chronicle of Battle Abbey, ed. E. Searle (Oxford, 1980).

The Chronicle of Joscelin of Brakelond, ed. H.E. Butler (London, 1949).

The Chronicle of Walter of Guisborough, ed. H. Rothwell (Camden Soc., 3rd ser., lxxxix, 1957).

The Chronicle of William de Rishanger of the Barons' War, ed. J.O. Haliwell (Camden Soc., xv, 1840).

Chronicon abbatiae Rameseiensis, ed. W. Dunn Macray (Rolls Series, 1886).

Chronicon monasterii de Abingdon, ed. J. Stevenson (2 vols, Rolls Series, 1852).

Chroniques Anglo-Normandes, ed. F. Michel (3 vols, Paris, 1839–40).

Chroniques des comtes d'Anjou et des seigneurs d'Amboise, ed. L. Halphen and R. Poupardin (Paris, 1913).

Clanchy, M.T., *From Memory to Written Record* (London, 1979).

Cligès, ed. A. Micha (Classiques français du moyen âge, 1957).

Close Rolls of the Reign of Henry III preserved in the Public Record Office (14 vols, PRO, 1902–38).

Cockayne, G.E., *The Complete Peerage*, ed. V. Gibbs and others (13 vols in 14, London, 1910–59).

Constitutio Domus Regis, in *Dialogus de Scaccario*, ed. C. Johnson and others (revised edn, Oxford, 1983).

Contamine, P., *War in the Middle Ages*, trans. M. Jones (Oxford, 1984).

Contamine, P., 'Introduction', *La Noblesse au moyen age, xie-xve siècles: essais à la mémoire de Robert Boutruche*, ed. P. Contamine (Paris, 1976).

Coss, P.R., 'Literature and Social Terminology: the Vavasour in England', in *Social Relation and Ideas: Essays in Honour of R.H. Hilton*, ed. T.H. Aston and others (Cambridge, 1983).

Coss, P.R., 'Knighthood and the Early Thirteenth-Century County Court', in *Thirteenth Century England*, ii ed. P.R. Coss and S.D. Lloyd (Woodbridge, 1988).

Coss, P.R., *Lordship, Knighthood and Locality: a Study in English Society, c.1180–c.1280* (Cambridge, 1991).

The Coucher Book of Furness Abbey, ed. J.C. Atkinson (3 vols, Chetham Soc., new ser., ix, xi, xiv, 1886–7).

Coulson, C., 'Structural Symbolism in Medieval Castle Architecture', *Journal of the British Archeological Association*, cxxxii (1979).

Coulson, C., 'Hierarchism in Conventual Crenellation', *Medieval Archeology*, xxvi (1982).

Coulson, C., 'Fortress-Policy in Capetian Tradition and Angevin Practice: Aspects of the Conquest of Normandy by Philip II', in *Anglo-Norman Studies*, vi, ed. R. Allen Brown (Woodbridge, 1984).

Coulson, C., 'Bodiam Castle: Truth and Tradition', *Fortress*, x (1991).

Cowdrey, H.E.J., 'The Peace and the Truce of God in the Eleventh Century', *Past and Present*, xlvi (1970).

Crouch, D., 'Geoffrey de Clinton and Roger, Earl of Warwick', *Bulletin of the Institute of Historical Research*, lv (1982).

Crouch, D., 'The Slow Death of Kingship in Glamorgan, 1067–1158', *Morgannwg*, xxix (1985).

Crouch, D., *The Beaumont Twins* (Cambridge, 1986).

Crouch, D., 'The Foundation of Leicester Abbey and other Problems', *Midland History*, xi (1987).

Crouch, D., 'Strategies of Lordship in Angevin England and the Career of William Marshal', in *The Ideals and Practice of Medieval Knighthood*, ii, ed. C. Harper-Bill and R. Harvey (Woodbridge, 1988).

Crouch, D., 'The Earliest Original Charter of a Welsh King', *Bulletin of the Board of Celtic Studies*, xxvi (1989).

Crouch, D., 'The Family of Martinwast of Noseley', *The Harborough Historian*, viii (1989).

Crouch, D., 'Urban, First Bishop of Llandaff, 1107–34', *Journal of Welsh Ecclesiastical History*, vi (1989).

Crouch, D., *William Marshal: Court, Career and Chivalry in the Angevin Empire* (London, 1990).

Crouch, D., 'The Administration of the Norman Earldom', in *The Earldom of Chester and its Charters: a Tribute to Geoffrey Barraclough*, ed. A.T. Thacker (Chester Arch. Soc., lxxi 1991).

Cruden, S., *The Scottish Castle* (London, 1960).

Curia Regis Rolls of the Reigns of Richard I, John and Henry III (16 vols, HMSO, 1922–79).

Dannenberg, H., *Die deutschen Münzen der sächsischen und fränkischen Kaiserzeit* (4 vols in 5, Berlin, 1876–1905).

Davidson, H.R. Ellis, *The Sword in Anglo-Saxon England* (Oxford, 1962).

Davies, J. Conway, 'Ewenny Priory: Some Recently Discovered Deeds', *Journal of the National Library of Wales*, iii (1943–4).

Davies, R.R., 'The Lordship of Ogmore', in *Glamorgan County History*, iii, *The Middle Ages*, ed. T.B. Pugh (Cardiff, 1971).

Davies, R.R., *Lordship and Society in the March of Wales, 1282–1400* (Oxford, 1978).

Davies, R.R., *Domination and Conquest: the Experience of Ireland, Scotland and Wales, 1100–1300* (Cambridge, 1990).

Davies, R.R., *Conquest, Coexistence and Change in Wales 1063–1415* (Oxford, 1987), repr. as *The Age of Conquest* (Oxford, 1991).

Davies, W., *An Early Welsh Microcosm* (London, 1978).

Davies, W., *Wales in the Early Middle Ages* (Leicester, 1982).

Davies, W., *Patterns of Power in Early Wales* (Oxford, 1990).

Davison, B.K., 'Early Earthwork Castles: a New Model', *Château Gaillard*, iii (1966).

De exordiis et incrementis quarundam in observationibus ecclesiasticis rerum, in *M[onumenta] G[ermanicae] H[istoriae], Capitularia regnum Francorum*, ed. A. Boretius and V. Krause, ii (Hanover, 1897).

De Expugnatione Lyxbonensi, ed. C.W. David (New York, 1936).

De Gray Birch, W., *Catalogue of Seals in the Department of Manuscripts in the British Museum* (6 vols, London, 1887–1900).

De ordine palatii, ed. T. Gross and R. Schieffer (M.G.H. Fontes Iuris Germanici Antiqui, iii, 1980).

Denholm-Young, N., *Seigniorial Administration in England* (London, 1937).

Denholm-Young, N., 'Feudal Society in the Thirteenth Century: the Knights', in *Collected Papers* (Cardiff, 1969).

The Description of Penbrokeshire, ed. H. Owen (Cymroddor Record Series, no. 1, 1897).

Devailly, G., *Le Berry du xe siècle au milieu du xiiie siècle* (Paris, 1973).

Devoisins, A-J., *Histoire de Notre-Dame du Désert* (Paris, 1901).

Dhondt, J., 'Le titre du Marquis à l'époque carolingienne', *Bullétin Du Cange*, xix (1948).

Dialogus de Scaccario, ed. C. Johnson and others (revised edn., Oxford, 1983).

Die 'Institutes of Polity, Civil and Ecclesiastical': Ein Werk Erzbischof Wulfstans von York, ed. K. Jost (Schweizer Anglische Arbeiten, xlvii 1959).

Die Zeit der Staufer: Geschichte, Kunst, Kultur (4 vols, Stuttgart, 1977–9).

Doble, G.H., *Lives of the Welsh Saints*, ed. D. Simon Evans (Cardiff, 1971).

Domesday Book, seu Liber Censualis Willelmi primi regis Angliae, ed. A. Farley and others (4 vols, London, 1783–1816).

Douglas, D.C., 'The Earliest Norman Counts', *English Historical Review*, lxi (1946).

Douglas, D.C., *William the Conqueror* (London, 1964).

Duby, G., 'The Diffusion of Cultural Patterns in Feudal Society', in *The Chivalrous Society*, trans. C. Postan (London, 1977).

Duby, G., 'Lineage, Nobility and Knighthood: the Mâconnais in the Twelfth Century – a Revision', in *The Chivalrous Society*, trans. C. Postan (London, 1977).

Duby, G., 'The Nobility in Medieval France', in *The Chivalrous Society*, trans. C. Postan (London, 1977).

Duby, G., 'The Structure of Kinship and Nobility', in *The Chivalrous Society*, trans. C. Postan (London, 1977).

Duby, G., 'The Transformation of the Aristocracy', in *The Chivalrous Society*, trans. C. Postan (London, 1977).

Duby, G., *The Three Orders: Feudal Society Imagined*, trans. A. Goldhammer (Chicago, 1980).

Duby, G., *La Société aux xie et xiie siècles dans la région mâconnaise*, (repr. Ecole des Hautes Etudes, 1982).

Dugdale, W., *The Baronage of England* (3 vols, London, 1675–6).

Dumville, D.N., 'The Aetheling: a Study in Anglo-Saxon Constitutional History', *Anglo-Saxon England*, viii (1979).

Dunbabin, J., *France in the Making, 843–1180* (Oxford, 1985).

Dunbabin, J., 'From Clerk to Knight: Changing Orders', in *The Ideals and Practice of Medieval Knighthood*, ii, ed. C. Harper-Bill and R. Harvey (Woodbridge, 1988).

Duncan, A.A.M., *Scotland: the Making of the Kingdom* (Edinburgh, 1975).

Dyer, C., *Standards of Living in the Later Middle Ages: Social Change in England, c. 1200–1520* (Cambridge, 1989).

Eadmer, *The Life of St Anselm*, ed. R.W. Southern (repr. Oxford, 1972).

The Earldom of Chester and its Charters: a Tribute to Geoffrey Barraclough, ed. A.T. Thacker (Chester Arch. Soc., lxxi 1991).

Earldom of Gloucester Charters, ed. R.B. Patterson (Oxford, 1973).

Early Medieval Settlements in Wales AD 400–1100, ed. N. Edwards and A. Lane (Cardiff, 1988).

Early Mysteries and other Latin Poems of the Twelfth and Thirteenth Centuries, ed. T. Wright (London, 1838).

Early Scottish Charters, prior to AD 1153, ed. A.C. Lawrie (Glasgow, 1905).

Ellis, G., *Earldoms in Fee* (London, 1963).

Ellis, W.S., *The Antiquities of Heraldry* (London, 1869).

English Coronation Records, ed. L.G. Wickham Legg (Westminster, 1901).

English Historical Documents, i, c.AD 500–1042, ed. D. Whitelock (London, 1955).

English Mediaeval Rolls of Arms, i 1244–1334, ed. R.W. Mitchell (Peebles, 1983).

English Romanesque Art, 1066–1200 (Arts Council, 1984).

English, B., *The Lords of Holderness, 1086–1260* (Oxford, 1979).

Erec et Enide, ed. M. Roquez (Classiques français du moyen âge, 1952).

Eulogium Historiarum sive Temporis, ed. F.S. Haydon (3 vols, Rolls Series, 1858–63).

Excerpta Historica, ed. S. Bentley (London, 1833).

Facsimiles of the National Manuscripts of Scotland (London, 1867–71), i.

Farnham, G., 'The Manor of Noseley', *Transactions of the Leicestershire Archaeological Society*, xii (1922).

Les Fastes du Gothique: le siècle de Charles V (Paris, 1981).

Faulkner, P.A., 'Domestic Planning from the Twelfth to the Fourteenth Centuries', *Archaeological Journal*, cxv (1958).

Fell, C., *Women in Anglo-Saxon England* (Oxford, 1986).

Fery-Hue, F., 'Le Cérémonial du couronnement des ducs de Bretagne au xve. siècle édition', *Questions d'histoire de Bretagne* (Paris, Comité des Travaux historiques et scientifiques, 1984).

Feudal Documents from the Abbey of Bury St Edmunds, ed. D.C. Douglas (British Academy, 1932).

The Fifth Report from the Lords Committees touching the Dignity of a Peer of the Realm (London, 1829).

Fleming, D.F., 'Landholding by Milites in Domesday Book', in *Anglo-Norman Studies*, xiii ed. M. Chibnall (Woodbridge, 1990).

Fleming, D.F., '*Milites* as Attestors to Charters in England, 1101–1300', *Albion*, xxxii (1990).

Flores Historiarum, ed. H.R. Luard (3 vols, Rolls Series, 1890).

Flori, J., 'Qu'est-ce qu'un bacheler?', *Romania*, xcvi (1975).

Flori, J., 'Chevalerie et liturgie', *Le Moyen Age*, lxxxiv (1978).

Flori, J., 'Les Origines de l'adoubement chevaleresque: étude des remises d'armes et du vocabulaire qui les exprime dans les sources historiques latines jusqu'au début du xiiie siècle', *Traditio*, xxxv (1979).

Flori, J., *L'Idéologie du glaive: préhistoire de la chevalerie* (Geneva, 1983).

Flori, J., *L'Essor de chevalerie, xie-xiie siècles* (Geneva, 1986).

Fossier, R., *La Terre et les hommes en Picardie jusqu'à la fin du xiiie siècle* (2 vols, Paris, 1968).

Foulet, L., 'Sire, messire', *Romania*, lxxi (1950).

Frame, R., *The Political Development of the British Isles* (Oxford, 1990).

French, A., 'Meilyr's Elegy for Gruffudd ap Cynan', *Etudes Celtiques*, xvi (1979).

Fuhrmann, H., *Germany in the High Middle Ages, c. 1050–1200*, trans. T. Reuter (Cambridge, 1986).

The Gaelic Notes in the Book of Deer, ed. K. Jackson (Cambridge, 1972).

Galbraith, V.H., 'An Episcopal Land-Grant of 1085', *English Historical Review*, xliv (1929).

Galbreath, D.L., *Manuel de Blason* (Lausanne, 1942).

Gatin, L.A., *Un village: St-Martin-la-Garenne* (Paris, 1900).

Gem, R., 'Towards an Iconography of Anglo-Saxon Architecture', *Journal of the Warburg and Courtauld Institutes*, xlvi (1983).

Génicot, L., 'Recent Research on the Medieval Nobility', in *The Medieval Nobility: Studies on the Ruling Classes of France and Germany from the Sixth to the Twelfth Century*, ed. and trans. T. Reuter (Amsterdam, 1979).

Geoffrey of Monmouth, *Historia regum Britanniae*, i, *Bern, Burger-bibliotek ms. 568*, ed. N. Wright (Cambridge, 1985).

Géographie du Perche et chronologie de ses comtes (2 vols, Mortagne, 1890–1902).

Gerald of Wales, *Omnia Opera*, ed. J.S. Brewer, J.F. Dimock and G.F. Warner (8 vols, Rolls Series, 1861–91).

Gerald of Wales, *Expugnatio Hibernica*, ed. A. Scott and F.X. Martin (Irish Academy, 1980).

Gervase of Canterbury, *The Historical Works of Gervase of Canterbury*, ed. W. Stubbs (2 vols, Rolls Series, 1879–80).

Gesta Francorum, ed. R. Hill (Oxford, 1962).

Gesta Henrici Secundi, ed. W. Stubbs (2 vols, Rolls Series, 1867).

Gesta Stephani, ed. K. Potter and R.H.C. Davis (Oxford, 1976).

Gillingham, J., 'The Context and Purposes of the History of the Kings of Britain', in *Anglo-Norman Studies*, xiii, ed. M. Chibnall (Woodbridge, 1990).

Given-Wilson, C., *The English Nobility in the Later Middle Ages* (London, 1987).

Glamorgan County History, iii, *The Middle Ages*, ed. T.B. Pugh (Cardiff, 1971).

Gras, P., 'Aux Origines de l'héraldique: la décoration des boucliers au début du xiie siècle d'après la Bible de Cîteaux', *Bibliothèque de l'Ecole des Chartes*, cix (1951).

Gui de Warewic: roman du xiiie siècle, ed. A Ewert (2 vols, Classiques français du moyen âge, 1932).

Guibert de Nogent, *De Vita Sua*, ed. E.R. Labande (Paris, 1981).

Guilhiermoz, P., *Essai sur la noblesse du moyen âge* (Paris, 1902).

Guyotjeannin, O., *Episcopus et Comes: affirmation et déclin de la seigneurie épiscopale au nord du royaume de France* (Geneva, 1987).

Harper-Bill, C., 'The Piety of the Anglo-Norman Knightly Class', in *Proceedings of the Battle Conference 1979*, ed. R.A. Brown (Woodbridge, 1980).

Hart, C., 'Athelstan "Half-King" and his Family', in *Anglo-Saxon England*, ii, ed. P. Clemoes and others (Cambridge, 1973).

Hartopp, H., 'Some Unpublished Documents relating to Noseley, co. Leics.', *Associated Architectural Societies: Reports and Papers*, xxv, pt 2 (1900).

Harvey, P.D.A., 'The English Inflation of 1180–1220', *Past and Present*, no. 61 (1973).

Harvey, S., 'The Knight and the Knight's Fee in England', *Past and Present*, no. 49 (1970).

Haskins, C.H., *Norman Institutions* (Cambridge, Mass., 1925).

Henderson, G., 'Romance and Politics on some English Seals', *Art History*, i (1980).

Henrici de Bracton de Legibus et Consuetudinibus Angliae, ed. T. Twiss (6 vols, Rolls Series, 1878–83).

Henry of Huntingdon, *Historia Anglorum*, ed. T. Arnold (Rolls Series, 1879).

Heslop, T.A., 'English Seals from the Mid-Ninth Century to 1100', *Journal of the British Archeological Association*, cxxxiii (1980).

Heslop, T.A., 'Romanesque Painting and Social Distinction: the Magi and the Shepherds', in *England in the Twelfth Century*, ed. D. Williams (Woodbridge, 1990).

Hilton, R.H., *The English Peasantry in the Late Middle Ages* (Oxford, 1975).

Hilton, R.H., 'Agrarian Class Structure and Economic Development', *Past and Present*, no. 80 (1978).

Hinnebusch, W.A., *The Early English Friars Preacher* (Rome, 1951).

Histoire de Guillaume le Maréchal, ed. P. Meyer (3 vols, Paris, 1899–1909).

Historia et Cartularium monasterii sancti Petri de Gloucestria, ed. W. H. Hart (3 vols, Rolls Series, 1896).

The History of Gruffydd son of Cynan, ed. A. Jones (Manchester, 1910).

The History of the King's Works: The Middle Ages, ed. H.M. Colvin and others (2 vols, HMSO, 1963).

Hoffmann, H., 'Französische Fürstenweihen des Hochmittelalters', *Deutsches Archiv für Erforschung des Mittelalters*, xviii (1962).

Holt, J.C., *Magna Carta* (Cambridge, 1965).

Holt, J.C., 'A Vernacular-French Text of Magna Carta', *English Historical Review*, lxxxix (1974).

Holt, J.C., 'The Prehistory of Parliament', in *The English Parliament in the Middle Ages*, ed. R.G. Davies and J.H. Denton (Manchester, 1981).

Holt, J.C., 'Feudal Society and the Family in Early Medieval England: III. Patronage and Politics', *Transactions of the Royal Historical Society*, 5th ser., xxxiv (1984).

Honorius Augustodunensis, *De imagine mundi*, in *Patrologia Latina*, clxxii.

Howell, M., 'Regalian Right in Wales and the March: the Relation of Theory to Practice', *Welsh History Review*, vii (1974–5).

Hume, K., 'The Concept of the Hall in Old English Poetry', in *Anglo-Saxon England* iii, ed. P. Clemoes and others (Cambridge, 1974).

Hunt, T., 'The Emergence of the Knight in France and England, 1000–1200', in *Knighthood in Medieval Literature*, ed. W.H. Jackson (Woodbridge, 1981).

Hunter Blair, C.H., 'Armorials upon English Seals from the Twelfth to the Sixteenth Centuries', *Archaeologia*, 2nd ser., lxxxix (1943).

Inquisitio comitatus Cantabrigiensis; subjicitur Inquisitio Eliensis, ed. N.E.S.A. Hamilton (London, 1876).

Intitulatio, i, Lateinische Königs- und Fürstentitel bis zum Ende des 8. Jahrhunderts, ed. H. Wolfram (Mitteilungen des Instituts für Österreichische Geschichtsforschung, xxi, 1967).

Intitulatio, ii, Lateineische Herrscher- und Fürstentitel im neunten und zehnten Jahrhundert, ed. H. Wolfam (idem, xxiv, 1973).

Inventaire des sceaux de la Bourgogne, comp. A. Coulon (Paris, 1912).

Jenkins, D., 'Kings, Lords, and Princes: the Nomenclature of Authority in Thirteenth-century Wales', *Bulletin of the Board of Celtic Studies*, xxvi (1974–6).

John of Salisbury, *Policraticus*, ed. C.C.I. Webb (2 vols, Oxford, 1919).

Jones, A.H.M., *The Later Roman Empire, 284–602* (2 vols, Oxford, 1964).

Jones, F., *The Princes and Principality of Wales* (Cardiff, 1969).

Jones, T., 'Cronica de Wallia', *Bulletin of the Board of Celtic Studies*, xii (1946).

Jones, T.B. and A.M. Robinson, *Clarendon Palace* (Society of Antiquaries Report no. 45, 1988).

Jordan Fantosme's Chronicle, ed. R.C. Johnston (Oxford, 1981).

Keefe, T.K., *Feudal Assessments and the Political Community under Henry II and his Sons* (Berkeley, Calif., 1983).

Keen, M., *Chivalry* (London, 1984).

Keynes, S., *The Diplomas of King Aethelred 'the Unready', 978–1016: A Study in their Use as Historical Evidence* (Cambridge, 1980)

King, E., 'Mountsorrel and its Region in King Stephen's Reign', *Huntington Library Quarterly*, xliv (1980).

King, E., 'The Anarchy of King Stephen's Reign', *Transactions of the Royal Historical Society*, 5th ser., xxxv (1984).

King, E., 'Waleran, Count of Meulan, Earl of Worcester (1104–1166)', in *Tradition and Change in the Central Middle Ages: Essays in Honour of Marjorie Chibnall*, ed. D.E. Greenway, C. Holdsworth and J. Sayers (Cambridge, 1985).

Knowles, D.M., *The Monastic Order in England* (Cambridge, 1941).

Les Lais de Marie de France, ed. J. Rychner (Classiques français du moyen âge, 1983).

Lambert of Ardres, 'Historia Comitum Ghisnensium', in *M.G.H. Scriptores*, xxiv.

Langlois, C.V., 'Project for Taxation presented to Edward I', *English Historical Review*, iv (1889).

Laporte, J., '*Epistulae Fiscannenses*: Lettres d'amitié, de gouvernement et d'affaires (xie-xiie siècles)', *Revue Mabillon*, xliii (1953).

Larson, L.M., *The King's Household in England before the Norman Conquest* (Madison, 1904).

Latimer, P., 'Grants of "Totus Comitatus" in Twelfth-Century England: their Origins and Meaning', *Bulletin of the Institute of Historical Research*, lix (1986).

The Latin Texts of the Welsh Laws, ed. H.E. Emmanuel (Cardiff, 1967).

La Touche, J.D., 'Stokesay Castle', *Transactions of the Shropshire Archaeological Society*, i (1878).

The Law of Hywel Dda, trans. D. Jenkins (Llandysul, 1986).

The Laws of the Earliest English Kings, ed. F.L. Attenborough (Cambridge, 1922).

Lay Subsidy Rolls, 1225, 1232, ed. F.A. and A.P. Cazel (Pipe Roll Soc., 1983).

Le Charroi de Nîmes, ed. J-L. Perrier (Classiques français du moyen âge, 1982).

Leges Henrici Primi, ed. L.J. Downer (Cambridge, 1972).

Le Goff, J., *La Naissance du purgatoire* (Paris, 1981).

Le Maho, J., 'De la *Curtis* au château: l'exemple du Pays de Caux', *Château Gaillard* viii (1977).

Lennard, R.V., *Rural England, 1086–1135: a Study of Social and Agrarian Conditions* (Oxford, 1959).

Le Patourel, J., 'King and Princes in Fourteenth-Century France', in *Europe in the Late Middle Ages*, ed. J. Hale and others (London, 1965).

L'Estoire des Engles, ed. A. Bell (Anglo-Norman Text Soc., xiv–xvi, 1960).

The Letters and Charters of Gilbert Foliot, ed. A. Morey and C.N.L. Brooke (Cambridge, 1967).

Lewis, A.R., 'The Dukes in the *Regnum Francorum*, AD 550–751' *Speculum*, li (1976).

Lewis, A.W., 'Fourteen Charters of Robert I Count of Dreux (1152–88)' *Traditio*, xli (1985)

Lewis, C.P., 'The King and Eye: A Study in Anglo-Norman Politics', *English Historical Review*, civ (1989).

Lewis, C.P., 'The Early Earls of Norman England', in *Anglo-Norman Studies*, xiii, ed. M. Chibnall (Woodbridge, 1990).

Lewis, C.P., 'The Formation of the Honour of Chester', in *The Earldom of Chester and its Charters: a Tribute to Geoffrey Barraclough*, ed. A.T. Thacker (Chester Arch. Soc., lxxi 1991).

Libellus de Vita et Miraculis sancti Godrici heremitae de Finchale, auctore Reginaldo monacho Dunelemensi, ed. J. Stevenson (Surtees Soc., xx, 1847).

Liber Eliensis, ed. E.O. Blake (Camden Soc., 3rd ser., xcii, 1962).

Liber Insule Missarum, ed. H. Drummond (Bannatyne Club, 1847).

Life of Gruffudd ap Cynan, ed. D. Simon Evans (Lampeter, 1990).

Llandaff Episcopal Acta, ed. D. Crouch (South Wales Record Soc., v, 1988).

Llyfr Blegywryd, ed. S.J. Williams and J.E. Powell (2nd edn, Cardiff, 1961).

Lot, F., *Etudes critiques sur l'abbaye de St-Wandrille* (Paris, 1913).

Loud, G.A., 'The *Gens Normannorum* – Myth or Reality', in *Proceedings of the Battle Conference*, iv, ed. R.A. Brown (Woodbridge, 1981).

Mabillon, J., *Annales Ordinis Sancti Benedicti Occidentalium Monachorum Patriarchae*, v (Paris, 1738).

Macdonald, W.R., *Scottish Armorial Seals* (Edinburgh, 1904).

McFarlane, K.B., *Lancastrian Kings and Lollard Knights* (Oxford, 1972).

McFarlane, K.B., *The Nobility of Late Medieval England* (Oxford, 1973).

Mackenzie, W.M., *The Mediaeval Castle in Scotland* (London, 1927).

Magna Vita Sancti Hugonis, ed. D.L. Douie and H. Farmer (2 vols, London, 1961–2).

Magni Rotuli Scaccarii Normanniae sub regibus Angliae, ed. T. Stapleton (2 vols., London, 1840–4).

The Manuscripts of his Grace the Duke of Rutland, G.C.B., preserved at Belvoir Castle (4 vols, Historical Manuscripts Commission, 1888–1903).

Martin, D., N. Saul and others, 'Three Moated Sites in North-East Sussex. Part 1: Glottenham', *Sussex Archaeological Collections*, cxxvii (1989).

Martindale, J., '*Conventum inter Guillelmum Aquitanorum comes et Hugonem Chiliarchum*', *English Historical Review*, lxxxiv (1969).

Mason, E., 'The Resources of the Earldom of Warwick in the Thirteenth Century', *Midland History*, iii (1975–6).

Mason, J.F.A., 'The Officers and Clerks of the Norman Earls of Shropshire', *Transactions of the Shropshire Archaeological Society*, lvi (1957–60).

Mason, J.F.A., 'Roger of Montgomery and his Sons', *Transactions of the Royal Historical Society*, 5th ser., xiii (1963).

Mason, J.F.A., 'Barons and their Officials in the Later Eleventh Century', in *Anglo-Norman Studies*, xiii, ed. M. Chibnall (Woodbridge, 1991).

Materials for the History of Thomas Becket, Archbishop of Canterbury, ed. J.C. Robertson and J.B. Sheppard (7 vols, Rolls Series, 1875–85).

Matthew Paris, *Chronica Majora*, ed. H.R. Luard (7 vols, Rolls Series, 1872–83).

Mayhew, N.J., 'The Circulation and Imitation of Sterlings in the Low Countries', in *Coinage in the Low Countries (880–1500): The Third Oxford Symposium on Coinage and Monetary History*, ed. N.J. Mayhew (British Archeological Reports, International Series, liv 1979).

Mayr-Harting, H., *The Coming of Christianity to Anglo-Saxon England* (London, 1972).

Memorials of St Anselm, ed. R.W. Southern and F.S. Schmitt (Auctores Brittanici medii aevi, i, British Academy, 1969).

Mertes, K., *The Noble Household, 1250–1600* (Oxford, 1988).

Metcalf, D.M., *Coinage of the Crusades and the Latin East* (London, 1983).

Monasticon Anglicanum, ed. J. Caley, H. Ellis and B. Bandinel (8 vols, London, 1817–30).

Monumenta Germaniae Historica [M.G.H.] Capitularia, Epistolae, Leges, Scriptores rerum Germanicarum.

Moorman, J.R.H., *Church Life in England in the Thirteenth Century* (Cambridge, 1946).

Morganniae Archaiographia, ed. B. Ll. James (South Wales Record Soc., i, 1983).

Morris, C., '*Equestris Ordo*: Chivalry as a Vocation in the Twelfth Century', in *Studies in Church History*, xv (1978), ed. D. Baker.

Mortimer, R., 'Religious and Secular Motives for some English Monastic Foundations', in *Studies in Church History*, xv (1978), ed. D. Baker.

Mousnier, R., *Les Hiérarchies sociales de 1450 à nos jours* (Paris, 1969).

Muratori, L.A., *Antiquitates Italicae medii aevi* (6 vols, Milan, 1738–42).

Musset, L., 'Recherches sur les communautés de clercs séculiers en Normandie au xie. siècle', *Bulletin de la Société des Antiquaires de Normandie*, lv (1959–60).

Musset, L., 'L'Aristocratie Normande au xie siècle', in *La Noblesse au moyen âge, xie–xve siècles: essais à la mémoire de Robert Boutruche*, ed. P. Contamine (Paris, 1976).

Mütherich, F., 'Das Evangiliar Heinrichs des Löwen und die Tradition des mittelalterlichen Herrscherbildes', in *Das Evangiliar Heinrichs des Löwen und das mittelalterliche Herrscherbild* (Munich, 1986).

Navel, H., 'L'Enquête de 1133 sur les fiefs de l'Eveché de Bayeux', *Bulletin de la Société des Antiquaires de Normandie*, xlii (1935).

Nelson, J., 'The Church and Military Service in the Ninth Century', in *Politics and Ritual in Early Medieval Europe* (London, 1986).

Nelson, J., 'Ninth-century Knighthood: the Evidence of Nithard', in *Studies in Medieval History presented to R. Allen Brown*, ed. C. Harper-Bill and others (Woodbridge, 1989).

The New Statistical Account of Scotland, xii, *Aberdeen* (Edinburgh, 1845).

Nichols, J., *A Collection of all the Wills now known to be extant of the Kings and Queens of England* (London, 1780).

Nichols, J., *The History and Antiquities of the County of Leicester* (4 vols in 8, London, 1795–1815).

Oakeshott, R.E., 'An *Ingelri* Sword in the British Museum', *Archaeological Journal*, xxxi (1951).

Orderic Vitalis, *The Ecclesiastical History*, ed. M. Chibnall (6 vols, Oxford, 1969–80).

Otto of Freising, *Gesta Frederici seu rectius Cronica*, ed. A. Schmidt (Ausgewählte Quellen zur Deutschen Geschichte des Mittelalters, xvii, 1965).

Oeuvres complètes de Suger, ed. A. Lecoy de la Marche (Paris, 1867).

Owen, H., and J.B. Blakeway, *A History of Shrewsbury* (2 vols, London, 1825).

Pastoureau, M., 'L'Apparition des armoiries en Occident: état du problème, *Bibliothèque de l'Ecole des Chartes*, cxxxiv (1976).

Pastoureau, M. 'L'Origine des armoiries: un problème en voie de solution?', in *Genealogica & Heraldica: Report of the 14th International Congress of Genealogical & Heraldic Sciences in Copenhagen, 25–29 August 1980*, ed. S.T. Achen (Copenhagen, 1982).

Pastoureau, M., 'La Diffusion des armoiries et les débuts de l'héraldique', in *La France de Philippe Auguste: le temps des mutations* (Colloques internationaux, C.N.R.S., dcii, n.d.).

The Peterborough Chronicle, ed. C. Clark (Oxford, 1970).

Petit, P., *Le Paix romaine* (Nouvelle Clio, ix, 1967).

Philip de Novara, *Les Quatres ages de l'homme*, ed. M. de Fréville (Paris, 1888).

Pierce, I., 'Arms, Armour and Warfare in the Eleventh Century', in *Anglo-Norman Studies*, x, ed. R.A. Brown (Woodbridge, 1987).

Pierce, T. Jones, 'The Age of the Princes', in *Medieval Wales: Selected Essays*, ed. J. Beverley Smith (Cardiff, 1972).

Pipe Roll of 31 Henry I, ed. J. Hunter (Record Commission, 1833).

Pipe Rolls (cited by regnal year), edited in Pipe Roll Society Publications (London, 1884–).

The Pleas of the Crown for the County of Gloucester, A.D. 1221, ed. F.W. Maitland (London, 1884).

Poey d'Avant, F., *Monnaies féodales de France* (3 vols, Graz, 1961).

The Political Songs of England from the Reign of John to that of Edward II, ed. T. Wright (Camden Soc., vi, 1839).

Pollock, F. and F.W. Maitland, *The History of English Law* (2 vols, 2nd edn, Cambridge, 1898)

Poly, J-P. and E. Bournazel, *La Mutation féodale, xe–xiie siècle* (Nouvelle Clio, xvi, 1980).

Poupardin, R., 'Les Grandes Familles comtales à l'époque carolingienne', *Revue Historique*, lxxii (1900).

Powell, J.E. and K. Wallis, *The House of Lords in the Middle Ages* (London, 1968).

Powis, J.K., *Aristocracy* (Oxford, 1984).

Pryce, H., 'Church and Society in Wales, 1150–1250', in *The British Isles, 1100–1500: Comparisons, Contrasts and Connections*, ed. R.R. Davies (Edinburgh, 1988).

Quick, J., 'The Number and Distribution of Knights in Thirteenth-Century England: the Evidence of the Grand Assize Lists', in *Thirteenth-Century England*, i, ed. P.R. Coss and S.D. Lloyd (Woodbridge, 1986).

Rackham, O., *Trees and Woodland in the British Landscape* (London, 1976).

Rackham, O., *The History of the Countryside* (London, 1986).

Ralph de Diceto, *Ymagines Historiarum*, in *Opera Historica*, ed. W. Stubbs (2 vols, Rolls Series, 1876).

Records of Harrold Priory, ed. G.H. Fowler (Bedfordshire Historical and Records Soc., xvii, 1935).

Recueil de chartes et documents de St-Martin-des-Champs, monastère Parisien, ed. J. Depoin (5 vols, Paris, 1912–21).

Recueil des actes des ducs de Normandie (911–1066), ed. M. Fauroux (Caen, 1961).

Recueil des chartes de l'abbaye de Cluny, ed. A Bruel (6 vols, Paris, 1876–1903).

Recueil des chartes de St-Nicaise de Meulan, ed. E. Houth (Paris, 1924).

Recueil des historiens des croisades: historiens occidentaux, iii (Paris, 1886).

Recueil des historiens des Gaules et de la France, ed. M. Bouquet and others (24 vols, Paris, 1869–1904).

Red Book of the Exchequer, ed. H. Hall (3 vols, Rolls Series, 1896).

Regesta Regum Anglo-Normannorum, ed. H.W.C. Davis, C. Johnson, H.A. Cronne and R.H.C. Davis (4 vols, Oxford, 1913–69).

Regesta Regum Scottorum, ed. G.W.S. Barrow and others, 5 vols (Edinburgh, 1960–).

Register of Bishop Godfrey Giffard, 1268–1301, ed. J.W. Willis Bund (2 vols, Worcester Historical Soc., 1902).

The Register of Henry Chichele, Archbishop of Canterbury, 1414–43, ed. E.F. Jacob and H.C. Johnston (4 vols, Canterbury and York Soc., 1937–47).

Registrum de Dunfermlyn, ed. anon. (Bannatyne Club, 1842).

Registrum episcopatus Glasguensis, ed. C. Innes (Maitland Club, Edinburgh, 1843).

Regula Pauperum Commilitonum sanctae Civitatis, in *Patrologia Latina*, clxvi.

Renoux, A., 'Recherches historiques et archéologiques sur le château de Fécamp, ancien palais des ducs de Normandie', *Château Gaillard*, vii (1975).

Report on the MSS. of Lord Middleton preserved at Wollaton Hall, Nottinghamshire (Historical Manuscripts Commission, 1911).

Report on the MSS. of the late Reginald Rawdon Hastings, Esq., of the Manor House, Ashby de la Zouche (4 vols., Historical Manuscripts Commission, 1928–47).

Reports of the Lords Committees touching the Dignity of a Peer of the Realm (5 vols, London, 1829).

Reynolds, S., 'Medieval *Origines Gentium* and the Community of the Realm', *History*, lxviii (1983).

Reynolds, S., *Kingdoms and Communities in Western Europe, 900–1300* (Oxford, 1984).

Richardson, H.G. and G.O. Sayles, *The Governance of Medieval England* (Edinburgh, 1963).

Richeri Historiarum Libri Quatuor, ed. J. Guadet (2 vols, Paris, 1845).

Richmond, C., 'The Rise of the English Gentry, 1150–1350', *The Historian*, xxvi (1990).

Richter, M., 'The Political and Institutional Background to National Consciousness in Medieval Wales', in *Nationality and the Pursuit of National Independence*, ed. T.W. Moody (Belfast, 1978).

Robert de Torigny, *Chronica*, in *Chronicles of the Reigns of Stephen, Henry II and Richard I*, ed. R. Howlett (4 vols, Rolls Series, 1884–9).

Robinson, J. Armitage, *Gilbert Crispin, Abbot of Westminster* (Cambridge, 1911).

Rodulfi Glaber: Historiarum Libri Quinque, ed. J. France (Oxford, 1989).

Rogerii II regis: Diplomata Latina, ed C. Brühl (Codex diplomaticus regni Siciliae, ii, pt 1, 1987).

Rolls of Arms: Henry III, ed. T.D. Tremlett (Harleian Soc., 1967).

Roman de Rou, ed. A. Holden (3 vols, Société des anciens textes français, 1970–3).

Rotuli Litterarum Clausarum ed. T.D. Hardy (2 vols, Record Commission, 1833–44).

Round, J.H., 'The "Tertius Denarius"', in *Geoffrey de Mandeville* (London, 1892).

Round, J.H., 'The Families of Mandeville and De Vere', in *Geoffrey de Mandeville* (London, 1892).

Round, J.H., *Geoffrey de Mandeville* (London, 1892).

Round, J.H., 'The Introduction of Armorial Bearings to England', *Archaeological Journal*, li (1894).

Round, J.H., 'The Introduction of Armorial Bearings into England', *Archaeological Journal*, li (1894).

Round, J.H., 'The Family of Clare', *Archaeological Journal*, lvi (1899).

Round, J.H., 'The Introduction of Knight Service into England', in *Feudal England* (repr. Westport, Conn., 1979).

The Rous Roll, ed. C. Ross (Gloucester, 1980).

Royal and other Historical Letters illustrative of the Reign of Henry III, ed. W.W. Shirley (2 vols, Rolls Series, 1862–6).

Sanders, I.J., *English Baronies* (Oxford, 1960).

Sandford, F., *A Genealogical History of the Kings of England and Monarchs of Great Britain* (London, 1677).

Saul, N., *Knights and Esquires: The Gloucestershire Gentry in the Fourteenth Century* (Oxford, 1981).

Saul, N., *Scenes from Provincial Life: Knightly Families in Sussex, 1280–1400* (Oxford, 1986).

Schmidt, G., *Die Malerschule von St Florian* (Forschungen zur Geschichte ober Ostererreichs, vii, 1962).

Schramm, P.E., *A History of the English Coronation*, trans. L.G. Wickham Legg (Oxford, 1937).

The Scots Peerage, ed. J.B. Paul (9 vols, Edinburgh, 1904–14).

Selden, J., *Titles of Honor* (2nd edn., London, 1631).

A Selection of Latin Stories, ed. T. Wright (Percy Soc., viii, 1842).

Siddons, M.P., 'Welsh Equestrian Seals', *National Library of Wales Journal*, xxiii (1983–4).

Simeon of Durham, *Opera omnia*, ed. T. Arnold (2 vols, Rolls Series, 1882–5).

Simms, K., *From Kings to Warlords* (Woodbridge, 1987).

Simpson, G.G. and B. Webster, 'Charter Evidence and the Distribution of Mottes in Scotland', in *Essays on the Nobility of Mediaeval Scotland*, ed. K.J. Stringer (Edinburgh, 1985).

Sir Christopher Hatton's Book of Seals, ed. L.C. Loyd and D.M. Stenton (Oxford, 1950).

Skene, W.S., *The Four Ancient Books of Wales* (2 vols, Edinburgh, 1868).

Smith, Ll. Beverley, 'The *Gravamina* of the Community of Gwynedd against Llywelyn ap Gruffudd', *Bulletin of the Board of Celtic Studies*, xxxi (1984).

The Song of Dermot and the Earl, ed. G.H. Orpen (Oxford, 1892).

Southwick, L., 'The Armoured Effigy of Prince John of Eltham in Westminster Abbey and some closely related Military Monuments', *Church Monuments*, ii (1987).

St John Hope, W.H., *Heraldry for Craftsmen and Designers* (London, 1913).

Stenton, D.M., *English Justice between the Norman Conquest and the Great Charter, 1066–1215* (London, 1965).

Stenton, F.M., *Norman London: an Essay* (London, 1934).

Stenton, F.M., *Anglo-Saxon England* (Oxford, 1943).

Stenton, F.M., *The First Century of English Feudalism, 1066–1166* (2nd edn, Oxford, 1961).

Stephen de Fougères, *Le Livre des manières*, ed. R.A. Lodge (Geneva, 1979).

Stephenson, D., *The Governance of Gwynedd* (Cardiff, 1984).

Stevenson, J.H., *Heraldry in Scotland* (2 vols, Glasgow, 1914).

Stringer, K.J., *Earl David of Huntingdon: A Study in Anglo-Scottish History* (Edinburgh, 1985).

Stubbs, W., *Select Charters and other Illustrations of English Constitutional History*, ed. H.W.C. Davis (9th edn, Oxford, 1913).

Tabraham, C.J., 'Norman Settlement in Galloway: Recent Fieldwork in the Stewartry', in *Studies in Scottish Antiquity presented to Stewart Cruden*, ed. D.J. Breeze (Edinburgh, 1984).

Tellenbach, G., 'Uber Herzogskronen und Herzogshüte im Mittelalter', *Deutsches Archiv für Geschichte des Mittelalters*, v (1942).

Testamenta Vetusta, ed. N.H. Nicholas (2 vols, London, 1826).

The Text of the Book of Llan Dâv, ed. J. Gwenogvryn Evans (Oxford, 1893).

Thompson, M.W., *The Decline of the Castle* (Cambridge, 1987).

Tout, T.F., 'The Earldoms under Edward I', *Transactions of the Royal Historical Society*, new ser., viii (1894).

Tractatus de adventu fratrum minorum in Angliam, ed. A.G. Little (Manchester, 1951).

The Treatise on the Laws and Customs of England commonly called Glanvill, ed. G.D.G. Hall (London, 1965).

Turner, R.V., *Men Raised from the Dust* (Philadelphia, 1988).

Turner, R.V., 'Changing Perceptions of the New Administrative Class in Anglo-Norman and Angevin England: the *Curiales* and their Conservative Critics', *Journal of British Studies*, xxix (1990).

Van Luyn, P., 'Les *Milites* dans la France du xie siècle: examen des sources narratives', *Le Moyen Age*, lxxvii (1971).

Van Winter, J.M., 'Uxorem de militari ordine sibi imponens', in *Miscellanea in memoriam J.F. Niermeyer* (Groningen, 1961).

Van Winter, J.M., 'The Knightly Aristocracy of the Middle Ages as a "Social Class"', in *The Medieval Nobility*, ed. T. Reuter (Amsterdam, 1979).

Vaughn, S., *The Abbey of Bec and the Anglo-Norman State, 1034–1136* (Woodbridge, 1981).

Vendryès, J., 'Le Poème du livre noir sur Hywel ab Gronw', *Etudes Celtiques*, iv (1948).

Vendryès, J., 'Trois poèmes de Cynddelw', *Etudes celtiques*, iv (1948).

Vita Connuoionis, in *The Monks of Redon*, ed. C. Brett (Woodbridge, 1989).

Vita Domni Willelmi abbatis, ed. N. Bulst and P. Reynolds in *Rodulfi Glaber: Opera* (Oxford, 1989).

Vita Eadwardi Regis, ed. F. Barlow (Oxford, 1962).

Vita et Passio Waldevi comitis, in *Chroniques Anglo-Normandes*, ed. F. Michel (Rouen, 1836).

Vita sanctae Margaretae reginae, in *Symeonis Dunelmensis Opera et Collectanea*, i, ed. J. Hodgson Hinde (Surtees Soc., li, 1867).

Vitae Sanctorum Britanniae et Genealogiae, ed. A.W. Wade-Evans (Cardiff, 1944).

Vogel, C. and R. Elze, *Le Pontifical Romano-germanique du xe siècle* (2 vols, Vatican, 1963).

Wagner, A.R., *Heralds and Heraldry* (Oxford, 1956).

Walker, D., 'Ralph Son of Pichard', *Bulletin of the Institute of Historical Research*, xxxiii (1966).

Walter Daniel, *The Life of Ailred of Rievaulx*, ed. F.M. Powicke (repr. Oxford, 1978).

Walter Map, *De Nugis Curialium*, trans. M.R. James (revised edn, Oxford, 1983).

Walter of Henley and other Treatises on Estate Management and Accounting, ed. D.M. Oschinsky (Oxford, 1971).

Warlop, E., *The Flemish Nobility before 1300* (4 vols, Coutrai, 1975–6).

Waugh, S.L., *England in the Reign of Edward III* (Cambridge, 1991).

Webster, G., *The Roman Imperial Army of the First and Second Centuries* (3rd edn., London, 1985).

Werner, K.F., 'Kingdom and Principality in Twelfth-century France', in *The Medieval Nobility*, trans. T. Reuter (Amsterdam, 1978).

White, G.H., 'The Beaumont Seals in the British Library Catalogue', *Notes and Queries*, 11th ser., cli (1926).

Whitelock, D., *The Beginnings of English Society* (repr. Harmondsworth, 1979).

Whitwell, J.B., 'Excavations on the Site of a Moated Medieval Manor House in the Parish of Saxilby, Lincs', *Journal of the British Architectural Association*, 3rd ser., xxxi (1969).

William of Ardres, 'Chronica', in *M.G.H. Scriptores*, xxiv.

William of Malmesbury, *Gesta Regum Anglorum* (2 vols, Rolls Series, 1887–9).

William of Malmesbury, *Historia Novella*, ed. K.R. Potter (London, 1955).

William of Newburgh, *Historia rerum Anglicarum*, in *Chronicles of the Reigns of Stephen, Henry II and Richard* (4 vols, Rolls Series, 1886).

William of Poitiers, *Gesta Guillelmi ducis Normannorum et regis Anglorum*, ed. R. Foreville (Paris, 1952).

Williams, A., 'The King's Nephew: the Family and Career of Ralph, Earl of Hereford', in *Studies in Medieval History presented to R. Allen Brown*, ed. C. Harper-Bill and others (Woodbridge, 1989).

Williams, A., 'A Bell-house and Burh-geat: Lordly Residences in England before the Norman Conquest', in *The Ideals and Practice of Medieval Knighthood*, iv, ed. R. Harvey and C. Harper-Bill (Woodbridge, 1992).

Wolfram, H., 'The Shaping of the Early Medieval Principality as a Type of non-royal Rulership', *Viator*, ii (1978).

Wood, Margaret, *The English Mediaeval House* (repr. London, 1983).

Wood, Michael, 'The Making of King Athelstan's Empire', in *Ideal and Reality in Frankish and Anglo-Saxon Society*, ed. P. Wormald and others (Oxford, 1983).

Wood, S., *English Monasteries and their Patrons in the Thirteenth Century* (Oxford, 1955).

Woodruff, C.E., 'Some Early Visitation Rolls at Canterbury', *Archaeologia Cantiana*, xxxii and xxxiii (1917–18).

Yver, J., 'Les Châteaux forts en Normandie jusqu'au milieu du xiie siècle', *Bulletin de la Société des Antiquaires de la Normandie*, liii (1957 for 1955–6).

Yver, J., 'Autour de l'absence d'avouerie en Normandie', *Bulletin de la Société des Antiquaires de Normandie*, lvii (1965).

Zadora-Rio, E., 'L'Enceinte fortifiée du Plessis-Grimoult', *Château Gaillard*, v (1970).

INDEX

INDEX

Saul, Nigel 239
Saulseat, abbey of 342
Saumur, abbey of St Florent 331
Say, family of 223
Scone 83, 279, 342
Scotland, earls in 80–3; thanes in 32
Scott, Sir Walter 295
Scroby 142
Scrope, family of 238
seals 138, 152, 190–1, 206–7, 219, 242–7, 248; in Scotland 155; in Wales 94n
Séez, bishop of (see Serlo)
Selkirk, abbey of 342
Semilly 261
seneschals 282, 283, 289–91, 292–3, 302–3
Senlis, family of (see Simon I, Simon II, Simon III, Simon the bastard)
sergeant (serviens) 33, 164, 165–6, 165n, 169
Serlo, bishop of Séez 249–50
Sèry, abbey of 312
Seymour, family of 233
Sherborne 261; abbey of 12n
sheriff (vicecomes) 63, 100–2
shire courts 61–2, 108 and n, 109, 111, 142–3, 172
Shouldham, priory of 329
Shrewsbury, abbey of 316, 338; earls of 58, 60, 63n, 291 (see Hugh, Robert de Belleme, Roger de Montgomery)
Shropshire, barons of 111
Sicily, kingdom of 93
Sico, duke of Benevento 200
Silsoe 309
Simeon of Durham 59
Simon I de Montfort, earl of Leicester 71, 236–7
Simon II de Montfort, earl of Leicester 13, 147, 216 and n, 235, 240, 301, 305
Simon de Senlis, bastard of Northampton 229
Simon I de Senlis, earl of Northampton 76–7

Simon II de Senlis, earl of Northampton 64–5
Simon III de Senlis, earl 64–5
Simon of Clifford 137
Siward, earl of Northumbria 182
Siward of Arden 135, 342
Slebech, preceptory of 340
Snettesham, church of 319
Snowdon, earl of 45; lord of 93 (see Gwynedd)
Solomon, Franciscan friar 300
Somerset, earls of 64 (see John Beaufort)
Song of Dermot and the Earl 32–3
Song of Roland 127, 129, 131n, 150, 161, 196, 229
Southwark 265, 270 (see also Winchester Place)
Spurgeon, Jack 157
spurs 127–8
squires 138, 147, 164–71, 229, 236, 251, 293
St Andrews, bishop of (see Eadmer)
St Asaph, bishop of (see Geoffrey of Monmouth)
St-Bertin, abbey of 14n, 194, 199
St Davids, bishop of 339; cathedral of 338
St-Denis, abbey of 183
St-Evroult, abbey of 174
St-Georges-de-Boscherville, abbey of 333
St Georges Roll of Arms 235
St-Martin-au-Bois, priory of 312
St-Martin-des-Champs, priory of 127
St Mary le Grand, college of 327
St Mary Woolchurch, church of 292
St Michaels Mount, priory of 67
St-Ouen, abbey of 76, 324
St-Pol, counts of 52, 225 (see Enguerrand, Anselm)
St-Wandrille, abbey of 324
Stafford, earl of 211; family of 23, 111–12, 113 (see Robert)
staller (constabulator) 285
standard of England 220–1, 221n
status, levels of 15, 27ff, 152–3